OURSELVES AND OTHERS

The Washington Post
Sociology Companion

OURSELVES AND OTHERS

The Washington Post Sociology Companion

The Washington Post
Writers Group

Allyn and Bacon

Boston London Toronto Sydney Tokyo Singapore

Project Editor: Hannah Rubenstein
Editorial Director: Bill Barke
Executive Editor: Susan Badger
Series Editor: Karen Hanson
Editorial Assistant: Laura Lynch
Cover Administrator: Linda Dickinson
Manufacturing Buyer: Megan Cochran
Cover Designer: Suzanne Harbison
Production Service: Greg Johnson

This book is printed on
recycled, acid-free paper

Contents

Chapter 6 Race and Ethnicity   117

Chapter 7 Gender   145

Chapter 8 Crime and Deviance   165

Chapter 9 Social Institutions   184

Marriage and Family

Politics

Foreword

Each of the articles in this reader addresses important aspects of sociological inquiry as enacted in real-world events. Written by many of America's foremost journalists and based on interviews with sociologists worldwide, the articles, in their focus on changing social conditions, capture the essence of the discipline and bring timeliness and relevance to the classroom. The impact of culture, socialization, stratification, social control, and development on societies worldwide is painted in vivid language and accompanied by cogent analysis. Each selection provides links between important sociological concepts and today's rapidly changing world. Both developed and developing nations are investigated, and the interdependence of a shrinking world is a major theme that is woven throughout. The result is a careful mix of pieces focusing on U.S. society and societies around the world.

In organization, *Ourselves and Others: The Washington Post Sociology Companion* parallels the structure of the usual beginning course in sociology. Separate chapters include Sociological Research, Culture, Groups and Social Structure, Socialization, Stratification, Race and Ethnicity, Gender, Crime and Deviance, Marriage and the Family, Religion, Politics, Education, Health and Medicine, Population, Urbanization, and Modernization. Full-page introductions, which appear at the beginning of each chapter, help students recall core concepts and provide a brief overview and context for the articles that follow.

The world glimpsed in this reader is a rich and complex one, full of cause for concern, hope, and action. The important subject matter of sociology—life in groups in a rapidly changing universe—is seen here through a multifocused lens. It is our hope that this lens will become part and parcel of the sociological imagination of the reader.

The Publishers

OURSELVES AND OTHERS

The Washington Post
Sociology Companion

Chapter 1

The World According to Sociology

Sociologists do not seek to explain human behavior at the individual level. Instead, they examine the various groups that individuals form, as well as changing conditions within the social environment. The first article in this introductory section describes the life of a Ghanian sociologist named Kwasi Oduro, who finds himself straddling two worlds, each of which makes very different demands upon him. As a university professor, Mr. Oduro lives in modern Accra, the capital city of Ghana located in West Africa. As a member of the Ashanti tribe, Mr. Oduro remains tied to his extended family, who live in his ancestral village of rural Dawu. This fascinating glimpse of a life split between ancient and modern worlds is an apt introduction to a key concern of sociologists—how the social environment determines individual choice. The forces of modernization are everywhere apparent in this introductory article.

An introduction to sociology also must begin with an investigation into how sociologists conduct research—the methods by which they study patterns of behavior. The second and third articles in this section describe large-scale surveys conducted by sociologists in the Soviet Union and in China. In the first, a public opinion poll was taken in Russia, the Ukraine, and Lithuania measuring attitudes regarding the desirability of U.S.-style capitalism. The second article reports on the first nationwide survey of sexual behavior ever conducted in China.

The final article in this section describes a rash of suicides among adolescent members of a Brazilian Indian tribe. When existing social structures are disturbed and not replaced with satisfactory alternatives, confusion and despair almost always follows.

Ancient Family Ties and Reluctant Sense of Duty Draw Ghanaian Teacher to His Native Village (Part 1)

Blaine Harden

Kwasi Oduro, the only member of his family with a university degree and a government job in the capital, is needed here at home.

In this upcountry village of mud houses and bad water, his kin want a piece of what they imagine to be Oduro's prosperity.

His father needs money to pay a hospital so a "computer can test my blood to know the particular place where the sick is." His mother needs money to install wiring that would, for the first time, bring electricity to her house. His sister, unhappily married to a polygamous village subchief, needs money for school fees for her five children. His aunt, who is believed to have magical powers and has professed in public to being a witch, needs money for a dentist.

The list of needs, bubbling up from the ranks of distant cousins, goes on and on. At times, Oduro, 38, a lecturer in sociology at the University of Ghana, says he despises his extended family.

His $83-a-month university salary is riot enough to feed, clothe and educate his own five children, who live with him and his wife in the capital, Accra. The demands of the folks back home, Oduro says, fill him with "dread."

"They are vultures," he says. "I say they are pickpockets. They are very cunning. They want money from you and they know how to get it. They will tell you lies calculated to soften your heart. Your grandmother talks to you about some chest trouble and you give her money and the next thing you know she is drinking gin."

At other times, his cynicism gives way to guilt. Oduro's family, especially his mother, sacrificed to put him through school. He owes them. There is a saying in his tribe, the Ashanti: "If your elders take care of you while you are cutting your teeth, you must in turn take care of them while they are losing theirs."

"My guilt is an expression of my failure to measure up to their expectations," he says. "Sometimes you crawl back home with certain gestures. The crawling back can only happen to the guilty."

After more than a year's absence, Oduro went home last month. This is an account of that three-day journey back into the West African forest, back into the smothering embrace of a medieval culture that Oduro says he can neither accept nor escape.

It was a bittersweet, expensive and emotionally draining homecoming of a sort that is replayed millions of times every weekend across this continent as the African extended family recalls its own.

2

The extended family system hooks into the hearts and pocketbooks of almost every African man and woman. Unlike tribal loyalty, which divides Africa along ethnic lines while dictating patterns of government patronage and sometimes boiling over into civil war, family loyalty operates on a smaller, more intimate stage—a stage populated exclusively by blood relatives.

With its labyrinthine web of rights and duties, the extended family is a day care, social security and welfare system. It babysits the children of working parents and keeps the elderly from feeling useless. It feeds the unemployed and gives refuge to the disabled and mentally ill.

It pays for all this by redistributing resources between haves and have-nots. Money, medicines and manufactured goods filter out to the village. Country cousins come knocking on doors in the city in search of familial favors. This system of commerce and welfare does not follow free-market precepts, Marxist dogma or the rule of law. It is governed by ties of blood, of tradition, of guilt.

As independent Africa stumbles through three decades of hard times—with corrupt leaders bleeding national economies, commodity prices skidding downward on world markets and the average African growing poorer each year—the extended family functions as a kind of homemade glue, holding together the world's most impoverished and politically brittle continent.

"There is really no alternative in Africa to the extended family," says Akilagpa Sawyyer, vice chancellor of the University of Ghana and a well-known social commentator in this country. "Its functioning is a major way to distinguish African society from that of Europe or the United States. And it is not going to go away. Every single person you meet in Africa who has got anything is sharing it with his kin."

Most African governments, despite socialist rhetoric and well-intentioned laws, cannot afford social security or unemployment benefits. Here in Ghana, for example, the government has an elaborate unemployment benefit program. But the program exists only on paper. Since it was introduced in 1972, government figures show that a total of three claimants have been paid.

"Compared to what African governments can do, the family is a marvelous welfare system," says Bernard Travallion, a British adviser to Ghana's government for development planning. "To dismantle it without an alternative would be a disaster."

Yet, as the journey home of Kwasi Oduro suggests, the extended family in Ghana, and across Africa, is under immense stress. Like a bridge that has borne too much high-speed traffic for too many years, its foundations are cracking. Decades of western education and urban migration have lured family members into different worlds. The rural old and the urban young are separated by hundreds of miles of bad roads and centuries of development.

At the University of Ghana in Accra, where Kwasi Oduro lives on campus in a house provided by the university, there is a nuclear physics research laboratory. Here in Dawn, 100 miles upcountry, fetishes hang in each house to ward off evil.

When Oduro goes home he does not bring along his city-bred children; the village water gives them diarrhea, and village cousins steal their food. Nor does he, a nondrinking, born-again Christian, bring home the traditional bottle of schnapps that his uncles pour on the ground as a libation to the ancestors.

Yet, he constantly worries about what his kin back home are saying about him.

There are 11 of his kin camped out in his three-bedroom house in Accra, not counting his wife and five children. The number has gone as high as 18. They are job-seekers and refugees from this village. Most are described by Oduro as "cousins of a sort." They pay no rent; they often eat for free.

"I suppose I should be thorough and dislodge all of these traditional obligations and call them humbug. If I decide for my urban family, I would be saved a lot of headache," says Oduro.

"But I cannot turn out anybody if there is space to sleep. You don't know what they will go to the village and say. That sort of thing counts a lot. I am not so worried about this talk of witchcraft. That is not what worries me at all. What worries me is my own conscience."

Oduro is a compact, well-muscled man, with a rounded face, a touch of gray in his hair and a booming voice toughened by long hours of monologue in large lecture halls.

As a student at the University of Ghana, he was an activist who led strikes that three times closed down the school. One of the strikes, in the late 1970s, precipitated the fall of a military government in Ghana.

"He caused a lot of trouble, but he has calmed down," recalls vice-chancellor Sawyyer. He now describes Oduro as one of the university's most energetic and popular lecturers. Oduro describes himself as riven among obligations to his own children in Accra, to teaching at the university and to his extended family here.

"In my situation, there are too many norms competing to guide my life," Oduro says. "The source of my trouble is that I have made a decision to combine all of them."

Though frayed by cultural stress and inimical to western concepts of efficiency, the extended family has proven itself adaptable to Africa's deepening poverty and political instability.

A remarkable demonstration of this occurred in Ghana five years ago when neighboring Nigeria, in a fit of xenophobia, ordered the expulsion of more than 1.3 million Ghanaian workers.

The mass deportation came at a time of severe drought and economic hardship in this country of 14 million people. (It was an invasion analogous to 20 million American expatriates returning in 14 days to the United States at the height of the Great Depression.)

Anticipating social upheaval and fearing starvation, western relief agencies drew up emergency plans to erect camps for returnees. Within two weeks, however, the deportees disappeared, absorbed back into their extended families like water into a sponge. What was potentially the greatest single disaster in Ghana's history was defused before donors could figure out what to do about it.

After six hours in a van on roads that deteriorated from good to bumpy to barbarous, Oduro was dropped off here in his home village late on a Friday afternoon.

Dawu has a population of about 1,500 people—when everyone's working-age children come home from the cities. Except at Christmas and Easter, they don't come home all that often. They drift back on the odd weekend to meet family obligations. Like tens of thousands of ancestral villages across rural Africa, Dawu is semi-abandoned and sleepy, with more than its share of the very old and the very young.

There is one unpaved street in the village and one shop, a kiosk that sells cigarettes, soap and bread. When Oduro arrived home, the kiosk appeared to have been freshly painted. It bore a portrait of Michael Jackson and the slogan, "No Hurry in Life."

The surrounding houses were made of reddish mud with rusted tin roofs. Greenish trails of sewage leaked from beneath each house into shallow ditches that crisscrossed the village. Between the houses, cocoa fruit (plucked from trees that surround Dawu) dried on woven mats in the sun.

Even in the late afternoon, it was very hot—the humid air heavy with the sweet fermenting aroma of cocoa and the biting odor of excrement.

Oduro had left his wife, Margaret, back in Accra with their children. Instead, he brought home Stella Adgei, 27, who works with him as a researcher at the university. He and Stella have been seeing each other for a long time. Last year he met her parents for drinks, proposed marriage and received their blessing. Although there has been no formal ceremony, Oduro has told a few of his university colleagues that Stella is his second wife.

He has not, however, mentioned his second marriage to his first wife. Margaret does not like Stella. The two have met only once, and it was not pleasant. Margaret charged into Oduro's office at the Department of Sociology and ripped Stella's dress.

When Oduro climbed the broken front steps and walked into his family's house, a structure he was born and raised in, his mother greeted him with a curtsy and immediately turned away to fetch water. It is an Ashanti tradition that water must be offered to guests before inquiries are made. Tradition, too, demanded that Oduro's satchel bag be carried immediately to the bedroom in which he was born and that his maternal uncles be sent for.

Going home to rural Africa means succumbing to, if not suffocating in, the traditions of one's elders. This is especially true among the Ashanti, Ghana's largest tribe. Before the British subdued their nation in the late 19th century, the Ashanti Empire was one of the most religiously intricate, commercially astute and militarily adventurous civilizations on the continent.

The Ashanti traded in gold, ivory and slaves. While subjugating neighboring tribes, they ruled themselves with a monarchy that had a strong component of participatory democracy. The symbol of Ashanti unity was the Golden Stool, which by legend descended from heaven only 25 miles from this village, at Kumasi, the Ashanti capital. No one, not even the Ashanti king, was allowed to sit on the gold-encrusted stool; it was the soul of the nation.

Devoted to the idea that the elderly and the spirits of the recently dead can intercede with the gods in behalf of the living, the Ashanti developed elaborate rituals to keep elders and the recently dead happy. Elders were revered and sought out for advice on key issues such as marriage, funerals and war. Every 43 days, recently departed kin were offered food and drink. When an important chief died, his contentment in the netherworld was ensured by slaughtering a retinue of servants, wives and advisers.

These beliefs, of course, have been pared down by time, Christian missionaries, western education and English common law. Ceremonial murder is now as repulsive a notion in Dawu as crucifixion is in Cleveland Park.

But many traditions remain. The most important among these is the Ashanti concept of matrilineal descent, a complex practice common among the peoples of central and west Africa. Family property can only be inherited from the mother's side of the family. In the Ashanti tribe, it is much better to have a rich mother than a rich father. A father's wealth goes to his sisters' children, but a mother's wealth goes to her own children.

When Oduro entered his mother's house, he knew his father would not be there. He has never lived there. The only kin entitled to live in the house are the "products" of his grandmother's and his mother's wombs. Oduro's father lives down the road in his mother's house. Maternal uncles, who manage family property and family affairs, loom large in the life of every Ashanti. That is why, when Oduro came home, someone ran to the forest to fetch them.

While waiting for his uncles, Oduro drank the welcome water his mother brought him. Stella, a city woman who grew up in Accra and who had never before come home with Oduro, rejected it, fearing gastroenteritis.

All around them, a legion of bare-foot children gaped and whispered. In Ashanti, there is a proverb that says "the family is a crowd." This rather large house, with its eight rooms built around an open concrete courtyard populated with chickens, goats and no fewer than 21 small children, bears it out. They are the children of Oduro's sisters, or the grandchildren of his aunts.

The senior uncle and head of the house lumbered into the courtyard after about 10 minutes. Yaw Bekoe, 66 years old, 21 children of his own (all of whom live elsewhere with their four respective mothers), was wrapped in a blue and red paisley print cloth that he wore, in the Ashanti way, off one shoulder, like a Roman toga. He shook hands, brought out a carved wooden stool and sat down to wait for uncle number two.

Peter Amoakahene, in his late fifties, with 14 children who also live elsewhere, arrived in a similar toga-like wrap, carrying a large transistor radio. A retired sanitary inspector with a government pension, he manages the family's cocoa farm, which is owned collectively by the maternal side of Oduro's family. It is the largest farm in the village and, in a good year, can earn $15,000. Uncle Peter is a powerful and feared man in Dawu. Oduro says he once declared publicly that he was a wizard.

The uncles quickly located a bottle of home-brewed gin, poured a bit on the ground for the ancestors and tossed back a little themselves. They ended the traditional interval of silence by asking Oduro why he had not been home for a year and why he had not written.

Prepared for these questions, Oduro lied about why he had not been home. He said he had planned several times to come back, but university business had intervened. He did not write, he continued, because he had always believed he would be home ahead of a letter.

He did not mention the real reason for staying away.

"I don't go home because I can't afford it," he said later. "My last trip home (in August 1987) was for my grandmother's funeral and it cost me more than three months' pay. I had to get loans from three colleagues at the university."

The funeral celebration went on for two weeks. Oduro said it was costly because his mother is the "queen mother" of Dawu, a traditional Ashanti title. Among other duties, queen mothers supervise the morals of local women and can publicly rebuke the village chief. They also attend a lot of funerals and when one of their own kin dies, they, in turn, are expected to put on a good feed with lots of drink.

"My mother believes she has a son in the university who can help her," said Oduro.

Oduro did not tell his uncles that he only came home this time because he had heard that his father needed money for a blood test, that his mother was complaining of an ulcer, that his aunt's teeth were giving her pain—and he happened to have $160 from a research grant. For the first time since the funeral, he could afford to come home without embarrassment.

He told his soothing lies and then sat in silence with his uncles as the late afternoon turned quickly to night. Fireflies cut curlicues of light across the darkening courtyard. Oduro's mother and younger sister pounded yam and prepared a meat soup for supper. Hungry children fought with each other as they waited for their yam.

Since it was Oduro's first night home, no relative even hinted that he or she needed money.

"It would be indecent," Oduro said later. "Tactically, on the second day home, everyone wants to know when you are leaving. Because then they can figure when best to ask for something."

On Saturday, Oduro went calling on his kin, as tradition requires. For this second day, he had tactics of his own. He was planning to leave Sunday, but he told his lesser relatives he was leaving Monday. Only to his parents, his sister and his aunt—whom he figured he could afford to help—did he tell the truth.

The trip was going smoothly when, late Saturday afternoon, as shadows lengthened and the heat began draining out of the day, he and Stella went for a stroll. Turning onto the main street of the village, they walked into a problem.

Margaret, Oduro's first wife, who was supposed to be back in Accra minding the children, had followed them home. She began shouting obscenities at Stella and moved menacingly toward the dumbstruck young woman.

(Part 2 of this article appears in Chapter 9: Marriage and Family.)

November 20, 1988

Majority of Soviets in Survey Reject U.S.-Style Capitalism; Democratic Socialism Favored Instead; Political Changes Backed

Richard Morin

Soviet citizens are deeply divided over their leadership's desire to change to a free market economy and large numbers reject many of the underlying beliefs necessary to nurture a capitalistic system, according to preliminary results of a public opinion poll conducted in Russia, the Ukraine and Lithuania.

The survey found that barely half of all citizens interviewed said they support Soviet President Mikhail Gorbachev's efforts to create some version of a free market economy. When asked to choose, the overwhelming majority rejected U.S.-style capitalism in favor of some version of democratic socialism.

But there are some signs that the economic reforms currently being pressed by Gorbachev may eventually achieve popular support.

"If there's any hope, it's because young people are far more sanguine about the future and far more ready to embrace these new values," said Donald S. Kellermann, director of the Times Mirror Center for the People and the Press, which sponsored the study.

"Those most opposed are the older members of the population," he said. "The minute you get below 50 years old, there is a turning point to increasing acceptance of change."

The Times Mirror study reported that among Russians under 25 years old, seven out of 10 favored a free market economy, a view shared by fewer than 20 percent of those over age 70. Similarly, more affluent and better educated Russians were more likely to have a favorable view of a free market economy.

Overall, 54 percent of those questioned in Russia, 53 percent of those interviewed in the Ukraine and 76 percent of all Lithuanian respondents said they favor efforts to establish a free market economy. (The proportionally larger share of Lithuanians who supported a free market economy was reflected in other questions as well. "Lithuanians are much c,ser to Western values than Russians or Ukrainians on many economic dimensions," the study found.)

A total of 2,210 randomly selected adults were interviewed in the European part of Russia, the Ukraine and Lithuania in April and May. Half the interviews were conducted in Russia. while the results do not necessarily reflect the views of all Soviets, they do highlight some of the internal pressures Gorbachev faces as he prepares to welcome President Bush to Moscow.

Although many Soviets view economic reforms with suspicion, the poll suggests that many have embraced the political changes that have reduced the role of the Communist Party. Six of 10 questioned favor free elections and a multi-party political system over one-party rule.

The apparent acceptance of political, but not economic, pluralism reflects the vastly different impacts of glasnost and perestroika on the average Soviet citizen, Kellermann said.

"Remember, glasnost has had a tremendously positive effect on the people," he said. "It has made them able to complain, to vent their unhappiness, to open up. Glasnost is related in the minds of Russians directly to political pluralism."

On the other hand, the first attempts to restructure the economy have hurt the average Soviet.

"Since perestroika began, the economy has gone into a sharper decline than it was in before," Kellermann said.

In fact, economic problems overwhelm all other concerns in the minds of the average citizen, the survey found.

The Soviet Union's first capitalists also are giving capitalism a bad name, Kellermann said.

"There is real resentment of the new capitalists; they call them the Mafia," he said. "These new capitalists are those running the cooperatives. But the average person can't afford the goods and services made available through the cooperatives, yet they see the owners getting rich."

Asked which economic system they wanted, just 17 percent favored a U.S.-version free market form of capitalism, while 10 percent longed for a return to "a socialist society along the lines we have had in the past." The plurality—36 percent—favored "a more democratic type of socialism" and 23 percent favored a Swedish-style version of capitalism.

Only in farming—among 15 types of enterprise from banks to newspapers to restaurants—did a majority favor private ownership.

The survey found that many Soviets reject many of the values that underlay the capitalist system. Nearly half believe that people who "get ahead do so at the expense of other people." Barely a third "see success as a consequence of some people having more ability or ambition than others."

Many Russians also have difficulty with the concept of personal accountability for failure, the Times Mirror study found. Forty-five percent of people interviewed in Russia think most people who fail in life do so because of personal shortcomings, "but almost as many think personal failure is society's fault."

"There is little evidence," the study concluded, "that the Russian public is ready, willing or able to easily adapt to a free market economy."

July 28, 1991

Limited 'Sexual Revolution' Seen in China: Nationwide Survey Shows More Liberal Attitudes Developing in Conservative Society

Daniel Southerland

Researchers who conducted the first nationwide survey of sexual behavior in China said the country's opening to the outside world has led to a more liberal attitude toward premarital and extramarital sex in China's largely conservative society.

The breadth of the new study is considered remarkable in China, where just 10 years ago it would have been impossible to conduct such a survey. Open discussion of sex has long been taboo under Communist Party rule, and even today it is likely to be difficult to publicize the results of the survey.

Chinese society has never been prudish as its facade of propriety would suggest. The country has a long tradition of concubines and prostitutes, and individual Chinese suggest that even under restrictive Communist rule, there has been much more premarital and extramarital sexual activity than many foreign observers realized.

However, after the Communists came to power in 1949, such sexual activity was severely discouraged. China gained a reputation as one of the most puritanical societies in the world. Since the opening of the country to the outside world in the late 1970s, there has been a limited "sexual revolution."

About 23,000 Chinese were questioned for the survey, which took 18 months to complete. Hundreds of volunteer interviewers went to three large cities and 12 provinces to question middle school students, college students, urban and rural citizens and a number of sex criminals. Queries were devised for each category of respondents, and each group was asked to answer between 50 and 60 questions.

Prof. Liu Dalin, a Shanghai-based sociologist, founder of China's first magazine on sex education and chief organizer of the study, said researchers encountered a number of difficulties, including a shortage of funds, a traditional Chinese prejudice against revealing sensitive information and problems in interviewing peasants, some of whom are illiterate.

Liu, who has played a leading role in sex education in China, said the survey will help to educate people and lead them to a healthier life.

The evidence of increases in premarital and extramarital sex did not come as a surprise to specialists such as Liu. More limited studies several years ago showed such a trend.

The survey reveals that young people in China are maturing more than a year earlier than their grandparents did, partly because of better nutrition. But Sill said that young people in China still have less interest in sex on the whole than their counterparts in Western countries. This, he said, is partly a matter of tradition and culture.

In fact, "sexual liberation" as it is known in the West differs greatly from premarital sex practiced in China. Here, some couples in their late twenties engage in sex before marriage because they must postpone their nuptials until scarce state-assigned apartments are allotted to them.

And while the government has adopted a more lenient attitude on sex education than it had in the past, there is little open discussion about the subject and people are sometimes punished for engaging in what are considered to be illicit sexual activities.

For example, authorities expelled a male student from one of Beijing's leading universities last month when he was discovered having sexual relations with a young woman. Other students said that the punishment was typical.

The survey also found that women are demanding more of a say in their sexual lives and marriages. Liu said that about 60 percent of today's divorces in China are initiated by women.

Eighteen percent of those who were interviewed in Chinese cities, and 15 percent in rural areas, acknowledged to having sexual intercourse with their marriage partners before they were married, Liu said. About 50 percent of youths in both the cities and countryside engage in premarital sex, and 86 percent of all of those surveyed condoned such affairs, he said. These represented increases from earlier studies.

Extramarital affairs have also increased and were approved by 69 percent of the respondents, Siu said. About 14 percent of the women surveyed in cities acknowledged that they had had extramarital sex.

The Chinese survey, referred to in Shanghai as China's "Kinsey report," reached more people than Alfred Kinsey did in his reports on Americans' sexual behavior in the late 1940s. The Kinsey report, which included responses from 16,000 people, was considered a breakthrough in research on sexual behavior.

Liu said in an interview that two Chinese newspapers and a women s magazine would begin publishing a limited summary of the findings this month. Academic specialists will be given a full, book-length report. A series of smaller books summarizing the results will be published for the "masses," he said. But full-blown publicity such as heralded the Kinsey reports in the United States would be unthinkable in China's current repressive climate.

The survey suggests that alongside a tradition of sexual sophistication among the elite, seen in Chinese literature, there has also been much ignorance of sexual behavior.

The study shows, for example, that many Chinese engage in a minimum of foreplay, with the result that 44 percent of urban wives and 37 percent of rural wives feel some pain at times during intercourse. But the trend is toward less shyness and more sexual experimentation, Liu said.

Liu, who is director of the Shanghai Sex Sociology Research Center, has actively promoted sex education in Shanghai. Secondary schools in China's largest city began introducing courses on an experimental basis for the first time in 1985.

But Liu said that in Shanghai and other cities, only a relatively small number of physicians, psychologists and others are qualified to deal with sexual problems arising from the rapid changes in Chinese society.

Several years ago, the Chinese press began to report the reemergence of venereal diseases long thought to have been eliminated in China. This was attributed by Chinese officials to growing sexual promiscuity, or what they described as the adaptation of Western-style sexual freedoms by a growing number of Chinese youths.

The number of AIDS cases reported in China has been extremely small compared with the numbers reported in many other countries. Chinese medical authorities say that most Chinese who have been detected either carrying the AIDS virus or suffering from acquired immune deficiency syndrome in this country have been foreigners or Chinese who infected themselves through using dirty needles to inject drugs.

But only a few weeks ago, an official at the Chinese Ministry of Public Health admitted that five years after the discovery of the first AIDS victim in China, it is still uncertain to what extent the AIDS threat is affecting the population, because only a very limited number of people in high-risk groups have been tested for the fatal disease.

The cost of conducting the recently completed nationwide survey was extremely low—about $20,000—in part because volunteers worked for a pittance and a Shanghai college offered computers.

Liu contributed some of his own money from royalties earned on books he has written on sex and marriage.

May 27, 1990

Despair of Brazilian Tribe Reflected in Suicides: As Development Erodes Traditional Life, Youths Turn to Alcohol, Violence, and Death

Julia Preston

Cida Martins, a 13-year-old Guarani Indian girl, hanged herself on April 8 from a tree in the manioc field behind her house.

Claudete Cabreira, also 13, poisoned herself with insecticide last December. Of five members of her Guarani family to commit suicide, she was the youngest.

Susana Nunes was 17 years old, four months married and two months pregnant when she hanged herself in March, three weeks after her 14-year-old husband had taken his own life.

In an epidemic of youth suicides that has hit the Guarani Indians of midwestern Brazil, 34 deaths and 36 attempts—all by hanging or poison—have been reported since the beginning of 1990. Most occurred on a reservation here that is home to 7,300 Indians, the largest concentration of Guaranis in Brazil.

There were six suicides in 10 days at the end of last year. The reservation nurse, Ine Brasil Caraja, said seven Indian youths on the reservation are under observation after trying to kill themselves in the past two weeks.

Indian leaders and anthropologists say the suicides reflect the despair of Brazil's largest Indian tribe after its way of life was shattered by the expansion of agribusiness in this region during the past 30 years.

"The material conditions for the survival of their culture are disappearing," said Odenir Pinto de Oliveira, regional director of the government agency for Indian affairs, known as FUNAI.

In the early decades of this century the Guarani were still the undisputed masters of the vast and fertile forested plains of the state of Mato Grosso do Sul. They farmed, hunted and fished, and celebrated their belief that they were descendants of the sun. Each extended family had its own settlement, spread widely apart from other families.

Carlito de Oliveira, 32, a leader of the Guaranis on the Dourados reservation, recalled that during his lifetime, "Whites came from outside to make huge farms. The forest was cut, the birds flew away, the fish died."

Successive Brazilian governments encouraged the development and sought to integrate the Indians into white society as stoop laborers. For those Indians who clung to their culture, Odenir de Oliveira said, "minuscule" reservations were set aside.

Today 23,000 Guaranis live on 7,900 acres in 16 reservations, eight of which are embroiled in legal disputes with private landowners because their borders were never clearly defined by the government. In some areas Guaranis have been thrown off their reservations by ranchers and are waging court battles to regain their lands. Many Guaranis are no longer able to farm at all.

Another tribe, the Terenas, shares the Dourados reservation. No suicides have been reported among the Terenas, who are more prosperous than the Guaranis but who no longer speak their own language or practice distinctive customs.

The Dourados reservation is being engulfed by a booming city. With 10-story bank buildings in view, many Guaranis live like refugees, in huts with no walls and only plastic bags for roofs.

Among Guarani teenagers, alcoholism and violence are high. Medical examination of the body of Cida Martins showed that she had been raped shortly before her death.

Jose Nunes, father of suicide victim Susana, said his son-in-law Florencio killed himself during a binge on cane alcohol. One evening Florencio attacked Susana and two small children with a knife before hanging himself.

"I told Susana that the violence of the world is great, and we can't allow our minds to weaken," the mourning father said. But Nunes said his daughter couldn't bear the "shame" of being widowed and pregnant.

Many young Guaranis are sent by their parents to cut cane and pick cotton on big farms. According to anthropologist Maria Aparecida Pereira, this has been devastating to the Guaranis. "They are out of contact with their gods," Pereira said.

Reginaldo Valdes was 13 when he hanged himself from a rafter in a farm barracks last year. "He was all alone," said his mother, Laurinda Valdes.

April 20, 1991

Chapter 2

Culture

In addition to studying "American" (that is, United States) culture, an understanding of other societies' cultural elements broadens and deepens our ability to place important world events in context and sheds new light on our own experience. The writers of the following articles investigate the cultural practices of other peoples and provide us with some fascinating glimpses of life in five very different societies.

Beginning on a light note, the first three articles in this section describe some interesting cultural traditions in Japan, Hungary, and China, including, respectively, one-night dates that cost $1,000; a nation of dog lovers; and fashion and beauty, Chinese style.

Article 4 describes a prosperous Japan that nevertheless finds many Japanese worried that their core values of hard work, loyalty to the group, and aversion to things foreign are now being threatened by that same prosperity.

U.S. troops stationed in Saudi Arabia during the 1991 Persian Gulf War encountered vastly different cultural practices than their own. Some of their experiences are recounted in the next two articles.

The final article in this section describes some of the cultural clashes that are an ongoing part of life in the new Germany. When the Berlin Wall fell, and East and West Germany was reunited after a forty-year separation, great joy was felt by both countries. However, the reality of integrating two peoples—brothers and sisters, perhaps, but strangers with distinctive cultures as well—is proving difficult.

Snug in Their Beds for Christmas Eve; In Japan, December 24th Has Become the Hottest Night of the Year

T.R. Reid

For young people all over the Christian world, this evening will be a night of magic and wonder. Here in Japan as well, Christmas Eve has become immensely important—but for rather different reasons.

It has become the sexiest night of the year.

Japanese popular culture has made Christmas Eve a night when every unmarried person must have a date, and it is now de rigueur for the date to include an overnight stay. For weeks now TV shows, magazines and manga (adult comic books) have been full of reports and advice on which hotels are best for young couples to stay in on Christmas Eve, what each partner should wear, and where the pair should have breakfast the next morning.

Virtually every major hotel in Tokyo reports that Dec. 24 has been sold out for months. At the popular Sheraton Grande Hotel, which has installed a larger-than-life plastic Nativity scene in its lobby to add to the ambiance, all rooms have been reserved—and paid in advance—since April.

"Christmas Eve is now important as a night for making love," complains poet and social critic Hazuki Kajiwara. This is such a widely accepted aspect of the day known here as eebu, the Japanese pronunciation of "eve," that Dec. 24 is frequently referred to as "H-Day." The letter H, taken from the English word "hormone," is a common symbol here for sex.

The eebu phenomenon is carried out in an intensely materialistic, free-spending atmosphere, reflecting the commercial nature of the Christmas season in Japan. In a country less than 1 percent Christian, Dec. 25 is just another working day; yet stores and restaurants here have more Christmas trees, wreaths and reindeer on display than most places in the United States.

For a couple's Christmas Eve fling, the man is expected to bear all costs. Many "salary men" save all year for this one date. Media reports here estimate that the cost of a typical couple's Christmas Eve will exceed $1,000.

The newsmagazine Asahi Journal last week printed a breakdown of a fairly standard "Eve course"—that is, the itinerary of a Tokyo couple's Christmas Eve date. The itinerary, incidentally, gives the lie to the notion that Japanese people won't spend their money on American goods.

When the man arrives to pick up his date, the magazine said, he should present her with a $215 silver heart pendant from Tiffany and then take her out for an evening at Tokyo Disneyland, where admission and extras will cost $100 or so. Then it's on to dinner for two at a French or American restaurant ($385) and a

17

room for the night overlooking Tokyo Bay at the Hilton or the Sheraton Grande ($300, or $650 for a suite). Breakfast in the hotel coffee shop should cost only $35, but a rental limousine to take the couple to their homes so they can quickly change and go to work will cost another $150.

Things would be cheaper if the couple could just go to one of the thousands of "love hotels" here, where a room costs about $30 for two hours. But the popular magazines have decreed that this is too tacky for such a special night.

But eebu is hardly a free ride for Japanese women. They must pay the emotional cost.

Women between college age and their mid-thirties have more money and more independence today than ever before in Japanese history. But they are losing connection to family and peer groups, and are struggling to survive on their own.

"Behind the traditional Japanese groupism is a fear of being alone," says Hikaru Hayashi, senior research director at the Hakuhodo Institute, a sociological think tank. For single women, "Christmas Eve enhances the fear that they are not rooted to society."

With everybody making elaborate plans for eebu, it is a social necessity for single women to have a date that night. The tribulations of those who don't have become the subject of enormous media attention.

A travel agency called Kinki Nihon Tourist (the word "kinki" here is strictly geographic, referring to the central section of Japan's main island, Honshu) has been advertising excursion trips for singles this fall under the headline "Find a Boyfriend by Christmas!"

This fall, the Tokyo Broadcasting System ran a 12-part miniseries called "Christmas Eve." The story concerned a young "office lady" who listened to her friends chattering about the fancy restaurants and hotels they were going to for eebu but was ashamed to admit she had no date. Last week, in the final episode, a young man called her at the last minute. The two walked off happily into the night, presumably in search of a hotel with a vacant room.

The popular comic book serial "Office Lady Story" this month features an episode called "29-Year-Old's Christmas." It features an office worker who comes home to her one-room apartment to find a piece of junk mail advertising a Christmas party where single women can meat men. When she sees the price, $400, she angrily throws the flier away. Later that night, though, sitting alone with her hair in curlers, she pulls it out of the trash and says, "Well, it's only $400... .

The idea that it might be shameful for a single woman to spend the night with her date is less commonly expressed, but it does occur. Sampei Sato, the widely followed editorial cartoonist for the national newspaper Asahi Shimbun, devoted his space one day this month to an appeal to young unmarried women to sleep at home rather than in a hotel on Christmas Eve.

While young men are emptying their wallets and young women are waiting for the phone to ring, the rest of Japanese society, never shy about analyzing itself, is busily talking about how Christmas Eve became a time for sex.

One theory involves a pop singer named Yumi Matsutoya, who had a hit record titled "My Boyfriend Is My Santa Claus." In a homogeneous society where people swarm to each new fashion, some analysts say that song helped turn Christmas Eve into the most important date of the year.

The calendar may also have fed the fad. Last year, Dec. 24 fell on a Sunday, the only day when almost every Japanese worker is off. This year, the 24th is a national holiday because of the birthday of the newly enthroned emperor, Akihito.

For whatever reason, the new view of eebu has increased the Japanese people's belief that they are unique. "In the whole world," said the lead-in to a TV talk show last week, "only Japan has turned the day before Christmas into a day for sex."

December 24, 1990

In Eastern Europe, Every Dog Has Its Day; Trims & Tradition at a Canine Salon

Blaine Harden

Sammy needs a haircut.

Last time he needed a haircut—that was in January—he bit his hairdresser on the breast.

Sammy has an appointment here at Kosmetika, a downtown salon where most clients do not even bark under the blow-dryer, let alone bite. Naturally, not everyone is looking forward to Sammy's arrival. Yet he is a longtime customer and he does live with a Budapest actress. The schnauzer is due at 1 pm.

"We try to make every dog feel that he or she is a part of what is happening here," explains Marika Szucs, who has been trimming dogs in the Hungarian capita] since 1961, trimming Sammy since 1985.

She has given a lot of thought to the unpleasantness that transpired back in January.

"Sammy was preparing to bite me for five years. It was the owner's fault really. She took off the muzzle too soon. I was very fast and he didn't get a really good bite. And you know, after he bit me, he felt much better about himself. Now we are good friends," says Szucs, puffing thoughtfully on an extra-long filter cigarette, awaiting her 1 o'clock. "Of course, you still have to steal the hair off that dog."

European culture is, by American standards, notably indulgent when it comes to dogs. From Paris to Prague, Ljubljana to Leningrad, dogs accompany their owners—to dinner at the finest restaurants, to weekends at the finest hotels. They ride trains, trams, subways and buses, often sitting side by side with their masters. Dogs in Europe go shopping, attend conferences and frequent parties.

By and large, they do it with less whining, growling, leash-jerking, spitting up and biting than might be expected of American canines. It is not at all unusual to see a European dog behave better in a restaurant than its owner, particularly in a German beer hall.

In Eastern Europe, where communism kept consumerism under grim wraps for half a century, dog ownership flourished as a link to the dignity and manners of the prewar urban bourgeoisie. Not only does the average mutt one encounters in the cities of Eastern Europe behave him- or herself, such a dog is likely to be well-fed, well-exercised and well-groomed.

A handsome, disciplined, nattily coiffed dog on a leash once served as a civilized symbol of dissidence. While Communists could ruin the economy, defile the environment and build hideous neighborhoods out of concrete, they could not come between a cultured European and his dog.

Budapest, which has endured as the most ostentatiously elegant of Eastern European capitals, has 14 downtown dog parlors. Pending privatization of the economy, which will come as part of the new democratic government, these parlors are state cooperatives.

The former Communist government here tried (and failed) to split the difference between a Soviet command-style economy and a socialist market economy. In its failure, however, it mildly encouraged dog care. Besides coop dog parlors catering to non-working-class canines such as Lhasa apsos and Shih Tzus, there were state-sponsored seminars to educate people in how to wash and trim dogs.

Szucs, a lifelong dog lover who owns five dogs and breeds Kerry blue terriers, lectured at these seminars for two decades. Her dog-care theories are built around a central axiom: A dog that looks good feels good.

"Dogs like coming here," she says while waiting for Sammy to show up. "Some may act as if it is beneath their dignity. But when these dogs go back home, they are the ones who are most proud of the way they look. Oh, they absolutely know they look better. I know one dog, a white poodle, that will not go home after a cut until he shows off for all the neighbors."Kosmetika—a sign out front says "The Salon Awaits Its Favorites"—caters to the vanities of its clients. Like many beauty parlors where human beings are shampooed, scissored and blow-dried, the walls are hung with brilliantly colored photographs of impossibly handsome creatures fresh from a perfect cut. There are Pekingese with ribbons in their hair and close-ups of cocker spaniels, their heads tilted coyly.

After a few bracing minutes with the shampoo girl (who works in a rubber apron at a long deep sink), Kosmetika clients are carried out to the trim tables, where they stand shivering, waiting to be toweled off.

The smaller and skinnier clients, such as miniature schnauzers, seem to shrink in the minutes they spend in the shampoo sink. They emerge looking like bony, long-legged rats.

All of which brings to mind Sammy, a black miniature schnauzer who has always hated and has always tried to bite the shampoo girl.

A brother of the Budapest actress who owns Sammy brings him in for his 1 o'clock. When the brother lifts him into a waiting-room cage, Sammy nips him on the hand. The brother, hardly wounded, not complaining, leaves.

The Encyclopedia of Dogs, which is available for light reading in Kosmetika, goes on at some length about the difficulties of being a schnauzer.

"Faults include a level bite, a soft slick coat, toyishness, light or prominent eyes, shyness and viciousness, sway or roached back, loose elbows, and bowed or cow-hocked hindquarters," the encyclopedia says.

His elbows seem fine, but Sammy clearly is not in a good mood. When it is time for his cut, Szucs collects him from the cage and carries him, growling, to her trim table.

On the table next to Sammy is a giant Russian terrier, a cheerful, clumsy-footed pup roughly 10 times the size of Sammy. The Russian terrier pokes a play-ful nose in the schnauzer's direction, an overture that Sammy haughtily ignores.

"I am sure this dog likes me," says Szucs as she begins to trim Sammy's strag-gly hair. "But I can see in his eyes what he thinks about haircuts. He thinks, 'I can't take much of this.'

After a quarter hour of squirming and feinting, sitting and lying down—all to evade the electric clippers—Sammy bares his teeth and starts snapping. For the next two hours, Szucs trims painstakingly at those hairs Sammy seems willing to lose.

"You should be ashamed of yourself," Szucs keeps saying.

When it is over, Sammy is noticeably less ornery. The actress will be coming for him soon. Szucs says that Sammy's friends describe him as a wonderful, affec-tionate schnauzer outside the salon.

He is, after all, a middle-aged Central European dog of good family.

May 7, 1990

Foreign Journal: The Makeup of China

Lena H. Sun

In downtown Shanghai, not far from the city's Communist Party headquarters, well-dressed women wait for beautician Zhu Lanying to make over their faces. Some want their eyebrows dyed darker; others want their eyelashes curled. A daring few opt for "dream makeup"—tiny moons and stars painted on their cheeks.

"People need to pay attention to their looks," explained Zhu as she put the finishing touches on a 21-year-old woman who had come to the Huaan Beauty Parlor to get a "new wave" look for her eyebrows. "No one thinks about beauty as bourgeois any more. Most people think that looking nice has become a kind of courtesy."

And it is not just here in China's largest and most cosmopolitan city that fashion and beauty reign. On the streets of the country's major cities, heavily made-up faces, nail polish and elaborate hairdos are common sights.

Wig stores are all the rage as fashion-conscious women try to stay abreast of the latest styles. Surgery to change eyelids to resemble Caucasian eyes has been popular for several years. And it is even common for young men, especially those working with foreigners in joint-venture companies, to have their hair permed.

The history of the Huaan Beauty Parlor, on bustling Nanjing Road, reflects the fortunes of fashion and beauty in up-to-date China. Huaan dates back 70 years, when it was opened by a Russian in the days when Shanghai was known as the "Paris of the East" for its freewheeling economy, casinos, opium dens, brothels and dance halls.

Nanjing Road was then one of Shanghai's four famous streets, lined by the city's most expensive shops and restaurants. "The beauty parlor was so expensive that the Chinese could not afford to come, and most of its customers were foreigners and most of the employees were Russians," said Du Dongping, who handles public relations for the beauty parlor. Sun Yat-sen, the founder of the Chinese republic, was one of its most famous customers, she said.

In those times, what a customer wanted, a customer got. But the rise of the Communists in 1949 changed things. The leadership in Beijing considered such enterprises bourgeois and the beauty parlor eventually came under severe restrictions.

During the 1966-76 Cultural Revolution, Chinese who wore Western clothes or makeup were labeled capitalist and subject to physical attacks by leftist Red Guards. During those days, fashion was confined to varying shades of the ubiquitous, unisex Mao suit.

But the era of economic reforms and opening to the West that began in the late 1970s allowed the display of a different aesthetic sense among Chinese, and fashion and beauty here came under decidedly Western influence. Even now, as the hard-line Communist leadership proclaims China's unwavering socialist future and tries to keep out Western influences, party apparatchiks know they no longer have the power to dictate a uniform dress code for the country's 1.1 billion citizens.

Today, several cities have modeling schools and China's first televised beauty contest aired on Beijing television last month, although it was different from American versions: There was no swimsuit competition and the entrants were judged by their skill in making others look good, not on how they looked.

An American suntan-lotion manufacturer, however, hopes to change that. It plans to tape the finals of the Miss Hawaiian Tropic pageant, featuring contestants wearing one-piece swimsuits, in Beijing's Forbidden City. To help promote the event, the manufacturer brought in a Playboy magazine centerfold model, a sixth-generation Chinese-American.

Here in Shanghai, at the forefront of fashion, it is clear that beauty and style are no longer defined by political trends. Not long ago, the faded but elegant Peace Hotel, one of the city's most famous landmarks, held a lavish ball that drew jetsetters from all over Asia.

Along the Bund, the wide boulevard lined with 1930s-era European architecture reminiscent of the Western powers' occupation of the city, affluent men and women sport tastefully coordinated Western-style outfits. Among Chinese youth, tight bluejeans, leather jackets, and designer sports shoes are the common garb.

The Huaan salon, an unusually profitable state-owned enterprise, now boasts a clientele that includes movie stars, pop singers and the wife of one of Shanghai's deputy mayors. On a busy weekend day, the salon is crowded with as many as 70 young women—brides and their attendants—who need to have their hair and faces done and nerves soothed.

"For the brides, we mostly use imported cosmetics from Hong Kong and Japan," Du said. "For the maids of honor, we generally use the Chinese-made cosmetics."

Starting last year, the beauty parlor began offering its "dream makeup" to customers who wanted something special for a night out. As in many other cities, Shanghai's karaoke, or sing-along, bars and dance halls are popular gathering places for the young and for affluent private entrepreneurs, the Chinese nouveaux riches who made money as a result of senior leader Deng Xiaoping's economic reforms.

"Very few people want to have [dream makeup] on their face during the day, but they like to use it for dances and parties," Du said.

For a more conventional look, dying eyebrows a darker black has become very popular, Shin said. The price is steep—70 yuan, about $13.40, nearly half of the monthly wages of an average worker. But, as Zhu pointed out, "You will have these eyebrows for the rest of your life."

In the next few months, the salon plans to introduce a line of women's wigs as well as imported massage and steam machines to help people lose weight, another decidedly Western obsession. "After the reforms, who doesn't want to look a little younger and prettier?" said Zhu.

April 8, 1991

Crossing the Culture Gulf: For the U.S. Troops, an Arab Primer

Amy Goldstein

For the U.S. troops in Saudi Arabia, transplanted abruptly to an alien part of the world, standard-issue equipment includes a booklet with this advice:

Arab women aren't allowed to date, so don't try to ask one out.

If you get into an empty elevator with an Arab, don't be surprised if he stands so close that he is touching you.

When sitting with an Arab, be careful not to expose the sole of your shoe, because the gesture would be construed as a "grievous insult."

These lessons are part of a hasty primer to the Middle East that the U.S. military is providing its troops. According to educators and members of the armed services, these are vital lessons for many of the tens of thousands of soldiers and sailors arriving in the Middle East unfamiliar with the region's history, politics and culture.

"I think [the soldiers] understand the global picture, that right now we are a deterrent helping Saudi Arabia with their own defense," said 2nd Lt. John Ford, 23, a West Point graduate who oversees a 10-member fire support unit preparing to leave from Fort Stewart, Ga.

"But if you're talking about factions within the Islam world, the national sphere... they are not overly inquisitive," Ford said of his soldiers. "To be quite honest with you, the main concern... [is] not world geography or political science."

With the mobilization too sudden for detailed history lessons, what most of the troops know about Saudi Arabia depends on what they have seen on television or learned in high school.

According to a Pentagon spokesman, 94 percent of the U.S. armed forces' enlisted personnel have not attended college. The Pentagon has not kept separate figures for the troops sent to Saudi Arabia, but the spokesman, Maj. Doug Hart, said that their education level is probably similar to that of the armed forces as a whole.

And as elementary and secondary school students, the troops were likely to have learned little about the Middle East. Half of the nation's high school graduates have been taught nothing about the region beyond its location on a map, according to a recent survey by the Middle East Outreach Council, a national group of teachers and college professors trying to promote education about the area.

"If students in a 12-year education get more than three weeks on the Middle East, I would be shocked," said Andrew Smith, president of the American Forum for Global Education, a nonprofit group in New York.

What lessons are taught, educators said, may be counteracted by negative stereotypes in movies, television and comic strips. "All these soldiers have spent their childhoods in a society that has regularly depicted the Arab as a greasy person with a long headdress and a big nose," said Sandra Batmangelich, outreach coordinator for the University of Chicago's Center for Middle Eastern Studies, which runs workshops for teachers around the country.

There is little concrete evidence of what Americans—and military personnel, in particular—know about the Middle East. But a 1988 National Geographic survey found that 75 percent of U.S. adults could not locate the Persian Gulf on a world map.

Lt. Denise McDowell, a Navy nurse from Gaithersburg, said she felt ill-prepared when she learned she was to leave Bethesda Naval Hospital to join the hospital ship USNS Comfort. "I knew of Kuwait," she said. "I really wasn't sure where Iraq was, to be honest with you." Before she left this week, McDowell said, she contacted a University of Maryland instructor for recommended reading.

In some cases, perceptions of the region are tinged with military fervor. Navy Petty Officer 2nd Class Jim Johnson, who is from Hershey, Pa., and is stationed in Norfolk, said, "In high school, I had a real good social studies teacher" who taught about the Koran, the Islamic holy book. "Allah is everything. They are willing to die for him."

As a Middle East primer for departing troops, each unit in all military branches has been given one of two booklets — one on the region, the other on Saudi Arabia. Each unit commander is responsible for briefing his troops.

The more general booklet includes a four-paragraph section on history. "The Arab world is a land of ancient yesterdays, a thriving today, and tomorrows of great promise," it begins. Other sections deal with customs, the importance of religion and the role of women.

At Fort Stewart, Army Pfc. Thomas Olschewski, 21, from Vancouver, Wash., said he had been "drilled over and over" during the previous week on Arabic vocabulary and Middle Eastern culture.

"You can't hold hands with the opposite sex. You don't lift up any veils of the women, because then they're yours for life," Olschewski said. "I don't know a lot, but I feel like I know enough."

Staff Sgt. Ervin J. Jennings, 30, a communications specialist who also was preparing to leave from Fort Stewart, said he had been stationed in the Middle East from 1987 to 1989. In preparation this time for Saudi Arabia, Jennings said, he has briefed his 20-man platoon, whose members have asked him "just little things: How did they come to the custom of having a king? Who is the king?"

But Jennings said such issues are ancillary. "Right now, we could care less about the religion, the politics, the history," he said. "We are training them {in} things that are going to save their life in the desert, in the front lines."

Educators, far from the Saudi desert, think cultural lessons may be more important.

"You're going to have 45,000, 100,000 people or more going into a traditional Moslem county where drinking is prohibited, where there is [little] language capacity," said Smith, of the Forum for Global Education. "A year from now, or two years, you are going to have huge problems of local population with regard to the military."

Added Jonathan Friedlander, who runs summer workshops for teachers through the Near East Center at the University of California at Los Angeles: "It seems to me, if you fight for something that endangers your life, you better know what the issues are."

August 23, 1990

Crossing the Culture Gulf: For Female Soldiers, Different Rules

Molly Moore

After a grueling, hot, dusty day on the edge of one of the busiest military airstrips in Saudi Arabia, U.S. Air Force Lt. Col. Lois Schwartz would like nothing better than to relax the way she would back home: shopping, but in this case at the small arcade across the steamy street from the schoolhouse-turned-barracks where she bunks.

But in this society, where Arab women often see the world from behind black veils, Schwartz, like other women among the American troops deployed to Saudi Arabia, cannot take her sandy clothes to the laundry or even buy a bar of soap at a store. She can run errands only if escorted by a male who must pay for her toiletries while she stands nearby, eyes focused on the floor to avoid offending Arab shopkeepers.

"It's frustrating," said Schwartz, who runs the Air Force 1st Tactical Fighter Wing's field hospital at this air base, the location of which cannot be named under u.S military rules. "We work long hours, it's hot, and we can't even have the release of going across the street to the store."

For many Arabs here, the independence and lifestyle of American military women seem perplexing and sometimes disconcerting. And for American military women, who are used to struggling for rank and status in a male-dominated institution, the restrictive Arab culture is an added strain in an already austere environment.

Deferring to Arab sensibilities can be nothing more than a minor irritation, but at other times it can be oppressive. For example, when desert temperatures soar above 120 degrees, the men strip off their heavy battle fatigue jackets and work in their T-shirts. But the women smother; they must continue to wear their desert jackets—fully buttoned—as well as T-shirts underneath.

The U.S. military obtained special permission from the Saudis to allow its many women drivers to operate trucks and forklifts in a culture that forbids women to drive.

The Saudis recently agreed to allow the 100 women of the airlift hospital to use, for a few hours each week, the gymnasium in the school where they are housed. But the gym is closed to men during these periods, and the women—even while swimming—must wear loose-fitting blouses and knee-length shorts.

Male and female Army troops sleep in the same tents during military exercises in the United States, Germany and elsewhere, but here the sexes are strictly segregated.

At an Army staging base on the edge of this airfield, most of the women troops—truck drivers, intelligence specialists, communications technicians and others—are housed in an unused Saudi military building, while men sleep in a tent city pitched in the nearby desert. When women soldiers are assigned to tents, they are kept segregated from the men, a base official said.

"We're just used to being so free," said a 21-year-old dental technician working at the field hospital. "We don't know where the rules are coming from. We get very mixed signals."

Women in the hospital unit say, for example, that while some shopkeepers will not allow them to enter stores without their heads covered, other merchants seem oblivious to bare heads.

And many of the women here have had conflicting reactions from Arab men.

A woman captain assigned to an airlift support unit in the neighboring United Arab Emirates said Saudi soldiers she has met have been curious but polite in their dealings.

"They stare a lot," she said. "But they treat us very well—better than a lot of American men."

But Schwartz does not share that view. "The men don't like to speak with us," she said "They have trouble dealing with women."

August 23, 1990

Sudden Riches Creating Conflict and Self-doubt: Nation Is Pressed to Define Its Values

Fred Hiatt and Margaret Shapiro

Beginning next month in the ancient capital city of Nara, you will be able to buy a cup of coffee for $350.

Your Evian water will be heated in a gold kettle, poured through Jamaican Blue Mountain coffee, dusted with real gold and served in gold-plated Royal Minton china. A genuine Renoir painting will hang on the coffee shop wall. And, as in many other such places in Japan catering to the very rich, you will be able to linger as long as you like.

"In and around Nara these days, there are many people with money, but they're not so good at spending it," said Nobuhisa Tomishige, spokesman for the department store where the coffee shop is located. "We hope to make their lives more colorful."

For 45 years, since the end of World War II, Japan doggedly worked to catch up to the United States, eschewing any other ideology and postponing pleasure. Now, many Japanese are taking a crash course in spending money, buying $2 million golf club memberships and $700 steaks, gold-wrapped sushi and mink coats for dogs. Japan, with 123 million people, has triple the net assets, per capita, of the United States, and its per capita income has also surpassed America's.

But this sudden wealth is creating new conflict and self-doubt within Japanese society, just as Japan is being pressed by the world to define its values and intentions.

No one can predict how those values will evolve, whether prosperity and its pressures will revive the arrogant nationalism of the past or nurture stable democracy and international cooperation. Given Japan's increasing clout, the course it follows will have an important impact on the world at large.

True to form, Japan is changing cautiously. The changes are sometimes invisible, sometimes less than meets the eye and often less than what the outside world demands. But they are real.

Farmers and shopkeepers, long protected from outside competition, sense trouble ahead as the government slowly gives in to foreign pressure for open markets. The postwar compact of equal labor for equal gain, in which all Japanese worked hard, confident they would get a fair share of the nation's prosperity, is being tested as rivers of cash flow unevenly through society.

An aging political leadership that many view as corrupt is seeking to bequeath power to sons and sons-in-law, threatening the meritocracy that rose out of the ashes of Japan's wartime defeat. Women, though still shut out of most positions of power, are becoming more assertive. The young generation is seeking a new balance between work and pleasure. Many Japanese want more creativity and less conformity, and are eager for Japan to play a more active role in the world.

Some Look to Past

For some, the changes, like the wealth, have come too fast. In its headlong sprint to prosperity, Japan has sacrificed much of its natural beauty and, some conservatives say, its values. Having become, by many measures, the richest people in the world, these Japanese now wonder for what they worked so hard.

Some seek answers in Japan's past, and in an inward-looking nationalism. For others, the changes are coming too slowly.

Japan has been "internationalizing" for more than a century, yet remains peculiarly insular, many Japanese complain. It has achieved wealth, yet remains focused on producing more, not on enjoying what it has achieved. Its closed world of endless study, brutal examinations, lifetime employment and 12-hour workdays demands full allegiance; those who step out even briefly still have trouble getting back in.

"If you look at our generation, we prefer time over money, and we don't want to work as hard as our parents," said Fujika Motoyama, 22, a literature student at Keio University. "But Japanese, from a small age, are brought up into a competitive society, and if we fall one step behind, we feel anxiety.

"So maybe without intending to, when we grow up and enter the adult world, we may not be so different from our parents," he said.

Outside critics also remain skeptical of change. Japanese may buy more Van Gogh paintings, spend more days than they used to on Hawaiian beaches, even take Saturdays off, but, the critics say, the basic values of hard work, loyalty to group and authority, reluctance to speak out and aversion to anything foreign—people, cars or semiconductors—will never change.

"Anyone who has ever worked on Japan has a file full of articles on Japan at the crossroads," said Chalmers Johnson, a professor of international relations at the University of California in San Diego. "Whereas all Japan has ever done is stand at the crossroads. They don't change."

Those who live here often feel differently.

"If you look day by day or month by month, nothing changes. It is so frustrating," said Sadako Ogata, director of the Institute of International Relations at Sophia University. "But compared with five years ago, the changes are amazing."

Indeed, portraits of change and the anxiety it is causing can be found throughout this island nation:

As evening descends on his steep hillside farm, Katsuyuki Suzuki can almost hear Japan in flux. A heavy truck grinds its gears as it climbs a nearby expressway. A young woman's voice recites the next day's weather forecast in echoing singsong from loudspeakers strung from ridge to ridge.

Through the mist, the twinkling lights of the encroaching city of Mishima seem to dance into Suzuki's neat rows of cabbages and carrots as he talks about his struggle—and that of many others—to continue working the land in modern, crowded Japan. Suzuki, 40, wants his son to succeed him, as he followed his father and his father's father before him.

"This is my intention," Suzuki said softly, kicking at some mud with his boots as the loudspeakers break into chimes. "But 10 out of 10 of my friends say, 'I don't want my son to take over the business.' Because they don't have any hope."

'Taking a Chance'

Naoki Iwata, 23, will graduate from Keio University this spring. Unlike most classmates at his prestigious private college, Iwata will not enter a corporation to begin what many see as the real education in Japanese life. Instead, fascinated by political change in Europe, Iwata will head to West Germany to study.

"I'm taking a chance," Iwata said. "My dad wanted me to get into a big company, but it's not my lifestyle. I probably wouldn't make it, and I'd just make problems for my co-workers.

"I don't want to go through all the hassles before I get to the top," he said.

Iwata isn't unique, though he is an exception. His classmate, Hideshige Saito, listens enviously as Iwata describes his plans in a coffee shop near campus. Saito wants to go abroad too, he said, but instead will go to work for Sony Corp. "One has to give way to social conventions," he said.

High school teacher Sumire Ogawa and her husband saved for years to buy a house. In postwar Japan, it was understood: Everyone would work hard, everyone would share in whatever prosperity came Japan's way.

But the Ogawas found that when they reached their goal, housing prices had soared 10- and sometimes a hundredfold, as land prices climbed to an average 25 times higher than in the United States. Politicians with lower salaries seemed to have no problem buying homes, Ogawa wrote in a letter to the editor of Asahi newspaper. But for the Ogawas, "In just a few years, our dream became impossible."

Now, their daughter must commute by train three hours to school, standing each way. And Ogawa no longer believes that wealth and success are based on hard work.

"Those who don't own land live inhuman lives, while those who obtained land through improper means or were lucky enough to be born to landowners become even richer," she said.

The Ogawas are not alone. Although almost all Japanese still see themselves as middle-class, a growing number place themselves in the lower ranks of the middle, according to surveys by the prime minister's office. In a 1989 poll, 32 percent of respondents said they were worse off, while only 3 percent said their lives had improved compared to the previous year.

The resentments of the have-nots—or, more appropriately for Japan, the have-lesses—seemed to crystallize last year when almost every top ruling politician was revealed to have benefited from an insider-trading stock deal. The Recruit scandal, as it was known, involved few illegalities, according to prosecutors. But for many ordinary Japanese, it pulled back a curtain from the clubby political world, where one-third of ruling politicians have inherited their seats, and seemed to prove that the booming stock and land markets work for the benefit of a powerful few.

"We have begun to see a new type of inequality, beyond the control of personal endeavor or effort," said Koichi Kato, a leader in the Diet, Japan's parliament. "So people have started to feel that opportunity is going to be lost in this country. I think that is a very, very dangerous issue."

Equally perturbing to many Japanese is the conspicuous consumption in a culture where frugality has long been revered.

At least once a week, it seems, a record falls somewhere in the world to a Japanese purchaser: most expensive fur pelt, about a half-foot long, purchased at auction ($8,400); most expensive portrait of a living person (a painting of Michael Jackson, sold for $2.1 million); most expensive bed slept in by Marilyn Monroe (the bed she shared with Joe DiMaggio, purchased by a Japanese furniture company president for $60,300).

Many who object are people like the Ogawas, whose lives remain hard, the statistics notwithstanding. Others, like longtime political insider Shigezo Hayasaka, see the spending as a sign of weakness in the young and a portent of decline.

"I've never seen such luxurious consumption, and I've never seen such waste," Hayasaka said. "And like the end of the Roman empire, I think it's inevitable there will be some punishment."

'Something Is Lacking'

The most fundamental disquiet, though, seems to stem from a sense that, in chasing the West, Japan must have been seeking something more than $350 cups of coffee—and in a sense that no one now is sure what that elusive something should be.

"Japanese people are materialistically well-off, but not inside, not in our hearts, not how we enjoy life," said Saito, the graduating Keio student. "We're brought into this competitive world so young, and then we enter the company, and then we work so hard. We never have time to find ourselves, or what we should seek in life."

Added Motofumi Asai, a former diplomat now teaching at Tokyo University, "As the Japanese people have become more prosperous, they have come to feel as though something is lacking."

Some here fear that the search for meaning in prosperity will lead back, not to militarism, but to the kind of self-satisfied nationalism that let Japan believe before the war that it deserved to lead all of Asia. "One of the greatest dangers," Asai said, are Japan's Japanologists, who preach the theme of uniqueness while "disregarding the common values of liberal democracy."

"I am afraid they are increasing their market in Japan," Asai said.

The national flag and anthem, long neglected due to Japan's revulsion with anything smacking of wartime patriotism, soon will be required at school ceremonies again, by government decree. School rules have grown more rigid.

"Education is becoming more conformist again," said social critic Takashi Tachibana. "It worries me very much."

Asai and others said they worry in part because Japan's democracy was imposed by the United States after World War II, leaving them uncertain how deeply it has sunk roots in Japanese society.

In addition, unlike older Japanese who remember American magnanimity in victory, young Japanese feel no gratitude for their prosperity—and nearly two-thirds of the population was born after 1945.

Shuichi Kato, a leading liberal philosopher, said a kind of "GNP nationalism" is growing among such people, sparked by Japan's economic success—a feeling that "Japanese cars are good, therefore everything Japanese is good."

"It's a vague, diffused sentiment, shared by a great number of people, but not yet crystallized into a political ideology," Kato said. "If we mishandle these popular sentiments, the results will be quite disastrous."

To Kato, the greatest danger lies in Japan's insularity, a legacy of its island location, its relative homogeneity and perhaps its three centuries of total isolation before the American Navy demanded entry in 1854.

Ethnic Koreans, many of whom are third-generation Japanese, are still barred from teaching jobs and most other mainstream professions. What is by U.S. standards a trickle of foreign laborers, primarily from China and Southeast Asia, has caused widespread alarm and triggered scores of xenophobic letters to newspapers and the government.

"Our economy is very, very internationalized, but our psyche is still very, very closed," Kato said. "What is in desperate need of change is the Japanese mind. It should be more open to others."

Japan's Role in the World

Takakazu Kuriyama, vice foreign minister, agreed that Japan's "most urgent problem" is "to adjust our thinking and our perception" to Japan's new place in the world. But Kuriyama said the adjustment won't lead Japan down its prewar path, and its search for values won't lead to Japan seeking a "messianic" role.

"We aspire to a modest, yet useful, international role," Kuriyama said. "It is a fairly modest vision—not very ambitious, not very ideological—but fairly solid in terms of our commitment to a democratic, free market, non-military role."

"We made a bad mistake in the first part of this century," he said. "Ninety-nine percent of Japanese don't want to repeat that mistake."

Yukio Matsuyama, Asahi newspaper's editorial board chairman, also is optimistic that Japanese will develop more and more confidence in individual freedom. "A quiet evolution, if not a revolution, is well underway in Japan toward a mature democracy," he said. But, he added, "I feel as if the ship of Japan were now leaving the harbor to face stormy, misty, uncharted seas."

February 11, 1990

Germans Divided by 'Wall in the Head': Psychological Gap between West, East Affecting Unification

Marc Fisher

For 40 years, Germans on both sides of the Wall believed the people across the divide were essentially the same. Both spoke the same language, read the same literature and thought the same way, according to the common wisdom; easterners and westerners might have had different political systems, but they really did know each other.

That was, most Germans now seem to agree, wrong.

This reality is the barrier that was not supposed to be. Laymen call it "the wall in the head." You hear it in everyday language. TV newscasters in the west still refer to the former East Germany as drueben, or "over there."

Yesterday in Halle, a city in the formerly communist east, young leftists pelted Chancellor Helmut Kohl with eggs and tomatoes as he shook hands with about 400 friendly residents in the city's central square, news services reported. The chancellor, who has made only a handful of visits to the east since winning reelection last December, was struck on the side of his face by an egg.

Last week, on a visit to Leipzig, Kohl darted in and out of the city, meeting only with carefully selected churchgoers. "I am not afraid of the people," Kohl said. But then he slipped and called them the "people in the GDR," or German Democratic Republic, East Germany's official name.

Kohl is not alone. Easterners, more than anyone else, still refer to their region as the GDR, usually without the smile and self—correction—"Um, I mean, former GDR—western politicians tack onto their sentences.

Outwardly, despite unemployment that could hit 50 percent this summer, eastern Germany is changing with stunning speed. City streets are being made over, lined with bright facades of shops stocked with the bounty of the consumer society. Schools are changing radically. Adults flock to courses on the mechanics of western life—banking, filing, taxes, suing your neighbor.

Hard times still lie ahead: The Bonn government's plan to reconstruct the east in "a few years" was far too optimistic. It may take a decade or more to achieve a western standard of living.

What may linger for a generation or two is the deep emotional and psychological gap between east and west, the divide that Germans sum up as the battle between Ossies (Easties) and Wessies (Westies).

Foreign Minister Hans-Dietrich Genscher tells this joke: The Ossi says to the Wessi, "We are one people!" the battle-cry of the East German revolution.

The Wessi replies, "So are we!"

Relations between Ossies and Wessies can get downright nasty. Ugly stereotypes have become everyday assumptions. Ossies, many Wessies say, are lazy, dependent whiners with bad teeth, unwashed hair, shiny polyester clothes and endlessly outstretched palms. Wessies, many Ossies say, are arrogant, pseudo-sophisticated boasters with outlandishly colorful clothing, overly made-up faces and a deep-seated cheapness.

"It's like a bad marriage," said east Berlin teacher Monika Schmidt. "The discussion can be about nothing, maybe how you wash the teapot. But then someone says, 'Oh, you always pick on me,' and the partner responds, and the argument takes off.

"We and the Wessies have communication problems. A Wessi might try to be friendly, but they treat you like newborn children. Aunt Emily tells you how to run your life.

"The western school officials gave us a course on the new literature curriculum and there was a lesson on short stories. The teacher, a Wessi, began with 'What is a short story? Have you heard of them? Have you heard of Hemingway?' " Schmidt said.

"I said, yes, and our students read him in the English. The bloody nerve."

The divide is most palpable in the hopelessness of many eastern adults. "So many people just gave up," Schmidt said. "They say, 'I'm waiting for a new job,' like it's just going to be given to them, like things were still the same as before."

This is the kernel of truth behind the ugly stereotype: Ossies are not lazy—300,000 new businesses have been founded in the east in the seven months since unification—but enough of them are stuck in the socialist way of behavior that, to Wessies at least, they look like they are refusing to change.

Professionals have a more scientific term for the syndrome: wendekrankheit, or turnabout illness, an identity crisis prompted by the overnight switch from socialism to capitalism.

The east is suffering from gut-wrenching trauma. Suicides are widespread. Eastern psychologists see dramatic jumps in crime, violence against foreigners, hooliganism at soccer games and traffic accidents as evidence of a collective cry for help amid soaring joblessness and even more frightening uncertainty.

"This is not unification, it's an annexation," said eastern psychologist Margit Venner. "A whole people have lost their integrity. We see depression, chronic psychosomatic illnesses, separation anxieties. We are different and we have to accept that."

"We speak differently," Venner told TV talk show host Margarethe Schreinemakers on a recent broadcast. "We think differently. We feel differently. Different things are important to me than to you."

Affronted, the TV host, a Wessi, said, "Like what?"

"Honesty," the Ossi said.

"You think that's not important to us?"

"Us!" the Ossi said. "Why do you all talk about 'us' and not what your own feelings are?"

They went on and on, as many such debates do.

In the new life, east Berliner Monika Newiger has discovered, you must learn how to find a job, borrow money, buy a car. There are so many decisions to make, and the changes have come too fast, she said.

"The old system is part of my life," Newiger said. "I still see things through the old view. Okay, we can get out of this cage now and see the world. But I don't think we'll ever really feel together with the west. Maybe it will happen with our children."

Newiger is still in high school. She is 18 years old.

Ossies knew great changes were coming, but many were stunned to see how little would remain of the society in which they grew up. Western laws and traditions have been adopted in almost every case. The sole exceptions are still unresolved: abortion—until a compromise is found, it remains legal in the east and largely illegal in the west—and the legal limit on drunken drivers—Bonn proposes a .05 percent limit for alcohol in the blood, up from the east's zero tolerance, down from the west's .08 law.

Ossies don't like to admit it in front of Wessies, but many in the formerly communist region still hunger for anything western. They have bought millions of western cars and video recorders.

To win access to western goods, easterners are willing to take on heavy loads. About 300,000 Ossies commute across the country to jobs in the west. Bus networks have sprung up to pick up easterners beginning at 3 am. and bring them to jobs as much as 250 miles away—the equivalent of a New York to Washington commute.

There are no public explosions of rage in the west, but opinion surveys and interviews show that the psychological unification is not going very smoothly even in Europe's most comfortable economy.

Last fall, 70 percent of West Germans told pollsters from Der Spiegel magazine that unification required sacrifices, but only 38 percent of the same group said they were willing to make them.

Seven months of unity have done little to connect the two visions of the world. A majority of westerners say east Germans complain too much. And on a range of topics, Ossies and Wessies continue to express starkly different views. While Ossies worry about unemployment and the continuing presence of Soviet troops in their region, a recent poll of west Germans found that they were most concerned about the environment, the economy, traffic and the shortage of kindergarten spaces, in that order.

"Basically, all Germans are extremely conservative," Roger de Weck, an essayist for the Hamburg weekly Die Zeit, wrote recently. "Even if they were willing to change, they cannot simply shake off the force of habit. This is true both for east and west Germans—perhaps even more so for west Germans. Many still refuse to believe that West Germany has become a different state" and that it too must change.

It wasn't supposed to be this way. From the moment the Berlin Wall fell, Germans on both sides embraced former Chancellor Willy Brandt's statement that "What belongs together can now grow together."

Western companies and governments quickly began trying to make that happen. Eastern radio stations are filled with programs on the joys of a multicultural society—an attempt to combat the increasing scapegoating of foreigners in the east.

The Kohl government spent $600,000 on a cartoon film that was supposed to explain market economics to Ossies. The ad agency that made it—western, of course—chose to portray the Ossi as a cute, if slightly dim-witted dog that barks happily when Ludwig Erhard, father of the 1950s West German economic miracle, throws it a one-mark coin. The film has been locked away, never to be seen, a government spokesman said.

Advertisers try to ease the Ossies' entrance into the consumer world. An ad for Pampers patiently explains what disposable diapers are—"Then you just throw it away!"—and adds a language lesson. The diapers are marketed with the English words "Girls" and "Boys" on the box, which is no problem in the west, where English is chic. Special ads for Ossies demonstrate how to pronounce and use the foreign words. "Not Geerls, Girls," a chipper announcer says.

The gap between east and west is most striking among the young. East Berlin's once-magnificent Ossietzky School is where the children of Communist Party loyalists were educated until the fall of the Wall. The school has a new principal, new textbooks from the west, a more open tone in class, and a curriculum that the students say is infinitely more interesting than the old one.

But asked how many of their parents already have lost their jobs, more than half the students in one class raise their hands.

"I want to compete," said Andreas Beckmann, 18, an Ossietsky student who has already found a job as a trainee at a west Berlin bank. "I must compete. But I don't know. Maybe I'm not on the same level."

Economic concerns also were said to be at the root of yesterday's scuffle in which eggs and tomatoes were thrown at Kohl, who was ending a day-trip to eastern Germany to meet workers and discuss the worsening economic situation there.

After one egg hit him on the side of the face and several more splattered on his suit, security men tried to drag him away from the demonstrators by his lapels.

But the burly chancellor moved back toward them and attempted to grab a banner from a young protester as another grabbed Kohl's sleeve and tried to get through a metal barrier.

The incident marred an otherwise uneventful trip to the east, where Kohl met east German workers for the first time since unification.

Across the country, on an idyllic island in the middle of the Rhine River just outside Bonn, the students of Nonnenwerth Gymnasium, a private Catholic school, are sympathetic toward their new countrymen in the east, but share the Ossies' doubts about how easily the divide can be bridged.

"I found it astounding how easily we could speak together when I was in Dresden" in the east, said Cornelia Russ, 18. "But it's so hard for them. We learned how to decide all our lives. Now they have to decide what am I going to study in school, what kind of career do 1 want."

"I'm thrilled every night when I see the weather map on TV" with east and west shown as one country, said Robby Fichte, 17, who was born in the east but has spent nearly all of his life in the west. "It's a pity that our young people feel closer to the French and British than to the Ossies."

"Sure, but we had a wall between us," said Marcos Bornheim, western born and bred.

Asked how long it would take before the terms Ossi and Wessi would become meaningless, Russ said, "There's 40 years of history there. It could take a generation or more."

But could you marry an Ossi?

"There's such a tremendous distance between us," said Renata Niffgen, 18.

"Why not?" Russ said. "I'll marry a person, not a country."

May 11, 1991

Chapter Three

Groups and Social Structure

The eight articles in this section all touch upon one or another aspect of groups and social structure. Recall that sociologists use the term "group" to describe a number of people who possess a feeling of common identity and who interact in a patterned and predictable manner. Groups can be as small as the two-person dyad and as large as a multinational formal organization (bureaucracy). The term "social structure" is used to signify the array of different groups within a given population, as well as the various patterned relationships that take place within and among these groups.

The first two articles focus on large-scale groups—government bureaucracies. Article 1 describes the controversial drive to rid India's mammoth socialist bureaucracy of some of its worst excesses. Article 2 relates Brazilian President Fernando Collor de Mello's fight to fire fully one-fourth of the federal workforce in an attempt to make the bureaucracy more responsive and efficient.

The next three articles examine issues of role and status within groups. "Single Parents in the Military" describes the role conflicts experienced by parents who are members of the armed forces. "Gender Games in the Gulf" reports on the role conflicts experienced during the Persian Gulf War by female soldiers who also are mothers. "An Amerasian Struggles to Belong" describes the plight of the daughter of a U.S. GI and a Korean mother as she struggles to find peer group acceptance.

When the stability of a society is disrupted, such as that which occurred when East and West Germany reunified in 1989, routine patterns of interaction also undergo upheaval. "New Sound Heard on Streets of East Germany: Gang Violence" reveals some of the consequences of reunification for a confused East German youth.

The power of a membership group to shape behavior is everywhere apparent in "Japan's White-Collar Clones," an article that investigates the values and norms of a typical Japanese "salaryman." The final article in this section describes life in a total institution—a Soviet women's prison camp.

Budget Axe Endangers India's Socialist Icons; Massive Bureaucracy under Attack

Steve Coll

India's socialist gravy train, the massive public bureaucracy that has fed, clothed and housed millions of government employees since independence, is running out of steam.

Consider, for example, ticket conductor S. M. Mahule, a 33-year veteran of the federal railway service, who exudes fatigue as he plods between passenger cars rumbling across central India.

Irregular blood pressure kept Mahule off the rails for two months last year, and he plans another extended leave soon. In the public sector, illness is no problem. Mahule said he receives 45 days of paid vacation, a dozen government holidays and up to 120 sick days each year.

"Most of our employees, they are sick," he said wryly.

So is the government that employs them. An unprecedented fiscal crisis on the subcontinent is highlighting the sorry condition of India's public sector, where many workers in guaranteed jobs seem proud to elevate organized inactivity to an art form.

During the 1988–89 fiscal year, the last for which complete statistics are available, 101 of the country's 222 largest nationalized companies lost money, contributing to a federal deficit five times larger in relative terms than the one in the United States, a ballooning external debt and a severe foreign—exchange crunch.

From railways to rubber, tea to tourism, sprawling state-owned enterprises in dozens of industries are under new pressure to cut costs, raise profits and stem the tide of red ink. For the first time since independence in 1947, even some nominally socialist politicians are talking about previously taboo ideas, such as labor-force discipline and privatization as parliament tackles a projected $7.7 billion federal deficit.

Still, despite deepening fiscal problems, there is widespread reluctance to shake up the bureaucracy. Paradoxically, India's vast public sector is seen here not only as a cause of national crisis, but as a bedrock of social stability.

The huge federal work force—1.6 million in the railway service alone—wields formidable political power. Indian courts continue to uphold laws that make it virtually impossible to fire a public worker, even if suspected of committing a crime. The bureaucracy has also become the main laboratory for experiments in affirmative action.

Challenging the socialist orthodoxy is a business-minded middle class that rose to influence during the 1980s and whose members are now demanding freedom from the government clerks and functionaries who regulate many aspects of their lives.

A 36-hour ride aboard the G.T. Express, which shuttles along the spine of India's British-built administrative infrastructure between New Delhi in the north and Madras in the south, offers a dusty window on the bureaucracy and the forces of change pressing against it.

At the head of the train is the engineer, H. N. Sharma, a neatly coifed advocate of public service and middle-class virtue who waves enthusiastically to villagers he passes along the way. With his son ensconced in a railway-built school, his wife at home in a railway-built house and his pension gathering interest in a state-owned bank, Sharma's principal lament is that India's younger generation does not seem to regard government service with adequate respect.

The young today, he argued, "are too busy making money." But what is wrong with that? "Money is a criterion of success, no doubt," he replied. "But side by side, you've got to see your reputation."

Behind him in an air-conditioned coach is electronics engineer N. Ramesh, 25, who sneers at what he sees as the lazy piety of government workers. Outlining his plan to start a computer company, Ramesh said that despite prodding from parents to join the bureaucracy, his generation is determined "to go on their own. They want to work, they want to make a go of it, they don't want to sit idle in government."

Such talk is unsettling to many of the railway service workers on the train, some of whom have used their government jobs to raise their families from crushing poverty and across caste barriers. They fear that all the recent talk of efficiency and privatization means their upward social progress will halt.

Without socialism, asked conductor Mahule, what would happen to the tens of millions of Indians who lack the skills and talent to earn a comfortable living in the private sector? His son, for example, is searching desperately for federal employment. "He's not so much brilliant or extraordinary. He is an ordinary boy. That is why he wants a government job."

February 26, 1991

Brazil's Leader Takes on Ensconced Bureaucracy; Having Cut Down Hyperinflation, Collor Vows to Eliminate 360,000 Federal Jobs

Eugene Robinson

Some political veterans call President Fernando Collor de Mello arrogant. Many economists say his policies are rash. His top advisers are widely considered inexperienced. He can be a grandstander, an evangelist, a showman.

All agree that whatever Brazil's 40-year-old newcomer to politics lacks in tact he makes up for with audacity. Having stunned inflation into dormancy with far-reaching measures that affect nearly every Brazilian, making life a little easier for the poor and much harder for the middle and upper classes, he now vows an all-out attack on what may prove to be a wilier, more entrenched foe—a suffocating bureaucracy.

Collor has ordered his ministers to fire or lay off 360,000 employees, one-fourth of the federal work force. He has set a deadline for coming up with the names of those to be let go, and this week he hectored his cabinet for not moving quickly enough.

The planned firings are not Collor's first attack on bureaucrats since his inauguration less than three months ago. He put up for auction thousands of their government cars, which he said were unneeded and undeserved. He is selling a score of lavish houses in and around the capital of Brasilia that had been kept for officials' use. All the while he has railed against "parasites" who collect salaries for little or no work.

But it is the notion of firing so many people that stuns Brazilians.

"Can you imagine what would happen in Washington if they fired a quarter of the government?" asked economist Edmar Bacha. "And remember this is Brazil, where nobody gets fired. Ever."

The bureaucracy, predictably, is resisting the job cuts. Cabinet ministers are said to be having trouble getting their departments to prepare the lists of those to be fired or laid off. Collor has had to clarify that he wants to fire only the "idlers," not workers who actually do a job. In addition, Brazil's constitution guarantees job security to workers with more than five years' service.

It now appears likely that only about 220,000 workers will be dismissed outright. The rest will be sent home and continue receiving reduced salaries.

A year ago, then president Jose Sarney pledged to fire up to 90,000 government workers but apparently did not bring about a single dismissal. Sarney's former top economic aide, Mailson da Nobrega, said recently that firing just 50,000 employees would be "a great success" for Collor.

A key Collor supporter in Congress, Sen. Jose Ignacio Ferreira, said Monday that the president's "emphasis on the numbers is almost a kind of anti-marketing," and that the administration should be emphasizing instead its intent to make the bureaucracy more responsive and efficient.

Collor, however, says he will not budge. "My will is firm," he said recently, "and the goals will be met."

Such vigor and inflexibility are typical of the young president, who seems to be trying to remake Brazil in one all-out assault before the country realizes what has hit it. "His team brings him a menu of options," said one person familiar with the way the administration works, "and he always chooses the toughest one."

Son of a wealthy politician from the sleepy Northeast state of Alagoas, Collor has brought dash to the presidency of the world's third-largest democracy, and he remains overwhelmingly popular. A recent poll showed him with a 74-percent approval rating.

Coming after the indecisive, unglamorous Sarney administration, the Collor show is as riveting as one of the flashy soap operas that keep Brazilians glued to their television sets each night.

On weekends, he stages high-profile photo opportunities—astride a speeding motorcycle, hurtling through the sound barrier in a fighter jet, dribbling a soccer ball, spiking a volleyball, practicing karate. His mother wrote an article in the news magazine Veja imploring him to cool it.

Collor replied with an official statement: "The president of the republic, as a good son, will attend to his mother's request and will no longer ride a motorcycle." He told reporters: "I'm a man of my times. I like motorcycles and jet-skis."

All the high-profile derring-do appears to win him popular support—and deflect attention from the many criticisms of his economic program.

Before Collor took over, inflation was running at 80 percent per month. Inflation for April was just 3.29 percent—not the zero that Collor had promised, but still a precipitous drop.

Collor achieved this by seizing about $100 billion in funds that savers had in "overnight" and monthly interest-bearing accounts, promising to begin returning the funds in 18 months.

The measure meant nothing to the vast majority of Brazilians, who are too poor to have bank accounts. But it was a blow to corporations, the rich and especially the middle class. The truly rich could make do "by eating caviar only once a week," said economist Bacha, "but the middle class is really ticked off."

Political scientist Helio Jaguaribe, who has conducted a massive study of Brazil's crushing social problems, said that the dramatic slowing of inflation has made a real difference in the lives of the poor.

"They have significantly more buying power," he said. "The poor are able to eat milk and meat for the first time in a long time. This is enormously significant."

Jaguaribe added, "Collor is always identified as being of the right, but he says he is center-left, and this is a profoundly center-left program. He has taken from the upper classes to give to the poor."

The big industrialists of Sao Paulo complained bitterly that the confiscation of funds would cause a deep recession and wreck the economy, and to emphasize the point they laid off tens of thousands of workers. But now it has begun to appear that the recession is only a minor one.

Economists agree, however, that Collor's economic plan is not an assured success. Inflation for May is estimated at about 6 percent. Corporations have taken advantage of loopholes to free up most of their frozen funds. Several courts have ruled that Collor must approve a whopping wage increase, although he has been able to block implementation of the decisions.

These inflationary pressures, economists say, are prompting Collor's urgency to get as many people off the federal payroll as soon as possible as a counterbalance.

In what is seen as an alarming new trend, Brazil may be starting to experience the "dollarization" that has plagued many other Latin economies. Brazil has suffered chronic inflation for many years, but wages and prices were so thoroughly indexed that Brazilians did not find it necessary to buy dollars as a hedge. Now Collor has shattered the indexation scheme, and by seizing savings accounts has demonstrated that the financial system is not inviolate.

As a result, the price of the dollar is shooting up rapidly, and increased numbers of money—changers are competing to snare tourists along the beaches of Copacabana and Ipanema.

Public confidence has not been increased by the performance of Collor's economic team, which is widely criticized as lacking in experience and technical expertise. One economist described Collor's economy minister, Zelia Cardoso de Mello, as "a nobody." Another called her "a smart woman, capable to a point, but not up to the job. More an assistant professor than a full professor."

Another question is whether Collor knows where his headlong rush is leading. For example, some 50,000 of the planned firings are in education, where there are seven administrators for every three actually teaching. Yet education is a critical issue if Brazil hopes to live up to its long-touted potential and join the first world. Study after study has recommended overhaul rather than shrinking of the educational system.

Said Bacha: "They seem to lack a flight plan. They had an excellent takeoff, but they don't seem to know where they're going."

June 1, 1990

Single Parents Struggle in the Military

Molly Moore

When Sgt. Charles Haskins reported for his new assignment at Fort Belvoir last fall, he discovered that the Army base in southern Fairfax County had no room for a single father with a 3-year-old daughter.

"All they tell you is go find the nearest hotel," said Haskins, 28, who at 11 pm. on an October night confronted the arduous task of trying to balance an Army career with single parenthood—the type of situation that has become one of the most difficult personnel problems for the U.S. military.

Winning custody of his daughter "was a shocker—I wasn't prepared for it," said Haskins, a supply sergeant who has spent 11 years in the Army. "Neither was the Army."

For Haskins, single parenthood has meant military transfers, reprimands in his personnel file for infractions such as bringing his daughter to physical training, and a continuous struggle to find child-care services compatible with the odd hours of military duty.

For the U.S. military, the dramatic increase in single parents comes as military leaders are trying to readjust to the needs of an all-volunteer force that is vastly different from the bachelor, male-dominated force of the Vietnam era. It is an issue, leaders say, that bears directly on the readiness of an all-volunteer service and the retention of troops in an era when the pool of potential recruits is dwindling.

Pentagon officials estimate that more than 50,000 single parents with custody of their children are serving in the armed services, although the total is unclear because the services use different methods to calculate their respective tallies. The single-parent population in the Navy has exploded from 5,100 in 1980 to an estimated 25,000 this year, according to officials at the Norfolk base's family services center.

Those growing numbers have meant increasing problems for the military as it seeks more money for day care centers and other special services at a time when budgets are tighter. Although many of those programs are aimed at helping all military families with children, officials say they are particularly crucial to single military parents.

In the past two years, the Defense Department and individual services have created high-level positions to organize family service programs. The Army's budget requests to Congress for child-development centers, of special importance to single parents, leaped from zero in 1985 to $45.6 million for fiscal 1987, according to a House Armed Services Committee report.

"The issue is being elevated and something is being done about it," said Bill Coffin, director of the Pentagon's family policy office. "In the early '80s, the initiatives came from military wives and people in the military were not listening."

Although the number of single parents in the military is increasing at about the same rate as the number in society at large, military officials say the problems for military parents are magnified.

"They have stresses civilian parents don't have—deployment, relocation, 24-hour duty," said Alice Stratton, the Navy's deputy assistant secretary for personnel and family matters, a position created a year ago.

To help single parents cope, the old-style family service centers that once existed primarily to lend pots and pans to new base residents have expanded programs to include special group counseling sessions for single parents. The Navy has established several shipboard counseling groups to provide emotional support for single parents at sea during long separations from their youngsters.

Even with the new attention on the issue, the demand for day-care centers and family services far outstrips what the military is providing, according to Pentagon officials. Housing for service members with children is limited on some bases and nonexistent at most remote and overseas locations. Almost every base day-care center in the United States and overseas has a long waiting list, officials said.

With a few exceptions, a single parent with child custody is barred from entering the military services. "We're growing enough of our own {single parents} without bringing them in from society," said Col. Donald S. Palmer, chief of the Air Force's human resources development division. "We can manage the situation now with the number we have."

But some parents, like Pfc. Connie Peresada, circumvent the regulation by signing custody of their children to another guardian during enlistment and basic training and resuming custody later.

Two months before Peresada, 28, was scheduled to move to her new assignment as an eye technician at Fort Belvoir, she telephoned to arrange base housing for herself and her two young daughters. But when she arrived in June, Peresada was told she would be put on a waiting list because of the shortage of family housing.

"I had a rude awakening," said Peresada, whose husband was killed in an accident two years ago. "I had two daughters, and I had no housing and no transportation."

She spent her first weeks living with her stepfather in Maryland. She left the house at 4 a.m. to reach her job by 8 a.m. With no automobile, she said, she hitchhiked the first 30 miles, caught a train from Brunswick, Md., to Rockville, took the Metro to Huntington and then a Metrobus to Fort Belvoir.

When she fell asleep from exhaustion one day while sitting in her supervisor's office, the supervisor "restricted me to the base two days a week just so I could get some sleep."

Peresada said she finally wandered into the base's Community Service Center for assistance. The center, which its director said is increasing efforts to assist single parents, found temporary housing for Peresada in northern Virginia. She hops a

Metro bus with Joy, 7, and Sarita, 5, for the two-hour commute to Fort Belvoir, then drops off the youngsters at separate base day-care centers on her way to work.

"Everyone at the eye clinic is very lenient," said Peresada, noting that she frequently is late to work and remains on the waiting list for on-post housing. "But it upsets me that I can't be here when I have to be. One year in the service, I'm trying to establish myself."

The increasing number of single parents—as well as the proliferation in recent years of married enlisted troops with families—has forced the military to reassess many of its requirements for troop deployment. Most of the services refuse to allow children to accompany parents assigned overseas if there are no family housing or child-care services.

Sgt. Haskins' experience is representative of the problems facing many single military parents, according to military officials. Soon after he won custody of his daughter following a divorce, Haskins was transferred to Fort Belvoir from the unit in Germany where he had served 10 years.

"It was a deployable unit," Haskins said. "We weren't welcome there."

Haskins said he discovered his supervisors weren't much more receptive at his new assignment.

Because babysitters were difficult to find at 5 a.m., when Haskins was required to report for physical training, he brought young Natalie with him. That ended with letters of reprimand in his personnel file and orders forbidding him to bring his daughter.

Haskins eventually was transferred to a new battalion where he said the commander is more tolerant of his hardships as a single father. A neighbor looks after Natalie in the morning during physical training until Haskins can drop her off at the base day-care center before reporting to his job at 8 a.m.

In contrast to the civilian population, in the military most single parents are men—primarily because the services remain overwhelmingly male. Navy officials said 80 percent of the single sailors with children are men.

The attitude of the military toward single parents has changed significantly since the General Accounting Office reported in 1982 that the Army was considering discharging all sole parents or assigning them to positions coded as "nondeployable," which would not require sudden, long trips into the field.

"Some commanders believe that, in the event of war, the parental responsibilities of these service members will take priority over their call to duty," the GAO study said.

But the proposal to discharge single parents "raises questions of equity. Would it be fair? Would it be legal?" said Lt. Col. Craig MacNab, an Army spokesman.

Military officials also said they place a premium on retaining service members because of increasing costs of training recruits.

"We're not wasting the money we spend on families," MacNab added. "If the family is not happy, we don't keep the soldier."

The services have tightened requirements that military parents prove that they have arranged guardians for their children in the event the parent is deployed. That has become particularly important for single parents, especially in the Navy, which often requires sea duty.

Single parents who cannot rely on other family members to serve as guardians frequently turn to outside private services because the military makes no provisions for long-term care of children while parents are deployed, according to Karen Blaisure, young families coordinator at the Navy's Norfolk family service center.

Blaisure said a private service in the Norfolk area will place military children in civilian households at costs from $300 to $800 per month for each child while parents are at sea, which can be six months or longer.

The Navy's Stratton said some civilians are preying on single military parents by charging up to $1,000 just for the use of their names as designated guardians. "It's heartrending," said Stratton. "They didn't have a name and they have to have somebody."

September 3, 1986

Gender Games in the Gulf; in Anonymity of the Military, Sex Does a Vanishing Act

Henry Allen

It's hard to carry the weight when you keep feeling like you're disappearing.

"I've got two kids, a girl, 5, and a son, 2, back in New Jersey with my husband," said Staff Sgt. Connie Gumulauskis-Hall.

She carried an M-16. She was in a corrugated metal shed by an airfield, a PK, sort of a ghost shopping mall surrounded by barbed wire and bomb-sniffing dogs. She is in intelligence and she was standing in front of a display rack trying to make up her mind which greeting card to send to her daughter.

"When I left, she said, 'Why not Daddy? Why doesn't he go to fight the war instead of you?' I don't know where she gets it. I think it's peer pressure. They learn it from the other kids in school."

Her husband, a civilian, is watching the kids. "He's a dependent. He cooks, he cleans," she said.

It was a joke, but it wasn't about him, it was about the last 20 years of wrangling over what men and women are and aren't—wrangling that began, maybe only coincidentally, at the end of our last good-sized war. That was Vietnam, a war in which there were no women like Gumulauskis-Hall and a war that the men lost, when all was said and done.

Now she is here and her husband is home. This time around about 10 percent of our forces are women.

You'd think that 20 years of feminist indoctrination would have persuaded the 5-year-olds, at least. She tries to explain it but it's hard, standing in line for hours to get to a telephone where you have to pretend to be you in this desert of military anonymity, this country where the native women wear full black veils so the men stare not at your body but at your naked face—the same effort of stare—and it makes you feel like nobody. You can buy a souvenir here, an English-language version of a Saudi sign showing a woman with an X drawn over her, and the words: "No women—women cannot be seated or served here."

It's hard to explain to a 5-year-old.

"I called and I talked to her, but something was wrong, I think the connection was bad. She didn't realize it was me talking to her," Gumulauskis-Hall said.

She studied the greeting cards. She had her choice down to two categories with a small but crucial difference between them: "When They Need You" and "They Need You." She thought about it for a while and then walked away without buying either one.

The men in the Persian Gulf are more used to this vanishing act than the women—it's part of male tradition, the sort of thing that Baghdad Betty, the radio propagandist, works on by broadcasting stuff like: "Listen to this, American men!

While you are lost in the desert, your wives are sleeping with famous movie stars!"

The other apocryphal story you hear is about a new twist on the old literary form known as the Dear John letter. You hear that some guy in the unit three clicks up the road got a videotape in the mail from his family.

The first part shows his children standing in front of the Christmas tree and saying, "Hi, Daddy, we hope you come home soon." Then it cuts to his wife. It pulls back to show her making love to another man. The wife looks at the camera and says, "This is my way of telling you that this marriage is over." This story has everything you need: video, Christmas, children for an army in which a huge number of the troops are married. Best of all, it has the ironies that soldiers like to work away at like a tongue working at a sore tooth.

And it passes for titillation in a theater of operations where there are no camp followers, alcohol, drugs, brothels or "pornographies," where the local women hide even their faces and Saudi pin-up art shows merely the eyes of a veiled and shrouded woman.

If this army wins a great victory, and its veterans become our moral exemplars like the veterans of World War II, they could end an age in which we take it as gospel that sex is not only an undeniable need but a right, an age in which imprisoned felons sue for conjugal visits as their constitutional entitlement. This is an army that throws away the gospel of Freud, Havelock Ellis, Hugh Hefner, Donahue and Dr. Ruth and instead looks back to good old American puritanism, and forward to the stern egalitarianism of modern feminism.

How strange that chastity, virtue, even celibacy comes at a moment when men and women serve as equals on combat teams, even husbands and wives.

"Holding hands, kissing, none of it," said Sgt. John Erb, who is part of the same Marine communications unit as his wife, Cpl. Michelle Erb. "We'd get office hours," he said, referring to disciplinary proceedings just under the court-martial level.

"You're never alone. There's always somebody else around, 24 hours a day. You can't do that kind of thing on duty status, and we're always on duty status."

"You might get a minute here, a minute there, but that's all it is," his wife said.

"It's more like being in high school," he said.

If the great sex manual of the 1950s was "Love Without Fear," the manual of this standoff in the gulf is "Fear Without Love."

In earlier wars women were usually scarce, but all the icons of femininity traveled with the troops. Now, because the Saudis forbid the possession of "pornographies," as they say, and because pornographies include things like the swimsuit ads that American schoolchildren have been erasing with Magic Markers so that magazines can be sent to our defenders of freedom, you rarely see pin-ups that approach even the erotic value of Betty Grable peeking over her shoulder half a century ago in World War II.

Safe inside the inside of a tank, next to the toilet paper and the fly swatter, you might see a Guess Parfum ad torn from a magazine, some pictures sent by female pen pals writing to "Any Soldier" or "Any Marine." In the all-male units out in the desert, there are shy, wry euphemisms for sexual solitude: "nocturnal air bursts" or "clown punching."

As far as the theorists of both gender-free utopias and high—tech war are concerned, the grunts out in the field disappeared years ago. But as the grunts know, after all of the air strikes and high-tech, it will be they who will go in to make sure the enemies are dead, which they will have to do by killing them.

They will do this by picking up huge amounts of weight, strapping it to their backs, mile after mile, more than a hundred pounds for a mortar baseplate man or an A-gunner on a Dragon antitank team. Think of it as putting on boots, helmet, rifle, ammunition, pack, canteens, chemical-warfare kit, bayonet and grenades, and then strapping, say, the equivalent of two cases of beer and a 10-speed bicycle to your back and walking 20 miles in soft sand, carrying, say, the weight of a small-to-medium-size woman. This is what war is about, finally, and at some level it is what sex is about too.

"Actually, we sell a lot of condoms for guys to put over the muzzles of their rifles to keep the dust out," said Marine Master Sgt. Herbert Moffitt, who runs a post exchange out of a tent by a harbor. "You can shoot right through them."

This may be nothing but lore, a sort of bragging about coarse truths transcending middle-class niceties in the realities of battle. What you are far more apt to see on the muzzles of M–16s are black plastic muzzle caps. You can shoot through them as well.

The nurses seem to handle it best—they're officers, for one thing, and they've been part of the military for so long they've learned to keep war and sex from getting confused.

"It's not hard here being a woman," said Navy Lt. Sheila Weibert with a flash of the military nurse look, a bit of psychic triage that suggests she has just made some irrevocable decision about you, a look that makes you feel understood and ignored at the same time, reassuring but not encouraging.

Women with husbands and children seem to have a harder time.

Down near an airfield, Army Sgt. Christina Wall, an ammunition specialist, waited for her husband, a petroleum specialist, to fly in. "We'll get 10 or 15 minutes together," she said, and then she'll go back to her tent. "We have a husband-and-wife team in our unit but they spend no time together. The other people would think it's unfair. The majority of men think that just because it's your wife, that doesn't mean that you get to have something they don't.

"When we got here, it was difficult between the men and the women. We've got guys raised to protect a female, and they treat us like we can't do our job. Then they approach you, but the female always controls that situation—she has to. If she goes off with a guy it makes all the women look bad. We always travel in pairs. There are some times I'll go to bed, I'll think maybe somebody will get me and take me off.

"It puts you to the test. I've got two kids living with neighbors back in Kansas now that my husband is coming over. Son, 6, and a daughter, 3. My son thinks Daddy is coming over here to get me and protect me. I just let him think it so he'll feel better."

The problem, the women said, is that it's not anything a man might say or do, but a look, a tone of voice, a way they might have, say, of getting all earnest for no apparent reason, they might be talking about preventive maintenance on the M-60 tank but they sound as if they're confiding in you, making you feel that only you can make them feel like they exist out here, all the old jive, one line or another.

A Marine admin clerk named Cpl. Heather Robinson said: "The men are getting used to us. They'll give you that look, you know, but you stop it right there, a thing you do with your face, you give them your look."

In the new model Army, the idea is to become invisible, psychic camouflage, the countermeasures of sexual radar, watch out for the Dear John video, and all pornographies to stay inside the tank, please.

December 31, 1990

An Amerasian Struggles to Belong; Teenager Finds Herself Isolated in Both United States and South Korea

Fred Hiatt

As a high school student in California, she felt isolated, unable to keep up with her classmates and their easy familiarity with American pop singers, opening bank accounts, driving the freeways.

As a college student in South Korea, she feels isolated again, scorned by her classmates for her round eyes and slightly American looks, personally threatened by their anti-American demonstrations.

She is what South Koreans insultingly call a "half"—daughter of a U.S. GI stationed here 19 years ago and a Korean mother. Like about 1,000 other Amerasians here not fully accepted by their U.S. fathers, her face reflects South Korea's turbulent history—and her own unhappy tale reflects Korea's ambivalence about its relationship with the United States and the world.

"My heart belongs to Korea, but people around me don't accept me, because I look different," said Lydia Weimer, 19, now an English literature major bearing her father's last name. "I'd like to walk to school straight, with my head up, but I can't. I feel like I don't belong here.

"But when I was in the United States, I felt like I didn't belong there, either."

The U.S. Army has stationed troops here since World War II ended in 1945; 41,000 soldiers at the moment, most on one-year tours. Some bring Korean wives home when they depart, while others leave unacknowledged children behind.

Those children, who have received less publicity than their counterparts in Vietnam, often are taunted as offspring of prostitutes, whether true or not. They also sometimes bear the brunt of rising Korean nationalism and resentment of the longtime "big brother-little brother" relationship with the United States.

Weimer grew up poor, living in a small, newspaper-lined room with her mother and older sister, scrounging for charcoal to heat their home in the winter, eating kimchi, a spicy Korean vegetable dish, and rice. Elementary school classmates would taunt her and demand candy, telling her that because her father was American, she must be rich.

Unlike many soldiers, her father never abandoned the family. He would visit every few months, bringing candy and occasionally some money; he spoke no Korean, and at the time she spoke no English.

Finally, when she was approaching high school age, her father adopted Lydia and her younger brother, who had been dyeing his reddish hair black in an attempt to escape some teasing. She attended American high schools, first on an Army base in South Korea and then, for a year, in Fall Brook, Calif.

Parts of the "American style" appealed to her. "They mind their own business, they do everything on time, everything is clean," she said. "Americans have so much opportunity, you can do anything."

But after her Korean upbringing, she felt out of place, she said; not because of the kind of racial discrimination she encountered in Seoul, but simply because she felt Korean.

"I went to school Korean-style—I listened and didn't ask questions," she said. "But it seemed the American students didn't have as much respect for the teachers as the Orientals."

And little things, even automatic doors, made her feel out of place. After graduating in California, she came home to South Korea, where the Pearl S. Buck Foundation, which helps Amerasians throughout Asia, helps pay her tuition.

Today, Weimer said she is not fluent in either language. When protesting classmates demand, among other things, the expulsion of U.S. troops—she feels as if they are speaking directly to her.

"They tell me, `You should have stayed in the States. You don't belong here. Korea is for Koreans,' " she said.

There are times, too, when she rages against South Korea: its relative poverty, the importance of social connections and family background. But for all the difficulties, she said, Seoul remains her home.

"No matter what, I love this country," she said.

September 7, 1988

New Sound Heard on Streets of East Germany: Gang Violence

Marc Fisher

They have names like Hitler Youth Schoenefeld, the Fascist Storm Youth, the Rautnitzer Rightists. They are young boys and girls of 17, 15 and 13.

On weekend evenings, they chant "Heil Hitler" and smash storefront windows along the same boulevards where tens of thousands of Leipzigers walked by candlelight a little more than a year ago, silently pressing the case for more democracy in rigidly run Communist East Germany.

In this city where East Germany's peaceful revolution began, young people are challenging the shrinking police force, rioting at soccer games and using a mix of Nazi slogans and street crime to rebel against the new society.

Leipzig is not alone. Neo-Nazi and skinhead groups also have taken to the streets of eastern Berlin and Chemnitz. Berlin was rocked in mid-November by hand-to-hand combat between police and more than 1,000 youths—some of them squatters but many of them from west Berlin's anarchist scene—who had occupied empty apartment buildings in the eastern part of the city.

The German Constitutional Protection Office, which monitors extremist groups, estimates that there are about 30,000 neo-Nazis in eastern Germany, about the same number as in the west.

The outbreak of street violence in the first months after German unification has sent a shock wave across a country where many had been marveling at how smoothly the historic transition had been going. Plans for a final east-west soccer game last week were canceled because of fears of violent hooliganism. On Nov. 3, Leipzig police shot and killed a soccer hooligan.

Those who have studied the surge of violence argue that it is not an expression of political extremism so much as a cry for attention by east German youths who, freed from the tight structure of Communist society, are lost in the relative insecurity of Western life.

Every child who grew up in the former East Germany spent not only school hours but also many afternoons, evenings and weekends under the close watch of the Free German Youth. The East German Communist Party decided school and career paths, and any anti-social adolescent expressions were quickly and efficiently suppressed or punished. Youth workers say that for any youngster who grew up under such conditions, the sudden switch to the vagaries of a market economy can be terrifying.

"In our newly discovered freedom, we've also imported a lot of violence," said Markus Zimmermann, a 25-year-old east Berlin councilman who is in charge of the city's youth programs. "Homelessness, drugs, youth gangs and hatred of foreigners were always here, but with unification, they are actually being expressed for the first time."

Zimmermann and several German sociologists say the violence has been building for years and only now has been allowed to flourish.

"It is very difficult for youth to suddenly be without leadership," Zimmermann said. "An East German was always led, from childhood through education to work and party activities. Now they have to lead themselves. So alcohol consumption is up, violence increases.

"It's a real identity question. What do our souls do with this new freedom?"

"These young people are crying out for recognition," said Jan Peter, the 21-year-old founder and editor of Die Andere Zeitung, eastern Germany's first independent newspaper. The paper has reported extensively on the extremist youth scene.

"They feel like second-class citizens, like they don't belong in this new Western country," Peter said. "Their future is nothing but a hole.

"These are generally not workers' kids. They are mostly kids of teachers, professionals and civil servants. They have a good social background. They are not fascists. They are bad boys and girls who just want to say what people don't like to hear."

According to this view, they get dressed up in black capes and white hoods on weekends largely to have something to do, and preferably something that will upset their elders; they know that any reference to Nazi tactics or slogans will especially frighten the authorities, so they specialize in Hitler salutes and chants.

The surge in violence in eastern Germany coincides with a reduction in the number of police on the street, both to free citizens from the police-state atmosphere of the former Communist government and to save money. More than 1,000 officers have been laid off in Leipzig alone.

But the combination of fewer police and more trouble has increased worries of political disarray. "I'm afraid of polarization like we had in the '20s," Peter said, referring to the period of turmoil in Germany that preceded Adolf Hitler's rise to power. "These militant groups can destabilize the system very easily."

Zimmermann and Berlin police say they suspect that some of the youth gangs are being supplied with weapons and strategy by former employees of East Germany's disbanded Stasi secret police. Earlier this month, Berlin officials found right-wing demonstrators equipped with radio phones and other high-tech communications devices that they suspect came from the Stasi.

Those who have studied the violence are worried about another aspect of the new Germany: the thriving black market in Soviet weapons. Disgruntled and bored Soviet soldiers, whose bases are close to every major east German city, sell everything from pistols to rocket launchers, making the new gangs potentially dangerous.

In the old East Germany, the idea of teenagers rampaging through the streets on a Saturday night was inconceivable. Instead, young people were required to be members of the Free German Youth, a Communist Party-sponsored group that embraced some of the mass demonstration techniques of earlier times, including torchlit parades.

Beginning in eighth grade, all East German students became members of the organization. Earlier, they participated in the Young Pioneers, uniformed child brigades that met in afternoon study sessions and military-style outdoor activities.

"The youth of any country are opposed to the state," Zimmermann said. "But this attitude was not allowed in the Free German Youth. Discussions about the biggest political problems—the [Berlin] Wall, freedom to travel, why the Communist Party was alone in power—were strictly forbidden."

The youth organization still exists, but only 30 youths in Berlin still belong, Zimmermann said. A year ago, there were 2 million members.

The government is trying to fill the gap by opening youth clubs, starting a telephone hot line for troubled youths and offering counseling. But youth workers say there are not enough resources.

"No one can change overnight," Zimmermann said, "and that is true for young people, too."

December 1, 1990

Japan's White-Collar Clones; the New Industrial Warriors Live for the Firm, the Future, and Occasionally the Family

John Burgess

He is hailed here as an "industrial warrior," the driving force behind Japan's economic success. He is also ridiculed in cartoons and commercials as a wimp who lives in terror of the boss' glower and chews antacids by the case.

He is as much a part of the Japanese cityscape as neon and sushi bars. He is found in dark suit, imported necktie, short hair parted on the left. No beards or moustaches. Accessories are standard, too—pocket calculator, leather briefcase, commuting pass, business cards, pornographic comic book for long subway rides.

Most of all, he is mass-produced. The "salaryman," as the male white—collar worker is called in Japan, is what most of the 280,000 young men who graduate from universities each year quickly become.

The good salaryman devotes himself body and soul to the company. If the company thrives, so will he. He loves his wife and children, but in a pinch he can be counted on to put the office first.

In few countries do such stereotypes hit so close to the truth. The Japanese joke endlessly about the salaryman, but not much is happening to replace him as an important bearer of the national standard. Some commentators predict that the new generation of young people, more devoted, it is said, to family and self-expression, will undermine the salaryman lifestyle. But for now, a good job at a good company is what the average young man aspires to and the salaryman lifestyle generally goes with that territory.

What follows is a day in the life of a prototypical salaryman, a portrait based on interviews, observations and reading over a three-year period of reporting in Japan. Salaryman represents no specific person and his company is no specific company. But when the Japanese think about a salaryman, someone like him comes to mind automatically, perhaps the guy living next door.

We join Salaryman as he rises from bed in the cramped master bedroom of his house, a thin-walled, heavily mortgaged affair deep in Tokyo's teeming suburban expanses ....

Salaryman's wife of 12 years has already been up more than an hour and gotten the two children off to school. Our man was too late getting home the previous night to see them. On Sunday, he is planning to take his wife and children to an amusement park a half hour's drive from the house—it's been a while since the family had a decent outing together.

After a wash, shave and quick dressing, Salaryman lights the first "Mild Seven" of the day, the brand that he and a third of all Japanese smokers favor. He wanders down the narrow stairs to the breakfast table, where his wife has laid out eggs, thick toast and coffee. He digs in and they talk about the new car they are planning to buy. "You're still against the Crown?" Salaryman asks. His wife doesn't answer. The Crown is a type of Toyota that she feels is not only too expensive but too flashy for someone of his rank at the company.

Salaryman opens his newspaper and sees another article about skyrocketing land prices. Good thing we bought when we did, he thinks. We could never afford this house now.

His wife drives him 10 minutes to the train station, where he slips into a throng of other salarymen embarking on the 70-minute journey to central Tokyo, site of the company where he has been employed since he graduated from college IS years ago. The train that stops before Salaryman is packed, as it always is.

He pushes his way in and, after staking out a strap, pulls from a pocket a book on computer science. Salaryman is 37, a shade too old to have grown up with computers. He is now determined to catch up and stop feeling the fool on this subject around the youngsters at the office. Thirty minutes later, a seat opens up and he drops into it. He is soon dozing, the book forgotten.

There are two kinds of salarymen, the elite and the run-of-the-mill. Salaryman counts himself among the former, the men heading for the top. But he is starting to slip. When he should be at home boning up on some new commercial skill or at a special night course, he is more likely to be out drinking with office buddies.

At 9:10, he steps into his real home, the sales division, on the 11th floor of the glass-skinned headquarters of his company. There are 40 cluttered desks in this room, and no partitions. Salaryman's is at the head of a bank of eight desks pushed head-to-head with four on each side. It is his little empire within the company. He fires up another Mild Seven and gets down to work.

There is no privacy in a Japanese office. Every phone call, every coffee break, is communal knowledge. A certain amount of slacking-off is permissible, but everyone does his or her best to look busy. No one, after all, wants a reputation for letting the section down.

Salaryman has risen to the rank of kacho, or section manager. His job consists largely of analyzing sales data sent up from field offices and processed by his own subordinates before being passed his way. This morning, he must assemble material for a contract the company is after. Finishing right on time, he runs into a 10:30 meeting.

The meeting lasts more than an hour and helps members inch toward a strategy for grabbing the sale. "Let's give our all to this contract," the dour-faced department manager tells the group as it breaks up after an hour. Perhaps the Sunday outing with the family could be squeezed into the morning, leaving the afternoon for the office.

Salaryman is 10 years younger than his manager and part of his batsu, or faction. The manager has done well, rising ahead of his due according to seniority. He has carried Salaryman along with him much of the way since Salaryman first worked for him in a provincial branch of the company years ago. Salaryman defers to his manager in the elevator, seeks advice on personal problems, and even volunteered for some heavy lifting one weekend when the manager was moving house. It meant cancelling the baseball game with his son, but what could he do?

Lunch today is noodles, grabbed in a shop in the building's basement. Salaryman eats with a fellow member of his "class" at the company, the group of 140 young men who were ceremonially inducted into its ranks 15 years before, singing for the first time the company song. Salaryman, like most of his type, can never converse with a co-worker without marking unconsciously whether he is ahead or behind in seniority.

With this colleague, though, things are more relaxed. The two men have become fast friends. Over the noodles, they talk of their passion, golf. Neither has the money, or the time, to join a golf club. But both have bought complete sets of clubs and imported clothes and shoes. At lunch, Salaryman sometimes manages to stop at a driving range on the roof of a building near his company, where under a pro's direction he whacks balls into a net eight yards away. His own clubs are used maybe one weekend a month on a larger range near his house, where the ball can actually fly 80 yards before being arrested by the net.

Soon talk turns to his colleague's interest in leaving his job in procurement for one in Salaryman's department. There is an opening, but it wouldn't do to apply for the job outright. He might not get it, after all, and the shame would be public. And the manager might be put off by a man who places his personal preferences ahead of what the company needs.

Salaryman promises to help, but his mind right now is more on his own future. Few people ever reach the rank of department manager and Salaryman is beginning to have doubts about his own chances. Salaryman knows of others from his class who are already assistant department managers, the next rung on the ladder. Salaryman thinks he will make assistant department manager but after that, who knows? He may hold steady at that grade until his mid-50s and then be farmed out as a senior executive to one of the smaller of the company's many subsidiaries.

Neither Salaryman or his friend would consider doing what one classmate did. This man quit the company two years ago to set up his own consulting business. He has prospered, but in Salaryman's mind lacks the most satisfying element of professional life, membership in a large and respected organization.

Waiting for the elevator, Salaryman decides to sprint up the stairs instead. By the third floor, he is breathless and cursing. Last year, he actually bought a membership in a sports center near the office, then used it only twice, wasting a wad of money. But how could he exercise when his colleagues remained behind to work?

Back at his desk, Salaryman groans. A new batch of sales orders has appeared during lunch to be analyzed. Ganbatte (Fight!), he thinks to himself, and hunkers down. Work is interrupted at 4 for another meeting, to which he has nothing to contribute but which he must attend to appear part of the team. It ends at just before 6.

By now most of the secretaries and tea-pouring women have gone home. By 7, Salaryman has finished his compiling. But he does not leave—in fact, the thought never occurs to him. None of the other men has. Besides, he has been included in a 7:30 dinner at a nearby restaurant, where the department is entertaining some people from the buying department of a client company.

There business cards are exchanged and the men, numbering four from each side, sit down in a private room. The restaurant is in a basement, but false paper windows and the gurgle of an artificial spring give the feeling of a feudal-era teahouse. Beer is poured, and on cue, everyone raises a glass and the dinner is officially underway.

It runs two hours, through course after course of raw fish and vegetables and rice. Women in kimonos glide in discreetly to fuss over the men, flirt a bit, and top off their beer glasses. Talk touches on the price of golf clubs, the fight for the Japan Central League Pennant, the weather. Everything, in fact, except the equipment sale that has brought them together.

They get up to leave. With drinks, the bill comes to about $1,600, which the restaurant will add to the company's tab and forward at the end of the month. Salaryman's manager is pleased with how the dinner has gone. "They seemed really to enjoy your story about the ski trip," he whispers as they walk out. Now the manager is going on with two of the client company men's to a pricey hostess bar, where he intends to ask for "kind consideration when you make a certain decision."

Salaryman is now free to head for a get-together with office mates. He rolls in to the drinking spot they have decided on at about 10, two hours after things have got under way. Three other friends arrive from a parlor where they have been playing mahjong and the gathering gets a second wind. Soon people are yelling at Salaryman to sing. He struggles to his feet and stumbles through his standard number in such a situation, a teary ballad called "At the End of a Journey." One of these days I've got to get new material, he thinks as he drops back down, feeling a bit boozed. Another Mild Seven is lit, the 45th of the day.

As ll p.m. rolls around, several friends are talking—it is unclear how seriously—about going to a sopurando (soapland), a type of bathhouse where young women suds up clients and offer sexual services. "Just call your wife and tell her the boss is making you work overnight," says one.

Salaryman has been to such places since his marriage. For a while, he had a thing going with a young woman from the audit department. But he broke it off when he felt she was making too many demands. Lately, he has lost interest in such diversions—they're too expensive, he tells himself. "No thanks," Salaryman tells them, and steps outside to flag a taxi for the ride to the station.

August 23, 1987

Soviet Women's Camp Depicted as Nightmare: Expose Says Conditions Lead to Drug Abuse, Lesbianism

Michael Dobbs

A Soviet newspaper today published the first expose from inside a women's labor camp, depicting a nightmare world of drug abuse and lesbianism, bad food and harrowing conditions for raising children.

The report, touching on an area of Soviet life that so far has received little attention in the official news media, was published in the conservative newspaper Sovyetskaya Rossiya.

It said that the inmates of women's camp No. 65-15 near the town of Kuybyshev in the Ural Mountains included nursing mothers who were expected to work up to 12 hours a day to fulfill state production quotas.

The newspaper, which until recently was regarded as a voice of muted opposition to the reform plans of Soviet leader Mikhail Gorbachev, quoted one inmate as saying that the women prisoners were quickly drawn into a cycle of viciousness and fear.

"The regime of the camp triggers off a destructive process in a woman. Marching in ranks, shapeless clothes, constant noise, obeying every command—all this exhausts you, makes you dull, forces you to find emotional outlets at any cost," said the inmate, a former technical school professor identified only as Kutsenkova.

"You can resist for two, three years, five years at a maximum. After that the organism gives out catastrophically and the camp infection takes over: smoking, lesbianism, narcotics," she added.

According to Sovyetskaya Rossiya, there were 1,200 women in the Kuybyshev labor colony, serving various terms for such crimes as murder, assault and theft. When 400 were given amnesty last year to mark the 70th anniversary of the Bolshevik revolution, the remaining 800 were forced to work even harder to fulfill the unchanged annual production target of 24 million rubles worth of padded cotton jackets.

In an accompanying commentary, Alexander Vlasov, minister of internal affairs, expressed concern about the presence of babies and young children at the camp but said there was no solution in sight.

"A woman who gives birth in the labor colony has to be with her child until it is 2 or 3 years old. It is necessary to improve the conditions for bringing up these children, to create greater comforts for them," he said.

There have been many revelations in the Soviet press about the network of prison camps known as the gulag established by Joseph Stalin, but few details about their present-day equivalents. A recent exception was an article in Moscow News, which described the present camp system as "a remnant of the Stalin era."

May 21, 1988

Chapter Four

Socialization

Each of the articles in this section focuses on some aspect of socialization—the social learning process we experience throughout our lifetime. Recall that there are many agents of socialization in contemporary society, including (but not restricted to) the family, the school, peer groups, and the mass media. The first three articles in this section share in common a focus on adult, or secondary, socialization. "Learning the ABC's of Parenting" examines the growing need to formally train adults to be parents. The decline of the extended family, in which members once learned how to raise children from grandparents, aunts and uncles, and others, has created a socialization vacuum that is now being filled by a growing host of specialized agents. "From Communism to Courtesy" depicts the attempts by Polish citizens to change their values and behaviors in a new, noncommunist society. In a similar vein, "Anxiety Spreads in the East" explores the pressing need felt by many East Germans to learn how to cope with life in a democratic, capitalistic system.

"A Matter of Form: In Conformist Japan, Even Rioters Go By the Book" describes the values and norms that affect the behavior of almost everyone in Japan. In "Immigrant Pupils Change the Face of Arlington, Virginia School," a key source of anticipatory socialization—the school—is the focus. This article describes the fears of a group of parents regarding the potential disruption of their children's socialization process by a influx of non-English-speaking immigrants into the classroom. The final article in this section also investigates the school as a socializing agent—this time, in Nicaragua.

Learning the ABC's of Parenting

Don Oldenburg

When Carol Ann Rudolph directed a day-care center at the National Institutes of Health in the mid-'70s, she recognized something unsettling about many of the parents: Most of them were new to parenting; few of them knew what they were doing.

"They didn't even know the first question to ask when looking for child care," recalls Rudolph, a Bethesda resident who has known the frustrations and self-doubts of raising two children as a single working mother. "But none of us were born knowing how to be parents."

Ten years ago, with a few exceptions, parent education meant childbirth classes—the now ubiquitous Lamaze-style sessions where couples haul along pillows and blankets to practice giving birth. Not coincidentally, those classes represented a new experience and attitude toward childbirth that, when induced by larger cultural shifts, also gave birth to a generation of parents unlike any before it. Never has there been one less prepared for raising children—nor one more eager to learn how.

Rudolph, who is considered a pioneer of multifaceted parent education in the metropolitan area, quit the day-care center and began promoting classes on bringing up baby. Initially, there were few takers. Her breakthrough came when Giant Foods penciled her class on choosing child care into its brown-bag seminar schedule of garden club lectures and tax advice. She has been talking with parents about parenting ever since.

"Some people have good nurturing abilities and that comes naturally," says Rudolph, who founded Child Care Management Resources to offer parenting seminars in the workplace. "But they don't really know what their children should be doing when they are 2 years old, 3 or 4. Parents today need to be taught those skills."

As national statistics and informal surveys of strollers parked at playgrounds confirm, there are more young children than anytime since the first baby boom. Some experts are calling it "the echo of the baby boom." In numbers alone, offspring of the original boomers have increased the population of infants to 5-year-olds since 1980 by more than 2 million.

And that has put a premium on research and information on how to raise Junior. It is particularly evident on bookstore shelves: Where Dr. Benjamin Spock once had the last word on matters of upbringing, his seminal book is now but one of dozens. With that escalation of expertise has come a proliferation of parenting classes, workshops and seminars—a phenomenon that sputtered in the '70s only to come of age a decade later.

"The customers are out there," says Mel Silberman, professor of psychoeducational processes at Temple University, whose book *Confident Parenting* is scheduled to be released by Warner Books in March. "And they're older... more educated and more mature parents today. There is a growing desire among couples to come together in parenting classes."

The early '80s, however, were a down period for parenting education. The population of newborns wasn't yet increasing and times were tough economically. "You couldn't give away parent education at that point," says Silberman, who credits the get-tough era of parenting that came in vogue with the Reagan era for helping couples to recognize their strength was in numbers. "Parents began to band together instead of being intimidated or desperate."

Linda Jessup has watched the phenomenon grow firsthand. An 11-year veteran of parent education, she is director of the Parent Encouragement Program (PEP), a Silver Spring-based program modeled on the family psychology of Alfred Adler. For the past five years, she has tracked the demographics of enrollment in PEP classes. "We attract a broad spectrum, from blue-collar parents to welfare mothers, with the bulk falling into the educated white parents category," reports Jessup.

"You hear a lot of talk about hurried kids? I see hurried parents," says Jessup, who reports the enrollment—which has jumped from 60 to 115 since the fall—consists of 40 percent men and a majority with children aged 2 to 5. "We're dealing with the Hurried Parent Syndrome. There's a real yearning for family life and connectedness ... what is missing is a feeling of control and competency among adults who in most every other aspect of their lives feel proficient. But as parents they feel inadequate."

In more than 1,500 classes that Noel Merenstein has taught, he has seen the same needs expressed by parents. "I was in a home in Westchester (N.Y.)," says the founder of Baby-Life, a New York-based group that now offers its emergency-response classes here. "These were very sophisticated people, yet they never blinked an eye for four hours. We are, without question, dealing with a new and unique generation of parents. They not only care for and love their children, but they are also taking the responsibility to learn how to bring them up."

That today's new parents would return to the classroom to learn parenting skills shouldn't be surprising. They make up the most formally educated generation in history. These are the same people who topped off their BAs and graduate degrees with extension classes like "Making Your own Sushi" and "Juggling to Beat Stress."

"This generation of parents are people who are used to going to books and classes and professionals for resources," says Deborah Benke, director of The Parent Connection, a Bethesda-based nonprofit group that offers a wide range of workshops and activities for parents and children.

"You can read and read and read, but somehow that human factor is really important," says Benke, adding that the biggest problem for today's parents is simply knowing what is normal in their children. "If you can give them a perspective of what's normal behavior, that's really what it is all about."

Experts say not knowing what is normal is a problem due to social and cultural realities. There was a time when new parents picked up tips on baby care from nearby grandmothers and aunts with friendly advice. Today's extended family has to kibitz long-distance. Meanwhile another training ground for parents dried up: As the babies born per family dropped below 2.0 over the past 25 years, fewer of today's parents ever had a runny-nosed sibling to help mama raise. "The old ways that we got information and help about our children no longer exist," says Rudolph.

The cultural change of more women punching the clock has almost overnight made parenting concerns an issue of the workplace. "Anywhere between 50 to 65 percent of mothers with young children in this area work, so if you want to go where the parents are, you've got to go to the workplace," says Sandy Kronsberg, a developmental psychologist who 16 months ago founded the Great Kids Program, sponsored by Children's Hospital National Medical Center.

Brad Sachs says the emergence of fathers in the '80s taking a hands-on role in parenting also has sent parents scurrying for help. "When men become involved with parenting in an intense way, it breaks some assumptions and mythology that parents of this generation have carried with them," says Sachs, a clinical psychologist who last September founded The Father Center, in Columbia, Md. "So as fathers become more involved, couples are asking what other myths have we been carrying around that aren't accurate anymore?"

Some experts say there may be a trickle-down effect from parenting education that, in the long run, will benefit all children. "Part of our whole purpose is to strengthen families and change attitudes," says Joan Danzansky, executive director of Family Stress Services, a District-based referral and information group.

Danzansky believes that information on good parenting is a realistic offense against child abuse in the United States. "A lot of parents don't know any other way of changing their child's behavior without relying on corporal punishment," she says. "We try to make the point that there are alternatives. We're trying to get across that we can all improve our parenting skills."

February 23, 1988

From Communism to Courtesy: At Poland's Only Charm School, Lessons in the Lost Art of Etiquette

Mary Battiata

"And now, the dinner party," said the teacher.

The pupils—43 bookkeepers, secretaries, college students and homemakers—pricked up their ears. It was table-manners night at Warsaw's School of Elegance and Charm.

"Each dinner guest should be placed 55 to 75 centimeters apart, never closer," the teacher said. "This will make your guests feel at ease."

The charm-seekers—most of them from cramped apartments where etiquette is often a casualty of other people's elbows—nodded gratefully and filed the advice away for a more affluent day. They put it in the same rose-colored envelope where they'd tucked away guidance about caviar—"always serve with a spoon of pearl or ivory; never silver, it changes the taste."

Etiquette is a growth industry in post-communist Poland. All the rules are changing. The smart money says that if you want to live well—with a big dining room full of caviar spoons—you'd better learn how to behave.

Poland's only charm school has seen such a surge in interest since the fall of communism in 1989 that it can't find enough classroom space to accommodate all who want to enroll.

"Part of the idea of communism was to be a member of the group, as opposed to having your own personality," said school founder Ryszard Swierczewski. "We teach people how to distinguish themselves from the others. Until now, there was no incentive or benefit for things like appearance or etiquette. But new horizons are opening up."

It's not just ambition that's filling the charm school. Many pupils, according to etiquette teachers, are searching for the common courtesies and a noble code eroded by four decades of communism.

Besides learning table manners, the students, most of them women, attend five weeks of night school on subjects including: the proper way to put on a coat, how to muzzle a drunken dinner guest, how to flourish a business card and how to win when dealing with the boss.

"It's not that I'm going to be a goddess after this course," said Marzena Szczudlinska, a 24-year-old bookkeeper at a Warsaw power station. "But if you want to find a new job, you have to present yourself."

"Maybe it's asking too much to think that the right clothes will cinch a job, but I think it can help a lot," agreed Elzbieta Hanusz, her 28-year-old co-worker.

"The changes in Poland are very fast now. I could lose my job tomorrow, so I'm trying to be prepared."

A rented classroom strewed with papier-mache petits fours and silverware diagrams may seem an unlikely setting for sea change, but the school is one of the staging grounds for Eastern Europe's next great revolution—the one inside people's heads.

The school, along with dozens of new self-help, fitness and holistic health centers in Warsaw, is part of a conceptual leap that millions of East Europeans are making in their pursuit of happiness, Western-style.

"People in Poland are traveling now, we watch Western television, and we notice that we have gaps in our own education," said Wanda Macialowicz, a restaurant school teacher who moonlights at the charm academy. "We want to catch up with the others, to stop being Cinderellas."

Director Swierczewski said his mission is to convince timid, self-effacing Poles of all ages that they can seize the day—whether that means opening a shop, finding a job, planning a business reception or simply standing up to a tyrant at home.

"People are used to the old system, a certain social insurance," said Swierczewski. "They have accepted the political changes, but only in theory. Really accepting the idea that your life depends on you is a big thing, a revolution!"

For many women the classes are the first time, in a culture where men run the show, that they have been encouraged to be ambitious for themselves.

"Many students come to us hunched over in the psychological sense," Swierczewski said. "We try to leave them more self-confident."

The school started out training hostesses for trade fairs, but Swierczewski, gauging his market, quickly broadened the curriculum to include everything from assertiveness training and the power of positive thinking to aerobics and how to dress for success.

On a recent evening, women rushed into the school's steamy vestibule, handed sleet-encrusted coats to the man behind the cloak counter and rushed to the bulletin board. Munching on hard rolls or puffing cigarettes, they scanned the offerings: a choreographer's tips on posture, a psychologist's lecture on how to get mad productively and an acting class where students rehearse imaginary job interviews.

"Self-promotion is a very new idea for us," Swierczewski said. He recalled the visiting American professor who'd presented his bona fides at Warsaw University by listing the VIPs with whom he'd shaken hands.

"We were shocked. In Poland you never promote yourself so openly. You do it behind the scenes, by giving gifts to people, or having someone else praise you. This is a big difference between Western European and American culture and ourselves, and one that we must bridge."

As unemployment rises and bankruptcies of state-owned companies increase across Eastern Europe this year, students can no longer afford to be squeamish about selling themselves.

"We learn that instead of saying, `I know Russian,' it's better to say at the job interview, `I know very well Russian,' " said Szczudlinska. "That way they are sure that you really do know it."

It wasn't just that the state ideology frowned on etiquette as a bourgeois affectation. The Eastern Bloc's rush to industrialize squeezed millions of country people into city apartment blocks, and then fractured family life by assigning parents to long and clashing work schedules.

"Before communism families had one common meal, but after, it became more difficult, because everyone worked and everyone worked different hours, and parents had no time to teach these things," said teacher Macialowicz.

The result is a society where in daily life, from the butcher shop to a snowy sidewalk, surliness is routine.

"For the last 45 years, all these things slept in human beings, because everyone was stuck in the same gray circle," said Ewa Piatek, a 29-year-old mother and full-time hospital bookkeeper.

"When I go into a shop or office, I would like to be treated with respect, and I'd like to be able to do it myself, but I'm not sure how," Piatek said. "But I figure if I learn how to show the best side of me, then I'll start treating people differently. And then I can bring my child up properly too."

At the moment, the Warsaw charm school is one of the few places for a courtesy-minded person to turn.

Post-communist Poland has plenty of advice sheets for fledgling entrepreneurs—Businessman magazine offers marketing know-how; Success profiles the nouveau riche and famous.

But there is no Polish Miss Manners, and etiquette manuals are scarce, except for prewar tomes such as "The ABCs of Table Manners."

The void leaves would-be well-mannered Poles gleaning etiquette tips from unlikely sources.

"I know that the way of eating tells you a lot about a person," said Piatek. "It's like in 'Gone With the Wind,' when Scarlett O'Hara's nanny tells her to eat before the party so she won't be seen stuffing herself in public."

One of the school's most popular lecturers is a dignified former ambassador, whose advice includes what to do and say in a receiving line.

"He told us that a woman who behaves correctly seems of a higher class," said Wanda Kamrat, a thirtysomething hairdresser and mother who said she was hoping to learn the composure to deal winningly with her "upper-class" customers.

Swierczewski said he thinks of the charm school as the proverbial drop of water in which a whole universe may be glimpsed. The effect of the lectures, students say, ripples out far beyond the classroom door.

"Three years ago, this kind of school would have made people laugh," Piatek said. "My friends would have said, 'What do you need charm school for? It's a waste of money.' Now they say, 'That's great. You can teach me.' "

One-third of the charm school students come from small villages outside Warsaw. For them the classes add extra hours to two- and three-hour commutes to the capital by train and bus, and to the heavy domestic and child-rearing responsibilities that fall almost exclusively on female shoulders here.

"It is a gamble for them, but they take it because they know that if they stay in the village, no one will ever find them," Swierczewski said.

For some, just signing up for night school was an act of rebellion. "My husband thinks this is a waste of time," said one student. "He said I should know enough about myself already."

Most students said they expect the $41 tuition (roughly one-fourth of the average monthly salary) to be the best investment they'd make this year, even if the metamorphosis from factory mouse to mistress of the universe is a slow one.

"I never tried to improve myself before," said Anna Gierak, a mop-headed 20-year-old secretary at a foreign trade firm. "There was too much work, and too much looking for food in the shops. A woman was just supposed to do shopping and cooking. But It's different now. On television they show businesswomen now, and I like that. You don't just see a woman with pots and pans around her."

"My mother told me she wants me not to suffer as she did and to have a better life—that's why she's paying for this class," said Joanna Wojcik, a high school student. She said her mother had stayed home to raise children but was often rebuked by her husband for not earning any money. "I wanted more courage, and I think already I'm stronger," she said.

"Like yesterday," added Szczudlinska, brightening.

The morning after the lecture on the power of positive thinking, she'd marched off to work at the power plant. Keeping her lessons in mind—"Be discreet but forceful!" "Smile when you see yourself in the mirror!"—she found the courage to enter the big boss's office for the first time in her five-year bookkeeping career.

There, in a clear, unwavering voice, she'd requested, no, made the case for, justice in the matter of company housing. The boss promised to investigate her appeal.

"I mobilized myself," she said, beaming.

March 12, 1991

Anxiety Spreads in East; Many Doubt Ability to Compete in West

Marc Fisher

At midnight as Wednesday begins, fireworks will flame over dozens of cities in both Germanys as the German Democratic Republic becomes the first country in modern history to erase itself from the map peacefully and democratically.

The physical changes are dramatic enough. From Ho Chi Minh Alley in East Berlin to Ethel and Julius Rosenberg Street in Oranienburg, place names will be scrapped, and statues of Marx, Lenin and the other socialist icons will fall. Industries collapse daily; under the economic prescription the Bonn government calls "creative destruction," nearly 2 million workers already have been let go or had their jobs cut to part time.

But the invisible changes are even deeper. After more than 40 years in isolation, under the constant and unforgiving eye of the Stasi secret police, East Germans have grown far from their cousins to the west. Now, when overnight they will become simply German again, they are expected to blend in.

It won't be easy.

"We needed more time to get to know each other," said Hans Modrow, the country's last Communist prime minister, now a member of his country's parliament. Modrow at first tried to slow the marriage of the two Germanys, then faced the reality on the streets and endorsed quick unity.

"I'm afraid what we will actually bring into the united Germany is quite little, almost nothing," Modrow said. "We're pretending that the last 40 years never happened, but without the past, one is nothing."

One year ago, East Germany was the Soviet Union's most important European partner, the economic pride of the East Bloc, a rigid society ruled by inflexible, corrupted old men—former idealists who had done time in Nazi concentration camps because they were Communists.

Now, in their country's last hours, the 16 million East Germans find themselves guinea pigs in the historic experiment emerging from the collapsed Soviet empire. Moving from communism to capitalism in a matter of weeks, they are losing their jobs, military, police, schools, flag, traditions and, many say, their identity.

East German churches are being merged with West Germany's. The number of plays by East German authors produced at East German theaters has dropped from 27 in the first half of 1989 to five in the same period this year. East Germans will lose their subsidized vacations and their ability to turn right at a red light, a practice West Germans derided as "the socialist right turn."

East Germany's teachers will be tested and retrained. Judges will simply be sacked. The government, other than a contingent of legislators who will go to

Bonn for an eight-week transitional session, will cease to exist. Everywhere East Germans turn, everything they know is becoming Western.

In the long run, most East Germans expect their financial status to improve. But many—especially people in mid-career or older—believe they will never be able to adjust completely.

A wave of nostalgia is sweeping over East Germany in its final moments. Not for the corrupt regime or the lack of consumer goods, but for a simpler, less competitive life, for rich friendships and the security of a system in which careers—assigned and organized by the state—were secondary to home life.

Prime Minister Lothar de Maiziere said in an interview that East Germans already are losing what they called the Nischengesellschaft or "niche society," in which people closed themselves off from the state's prying eyes and built tight circles of friends. Those deep private bonds—the only saving grace in a society that cast a political pall over much public discourse—were "often nothing more than a reaction to the pressures and constraints of the state system," de Maiziere conceded.

Despite their artificial foundation, the friendships were real. Now, many say, they have the wrong survival skills. East Germans tended to be inner-directed, finding the rewards of life behind their shuttered windows, away from neighbors and co-workers who might have been reporting every spark of individuality to the Stasi. Now they must compete in a society that measures success in places such as work and school—the very areas of life East Germans often tried to pass through unnoticed.

Much of the nostalgia for the vanishing life is, as East Berlin university student Mark Scheffler put it, "a bunch of over-romanticizing. But I feel justified in trying to hold onto something. We're just being taken over."

East Germans always lived two lives, a public, East German one during the workday and a private, West German one after 5:30 pm., when they got home, locked the door and tuned in to Western TV.

That secret life—evening upon evening spent soaking in the news, fashions and attitudes of their capitalist cousins—not only fed the desire for change, but also made it happen much more quickly once the Berlin Wall fell. East Germans, as they showed by voting for Bonn's business-oriented Christian Democrats in March, knew exactly what they had been missing. They chose the Western way instead of the "third way," a new, reformed socialism advocated by the leaders of last fall's revolt.

While revolutionary leaders in other East European countries now run those nations, the heroes of East Germany's bloodless uprising—leaders of the grassroots New Forum and Democratic Awakening groups—have become marginal, almost comical figures who occasionally appear on the evening news holding banners or complaining that their government is selling out to Bonn.

East Germans have watched this summer as their heroes were discredited one by one, as reports leaked out about pacifist ministers, revolutionaries and dissident writers who allegedly worked as informers for the Stasi.

Even now, after months of intense local political activity including three election campaigns and the unification blitz, East Germans know far more about West German politicians than they do about their own leaders.

In a national poll conducted by the West German newsmagazine Der Spiegel, only one-fifth of East Germans said their local leaders should be East German. Indeed, four of the 10 major candidates for premier of the new East German states are West Germans. After Oct. 3 there will be no local residency requirement for holding these offices.

As the impact of their July I overnight conversion to a market-based economy has hit hard, many East Germans have come to fear not only the change but themselves. Pointing to repeated attacks on foreigners, they worry that the masses of unemployed will turn to nationalism as an easy answer to a hazy future. A recent psychological study of East German youth found that 26 percent of them said all foreigners should be kicked out of the country—almost twice the anti-foreigner sentiment that West German youth expressed.

"We are so hesitant, so unsure of ourselves," said East German government spokesman Matthias Gehler. "No one really knows whether they will be able to make it in a competitive society."

Michael Froese, an East Berlin psychiatrist flooded with new patients straining to adjust to the new society, said the Communist system "drained the vigor from our society and left many of us with a sit-it-out mentality."

Even now, many East Germans facing unemployment sit at home and wait. They may know rationally that there is no more bureaucracy to give them a new position, but they cannot face going out to make their own way. In a West German TV network poll, 78 percent of East Germans said they expect to be second-class citizens in the new Germany for a long time.

Those who have had direct contact with West Germans often retreat to familiar ground, frightened by Western self-confidence or embarrassed by their own lack of knowledge.

Thomas Grube, a 20-year-old electrician who moved west to get a job, is going back home to Magdeburg this winter, because he cannot find friends in the West, because he cannot bear to see the "Easties Out!" graffiti in the streets of Hamburg, and because he cannot stand the smirks he gets when he walks into a car showroom and has to admit that he has no idea what financing is, let alone how it works.

"The mentality is so different," said Ulrike Jenss, 19, an East German who moved to Hamburg this summer to find work. "The way we talk, what we talk about, what we dream about—all so different."

Jenss found a job as a bartender at a luxury hotel in Hamburg. Out of a lifetime of Communist teaching about classless equality, she found herself addressing customers with the informal form of "you," du. Most West Germans use the formal sie with all but their closest friends and relatives.

"It's been so embarrassing," Jenss said. "But it's so strange to say sie to someone your own age."

One of Jenss's customers ordered an Irish coffee, but the East German had never heard of the drink. Her West German co-workers would not let her forget the lapse. " `Oh God, typical East German,' they say, like of course we have no experience with anything," Jenss said. "So I didn't know how to prepare Campari and soda. So what?"

Those who try to hold their own against their rich neighbors have found the going rough. "I feel I have to personally show the Westies what was good about the East," said Scheffler, the East Berlin university student.

"Why try to convince them?" replied his friend Guido Tuschke, a law student. "Nobody there believes it anyway."

But whatever their adjustment problems, most of those East Germans who chose to go west rather than reshape their own artificially created country, are prepared to stay. They are not about to give up the new life, with its rich variety of food, technological marvels and freedom to complain and create.

Those who stayed east live in a very different place, a land where the air makes you cough, the ground water is ruined, the phone system is pre-war and the railroads are largely unelectrified. Nevertheless, they have retained a strong strain of optimism.

Polls show that about half of East Germans believe their personal economic situation will improve in the next year and large majorities say that in five years, their part of Germany will look little different from the rest.

"We are, after all, one people," de Maiziere said. "A people which was able— unarmed—to overcome one of the best-organized secret services in the world will be able to manage the upcoming problems."

In the sweep of reunification, the problems in the East range from massive unemployment to the existence of DT-64, East Germany's youth radio station. On a cool September night, the music station suddenly fell silent, replaced seconds later by a popular West Berlin station.

The demise of a music station seemed so trifling that no one bothered to announce it in advance. But within minutes, loyal East Germans besieged the West German station with calls. Letters followed, as did a hunger strike by listeners, all to protest the loss of another piece of national identity, a place on the radio dial where East Germans could hear the language spoken their way, with their jokes and advice programs about their lives.

The outpouring stunned West Germans and, 72 hours later, PT-64 was back on the air, a small symbol that while East Germany was nearly gone, it would not be buried quite yet.

But like other state-controlled enterprises, DT-64 is spending money its government does not have. In the next weeks, it too will be shut down, this time forever.

October 1, 1990

A Matter of Form: In Conformist Japan, Even Rioters Go by the Book

John Burgess

Foreigners living in Tokyo aren't often asked to Japanese weddings. So when the invitation came, my wife and I were more than eager. This one took place in a tiny Protestant chapel in the city's toney Harajuku district. Bride and groom walked down the aisle in immaculate western dress, as an organ provided a matrimonial mood. Following the exchange of rings, vows and kisses before a stained-glass window, they were pronounced husband and wife. Afterwards, everyone retired to a reception hall, where we toasted the newlyweds, nibbled from a layer cake and lavishly stocked buffet and watched the bride make entrances first in kimono and then in another fancy western dress.

It wasn't until afterward that it occurred to me that the whole thing had been almost devoid of emotion. In fact, the mood was almost identical to that at a Japanese funeral I had attended earlier. Joy and sorrow were for other occasions. The paramount concern at both gatherings was flawless execution—for guests to stand and sit on cue, to voice the correct words of congratulation or condolence, for hosts to lead the groups smoothly through the rituals, to make sure that food and drink were adequate.

The Japanese have a right way and a wrong way to do everything. In three years of living in Japan, I came to believe that that is one of the fundamental differences between our society and theirs. This attentiveness to process, to form, to things that Americans see as the inconsequential means of reaching a desired objective, permeates Japanese life. The Japanese acknowledge this and sometimes lampoon it, but show little sign of giving it up. It is, in the end, part and parcel of the "Japaneseness" that they so treasure and the remarkable stability and security their society enjoys.

There is often talk in this country about fixing economic and social troubles by borrowing from Japan. But much of what Japan has achieved in the last four decades depends on deeply ingrained cultural traits that Americans cannot and in many cases would not want to adopt.

Not many of us, for instance, would be willing to suppress individuality to the extent that people do at the boot camps that pass for driving schools in Japan. Two years ago, a Wall Street Journal reporter visited one and found that the first hour of instruction focused on the correct way to open and close a car door: "Gently lift the handle, pull the door open exactly 10 centimeters, stop and look in both directions, pull the door toward you and proceed to enter the vehicle."

I don't mean to suggest that Americans are entirely scornful of form. We too take pride, for Instance, in pulling off a Thanksgiving dinner with all the traditional fixings. But in so much of what we do we try to leave a personal mark, to handle things a bit differently from the rest of the herd. The Japanese, in contrast, are more likely to devote that extra energy to making sure their version is exactly like everyone else's. It is not necessarily that they fear their neighbor's criticism. They take satisfaction in the act of doing things right.

Even when the right way defies common sense to our way of thinking, the Japanese cling to rules. During parliamentary elections in 1986, there was an unusual candidate, a deaf and mute man running with one of the opposition parties. When it came time for him to make the brief address on television that the rules accord to each candidate, he had a special request. Since sign language was not intelligible to the public at large, wouldn't he be allowed to do his message with subtitles or a voice-over? Bureaucratic brows furrowed. The rules were quite clear, it was explained. All candidates must be treated exactly the same. So the man did his message in sign and it was duly televised. That was not the end of it, however. The rules also specified that the sound track of each spot would be broadcast on radio. And so his was—several minutes of silence.

How could a society so set in its ways lead the world in technological innovation? How could it be so receptive to outside inventions like Chicken McNuggets, personal computers, Christian weddings and pro baseball? That is a question that bedevils the modern study of Japan. Part of the answer seems to be that there is less than meets the eye to the cultural impact of these borrowings. The Japanese are quick to borrow product and technical ideas from the outside world but they often do so without altering their society's underlying values.

Japan's devotion to form goes far back in history. Feudal society there was among the world's most tightly controlled, with specific occupations reserved for people of specific birth, and specific places for their homes. The small things in life were not left to chance either: One text that has survived gives exhaustive instruction in how to use a toilet.

The traditional Japanese arts are by western standards painstaking exercises in form. The tea ceremony, for instance, is an elaborate set of instructions for making and serving tea. The point is to gain fulfillment from carrying them out just so, not to make a better pot of tea. Karate, similarly, is a catalog of stylized moves, many of which have little utility in combat but are nonetheless the "correct" way. Likewise, Japanese flower-arranging, ikebana, gives little room for personal creativity—students learn arrangements devised by masters in which stem lengths must be so many times the diameter of the vase, stem angle precisely so many degrees, etc.

Personal relations in Japan today are also governed in large part by the notion of doing things right. Social encounters tend to unfold more closely according to set phrases and gestures. Exchange of namecards, for instance, is never overlooked on a first meeting. Nor are greetings, at every encounter. It is essentially impossible to start a conversation with a Japanese officemate without first saying good morning. Without the salutation, the inquiry about the Tanaka account or whatever will not make sense to the colleague, in the same way that a computer cannot comprehend incoming data unless it is preceded by the requisite codes.

The right way/wrong way tenet has helped build the much-documented ethic of conformism In Japan today, be it in dress, urban design or sushi bar decor. Every Japanese knows that dark, two-piece suit, conservative tie and tasseled loafers are the correct dress for a male middle-level office worker, so virtually every one of the millions of men in that niche dresses that way, or in a close variation. Moustaches are occasionally okay, but in three years of visits to Japanese company and government offices, I don't ever recall encountering a beard.

The same logic holds that every politician on the campaign trail must wear white gloves, every woman sales rep in a bank or department store a uniform (I recall a newspaper marking the arrival of spring with a photo of bank employees who had switched out of winter woolens) and every student radical at a demonstration a helmet with the group's faction name painted on the front.

American companies target particular products at particular social groups but would never dream of telling that group outright. American consumers want to believe they shop creatively. Not so in Japan. There advertisements occasionally include reassurances that the product is right for the target group. A particular grade of Suntory whiskey may be pitched as appropriate, say, for men of the section-manager rank In a company.

In the consumer world as a whole, fads and designer labels take grip with an unusual fervor. That way, people are spared the trauma of having to decide for themselves whether a new dress or a pop album is "right."

Thus, during the two traditional gift-giving seasons in Japan, there is no need to personalize what you buy. The point, rather, is to show you are a responsible member of society who is acknowledging a service performed during the year. Specially wrapped cooking oil and instant coffee are two common gifts. Department stores keep computerized gift lists for heads of families, who call in with instructions, say, to send oil to everyone in Category A and coffee to everyone in Category B.

The vaunted personal service of commercial Japan consists largely of a devoted acting out of approved gestures and phrases. Department store clerks memorize from a manual correct ways to greet customers, to point (fingers together, thumb along the palm) and to bow as they pass superiors in a corridor.

Similarly the Japanese police operate with very little creativity. If criminals think up something not in the patrolman's handbook, they can operate with near impunity, as has happened over the years with leftist extremists who make their political point by firing home-made rockets periodically at symbols of governmental authority.

In 1986, the police deployed thousands of helmeted officers to create an airtight security zone around world leaders meeting for an economic summit. Every square inch was checked and rechecked. Safety would be maintained, the police assured the public, because the radicals had never fired a rocket of more than so many hundred yards' range and the zone extended out further than that. At the height of the meeting, new, longer-range rockets, launched from an unguarded spot outside the zone, arced over the meeting hall (the only injury was to police pride). In practice, however, the police rarely lose control, as criminals are generally just as fixed In their ways as everyone else.

Japanese bureaucrats, with their reams of fine-print regulation, often take themselves to be the supreme guardians of the right-way/wrong-way ethic. Foreign companies trying to sell in Japan may feel that the inflexibility they encounter in interpretation of regulations is a ruse to close the market. However, the bureaucrats often treat fellow Japanese in just the same way.

Children in Japan are drilled in respect for form with an educational system that stresses memorization and unquestioning acceptance of teachers' words. This is partly because of the immense labor required to learn to read and write. The Japanese system is a mix of Chinese ideographs and two sets of phonetic scripts. Children spend years memorizing one-by-one the ideographs, which generally have more than one pronunciation, with context the only guide as to which should be used. Each character must be written in a particular way, with the strokes following in a set order.

Americans often wonder, why not simplify the writing system? That way children could learn to read faster—and that's the point of the study, isn't it? Japanese parents generally find the question off the mark. First, the way It is is the "right" way. Second, they believe firmly that children develop invaluable self-discipline and character as they hunker down over exercise books late into the night, year after year, plowing through the thousands of required characters, just as their parents did.

While Japanese companies are quick to adopt new technology, their corporate culture in many other respects remains chained to convention. Promotion is strictly by seniority. Big companies tend to move as groups and to be largely indistinguishable from the next. Toshiba, Sony, Matushita, Hitachi—all make basically the same mix of consumer products. If one Japanese bank wants to upgrade its office in a foreign capital, it will hesitate if none of its fellow banks has done so. But once it makes the plunge, all the others in its class are likely to feel they have to follow, as the maverick has changed the rules.

Doing things by the book is one reason why Japan continues to lag in creative endeavors like basic research (in exhaustive trial-and-error research, however, it does well). Great breakthroughs in science often depend on egocentric geniuses who feel comfortable declaring: I don't care what my teacher taught me, I know a better way. Talk of that sort makes the Japanese viscerally uncomfortable.

The Japanese like to say that they learned industrial quality control from an American, Dr. W. Edwards Deming. But his maxim—"do it right the first time"— meshes well with a culture in which people wake up with the objective of doing everything correctly.

As is well known, Japanese products in the 1950s were junk. But I would not be surprised if the poor quality was built into each type in precisely the same way. Then, once the production engineers got their lines designed correctly, they built in good rather than bad quality and Japan was ready to take on the world.

There is evidence that some Japanese are questioning their obsession with form and are trying to change. For some years now, blue-ribbon panels studying the educational system have been recommending that a bit more creative thought be encouraged in the schools and research world. That is slow in coming, so In the meantime they are trying to import a bit of this thinking. I once met an American researcher who had been brought to Japan to work on a research team partly in the hope that he would inject a measure of irreverence.

A Japanese colonel once suggested to me that the world's best army would have, among other things, Japanese foot soldiers (they would march by the book into the jaws of death) and American generals (they would quickly devise creative responses to every battlefield contingency).

And fatigue with the current ways is showing up in popular culture, too. Several years ago, movie-goers flocked to a comedy called "The Funeral." It was the saga of a middle-class family struggling to do things right after the aged father passes away. How much to pay the monks handling the rites? What words to use with the mourners? At one point the family watches a video tape that offers advice on such points. The instructor offers an elaborate expression of gratitude as appropriate for delivery to mourners. Or, says the instructor, you can just say, thank you so very much. That's just what I'm going to say, exclaims one of the bereaved in relief.

August 14, 1988

Immigrant Pupils Change Face of Arlington, Virginia School: Teachers Say Children's Needs Can Be Met

Dana Priest

Mary Hynes considers herself one of Key Elementary School's biggest boosters. Three of her children attended the Arlington, Virginia school. She served as PTA president and has high praise for the school's teachers and its rich mix of foreign-born pupils.

But this year, when it came time for her daughter Shannon to begin the first grade, Hynes broke the family tradition and transferred the child to Taylor, where an overwhelming majority of pupils speak English as their first and only language.

She says she made the decision when she saw the list of Key pupils who would have been in Shannon's first grade class. "I just looked down the list and everyone had a Spanish surname," she said.

Hynes' reaction reflects that of a growing number of middle-class Anglo parents in Arlington who have expressed concern that their children's educational and social experience in school is being adversely affected by concentrated numbers of newly arrived immigrant children.

Some Anglo parents have complained that typically American social traditions suffer in a setting where they are new to the student body. They complain of not being able to maintain Girl and Boy Scout troops and about foreign languages spoken on the playground. "There's nobody to play with," explained Judy Buchholz, a mother of three Key pupils.

Without exception, the pupils and six teachers interviewed at random during visits to Key agreed that the large immigrant population affected the instructional and social atmosphere at Key.

But, in contrast to some of the parents, the pupils and teachers described the effect only in positive ways, including the social benefits gained through knowing people of other cultures. In addition, the teachers argued that foreign-born pupils do not have a negative impact on classes because they have been able to adapt their lessons to accommodate them.

In the 1986–87 school year, Arlington had three of the 12 Washington area schools in which immigrants made up more than 50 percent of the student population, according to figures compiled recently by The Washington Post. Ten years ago there was none.

Arlington students are among the most ethnically diverse in the area, with 52 percent of its students being white, 18.4 percent Hispanic, 16.4 percent black and 13 percent Asian.

About 15 percent of Arlington's 14,258 students are enrolled in full- or part-time English-language classes. At Key, Barrett and Glencarlyn elementary schools, 40 percent of the pupils are in these courses. At Key, another 30 to 40 percent are immigrants who have learned English well enough to attend regular classes full time. About 35 percent of the non-English-speaking pupils are in preschool and first grade.

Of Key's 573 pupils, Spanish is the native language of 272 pupils, and English is the first language of 193. The other pupils speak one of 12 other languages as a mother tongue.

Last year, responding in part to parental concerns, Arlington Superintendent Arthur W. Gosling appointed a citizens committee to investigate the impact of these pupils on county schools. One goal of any solution, said school officials, is to stop the small but growing exodus of Anglo middle-class children from schools with large foreign-born student bodies.

This month, after six months of debate and investigation, the committee delivered a report that outlined alternatives, ranging from districtwide busing of all students to achieve linguistic desegregation to relocating immigrant students in special centers until they master English.

But John Crowder, the school official in charge of the committee, said the 33-member group could find no studies or hard evidence to support the perception by some parents that the language deficiencies of these students negatively affect the educational or social milieu at a school. Rather, he said, "the impact is in the eyes of the beholder."

Gosling contends that that perception alone is enough to merit School Board action on the matter. "It is important that we are able to sustain the support of the broad-based community," he said. The concerns include "a combination of (academic] performance, people's attitudes and people's views of what is a reasonable expectation of a school."

Last summer, members of the affluent Lyon Village community, part of which is contained within Key's attendance boundary, surveyed parents about their perceptions of neighborhood schools. More than 50 percent of the respondents described the school's "least desirable" qualities as "too many minorities," "low test scores," "inactive parents" and "overcrowded." Also, more than 50 percent said its "most desirable" characteristics included "good teachers" and "good facilities."

The survey was collected from the parents of 274 youngsters, 81 of whom were elementary or preschool children living in the Key boundary area.

School district officials said there are no reliable figures on the number of pupils who have been withdrawn from Key or the two other schools where foreign-born pupils dominate. But, they said, the numbers were disproportionately large among Anglo pupils when compared with withdrawals at other schools.

"It has been true that you have more instructional transfers out" of these schools, said School Board member Dorothy H. Stambaugh. "The most consistent reason that people transfer out is the instructional program... and that can relate to the number of {immigrant} students at the school."

Lori Maes, Key's PTA president and one of two Hispanics on the superintendent's committee, said that the Hispanic community supports Key and that the School Board should devote more resources to helping immigrant children learn English if they are worried about their impact on other pupils.

"These children are going to be around, and we have to educate them," she said.

Key, at 2300 Key Blvd., is in a largely stable, middle-class community next to the Arlington courthouse. Within its enrollment borders sits the low-income Lee Gardens apartment complex, where most of the school's Hispanic children live.

Pupils are placed in regular classes only when they meet certain school district criteria. Under these rules, pupils can be mainstreamed into a class appropriate to their age even if their reading ability is as much as two years behind their grade level. The belief is that once they reach that level, they can catch up more quickly if they are in regular classes.

Teachers, for the most part, argued that they were able to adapt their lesson plans so that neither the immigrant pupils nor the native-English speakers suffered.

"There are difficulties in science and health, for instance, where they need to get information from a book," Karen Spees, a third grade teacher, said of some of her immigrant pupils. "There are cases where vocabulary can slow down reading, but by {having the pupils} talk back and forth, what they don't get from reading they get in class discussion."

Said sixth grade teacher Joan Myers, "You've got to go a little bit slower. We do a lot of writing.... I make a point of making sure {immigrant pupils} participate. I fuss at them, and as far as they're concerned, every one of them is up on top of it or this lady gets ugly." Five of Myers' 22 pupils are native speakers of English.

Teacher Alan Tonelson has turned each of his sixth graders into a mentor for other pupils in the class. Many of the American-born children help immigrant pupils with reading. Some immigrant pupils take leadership roles in science and sports.

Tonelson said the device encourages strong self-esteem and enables the mentor pupil to work on verbal and organizational skills through developing one-on-one lesson plans.

In each class at Key, pupils are divided into three groups, based on their reading ability. In the lower grades, gifted pupils who do not choose the school's English-Spanish immersion program share the same classroom with other pupils their age. In higher grades, the gifted students and the high achievers attend a special class that combines the best students from two grade levels.

Pupils and teachers said they see many benefits to the cultural mixture at Key, and they note that the school is virtually free of cultural-based cliques, except among pupils who are just beginning to learn English.

"I don't see prejudice in this room," said Spees. "I don't see people making fun of people's names. It sort of renews my trust in people."

The children seem oblivious to the cultural concerns of their parents. Many take great pride in the school and describe their best friends as people from other countries.

"We don't have that many people from America, so we can learn new stuff about other countries," said Hynes' son Brendan, whose two best friends last year were Chinese and Vietnamese. "They always made me laugh and had fun things for me to do."

"Some of my friends ask me, 'What do you do at your school? How do you communicate?' " said student president Yael Latt, 11. "They say that their schools are better, but I don't think that's true. I think this school is better because it lets all sorts of people in."

February 1, 1988

Battle Looming over Nicaragua's Schools: Government Wants to Purge Education of Sandinista Influence

Lee Hockstader

For 11 years under Sandinista rule, Nicaragua's children were weaned on the revolution and the party.

They learned that 'G' is for guerrilla and 'C' is for Carlos Fonseca, founder of the Sandinista Front. They sang the Sandinista hymn and saluted the Sandinista red-and-black flag. And just in case the message did not get through, their textbooks reminded them that good boys and girls belong to the Sandinista Children's Association.

Now, as Nicaragua's 1 million public school students prepare to return to their classes this week for the first semester of the post-Sandinista era, they are the focus of a looming struggle that could pose the next major test for the newly elected government of President Violeta Chamorro.

The stakes involve the most basic issues of Nicaragua's recent history: What did the revolution represent? How will it be judged by time? And in a society still bitterly divided, who will judge it?

"Schools under the Sandinistas were not schools, but centers of Sandinista propaganda," said Sofonias Cisneros, the new education minister. "They were taking students and turning them into soldiers of the revolution, promoting class hatred."

"We may have exaggerated the party aspect of the revolution," conceded Carlos Tunnermann, who was the Sandinista minister of education in the early 1980s. "But the basic values we taught were good."

The new government is determined to exorcise Sandino and his revolutionary legacy from the classroom. As a replacement, officials have decided to stress fundamental Christian and democratic values.

But the Sandinistas, who proved in a violent strike by public workers this month that they are ready to defend the "conquests of the revolution," are gearing up to resist. Their weapons include a majority of the nation's 30,000 teachers, many of whoa got their jobs after being screened for ideological purity.

At eastern Managua's Angel Valentino Barrios school, named for a fallen hero of the revolution, Sandinista teachers outnumber pro-government teachers 17 to 3.

Despite an order by Chamorro that all Sandinista party imagery be removed from public buildings, photos of Fonseca and of Augusto Cesar Sandino, a rebel hero during the U.S. occupation of Nicaragua in the 1920s and eponym of the revolution, still hang on the wall of the main office. When school opens this week, a teacher said, students will be expected to sing the Sandinista hymn as well as the national anthem.

"We won't teach the generation of the future as if the struggle never took place," said Ricardo Danilo Espinoza, a 24-year-old teacher at the school. "We had a revolution. We must teach the historical reality of the country."

Government officials are taking a firm line but acknowledge that they face a daunting challenge in instituting their reforms. "The Sandinistas still control the system," said Cisneros.

To an outsider, the gathering storm over the curriculum seems just one of many challenges facing the school system. A tour of some of Managua's dilapidated schools, with their few sticks of broken chairs, dangling electrical wires and leaky roofs, reveals the overwhelming poverty of the system.

But upgrading the physical facilities of a system that includes 5,000 schools with a budget of just $30 million is slow work. New textbooks, on the other hand, are already being printed to replace the Sandinista books. The texts, called the "Blues and Whites"—the colors of Nicaragua's flag—are being published with the help of $4 million, earmarked for such a project, from the United States.

Sandinistas charge that the textbooks are being submitted to the U.S. Embassy for approval. The Chamorro government denies it.

The Sandinistas, like revolutionaries everywhere, began spreading the symbolism and mythology of their revolution in 1979, immediately upon ousting the Somoza family dictatorship that had ruled Nicaragua for 45 years.

Schools were named after fallen Sandinista heroes. New elementary texts—called the "Carlitos," after Carlos Fonseca—were designed with the help of Cuban advisers. Every child could recite the feats and wisdom of Sandino, renowned for battling U.S. Marines from his mountain redoubt during the occupation.

But the changes went even deeper. History courses took a Marxist line, emphasizing class struggle. Civics classes stressed the evils of capitalism and the benefits of socialism. "Yankee imperialism" was denounced, and sovereignty, autonomy and nonintervention proclaimed.

At the same time, the Sandinistas launched a literacy campaign that they say cut the nation's Illiteracy rate drastically—although the new government disputes that claim.

"The Sandinista revolution tried to transmit revolutionary values," said Tunnermann, the former education minister. "In designing our curriculum, we consulted with over 50,000 people as to how to produce the 'new man' " of Nicaragua's new society.

The Chamorro government's vision of the "new man" relies heavily on traditional Christian values, which the Sandinistas gave short shrift.

One focus of controversy in the proposed reforms is Humberto Belli, the new vice minister of education who is In charge of redesigning the curriculum.

Belli, a U.S.-trained sociologist, belongs to a small, charismatic Catholic sect known as the City of God. The Sandinistas have suggested that he is a religious fanatic bent on sneaking Catholicism into the classroom in defiance of Nicaragua's constitution, which calls for separation of church and state and bans religious classes during regular school hours in public schools.

A former Sandinista and a former Marxist, Belli grew disenchanted with the revolution before it triumphed and left the country to live in the United States.

There, he headed the Washington-based Puebla Institute, a fiercely anti-Sandinista human rights organization. He was also a tenured professor of sociology at a Catholic college in Ohio until this year. He returned to Nicaragua when Chamorro offered him the government job.

Belli and other education officials say they will ban references to political parties.

Belli also plans to commission a history textbook for secondary schools—there is now only an elementary school text—a project he acknowledges will ignite bitter debate. One way to blunt the criticism, he said, might be to include opposing interpretations of events surrounding the revolution and Sandinista rule. Merely presenting both sides, he said, "would be an eye-opener" In polarized Nicaragua.

Although Belli insists that his task is to "clean our system of propaganda," he makes no promise of ideological neutrality.

"We are not neutral," said Belli. "We do have a strong Ideology, influenced by strong Christian values which we share with a lot of Nicaraguan people.... I don't harbor any illusions that you can depoliticize an educational system and make it value-free. But in contrast with the Sandinistas, we are not obsessed."

New classes, Belli said, will teach human rights, monogamy and what he calls a "a pro-life message." Like many American conservatives, he rejects moral relativism and secular humanism.

July 30, 1990

Chapter Five

Social Stratification

The articles in the section explore various aspects of an important area of sociological investigation—that of *social stratification*, the systems of inequality that exist in all societies. The first three articles investigate societies that have a closed-caste structure—that is, societies in which one's position in the social structure is dictated by ascription, or personal characteristics such as parentage, race, sex, and age. "Caste Conflicts in India" describes the violent opposition by members of the upper castes to a recent proposal by India's Prime Minister calling for a doubling in the number of public-sector jobs reserved for the lower castes. The subject of "A Passage to India" is a recent novel written by a wealthy Indian, who confesses to his unwillingness to give up his privileges even while he believes India must become more egalitarian. "Guerilla War in Peru Feeds On Caste Schisms" describes the modern-day caste system in Peru, in which Peruvians of Spanish descent dominate the "mestizo" (mixed heritage) Indians.

While the United States has an "open-class" system in which positions in the hierarchy are obtained on the basis of achievement, unequal opportunity is very much a fact of life. "A Tale of Two Schools" describes the disparity between two schools—one rich, one poor—in the same district and the unequal resources to which each has access. "The Rich Get Richer" reports on the falling income of the nation's poor. "Poor People in Rich America" offers one writer's opinion on the gulf between rich and poor.

The final article in this section offers a fascinating glimpse of poverty in the Soviet Union—a condition that under communism was not supposed to exist, but most emphatically did.

Castes Conflict in India: Affirmative Action Ignites Protest, Suicides

Steve Coll

Shivaji Singh, a powerful upper-caste landlord who lives in this squalid village, is preparing for war with India's lower castes. "The situation is rising beyond tolerance," he said, because of an affirmative-action plan proposed by the faraway government in New Delhi that would set aside about half of all public jobs for lower- and lower-middle castes.

Enraged by the plan, rival upper- and lower-caste landlords with private armies are stockpiling weapons in this lawless region of Bihar state. "We're just waiting for the other side to come onto the battlefield," Singh said. "There are about 17,000 people in this area who will die for me."

All across India's densely populated north, an emotional debate over affirmative action is igniting ancient hatreds over caste, the countless separate social classes into which Hindus are born that affect virtually all aspects of their lives. The debate began in erudite courtrooms and political halls but now threatens to trigger mass violence.

"Because of {affirmative action}, the backward classes want to finish the forward castes," said Sahjanand Sharma, an upper-caste school principal who had four fingers chopped off last week when a lower-caste private militia attacked a train in which he was riding in Bihar. "I think there will be a civil war."

Behind such fears in rural areas lies a divisive struggle over economic power and national identity in modern India, a stratified society that encompasses the feudal countryside and cosmopolitan cities.

Immediately at issue is the proposal announced two months ago by Prime Minister V.P. Singh to more than double the number of public-sector jobs now set aside for lower castes. Members of certain tribal groups and some of the lowest castes already benefit from such job quotas. Singh's plan would extend them to other lower castes, lower-middle castes and possibly some underprivileged non-Hindu groups.

Implementation of the plan was suspended temporarily by India's Supreme Court after riots and protest suicides by upper-caste students. But caste violence has only accelerated since then, claiming more than 100 lives.

Arrayed on one side of the issue are those from India's privileged classes who oppose setting aside jobs on grounds that the country cannot afford it. Quotas, they say, entrench caste divisions and retard economic progress by rewarding people on the basis of birth, rather than merit.

"How are we going to break the shackles of poverty, ignorance and disease if we are going to institutionalize mediocrity?" asked Karan Singh, an upper-caste prince and former ambassador to the United States.

He and others argue that India's public sector already is bloated, inefficient and corrupt. More quotas for lower castes will discourage individual enterprise and bequeath the country incompetent doctors, pilots and scientists, they say.

Lower-caste activists counter that the country's biggest social and economic problem is rampant caste discrimination that strips a majority of Indians of personal dignity and the opportunity to improve their lives. Government job quotas may not be a perfect way to end such discrimination, they say, but setting aside jobs will encourage assimilation of the lower castes and quickly correct inequities.

The opposing camps disagree about how to promote American-style social and economic mobility in a country in which for the majority of people all actions of daily life—with whom you eat, how you bathe, where you live and what job you do—are heavily influenced at birth by caste, Hinduism's divinely ordained assignment of worldly worth.

There are thousands of castes and sub-castes in India, but they can be sorted roughly into three groups. An estimated 15 to 20 percent of the population belong to the dominant upper castes, including priestly Brahmins and martial Rajputs. At the bottom are the lowest castes, also about 15 to 20 percent of the population, including the destitute "untouchables" whose cause was championed by Mohandas K. Gandhi.

In between is India's impoverished majority, the so-called "other backward classes," lower and lower-middle castes ranging from landless laborers to subsistence farmers, fishermen, goldsmiths, potters and non-Hindu minorities such as Moslems and Christians. This great laboring mass is the target of Singh's new affirmative-action plan, which could affect as many as 500 million people, depending on how the final quota lists are drawn.

Some upper-caste quota opponents argue that caste barriers will only be broken by the spread of capitalism and the growth of a middle class that prides itself on the privileges of wealth, not of caste. They say that caste identities already are dissolving in the consumerist flotsam of partially Westernized cities such as Bombay and New Delhi. Since caste has long been tied to land ownership, they say that what is needed is rapid industrialization, urbanization and the nation's integration with the world economy.

There is evidence for this view. While some Brahmins still wear saintly sashes, and some peasant castes don distinctive turbans or other styles of dress, nowadays caste is not always easy to determine on India's chaotic city streets. In the north, upper-caste members tend to have lighter skin and more Aryan features than members of lower castes, a fact that contributes to widespread prejudice against dark-skinned Indians, even those of high birth.

But some urbanized youth say that while their parents could decipher caste with a few subtle questions about family names and geographical origin, they often cannot even guess at caste status without asking directly—a query they regard as impolite.

Because of all the confusion, city counterfeiters do a brisk business in false lower-caste certificates that allow upper-caste applicants to take advantage of job or education quotas.

As India's urban middle class grows—its size is now estimated at between 40 million and 80 million people—the cities have attracted large numbers of lower-caste members who have escaped their birth status to compete as equals with the upper castes in business and education, without the benefit of quotas.

Consider Chanchal Shekar, an honors anthropology student at prestigious Delhi University born to a lower-middle caste in Bihar, where upper-caste feudal warlords hold the strings of power. Shekar's illiterate father broke with generations of caste tradition to start a small trucking business with money raised by selling the family's jewelry. Through hard work, he parlayed the business into land and made enough money to send his children to boarding schools.

Now the younger Shekar is a hero at home—the only person from a lower-caste town of about 10,000 ever to attend a university. "It was due to the sheer efforts of my father," Shekar said.

Shekar won scholarships by excelling at competitive examinations. He says job quotas are essential to improve the lot of those he left behind. The problem, he said, is that in India "all kinds of mechanisms for controlling society are concentrated among the 12 to 13 percent" who belong to the highest castes. Only the rapid social change that quotas attempt to engineer can break that grip, he said.

Indians of lower birth say caste barriers—grounded in religion and social prejudice as well as in economics—are too strong to be broken in a significant way by individual effort alone. Even a rapid spread of market capitalism, itself a dubious prospect given the socialist outlook of most Indian politicians, would not erode the power of the highest castes, they say.

In the rancid villages and tent cities that are home to most of the subcontinent's estimated 100 million "untouchables," that argument acquires fresh power.

A few miles from Shekar's university, Om Prakash and his family have been living in a garbage dump for 20 years, working as shunned ragpickers—freelance trash collectors. "This is the place for us. We can't get out of here," Prakash said, flicking flies off a friend. "There's always hope, but we never reach anything. I'm sure my grandfather hoped, too."

Why doesn't Prakash's family take advantage of the educational and employment quotas available for untouchables?

Prakash answers coldly. His brother did that, earned a college degree and is now working as a ragpicker in Haryana state. "Even if I work hard, if I go forward one step, there are 10 people pushing me back again," he said.

Prakash's story suggests that India's oppressed classes do not necessarily see quotas as the key to success. Indeed, while Prime Minister Singh is widely accused of springing his quota plan to win support from the populous lower castes, it is not clear that affirmative action is a vote-winning idea in India.

Polls taken by The Policy Group in New Delhi before last year's national elections found that only about half of the members of India's lowest castes, called scheduled castes, favored more job quotas, while a strong majority of non-scheduled castes wanted existing quotas reduced or eliminated.

In dozens of conversations with upper- and lower-caste Indians held in city universities and villages populated by illiterates, not one upper-caste member supported quotas and not one lower-caste member opposed them.

Such polarization is being exploited by political leaders and feudal landlords on both sides of the issue. Not all lower-caste members are impoverished, and in states such as Bihar, Haryana and Uttar Pradesh, the fight in favor of quotas frequently is being led by economically powerful landlord-thugs who command sizable private militias. The presence of such private armies is one factor feeding fears of an open caste war in the countryside.

Quotas such as the ones now being proposed by New Delhi were imposed decades ago in some southern states following mass agitations by lower castes. But while quotas bought peace in the south, they have increased polarization in the north. Millions of upper-caste members locked out of government jobs in the south have migrated north, carrying resentments with them and increasing caste competition for jobs.

One complication is the high prestige attached here to jobs in the central government. India's massive federal bureaucracy wields wide powers over everyday life and offers privileged officials innumerable chances to line their pockets illegally. Despite tentative steps recently to liberalize the economy, businessmen are frequently looked down upon as vultures tainted by relatively low-caste status. These factors endow India's debate over government job quotas with a power it would not have in the West.

Free-market economists say the answer is to eliminate the government's role, forcing more competition on the playing field of economic merit. But Indian politicians depend on the bureaucracy's grip for influence and money, as do the largest government-sanctioned business houses. Nobody expects that interlocking complex of government and business, which is overwhelmingly dominated by upper castes, to be broken up soon.

October 18, 1990

A Passage to America: Indian Author Can't Shake Caste Consciousness

Steve Coll

Anurag Mathur, of blue eyes and high cheekbones and the polished pitch of a diamond salesman, is the toast of India's capital this summer. The Swiss ambassador adores him, Mathur says, and the British in town treat him "like royalty." At lunch in a posh Chinese restaurant, he waves to Vasu Scindia, the queen of Dholpur.

"Have you read the book?" he demands.

She has, and so it seems has much of India's elite reading public. "The Inscrutable Americans," Mathur's best-selling comic novel about a young heir to an Indian hair-oil factory who travels to Upstate New York to study chemical engineering, is headed for its third printing six months after publication here. About the only people in India's cosmopolitan big cities who seem unamused by the novel are the expatriate Americans.

"Everyone asks, 'What do the Yanks think of it?' " Mathur says with a grin. "My response is, I have no idea. Maybe they're gnashing their teeth in silence, fomenting potions to slip into me." If so, they will be too late to reverse the impression Mathur has made on the minds of India's governing elite.

Mathur's tale of a subcontinental bumpkin at sea in the American heartland has struck a chord with the Indian intelligentsia at a time when they are grappling with new and fundamental questions about whether and on what terms India should embrace the West.

The new questions about the country's identity have arisen because India's politics, economy and traditional ideology are up for grabs as they have not been for four decades. The long-dominant Nehru-Gandhi family dynasty has been depleted with the assassination of Rajiv Gandhi in May, leaving a void at the center of the country's political culture. India's socialist economic model is in disarray, with some in the governing elite pushing for radical free-market reforms and others holding fast to tradition. With a new government taking office, debate about the future is swirling, and frequently the talk centers on American ideas, American culture and fears of American hegemony.

By coincidence, Mathur's "The Inscrutable Americans" has splashed down in the midst of this intellectual whirlpool.

As a novel, it is slight and played for laughs. The plot traces the travails of Gopal Kumar, a middle-class Indian provincial who, when he leaves for New York, knows everything about Americans that can be gleaned from the collected letters of Penthouse magazine. Once stateside, he leers his way across a caffeine-charged, sex-obsessed university campus and wanders off to discover Holy Roller preachers, urban blight and Coca-Cola, all the while recording his impressions in letters home written in fractured Indian English.

"Everywhere, brother, as far as I am seeing there are lights, lights. It is like God has made carpet of lights," Kumar writes. "Then we are landing in New York and plane is going right up to door so that we are not having to walk in cold. I must say Americans are very advanced."

At the immigration desk, an officer asks him how it is going. "I am telling him fully and frankly about all problems and hopes, even though you may feel that as American he may be too selfish to bother about decline in price of hair oil in Jajau town. But, brother, he is listening very quietly with eyes on me for ten minutes and then we are having friendly talk about nuts and he is wanting me to go."

But what Kumar discovers when he steps outside is that prosperity in the United States—middle-class, egalitarian prosperity—is far different from what he expected and much more demanding than the feudal privilege he knew and aspired to at home. Nobody in New York pays homage to Kumar's high caste. There are no servants, cooks or drivers. He must even clean his own toilet, a job reserved for shunned "untouchables" in India.

This is the dilemma India is confronting at home in 1991. Because of the severity of the country's present crisis and its traditions of democracy and pluralism, many here are pushing American middle-class ideas of individualism, enterprise and egalitarianism as the way to reform and salvation. But the elite that must decide on the course of reform is wary of American prosperity precisely because it would undermine India's centuries-old system of feudal privilege.

Not only is this the theme of "The Inscrutable Americans," it is the story of author Mathur's life. He gathered the material for his novel as a student at Tulsa University during the late 1970s. But while he says that he was seduced by the United States and found a promising job at the Tulsa Tribune after school, he gave it up and returned to India because he was not prepared to trade feudal prosperity here for egalitarian prosperity in the United States.

"A lot of people ask me, 'Why did you come back from America?' My answer is that I came back to improve my standard of living," he says. "Here I have servants, club memberships, cars, a chauffeur and the works. Over there I did everything. To the end I couldn't manage to clean toilets without thinking there's something terribly wrong."

Yet Mathur, reflecting India's boundless capacity for self-contradiction, insists that he wants desperately for his country to move toward an American model of social and economic organizations. "I think we're at a seminal stage," he says. "The Indian people have great abilities, which they have shown in various places. But they've been repressed, very systematically, ruthlessly" by the stifling socialist state.

To progress, he argues, India must discover that "competition is really what keeps people working at their optimal level... that change I think will come. Finally, the individual will start to matter more."

But what will that mean for India's traditional privilegentsia, the bureaucrats, politicians and intellectuals who for four decades have payed homage to socialist ideals while sitting atop an inflexible social hierarchy?

Like many in this capital these days, Mathur looks out at the great Indian heartland—where the masses of peasant farmers, landless laborers, cobblers, fishermen and toilet cleaners toil passively—and he senses that a quiet middle-class revolution is brewing. But unlike some, he is not afraid of its consequences.

"When India changes, it does so at a speed that is incomprehensible," he says. "Video, for example, has only been in India for seven or eight years. And what a revolution! I keep wondering what goes on in the minds of those villagers where they've had [state-run TV] and now they have video. And in village after village, they're getting to see state-of-the-art blue films. What is the effect on their minds? What an incredible leap—from bullock carts to Swedish erotica! But the Indian people do accept change remarkably well. I'm not worried. Anyway, I don't think anyone can stop this."

Kumar, the protagonist of "The Inscrutable Americans," is a bumbler from India's heartland state of Madhya Pradesh—one of the greasy-haired, inarticulate, naive scions of the country's surging provincial middle class. By casting Kumar in that role, Mathur has turned his novel into a comic parable of the confrontation between India's elite and its rising challengers, as well as of the older, ambivalent relationship between India and the United States.

For the Indian elite who are buying and reading his book about Gopal Kumar, Mathur says, "This kind of Indian is almost as inscrutable" as America. "This [elite] reader identifies in many ways with the poor Yanks trying to cope with this bumpkin."

Nonetheless, Mathur continues, Gopal Kumar is the future of India. "There's more confidence even among the ruling elite" that the Kumars of India must be celebrated and accommodated. "It's a generational change," he says. "The younger generation is simply not willing to wait. The older generation said, our children are going to have a better life. Now the younger generation is here and they're saying, 'Where's the better life?'"

Not in the United States, according to Mathur and his novel. At the end of "The Inscrutable Americans," as Kumar is preparing to return to his hair-oil factory in Madhya Pradesh, Mathur describes the Indian future of his imagination, a place he believes will be connected to the West through the inculcation of American ideas and ambitions—but not, for decades, by mutual understanding.

Kumar "knew that the world he had been trained for was the real one for people of his inheritance, and this one [the United States] was relatively a vacation," Mathur writes. "He knew he would stand for many days on the shop floor of the factory, amidst the black stains, the oil smells, the roar of men and machinery, sweating in the heat, and the memories of this interlude would wash over him. ...

"Perhaps he would relive it all only when he sent his son here to study, to learn in their superb systems, to grow and be hurt and yet feel so alive in their strange world, amidst their alien and rude ways that somehow managed to be affectionate. But that would be a long time from now."

July 8, 1991

Guerrilla War in Peru Feeds on Caste Schisms: Peruvian Indian Culture Moves Uneasily from Highlands to City

Eugene Robinson

When police hauled 15,000 people off the streets for questioning in the killing of a former defense minister last month, the sweep was largely an exercise in rounding up the usual suspects: young, dark-skinned men with Indian features.

In a country where race is a delicate, seldom discussed issue, the 10-year Shining Path insurgency has thrown into relief a complex system of class and caste based largely on color and cultural identification. A light-skinned criollo minority, descended from the Spanish colonizers who made Lima the seat of their South American empire, feels surrounded and even under attack by a majority that stems mainly from Indian stock.

Some say Peru's deepening economic woes have sharpened racial divisions, which in recent decades had seemed to be lessening, and provided recruits for the Maoist guerrillas. Some young people in the countryside have reacted to the unrelenting poverty around them—and the indifference of the white power structure in Lima—by turning to Shining Path.

"With this crisis that's tearing the country apart, we're going backwards racially," said Carlos Ivan Degregori, a scholar with the Institute of Peruvian Studies. "In a real sense, Shining Path's fight is also an ethnic fight."

Most Peruvians are neither full-blooded white nor full-blooded Indian, but rather mestizo, of mixed heritage in varying proportions. But the pattern of power and influence is unmistakable—the economic and political elite is overwhelmingly white, and the society becomes poorer and more disenfranchised as it becomes darker and more Indian.

"If you go into a bank and look at the people in charge, you won't see any Indians," said Salvador Palomino, an anthropologist who heads the South American Indian Council, a coordinating group for Indian organizations. "In the newspaper you'll see an ad for a secretary that requires 'good presence.' That's a code word for white."

The word a person uses to describe someone with darker skin is cholo, which roughly translates as half-breed and can be a term of address between friends, a neutral physical description or a term to humiliate.

"No one will talk about race directly," said anthropologist Luis Millones, whose work has touched on racial and ethnic divisions. "Race isn't even a topic of very much academic research. Years ago, officials said that Peru is a mestizo country—we're all the same. In effect, the race problem was erased by decree."

Race is an unspoken but important factor in the war between the Peruvian state and Shining Path—in Spanish, Sendero Luminoso—the Maoist guerrilla group that has waged a bloody 10-year war against the Peruvian government.

Sociologist Degregori said: "It is clear that the spinal column of Sendero is drawn from one group. They are young men, from the provinces instead of the capital, from the mountains instead of the coast, mestizo or cholo, and more educated than the ordinary population. So, for the state, anyone who fits this description is a Senderista. Whites see Indians from the provinces and they are afraid."

Neither Shining Path nor the other major guerrilla group in Peru—the Tupac Amaru Revolutionary Movement, named after a rebellious Indian leader—makes an openly racial appeal. "You read their propaganda," said Degregori, "and you'd think we were in Sweden or Japan, someplace where everybody's alike." But prominent criollo society, which has the most to lose in the battle against the guerrillas, often behaves as if it sees the conflict in racial terms.

"People see it as an unspoken factor," said Millones. "The fact is that you don't see whites among Sendero's rank and file."

The military and the police have been accused by human rights groups of brutal excesses, mostly killings of Andean villagers, in the fight against Shining Path. Degregori and others said that part of the problem involves sending officers and troops from the coast to unfamiliar mountain areas, where they come to see almost everyone around them as a real or potential enemy.

The last few decades have seen tremendous migration from the mountains to Lima, now home to nearly 7 million people. The changes in the city are called "Andeanization." The Spaniards' graceful colonial capital of boulevards and plazas becomes less European, more Indian. The most recent arrivals live in peripheral shantytowns.

"We have come down from the mountains," said Palomino. "We are now surrounding Lima."

White elites have shifted their residential enclaves as the migrants from the hills settle throughout the city. Perhaps the most exclusive criollo redoubt these days is a hillside neighborhood called Casuarinas that has a guard station at the foot of the mountain.

Relatively few Peruvians think of themselves as Indian. In the mountainous countryside, people are more likely to consider themselves campesinos, or peasants. Those who have moved to the city tend to call themselves mestizo, whether they are of mixed heritage or not.

The two major indigenous ethnic-linguistic groups are the Quechua and Aymara, with the Quechuan language still widely spoken in the mountains and among recent arrivals in Lima. Scores of smaller Indian ethnic groups live in jungle lowlands. There is also a small Afro-Peruvian population, but it is declining steadily through intermarriage.

As for the numerically dominant Indians, "we were many millions, we existed as a culture," Palomino said, "but we didn't have the consciousness to say we were

Quechuas, we were Aymaras. The educational system emphasizes criollo values, and subliminally puts down our culture."

Degregori said that until the 1950s, the term "Indian" was equivalent to "servant." But migration to Lima and land reform in the countryside changed things somewhat. "Now, 'Indian' no longer means 'servant,' but it's not clear just what it does mean."

He said there is a ladder-like pecking order with criollos on top, then mestizos, then darker or cholo mestizos and finally Indians. There is a verb, he said—cholear—which means to put down someone lower on the scale, as in a father's telling his daughter not to go out with a young man because "he's cholo."

Palomino said that when people move from the hills to the city, they still tend to abandon their old cultural identification. But whereas 30 years ago it was unusual to hear Andean music on the radio, now there are stations in Lima that play music from the hills all day long. The government and other leading institutions celebrate the Indian artistic and cultural achievements.

And in the slums of Lima, some traditions imported from the countryside have been upheld. Important regional festivals, combining ancient celebrations with an overlay of Roman Catholicism, are still observed. As in the hills, weekends are a time for people from the same area to gather—not in the town square, but in social clubs around Lima for those from a certain region. The traditional value of community cooperation makes it possible for shantytown dwellers to work together on common projects, such as electrification.

There is also a cultural awakening among some urban young people, mostly the sons and daughters of migrants from the mountains. However, there is nothing so widespread as, for example, the black consciousness movement that began in the United States in the 1960s.

Degregori said he believes ethnic pride motivates at least some in Shining Path. But Palomino—who was born in Ayacucho, the Andean city where Shining Path was founded—said that while several young people from a community will support the guerrillas, the majority rejects them.

"But look at how society reacts," he said. "When a handful of reporters from the coast went up there a few years ago and got killed, there was a big outcry. But in the aftermath, hundreds of Indians were killed, either by Sendero or by the army. But you didn't hear anything about that."

"So in our villages we are caught in a fight between two grand forces, and there is a lot of racism on both sides. Our culture means nothing to either of them."

February 2, 1990

In Maryland, a Tale of Two Schools: Amenities, Staff Define the Gap between Rich and Poor Districts

Amy Goldstein

At Fields Road Elementary School in Gaithersburg, Beth Figura teaches her third-grade class to check subtraction problems in a new way.

She hands each child a bright blue calculator, part of a kit she borrowed from the school library. "It's fun. You just press the buttons," an 8-year-old named Nicolette said as the students eagerly inspected the device.

Nearly a hundred miles away on Maryland's Eastern Shore, Janet Fountain also is trying a new approach to math with her third-graders at Preston Elementary School.

But she skips the lessons that require calculators. "It is one of those things where you don't have money to buy everything the program calls for," Fountain said.

The need to scrimp in math lessons is one of many differences in how and what the two schools can afford to teach. Fields Road is in Montgomery County, where the schools spend $6,001 for each elementary student, the most in the state. Preston is in Caroline, a rural county at Maryland's easternmost edge, where the schools spend $4,031, the state's least.

For the 29 students in Fountain's class, that gap translates into more than $57,000.

Such disparities, and their effect on children's education, are of acute interest to educators, politicians and activists. Money alone doesn't account for how well students learn, and there is disagreement over whether rich schools are necessarily better ones.

But in Kentucky, New Jersey, Texas and Montana, courts recently have ordered the state to devote more money to students in poor communities, sometimes at the expense of more affluent ones. In Virginia, a gubernatorial commission is about to recommend ways to lessen disparities in school subsidies.

This winter, Maryland legislators also will reconsider the question. "We are trying to provide the poorer subdivisions greater opportunity for a quality education for their students," said Del. Howard P. Rawlings (D-Baltimore), who intends to introduce legislation in the General Assembly session that began last week that would infuse more aid into Baltimore and Maryland's rural schools.

In case legislation stalls, as many expect it will at a time of budgetary hardship, several Maryland groups such as the American Civil Liberties Union are exploring a lawsuit.

To find out the difference money can make, The Washington Post visited third-graders—students due to graduate from high school in 2000—in Maryland's richest and poorest school systems.

Montgomery's Fields Road and Caroline's Preston elementary schools are about the same size. Each contains what is for its county an average percentage of economically disadvantaged children.

Although it is poor, Preston is unlike a neglected inner-city school. Built in 1971, the school has gleaming waxed floors, enough textbooks to go around and teachers who say they are proud of where they work.

Like Fields Road, it can offer a sound education to average students. But it can't offer as many classroom amenities, as much guidance for teachers or the kind of special help needed by children who have trouble learning, or who are unusually bright.

Fountain said she would have liked to have been able to order the workbook that accompanies the new math text. "There are some things you feel are needed that you just can't get."

Figura, on the other hand, recently was issued an "artifacts kit" for a social studies unit on Japan, with pottery, maps, a Japanese comic book and tea. "A lot of things I ask for, we put in an order, and I usually get."

Preston is a community of 1,200 that is too small to warrant a stoplight. Many of the children's parents work at Preston Truck, a shipping company that is the largest local employer.

Some of Fountain's students live in town; more live in the flat countryside or in smaller hamlets with names like Harmony and Bethlehem. Four-fifths of the school's students are white, and one-third are poor enough to qualify for federal lunch subsidies.

Fields Road draws its students from the town houses, apartments and large houses that have sprung up within sight of the high-technology companies of Shady Grove. One-fifth of the students are black, one-fifth are Asian and one-tenth are Hispanic. The children come from 19 countries, and some are so new that they take special classes to learn English.

But when you walk into Fountain's and Figura's classrooms, one of the most striking differences is the number of students, a factor many educators think can affect how well students learn. Preston's 58 third-graders are divided evenly between two teachers, so that Fountain has 29. At Fields Road, Principal Gwendolyn Jones shifted some students so that Figura would not have more than 24 students.

Class sizes in Caroline have grown during the past few years as part of a deliberate but uncomfortable trade-off. While Montgomery has been shrinking its classes, Caroline has invested money in all-day kindergarten classes. It also has diverted money into teachers' salaries to try to stem what had been a 15 percent annual exodus in the county's teachers, many of whom left for higher-paying jobs.

Not all the differences between the schools are readily apparent. In Montgomery, educators and politicians attribute their higher spending mainly to the bigger salaries they must offer because of the high cost of living in the Washington suburbs.

With 16 years of experience and a master's degree, Fountain is paid $38,000 at Preston. If she worked in Montgomery, her pay would be $50,056.

Preston has no school gym, so children exercise on the cramped school stage. It has less money than Fields Road to buy textbooks. Preston's part-time art teacher would like to teach pottery, but the school has no kiln; Fields Road just got its second one.

In Figura's third-grade class at Fields Road, seven children attend a free homework and tutoring class after school once a week. Nine went to a free summer school for average students last year, and others get instruction tailored to gifted children. When they were preschoolers, some attended a Head Start class, a federal program that Montgomery augments. These amenities are unknown to Preston's students.

The teachers at Preston receive less help too. To get ready to teach from the new math book, Fountain glanced through a sample copy that the principal left in the teachers' lounge for a few days last year. At Fields Road, Figura gets coaching on how to use Montgomery's new math program by a curriculum specialist who works at the school 2 1/2 days a week.

In addition to smaller classes, Fields Road offers children more kinds of professional help: a full-time reading teacher, a full-time principal trainee and a part-time "disadvantaged" teacher that Montgomery has given the school because its test scores last year were relatively low.

There is a playground assistant to free teachers from supervising recess some days, and two math aides who keep computerized records of every child's progress in addition, subtraction, geometry, measurement and the use of money.

Without such specialized help at Preston, Fountain thinks her school can provide a decent education for average students. But for unusually bright children, or ones who have trouble learning, "there are some ... that need attention and aren't getting it," said Larry Anders, the school principal.

"We don't starve," Anders said. "We stretch."

Preston's school library doesn't have enough books or space to meet state standards, and last spring the librarian quit.

When Anders looked for a replacement, he couldn't find any applicants who were certified to do the job. So he gave it to a sixth-grade teacher, Agnes Sturtz, who had worked at Preston for 22 years but had no library training. She also is in charge of the school whenever the principal is away.

At Fields Road, the certified librarian, Tina Burke, is helped by two media aides.

Mary Sue Eldridge, the full-time counselor at Fields Road, has a daily routine this year for six boys in Figura's room who have been acting up in class.

First thing in the morning, they come to her office and sign a behavior "contract" for the day. They stop in again just before they go home, to review how the day went.

At Preston, counselor Mary McWilliams couldn't try such a technique because she must split her week between two schools. One boy in Fountain's class has been taken away from his mother this year, and his stepfather is in jail. "I am scheduled to see him once a week," McWilliams said. "But often he just appears at my door. Sometimes he just needs someone to sit down and play a game."

In the last seat in the last row of Fountain's class, a sweet, brown-haired boy named Trey fidgets most of the day. He scored at the very top last year on every part of the California Achievement Test. He also is hyperactive.

"Trey is very bored with paper and pencil things," Fountain said. "Here's a kid who would want to illustrate a story or tell someone about it."

If he were at Fields Road, Trey, like all Montgomery children, would have been tested during the spring of second grade to find out whether he is "gifted." And if he were in Figura's class, he almost certainly would be one of a small group of students to whom she assigns harder work and advanced library research projects.

But at Preston, Trey uses the same reading and math books as other children. No one has ever tested him to see what he might be capable of learning.

"Why identify gifted kids if we don't have gifted programs? What is the purpose?" Anders said. "When you're suffering for resources, let's face it, you're into the greatest good for the greatest number. Those children who are intelligent, we don't know how far they could go if given the chance."

January 14, 1991

The Rich Get Richer and ...: Study Shows That Income of Nation's Poor Down 11 Percent Since 1973

Spencer Rich

For the last six years, the Reagan administration took pride in rising incomes and falling unemployment after the deep recession of the early 1980s.

But at the same time, the gap between the richest and the poorest was getting larger, and the families at the bottom suffered an absolute decline in real purchasing power.

Put another way, while most Americans were better off, the lowest fifth fell further behind.

Here's how the numbers behind this paradox shape up, as reported in a study by the House Ways and Means Committee. Average household income, as measured in constant after-inflation dollars, rose from $27,568 in 1973 to $27,917 in 1979 and $29,487 in 1987—comparable high-prosperity years in the business cycle. Unemployment dropped to 5.1 percent, the lowest figure since the early 1970s.

Adjusted for family size and economies of scale, the committee calculated that the average income of Americans rose by 17.2 percent from 1973 to 1987, as measured by after—inflation 1987 dollars.

But the calculations clearly show that for the one-fifth of households at the bottom of society, average cash income in constant after-inflation dollars dropped from $5,507 in 1973 to $5,107 in 1987—even as the top fifth rose from $60,299 to $68,775.

Adjusted for family size and economies of scale, this means that the average income for the lowest fifth of all persons in the United States dropped nearly 11 percent from 1973 to 1987, with most of that drop occurring from 1979 to 1987, while average income for the top fifth was rising 24 percent.

These differences have been widening for some time and economists like Isabel Sawhill of the Urban Institute have said not all the reasons are readily evident.

But the committee said that at least some of the reasons include failure of welfare benefits to keep pace with inflation, cuts in eligibility for such programs, the growth of the one-parent female-headed family and the stagnation of wages for low-income and young workers.

The committee calculated that even if the value of noncash benefits such as food and housing assistance, plus tax changes, are taken into account, the trends would be the same.

For some time now, economists and domestic policy experts have said that these trends at the bottom of the economic ladder are linked to a dangerous development in American society.

That is the growth of what appears to be a self-perpetuating "underclass" with heavy crime and welfare rates, never able to climb up out of the bottom, poorly educated, disproportionately black and Hispanic, untrained to obtain good jobs and often unable to do a good job at even unskilled work.

The underclass, according to Sawhill, economist David Ellwood and sociologist William Julius Wilson of the University of Chicago, does not consist of all the poor—many of whom are disabled and elderly—but of a few million people packed into poor, squalid urban areas.

Arguments about the underclass have been going on long before Ronald Reagan became president, though it sharpened during his tenure.

Rep. George Miller (D-Calif.), chairman of the House Select Committee on Children, contends that poor health care, poor schooling and other disadvantages for children at the bottom are crushing any efforts they may make to move out of the underclass and provide little opportunity for them to succeed.

According to his line of argument, social policies that do not seek to redress more of these problems and prevent the continual economic grinding down of this group are perpetuating and enlarging the underclass. Society will pay for this, the argument runs, in increasing crime, disruption, and an increasingly inadequate labor force lacking the skills, education and work habits needed to keep the United States competitive with countries like Japan.

In its own selfish interests, Miller and his allies feel the United States must start enlarging programs to improve the income, health and education of this group.

Another line of thought, enunciated by Stuart Butler of the Heritage Foundation and author Charles Murray, contends that some of the very programs constructed by a compassionate nation in the interests of rescuing the poor from poverty are, ironically and unintendedly, contributing to the growth of the underclass.

Welfare—the battery of programs ranging from Aid to Families with Dependent Children to housing aid and food stamps—is the chief villain of this scenario. The availability of these forms of aid, with virtually no requirements until recently that the recipient do anything in return, makes it too easy to do nothing and live on the benefits. The remedy, under this argument, is much less permissive rules for receipt of welfare, with benefits not so high that welfare can be seen as a rational alternative to work, and much stronger work, training and education requirements for those who do get benefits.

Who is right in this policy debate is not absolutely clear.

But the Ways and Means study provides new evidence that the poorest fifth of the population is sinking. The average cash income of persons in the lowest fifth fell from 93 percent of the poverty line in 1973 to 83 percent in 1987, according to the committee. The next poorest fifth was found to live on an average income more than twice the poverty line. By contrast, the richest fifth enjoyed income 8 1/2 times as high as the poverty line.

March 28, 1989

Poor People in Rich America

Hobart Rowen

"I need my job, I want my job back—I'm the only one in my family who has a job," moaned a distraught nurse's aide at a New York City hospital, one of 6,300 municipal employees fired over last weekend. As she wept, the painful scene was recorded on national TV.

My sense of pride is marred on this Day of Independence, as we pledge allegiance to the flag and reflect on the nation's accomplishments. There is much to be thankful for, and I join with other Americans in our annual ritual.

But despite constitutional guarantees, the opportunities for health, happiness and economic security available to most seem an increasingly remote prospect for too many.

America is really two countries, one in which a privileged middle class and the wealthy have access to education, wealth and medical care that Roman emperors could only dream of. As recession fades, it means for them a gradual resumption of business profits and gains in the value of invested wealth.

In the other—an underclass America of mostly blacks, Hispanics and poor whites—millions have inadequate health insurance or none at all. Huge numbers are homeless. The bipartisan Jay Rockefeller Commission affirms that one out of five American children is brought up in poverty. For this part of America, the end of recession, when it comes, will be a statistic without meaning.

Poor people in rich America live in a cruel Third World of their own. The ugly side of our affluent society was recently reaffirmed by a Supreme Court ruling that effectively denies poor women the option of an abortion, easily available to richer women.

In his book, "The Work of Nations," Harvard economist Robert Reich demonstrates that the gap between managers and workers in America is getting wider. In 1960, the salary of chief executive officers at America's 100 largest corporations averaged $190,000 or, after taxes, 12 times a factory worker's pay.

By the end of the Reagan era, however, Reich says, these CEOs averaged $2 million in annual salary, and, given the benefit of tax cuts slanted to the upper brackets, the CEOs' multiple of factory pay skyrocketed to about 70.

In the 1960s under presidents Kennedy and Johnson, the Democratic Party articulated some goals to promote what might roughly be called social justice. One was a commitment to reducing unemployment to 4 percent or less, assumed to be the rough definition of an economy with "full" employment.

Now, Democrats want to appear as safely conservative as their Republican counterparts. Therefore, they accept 6 percent unemployment as the proper standard, because anything under 6 percent might trigger inflation. In today's single-party atmosphere, control of inflation has a higher priority than worries about recession and unemployment.

Find the Democratic leader in House or Senate who would repeat what Kennedy's labor secretary, W. Willard Wirtz, told me in 1962:

"Maybe I do get emotional about the unemployment problem. Maybe I am overconcerned by the fact that there are 4 million people unemployed in this country, people who are denied the essential right to work—using that term in the only true sense it should be. But I think the situation is so deplorable in human terms that it warrants an indignant intolerance of any explanation for it in terms of any kind of economic analysis."

As of the end of May, the unemployment rate was close to 7 percent, meaning there were 8.6 million people seeking jobs and unable to find them. Many losing their New York City jobs worked in hospitals, street maintenance or as garbage collectors, surely not the dream jobs to which college-educated, middle- and upper-income young people can aspire. They are filled mostly by nonwhite Americans trying to make an honest buck with which to put food on the table.

What's happening in New York is a microcosm of distress in scores of other cities and states that are struggling to meet added costs forced on them by the recession and shrinking federal outlays. In this bind, compromise is necessary, and union "give—backs" on wages will be needed to save jobs.

I have recently seen citizens at my local drugstore laboriously count out $60 or $70—sometimes in one-dollar bills—for a tiny vial of prescription drugs. It may be that they will recover most of the cost from Medicare, Medicaid or private insurance. But even if they are reimbursed, laying out the cash must be a hardship.

I have also seen citizens at the local supermarket watch as the cash register adds up their grocery bill, then carefully return one or two items because they can't pay the total.

Something's gone sour in this great country of ours, and it makes me sad as I contemplate Independence Day.

July 4, 1991

The Vast Landscape of Want: Poverty in the U.S.S.R.

David Remnick

How little the dreams of Russia have changed. A decent pair of boots here is still the stuff of fantasies and stratagems, the end of a dramatic guest through the poverty of everyday life. In the Soviet Union, few live otherwise.

Poverty is always clearest among the desperate. In the underpass near Pushkin Square, old people with pensions of 2 or 3 rubles a day slump against the wall and spread a rag for spare change. Others collect bottles in alleyways for 20 kopecks apiece or sell used shoes, used sheets, used tools at the Tishinski Market. At the Kazan Station, desperate vagrants dodge the police, buy some cabbage or a bottle and try to sleep the night through on a bench or in the bathroom.

But Soviet poverty more broadly defined reaches well beyond the broke and the lost. It is a state of being for tens of millions of people and is reflected less in salary levels than in daily, unending shortages of meat and apartments, medicines and vegetables, soap and shoes.

On Nikolai Ostrovsky Lane, the airy pre-revolutionary apartments of merchants and artists long ago were divided into communal flats. Five or six families, most of them with regular salaries or pensions, share a toilet and a kitchen and take turns complaining to blank-eyed local officials about the rusted pipes, the cascade of plaster. Evenings after work, they stand endlessly in lines, hunting for milk, oatmeal, toilet paper, whatever can be found.

Beyond Moscow, miners in Vorkuta in the polar north don't have enough soap to wash the coal dust from their faces; mothers on the Far Eastern island of Sakhalin give birth in rented rooms for lack of a maternity hospital there; Byelorussian villagers scavenge scrap metal, rags or even pig fat to pay for shoes, and the staff at a huge hospital in the Siberian city of Krasnoyarsk reuses needles after, as one doctor admits, "We sharpen them up, straighten them out and scrape off the rust." Such stories, and countless others, are now printed in official papers that once told only of the triumphs of the Soviet system.

Poverty in the Soviet Union is not bloated bellies and famine, but rather a common condition of need that seems only to widen and grow worse with every month. Just as dangerous, it haunts the heart as well as the stomach.

"I watch everything around us going downhill every day, and I think that life will be even worse for my children than it is for me. For a parent, there is nothing worse," said Vagid Bairamov, a truck driver who shares a five-room apartment with 15 people on Nikolai Ostrovsky Lane.

"Do you know what that is to a person?" he asked. "To know that working harder is useless because it makes no difference? My wife and I and our three kids live in one room, and we've been waiting 10 years for our own apartment. Ten years! I don't want to call us poor, but you go ahead, I'm not arguing."

Poverty: At first the government of Mikhail Gorbachev, like those before it, could hardly bring itself to pronounce the word. But from the start, poverty has been the precondition, the bottom line of the perestroika reform program. The open admission that the Soviet Union was a military superpower with a ruined, aimless economy influenced virtually every critical change in Europe over the past five years, from Moscow's decision to cut its troops and let Eastern Europe go its own way to the erosion of Marxist-Leninist ideology.

"How can we feed ourselves and live decent lives? That is what it's all about," said Tatyana Zaslavskaya, a sociologist who has long been a keen intellectual influence on Gorbachev. "Everything revolves around that."

Alexander Solzhenitsyn once remarked, with characteristic Russian insularity, that there are three standards of living in the world: the West, Moscow and the rest of the Soviet Union. But visitors expecting little more than long lines for vodka and a certain dowdiness are likely to be appalled—even in Moscow. Only the naive look at the opening of a few lush hotels and cooperative restaurants and speak of well-being.

To describe the Soviet Union in terms of overwhelming poverty is no longer the work of fire-breathing ideologues from abroad. Now even the press organs of the Soviet Communist Party ruthlessly survey the wreckage of everyday life. Nothing, it seems, poisons ideological purity more thoroughly than an empty shelf.

Komsomolskaya Pravda, the party's youth newspaper, blames the system (of which it is a part) as it points out that before the 1917 revolution, Russia ranked seventh in the world in per capita consumption and now is 77th—"just after South Africa but ahead of Romania."

"If we compare the quality of life in the developed countries with our own," the paper said, "we have to admit that from the viewpoint of civilized, developed society the overwhelming majority of the population of our country lives below the poverty line."

After decades of official concealment, numbers and statistics here are still notoriously unreliable. But the Soviet Union does have an official poverty line of 78 rubles a month. About 43 million people, many of them pensioners, fell below that line of "minimum material security" last year.

But no one, not even the government itself, takes the official poverty line seriously, and most officials and scholars here and in the West argue that figure should be raised to 125 rubles. At that level, about 131 million out of 285 million Soviet citizens would be registered as poor. Some Soviet experts believe the number is higher still.

"For decades we were striving to translate into life the idea of universal equality," economist Anatoli Deryabin wrote in the official journal Molodoi Kommunist. "So what have we achieved after all these years? Only 2.3 percent of all Soviet families can be called wealthy, and about 0.7 of these have earned that income lawfully.... About 11.2 percent can be called middle-class or well-to-do.

"The rest, 86.5 percent, are simply poor. What we have is equality in poverty."

Everyone agrees that income is hardly the point. Hardly anyone, save the government elite, can insulate themselves much from the Soviet version of poverty. "Even the 'millionaire' farm chairmen don't have hot water out here," a cotton farmer said in the Turkmenian countryside. Or as Soviet émigré Joseph Brodsky, the Nobel Prize-winning poet, remarked, "Money has nothing to do with it, since in a totalitarian state income brackets are of no great variety—in other words, every person is as poor as the next."

How, then, to get a sense of the problem, let alone the reasons and the solutions?

A few published figures only begin to give some sense of the scope of Soviet poverty: the average Soviet must work 10 times longer than the average American to buy a pound of meat; at least 500,000 internal refugees fled unrest in the Transcaucasus and other regions and now mainly live in ramshackle settlements; the press estimates between 1.5 and 3 million homeless, more than 1 million unemployed in Uzbekistan alone and a national infant mortality rate 250 percent higher than in most Western countries, about the same level as Panama ... .

... But the numbers begin to blur, like puzzle pieces scattered on a table.

The Communal Kitchen: Every Russian's Refuge

The adult dinner shift in a communal kitchen: the children still awake and racing through the hall, a Supreme Soviet session droning away on the television, the smell of beets and ammonia, sheets and shirts like pennants strewn across a cord, drying. Sixteen people live here in five rooms. The rooms feed onto a narrow hall leading into every Russian's sacred refuge: a kitchen table covered with a red-and-white checked oilcloth.

The Bairamovs, Vagid and Rhalbala, are here, as are Boris and Maria Kirval, Tanya Shukova, and Boris and Galina Pak. Workers, drivers, housewives, a teacher, an engineer. Ludmilla Gaidacz, who lives alone in the corner room, is depressed and would rather not eat. Her mother died just the other day. Soya Ivanovna Kuzmina, a pensioner in her late sixties, is on the phone, as always, to her sister.

Every family here—all but Soya Ivanovna, who said she likes the "family noise" of a communal apartment—has been waiting for a place of their own for years. Not that a new apartment would be paradise either. Invariably, a new apartment means a cramped two-room flat in one of Moscow's micro-raions, outer neighborhoods of almost preternatural ugliness where you can spend half a winter morning freezing and waiting for your bus into the center.

Everyone at the table works at least one job, spends hours in line and at the end of the day comes home to an apartment where noise is the norm and the toilet will fall over unless you sit on it just right.

"No one will come in to fix it—we've been calling for months—and we can't find the parts to fix it ourselves," said Vagid Bairamov. "It's 50 years old." He pointed to the bathroom ceiling, which hardly exists but for the random slabs of plaster that, for the moment, still stick. The bath is a corroded tub, used both for bathing and everyone's laundry.

"I came here to Moscow when I was still just a kid because I wanted to live better than we did in Azerbaijan," Bairamov said. "But to tell you the truth, I'm not sure Moscow is better than a lot of other cities now, not with the preyekhavshi," the more than 2 million people from out of town who arrive on electric trains and buses every day looking to fill their empty shopping sacks.

"It's true," said his wife, Khalbala. "By afternoon, there is nothing in the stores. If you work all day, you're forced either to look for hours or spend triple the price in the co-ops or the private market." Even without indulging at the private markets, where prices are three and four times higher, most people must spend about half their monthly salaries on groceries.

No one around the table used the word byedni, or poor, to describe their circumstances. Thanks to government subsidies, they have a roof, bread, free education and free hospital care. "Free. And it's worth every kopeck, too," someone cracked. Instead, they saved the word "byedni" for those with even less, those who sleep in foundation pits and empty railway cars.

But soon the talk turned to the price of a woman's winter coat (at least 400 rubles), and you realize that is two months' salary for a necessity. To buy a car these days is usually only possible on the black market, and there the price for a new Zhiguli (a kind of degraded mid-'60s Fiat) is 35,000 rubles.

The only way to buy such things is extra work, to trade services. Lately in Moscow one of the nastiest curses you can hurl at a person is, "May you live on one salary!"

And yet that is precisely what Tanya Zhukova, an engineer and a single mother, must do. Her salary is 140 rubles a month, plus the 20-ruble state subsidy she gets as a single mother for her 6-year-old son. Even by the state standard, Tanya is barely above the poverty line—but she never speaks the word.

"I have to struggle. I can get some food by ordering it through the institute where I work twice a month, but not much," she said. "To tell you the truth, this apartment is my refuge. We are lucky, because in a lot of communal flats there are arguments, scandals, one family doesn't talk to the other, and it goes on like that for years. We're the lucky ones."

Moscow's Uncountable Illegal Population

Sunday mornings you see them, tourists from across the country who have abandoned their sightseeing to roam the markets of Moscow. the Luzhniki Market, one child's sandal and a woman's dark boot dangle by their laces from a shop door. This is the "display" of what is on sale. The line is 50 yards long and the store does not open for another half hour.

"It's better than where I've come from," said Nadia Zinova, a young woman from the Urals. "It's expensive, but I could spend a month looking for shoes where I come from. Here it's just a day or two."

But soon Zinova will have to return home. Even if she wanted to move here, it is impossible without a Moscow propiska, or residence permit.

So bad is the economy throughout the provinces that hundreds of thousands of young people come to Moscow and either live illegally or agree to work for especially low wages at a factory in exchange for the promise of a propiska. Such people, and there are hundreds of thousands of them in Moscow, live in overcrowded dormitories and, because of their precarious situation, have few rights as Muscovites and even fewer on the factory floor. They are called limitchiki and constitute a sub-class whose poverty consists not only in their minimal salaries and access to housing, but also to their lack of freedom.

"That's how I got here. That's how I started out," said Olya Koshkin, a 25-year-old construction worker who shares a bare room in a dormitory near the Danilovski Monastery with her husband, Yuri, and their 4-year-old daughter, a moon-faced little girl named Zhenya. Their entire space is the size of a small Western sitting room. The television set in the corner represents their only luxury, and it is covered over, like a religious object, with a lace doily.

Native Muscovites, for their part, have problems of their own and deeply resent the influx of limitchiki. They accuse them of emptying out the stores and helping make Moscow just another Russian town—in other words, poor. But the state enterprises continue to hire the limitchiki, knowing full well that they are cheap and grateful labor willing to do the worst jobs.

Olya came to Moscow when she was 17 to study for a year at the city's main construction trade institute and then began work at various building sites for the state. Her salary is often as little as 80 rubles a month. Her husband, after years of the same sort of work and pay, is trying to work on his own, spending 12 to 14 hours a day, seven days a week, repairing apartments.

After lifting crates and plastering walls all day, Olya scours the stores, especially for children's clothes. For the last six months she has been on the lookout for a jacket for Zhenya. Furniture or a car is out of the question. By day's end, Olya is bone tired, and it becomes easy to see why Russians, especially women, age so quickly. A cup of tea is pure luxury. Olya has not been to a movie "since I don't know how long." The last time she and Yuri ate in a restaurant was on their wedding day in 1985.

Like the crowd around the table on Nikolai Ostrovski Lane, Olya has lost a certain sense of promise. She watched the first Gorbachev years with the hope and expectation that the stores would begin to fill up, that the daily feeling of resentment and uncertainty would begin to ease.

"We were all believers. We all thought things would get better, and just the opposite has happened," she said.

"Yuri works like a madman. Not to get rich, but because we need the money. He says he can't rest when a winter coat is 600 or 700 rubles—it was half that a few years ago. Sometimes I think he's working himself to death and all he can say is, 'It will be better someday, I know it will.'

But still, Moscow is that much better than her home town in the Urals. There is no going back. Olya's mother, who still lives in a village in Bashkir, has it worse. All she can depend on every day is bread. The rest is a search.

"So I stay in Moscow," Olya said. "The state construction people promise that they'll get you a propiska after a certain period if you work well. I was one of the lucky ones. I got it in five years. Some people wait 15, and others get fired and they have to leave. You can't yell back at the bosses. They say after 10 years they'll help find an apartment, so in a couple of years my name goes on a list.

"Then the real waiting begins. The bosses play games with the lists. They play favorites, they feather their own nest. I guess they have troubles, too. Well, we'll see. I've got to hope. Maybe we'll get a place when Zhenya has children of her own."

Police Work to Keep The Homeless Invisible

You will rarely, if ever, see a homeless person on the streets of Moscow. The police make sure of that. The Moscow bomzhi—the acronym for the homeless that stands for "without definite residence"—sleep in cemeteries, railway stations, construction sites and basements. A favorite spot is the empty, uppermost floor of Moscow high-rises, amid the ventilation pipes and heating ducts.

"There are all kinds of bomzhi," said Alexei Lebedev, a young poverty activist who runs a small research group on the homeless and unemployed. "People who've lost their propiski, prisoners who are let go but have nowhere to go, drinkers, an addict once in a while, lost souls."

As the Soviet Union has begun to acknowledge the problem of poverty, it has allowed churches and civic organizations to begin helping the, poor. No one dares any longer to maintain the fiction that the "first socialist state" requires no charity. There are now a few soup kitchens in Leningrad and Moscow. The Baptist Church here helps with clothes and food. But charity and the state are poor as well, and the homeless remain so.

Bomzhi sometimes work, sometimes for money, sometimes for a bottle of vodka. You can see them afternoons helping the local liquor store unload a truck. They collect empties in the park and on garbage heaps. At airports and train stations, bomzhi help the drivers hustle fares and then take a small cut. In Moscow they might hold a place in line; in Central Asia they'll take on migrant work at harvest time.

Many of the bomzhi around the Kazan train station say they are "between jobs" or have just lost, somehow, their propiska, or are escaping some private crisis far away. They'll do some work to get by and hope they can "get out of the hole," as one of the stalwarts of Kazan station said.

But Alik, a sawed-off man with a two-week beard and an empty bottle in his jacket, says he won't collect bottles. "Too humiliating. What am I, a dog?" he said. "I'll tell you what I do. When I need money, I take it. Like, one minute you've got your rubles, then you don't!"

Alik is 41 and has spent the better part of the last 20 years in prison camps and exile. When he gets out, he returns to the station life. He speaks pure mat, the ornate system of prison camp profanity. He is a bad drunk and will sometimes go three or four days without eating, "just 'cause I can't stomach it." Alik has no propiska, and hospitals can't bear him for long. He doesn't make it easy. He is irritable, by turns nasty and mean, and then, suddenly, sentimental, an autodidact who recites the poems of Pushkin and Yesenin, the songs of Vladimir Vysotsky.

"My father and mother worked morning till night just to support us kids," Alik said, sitting in a deserted courtyard. "My brother was killed in Hungary in `56. He was 19. Sometimes I think if he had survived I might not have started the way I did.

"I ran away when I was 16 or 17, went off to Kazakhstan. I was going hungry and so I lifted my first purse. That's how my prison career started. I got five years in the Tashkent camp for teenagers. I've been all over the Kritaya (the prison zone) ever since. You sit in a rank cell and get 20 minutes' exercise a day and you're hungry, lying there on the cold concrete. I started getting sick that way.

"We bomzhi stay in these places 24 hours a day and we're always worried we're gonna get clubbed by the cops, day and night. We have nowhere to go. I'm telling you this on behalf of the Soviet homeless who are punished for their destinies. No rights, no propiska, nothing. It's tough when you get out of jail. It's like you're a third-class citizen and nobody needs your life."

At times, Alik stops talking and begins humming and singing a Vysotsky song about a man going off to jail and never seeing his beloved again. And then he'll break it off and stare out into space and take another swig on his bottle:

"So how do I break this cycle? I just don't know. One of my buddies comes up to me the other day, yesterday maybe, and says he'll smash my face if I don't stop drinking, and I said, 'You son of a bitch, I can't stop. I can't.'

"I worked some in Uzbekistan, but it didn't last. Never got along with the bosses. Worked on an oil rig once, too. I've never worked a single day in Moscow. For me, 300 rubles a month and a flat, and I'd make it all right. But don't have it. So where should I go? You tell me."

May 20, 1990

Chapter Six

Race and Ethnicity

With the exception of Native Americans, all other people in the United States are from "somewhere else." Whether of English, German, Irish, Dutch, Spanish, Latvian, Polish, African, or Chinese Ancestry, at one time or another we all began as voluntary or involuntary immigrants. Upon arrival, each immigrant group had to adjust to becoming a member of a new society. Today's immigrants face the same tasks.

The first three articles in this section examine, in turn, the experience of Korean, Ethiopian, and Amerasian immigrants.

The fourth article, "To Be Young, Gifted, Black... and Preppie," reveals what life at an exclusive boarding school was like for author Lorene Cary. "Japan Discovers the Jews" uncovers some startling prejudices held by the Japanese toward this ethnic group, of whom only about one thousand actually live in Japan. The final article, "The Empire of Ethnic Russians Retrenches," describes the reverse flight of ethnic Russians living in several former Russian republics.

The High Price of Success: Korean Immigrants Suffer Alienation, Loneliness

John Mints and Peter Pae

Many Sundays, when the Rev. Hun Cho preaches to his flock of several dozen families at the Korean Presbyterian Church in Beltsville, Maryland, returns to the same theme: You must stop driving yourselves so hard, or you could be heading for physical and mental breakdowns.

Cho tells his parishioners—almost all of whom he describes as workaholic shopkeepers—that toiling 14 hours a day may earn them a good living, but also may be one reason so many feel lonely, empty, alienated from the country in which they live.

"That's my main message," said Cho, 34, who held several jobs earning his way through seminary in New York. "The Koreans want the Cadillac, the big house, to play golf... But they have no time to spend the money. After they buy the house, they can mentally collapse."

Psychological collapse is not the image most Americans have of Koreans here. The nation's approximately 800,000 Korean Americans, including 60,000 in the Washington area, have a reputation as "model ethnics" who have adapted quickly to the American way of life as they pursue material success and their obedient children bury themselves in schoolbooks.

In the District, Koreans own most of the mom-and-pop stores—about 1,300 grocery, liquor and convenience shops—plus another 1,000 businesses in nearby Maryland and Virginia suburbs, where the great majority live. In New York, Koreans control 85 percent of the city's fresh produce markets. In Los Angeles, they own banks, real estate and thousands of businesses, many of them clustered in the city's Koreatown section.

Despite this flair for commerce, Korean community leaders, social workers and academics across the United States concur with Cho that many Korean Americans are paying a price for their obsessive work habits. Many immigrants are encountering serious family problems—including wife abuse, divorce and juvenile delinquency—and a range of other emotional difficulties that are considered uncommon in their home country, experts said.

Such anxieties have not stopped an explosion in America's Korean population. Changes in federal immigration law in 1965 brought a huge increase in Korean immigrants, who now comprise one of the fastest growing ethnic groups in the United States.

The number of Korean Americans has risen more than tenfold since 1970, when the U.s. census found only 70,000 Koreans in this country. Many of them have come here to get their children into U.S. universities and skirt South Korean government quotas on college admissions back home.

Already, the round-the-clock neighborhood fruit and vegetable store often run by entire Korean families, with father, mother and children helping behind the counter, is making a serious imprint on key urban centers around the United States.

But the rapid economic success of many Korean immigrant families does not necessarily translate into social contentment.

Young-Ja Kim, the D.C. police's liaison to the Korean community, knows about their worries. Every week, Kim tapes a five-minute police announcement for a Korean-language television show. The program has made her famous among local Koreans. Now Kim—in the tradition of the advice columns in turn-of-the-century Yiddish newspapers—has become an adviser to hundreds of lonely and disoriented Korean immigrants who call her for counsel.

Some are shop owners insulted by anti-Korean comments. Others are upset because a child is in trouble with the police or dating an American. In keeping with Koreans' shyness about airing problems in public, some callers pretend to be soliciting advice for friends and not themselves.

Kim said she enjoys helping, but knows it may not be sufficient.

"I give them comfort, the best advice I can," she said. "But sometimes I get very frustrated."

Young Shik Kim also is frustrated. A juvenile delinquent counselor in Rockville, he handles Korean cases throughout D.C.'s suburbs. He said the Koreans' goody-goody image is a myth.

"The [Korean] Harvard student, the so-called 'model minority,' is just the tip of the iceberg," Kim said. "Below is a big chunk of troubled Koreans few Americans see.... The Korean community has been trying to hush up the problems. Every time they do that, the problem gets bigger, to the point where it's about to explode."

Kim said about one-fourth of Montgomery County's Korean teenagers are having serious personal problems or troubles with the law. They range from a boy who has robbed liquor stores to a 17-year-old girl who has had five abortions.

NIMH Study Sees "Vicious Cycle"

Korean family difficulties in the Washington area are symptomatic of adjustment problems elsewhere in the country. Across the United States, an array of academic studies of Korean immigrants has shown a disturbing pattern of trouble, particularly for those Koreans here less than five years.

A 350-page study of the Korean community, completed in June for the National Institute of Mental Health, found that while Koreans are satisfied with some aspects of their lives, they feel miserable about others. They lead "a mixed life of blessings and distress," the study concluded.

The study—undertaken by two sociologists at Western Illinois University, Won Moo Hurh and Kwang Chung Kim, and based on surveys of 630 Koreans in Chicago—offered an eye-opening list of afflictions, including severe time pressure, loneliness, alcoholism, mental disorders and family strife.

Rockville counselor Kim said Koreans' fear of admitting problems prevents many families, against all reason, from seeking aid.

"They're driving Mercedes-Benzes, but in the household, the family is rotting away," he said. "When they come to me, it's too late."

The Koreans' reluctance to seek professional help and their disdain for social services leads to a "vicious cycle," the NIMH study said, causing many Americans to dismiss the problems of the Asian immigrants because of their inclination to isolate themselves.

One reason for their insularity is that, like many Asian immigrant groups, Koreans have trouble learning English. Except for those who live here for decades, most of them rarely mingle with non-Koreans. In every major city, Koreans use a local Korean telephone directory more frequently than the Yellow Pages; the D.C. book is 388 pages long. They get most of their news from Korean-language newspapers. There are four dailies in this area alone.

Churches remain the tie that most binds Korean Americans. The Koreans' Presbyterian, Methodist and Catholic congregations—100 in the D.C. area alone—provide not only gospel study but also a social gathering place to hold parties, discuss business and teach Korean language to the children.

"They have to be in church to maintain ties to the community," said Pyong Gap Min, a Queens College sociologist and expert on Koreans. "Korean churches are a very important part of immigrant life."

While only 25 percent of Koreans attend church in their native country, up to 80 percent go to services here. Even many immigrants who were Buddhists become Christians in the United States because of the church's vital role in the community.

Many Koreans in the United States are Christians from North Korea, whose move here means starting a third life. They grew up in northern Korea, fled south when the communists took over in the late 1940s, and then, feeling few bonds to South Korea, emigrated to the United States after 1965.

The biggest Korean-American community is located in the Los Angeles area, with about 200,000 residents. The second largest is in New York City, especially the Flushing section of Queens. Washington has the fourth largest Korean population, after Chicago.

Their labors have placed them in the lore of the American work ethic. A study of New York's Korean grocers found they work 16 to 18 hours a day, six or seven days a week, or more than three times the work week of a 9-to-5 office worker.

Seo Kwang Won, owner of a tiny market at 11th and C streets NE, knows the problem. He says that each time he tries to eat, he has to jump up and serve a customer. So he often skips meals. "Many times, I only wish for sleep."

The overwork creates stresses of its own, but it is compounded by the embarrassment many Koreans feel at working in menial jobs like retailing. Most immigrants were well-educated professionals in South Korea, or midlevel corporate managers.

The merchants feel all the more disoriented because their stores are located mainly in low-income, crime-ridden areas, business leaders said.

Many blacks resent the Koreans' lack of proficiency in English and mistakenly believe they get government aid to buy neighborhood stores, police said. Many Koreans say they regard blacks as ill-educated and disrespectful of elders, and perceive many blacks as anti-Korean.

Whenever Korean-black tension boils over, police and city officials try to bring them together. Police urge Koreans to hire neighborhood youths. All agree that ethnic friction has declined in the past few years.

"We try to live with them in peace," said Henry Shin, president of the local Korean-American Chamber of Commerce. "But {many} look at us differently, like enemies."

While Koreans are often upset by the culture clash with their customers, sometimes the tensions are no less acute at home. The immigrants' confusion reaches into the family and inflicts damage on relationships, community leaders and academics said.

Korean culture stresses the Confucian ideals of discipline and hierarchy. The father is the unquestioned head of his household. Wife and children follow.

While wives in Korea rarely work, in the United States, two-thirds of married Korean women work—and usually at the side of their husbands in the family business. In addition to long hours on the job, wives also must care for the children, make dinner and clean house—taking on the role of a superwoman, social workers said. It often chafes.

"Korean women feel they have to do it all," Queens College's Min said. "Many feel guilty that they don't have enough time to be with the children."

The great majority of Korean wives "quietly carry out the double and triple roles imposed on them by the new environment, and are often frustrated," according to a study by Eui Young Yu, a sociologist at California State University/Los Angeles.

The women, working outside the home for the first time and tasting economic independence, sometimes complain, Yu said. Korean men, already frustrated by the outside world, cannot tolerate the griping, he said. In response, many men "keep silent, shout back, break things, indulge in drinking or sometimes resort to violence," Yu said.

Experts such as Min said that Korean Americans have the highest rate of wife abuse of any Asian-American group.

Theresa Yum, director of a Korean counseling center in Queens, said her group handles about 1,000 cases of wife abuse each year. But the government has not granted money for a women's shelter. So she takes an average of one battered woman a week into her own home.

Splits Between Parents and Children

While child abuse is uncommon, social workers said, the split between parents and children still can be substantial.

Because of work pressures, parents do not see much of their children. The adults often leave home at sunrise and return very late. Business leader Shin recalled a recent softball game that he believed showed a gap in Korean family life. The game at Anacostia Park pitted children of Korean merchants against children of D.C. police officers. While most of the American children were with their families, none of the Korean parents were there. "The Korean kids were envious," Shin said. "They would look over and see the {American} kids with their parents and family having fun."

The alienation of Korean children from their parents is ironic, community leaders said, since the main reason most Korean parents moved here was to improve life for their offspring.

In Korea, children are expected to be silent, studious and obedient. In America, immigrant parents pressure their children to work just as hard as in Korea, but in the United States, the children encounter a more freewheeling, chaotic culture that questions authority.

Meanwhile, Korean-American children are learning English faster than their parents. When police or school officials need to communicate with a parent, they may use the children as interpreters—often a humiliation for parents accustomed to exercising total authority over their children. This gives children leverage over their parents and makes family life seem topsy-turvy.

Sometimes, the childrens' newfound freedom goes haywire. Some Korean youth in Los Angeles and New York have formed gangs that prey on other Koreans, police officials said. While gangs are uncommon in the Washington area, Korean-language papers around the United States frequently run articles about crime by Korean youth.

More commonly, tension inside Korean families focuses on less sinister forms of youthful rebellion—such as when the children start dating. It can be especially dicey if they date Americans. Korean immigrants are less tolerant of interracial relationships than most other ethnic groups, Korean community leaders said.

Janet Han, 21, a University of Maryland senior from Silver Spring, said that she hid the fact that she was dating an American. Anytime he drove her home, she insisted he park his car a block away and not come in.

Many Korean parents struggle to preserve their children's "Koreanness" by sending them to Korean language school, as early as age 5. But parents said they are cautious in presenting their beloved Korean culture.

"Parents don't want to push too hard," said Tae Kyong Hahn, director of a Korean immigrant counseling center in Silver Spring. "You can lose them."

An open letter from a well-known Korean-American writer to his children, published in a Korean-American paper last month, gives a sense of Korean adults' sorrow at their childrens' losing Korean roots—and the Korean disorientation felt from living in this country.

"I feel an essential dimension of our life is inaccessible to you," wrote Kichung Kim, a professor in San Jose. "Even today your mother and I sometimes feel very strange speaking only English all day long. At those times we feel as if our speech is not our own, as if we were listening to someone else's words. Then we have to whisper some Korean words to ourselves to see if we're really awake and not sleepwalking."

September 2, 1988

New Firms Backed by Family, Friends: Tenacity, Pooling of Money Yield Visible Results for Ethiopian Immigrants

Sandra Sugawara and Elizabeth Tucker

Last year, while working as a waitress, Asmeret Seile, a 26-year-old Ethiopian, was watching carefully and thinking that some day she would like to have a restaurant of her own. Her reason for wanting a business was simple: "It's the freedom you get on your own," said Seile.

But when she got serious about the idea, she faced major obstacles. She had saved some money in the six years she had been in the United States, but nowhere near enough. Her collateral consisted of a 1974 Mustang, so she could not qualify for a loan. She had no familiarity with the complicated liquor laws and licensing requirements in the District of Columbia. And the competition was fierce—Ethiopian restaurants had already sprouted, it seemed, on every corner.

Nevertheless, last Valentine's Day, her restaurant opened for business in the heart of Adams-Morgan. It's still struggling, but it has survived nearly a year—one of those small entrepreneurial miracles that are among the most visible signs of the presence of recently arrived immigrants in the Washington area.

Seemingly overnight, thousands of small businesses owned by foreign-born entrepreneurs have blossomed: dry cleaners and convenience stores; flower shops and groceries; purveyors of jewelry and of bagels, of beer and wine and exotica from every continent; and restaurants, one after another, in a city that once was derided for having so few.

Interviews and studies suggest that the strongest forces at work on behalf of the immigrant business people are their own communities, the source tapped by earlier generations of immigrants. From the community and the family come advice, moral support and often labor. Most importantly, these businesses are able to get money from the community, from the "surrogate" banks they have created.

No two of the businesses have come into being in quite the same way. But Seile's story illustrates the common theme: Unable to call upon the conventional methods, she relied on friends, family and even one of her prospective competitors.

"I am very much impressed with my fellow Ethiopians," said Seile, reflecting on her good fortune.

'Cried All the Time'

Seile arrived in Philadelphia in 1980 on a tourist visa, but she said her real goal was to further her education. In Ethiopia, she had completed high school and business school, receiving a degree in bookkeeping, and she planned to study accounting here.

She had a brother-in-law here, but she knew few people. She was a frightened and lonely 19-year-old, she recalled. "I cried all the time," said Seile, who has large dark eyes and a shy smile.

When her tourist visa ran out, she said that she "kept getting letters from the government telling me to leave." But she was determined to stay, viewing the United States as "the land of opportunity," and she finally was granted political asylum by the government last year.

In 1981, at her invitation, her sister, LemLem, came to join her. The two gravitated to Washington because of the large Ethiopian community here and job possibilities. "I feel like at home when I came to Washington because I meet a lot of my friends and see people from home. It's just like meeting your relatives," she said.

They moved in with relatives in Arlington, and within a week, Seile summoned her courage and went in search of a job. She had passed the nearby Sheraton Hotel while taking a walk earlier in the week and thought it was a logical place to look. "I just walked in there on a Sunday afternoon," she recalled. "The manager was very helpful. He gave me a job right on the spot" as a cocktail waitress.

She also took on a part-time job waiting on tables at Fasika's, an Ethiopian restaurant, and she enrolled in an accounting program at the University of the District of Columbia, although she soon switched to computer science.

All her tips went into savings; her paycheck to food and tuition. Seile and her 27-year-old sister moved briefly into a room on 16th Street, and then into a downtown efficiency apartment on 15th Street NW that they still share for $279 a month.

It was her experience as a waitress—watching other Ethiopians managing their own businesses—that convinced her that she wanted her own restaurant. She would rather have the headache of working for herself than the headache of working for others, she said.

With little in assets, she and her sister were turned down when they applied for a bank loan. She contacted two cousins in Boston who owned a taxicab business. They had become increasingly concerned about the dangers of picking up strangers, however, and had been contemplating a switch in business.

A restaurant was not their first choice, but "they were fascinated because it was a prime place for a restaurant," Seile said. The cousins sold the cab business for $85,000. Seile, her cousins and her sister calculated that with their savings and the income from the sale of the business, they had about $120,000.

An Ethiopian they knew was about to close a boutique at 1819 Columbia Rd. NW and told them the place would soon be vacant. They rented it for $4,350 a month.

For help in mastering the licensing requirements and in finding suppliers, they went up the street, to the proprietor of the Asmara restaurant, a friend of Seile's.

Seile said she saw nothing remarkable in seeking help from a competitor, particularly because he is a longtime friend. She even suggested that the very presence of competitors nearby (there are 13 Ethiopian restaurants in the general vicinity) is helpful rather than threatening: They depend on each other for survival.

Neither did the owner of the Asmara, Tesfmichael Gebre, find it threatening, for he did indeed come to Seile's aid. "There is nothing to lose to be a nice person," said Gebre. "The God, what He gives you, He will never take away, no matter who comes."

The four did much of the renovation themselves, building the bar, painting, hammering and laying tile in the bathrooms. They decorated with handmade wooden and silver Ethiopian crosses, woven straw lids used to keep food warm, serving bowls made of animal skins and a gasha, an Ethiopian shield used in hunting. From Ethiopia, Seile's mother sent traditional straw serving tables and chairs, which now sit at the front of the restaurant.

The outside was painted a hot pink, an eye-catching color but a mistake. The painter they hired was told to use dark red but miscalculated when he laid down a base coat of white.

During this start-up period, Seile said, she called upon a unique Ethiopian tradition to help her meet personal expenses: the ekub, a kind of mutual assistance savings plan to which members contribute a set amount of money each week. The pot is given to a different member on a rotating basis. Those in need can be bumped to the front of the line.

Other friends helped, buying paintings for the restaurant. One friend, an Ethiopian doorman at a Marriott Hotel brought meals to them as they worked and contributed curtains for the restaurant.

After much discussion, the four decided to name the restaurant Selam, an Ethiopian greeting that means peace.

When Selam opened in February, about 15 friends helped out in the kitchen; others showed up to eat, ordering far more than they could consume.

The future of Selam is uncertain. The restaurant has six waitresses, who, incidentally, have now formed their own ekub. It is jammed on weekends but slow during the week. The rents are rising in Adams-Morgan. And there are those other 12 Ethiopian restaurants nearby.

But it is off the ground, another immigrant business born.

Mutual Assistance Is the Norm

According to estimates by ethnic business associations, there are at least 2,300 Hispanic-owned businesses in the area (about 500 in the District); well over 300 Indochinese-owned businesses; an estimated 2,000 small enterprises owned by Koreans; 500 owned by Chinese, and 85 to 100 owned by Ethiopians.

By most accounts, mutual assistance in one form or another is the motif for all these groups. The Ethiopian funds called ekubs have an equivalent in the Korean kehs, which Korean business people have used to help one another. The community, said a recent study of Southeast Asian refugees by the Refugee Policy group, "serves as a kind of surrogate banking institution."

The Southeast Asian community in particular has institutionalized the self-help in mutual assistance associations, which "are now important sources of educational services, employment services, translation and interpretation, mental health services and others," according to the study.

This pattern, it noted, follows a tradition "previously adopted by other immigrant groups" in American history.

"When you come to the U.S., it's a totally tough world," said Kassa Tesfaye, 34, owner of International Auto Care at 3426 18th St. NE, an auto repair shop. To survive, "you combine your culture with the present culture, and you come up with a kind of thoroughbred. And thoroughbred is the best."

What makes life work here for Ethiopian refugees, he said, is "the kindness and togetherness" that they bring with them. Thus, while the American saying is that lending money to a friend is the most effective way to end a friendship, the Ethiopians here say that the willingness to lend money is, in fact, a test of friendship.

Few of the newcomers qualify for bank loans or special subsidized loan programs. Tesfaye, as it happens, is one of the few who did. Tesfaye is a lean, handsome man with a melodic voice and a mischievous grin. He came to the United States in 1973 and was cut off from family funds in 1974 when the Marxists took power in Ethiopia. In order to finish his college education, he got numerous jobs, the first and the worst as a dishwasher at Blackie's House of Beef.

"That was a terrible time," he said. "I was pretty talented and {later} started cutting meat, cutting ribs, taking fat out of the round beef, spinal cords out of the ribs and working inside the freezer," he said.

He landed a car repair job in Maryland for $200 a week. He spent $50 a week on room and board, another $50 on pocket money, and he saved the rest. Eventually, he saved $3,000 and owned about $5,000 worth of auto repair tools. With a Jamaican partner who pitched in $2,000 and his own tools, the pair opened their own shop in 1980 at 1913 Franklin St. NE, a cramped alleyway.

At first, everything seemed to go wrong. His partner fell from a ladder and became a quadriplegic. "Due to that I started doing it by myself, and it was tough to deal with," said Tesfaye. In 1985, he moved the business out of the alley and into an abandoned gas station in a residential area in Northeast Washington.

What apparently enabled Tesfaye to get through the first shaky years of business was a bond of communication and trust that he built with his car parts dealers. "I never had a problem with him," said Warren Deavers, wholesale manager at Euromotor Cars in Bethesda. "He's honest, he's sincere, he'll tell you if he doesn't have the money and say he'll pay you next week. He's good about it.... He works harder than most people I know."

Over time, Tesfaye built up enough of a track record to qualify for a $250,000 loan package, which included a $98,000 loan from the D.C. Office of Business and Economic Development. The city, which is limited by law to lending 40 percent of the cost of the project, put Tesfaye together with American Security Bank for the remainder of the $250,000 that enabled Tesfaye to buy and refurbish the new premises.

Tesfaye is one of the few Ethiopian refugees to qualify for such a loan, according to District officials. "They want to see the last page of your financial statement," he said. "If you show a negative, you're in trouble. My bank record always showed a couple of dollars positive, and that meant I was taking care of all my bills." He said his business rings up about $750,000 a year in sales and more than $75,000 in profit.

Ethiopians say they would appreciate more government loan programs. But many, such as Tesfaye, say they are adamantly opposed to welfare. "There's a stigma that's attached to accepting it. It's that whole sense of pride Ethiopians have about themselves," said Wallace W. Lumpkin, director of the D.C. Office of Refugee Resettlement. He said that 25 percent of the Ethiopians refuse cash assistance outright, and another 50 percent are off welfare within a month. Of all the refugee groups, they receive the lowest amount of assistance, according to Lumpkin.

Much of the profit Tesfaye makes goes back into the company. But he has saved enough to help his sisters with more than half of the $80,000 they needed in August to open Twins' Lounge, yet another Ethiopian restaurant at 5516 Colorado Ave. NW.

Professionals Face Struggles

The ranks of the Ethiopians here are filled with former lawyers, accountants and corporate business people who are struggling to reestablish their professions. For them, the road seems more difficult.

"You can have an ice cream stand, and nobody cares if the owner is Korean or Ethiopian as long as the ice cream is good," said Feyissa Ghenene, a certified public accountant who started a K Street NW accounting firm in 1985 and employs three accountants. "It's not the case with accounting.... Because an accountant will learn the confidential details of a company's business, you need to have their trust and confidence as much as anything else."

Even those immigrants who are seeking work at established American firms rather than starting companies have problems getting their first job, Ghenene said. "I don't care how many years of experience they have. Employers are usually hesitant to hire you when you open your mouth and they hear the accent. You may have one of the most outstanding experiences, but they say that this is America and we do things differently here.... But then I get a job and I find they do things exactly the same way."

One stark example of the roller coaster existence faced by such professionals and corporate business people is Tedla Desta, a small, stately man with high cheekbones, intense eyes and an aquiline nose.

Desta, 68, is the proprietor of the Aenjera Bakery in Alexandria. He was an influential and wealthy businessman in Ethiopia before the 1974 Marxist coup and the overthrow of Emperor Haile Selassie.

Several of his closest friends were executed, and he was separated from his family for nearly a decade, Desta said. "They eliminated everyone. Two generals killed were my best friends. Three ministers killed were my schoolmates," he said quietly as tears welled in his eyes.

He escaped from Ethiopia in 1976 by telling government officials he needed a kidney operation. After a nomadic existence in Europe and the Horn of Africa, he got his wife and six children out of Ethiopia and came to the United States with about $300,000 he had been paid for representing American and British companies in Ethiopia and from the sale of a house in Paris.

Desta said that after arriving here he decided to rebuild his business life by turning to something every Ethiopian knew and loved—injera, the spongy flat bread used to scoop up the savory stews and other pungent Ethiopian dishes.

Standing amid steaming skillets and huge vats of pungent-smelling batter, Desta, wearing a white coat, demonstrated the slow, painstaking way injera is prepared.

At first, Desta planned to import teff seeds, the basic grain used in injera, from Ethiopia. But after importing four tons of teff seeds, he decided it was too expensive and located U.S. growers of the grain that is closest to teff—weeping love grass, which had been used in this country strictly for cattle feed.

Desta's request took Western grain suppliers by surprise. "I could hardly understand him, but I figured everyone to his own taste," said Leroy Mack of the Johnston Seed Co. in Enid, Okla., and one of Desta's suppliers.

Desta thought he had commitments from several Ethiopian restaurants to buy the injera, but those fell through. So the tenacious businessman headed straight to Southland Corp.—which owns the 7-Eleven stores—with an unconventional sales pitch that included a home-cooked Ethiopian meal.

Joe Keith, in charge of purchasing for 7-Eleven, had never tried Ethiopian food. But he was won over. Ten of their stores in the Washington area now sell the bread, mainly to Ethiopians. "Sales have been going very well," said Keith.

Desta's bakery is small compared with his operations in Ethiopia. But he hopes to expand by marketing dried chips made from his bread, by selling Ethiopian spices and drinks, and by cultivating the joia tree, a hard and aromatic wood indigenous to Ethiopia. He said joia is excellent for furniture and is a good tree to plant in arid areas because it helps prevent soil erosion and serves as a windbreak. He says he has already approached Saudi Arabian officials about selling the tree to them.

One of Desta's next big projects is to grow real teff in the United States, transplanting a small piece of Ethiopia here permanently. He said he has found a part-time farmer in Oklahoma named John C. Wisehart who has agreed to plant several acres of teff next summer.

In the meantime, though doing what he calls "women's work" in the bakery, Desta is full of hope. "I have found peace here, at least," he said.

December 16, 1987

Packing Hope, Amerasians Come to a New World

Karlyn Barker

Thu Kieu never knew her father, a young American soldier who left South Vietnam in 1966, shortly after she was born. Still, when the communists came to power, her mother's association with the enemy proved a harsh legacy.

First, she said, the new government terminated her education, pulling her out of school after third grade. Next, she and her entire family were moved to an "economic zone" outside Saigon, where they survived on one meal a day of rice and whatever they could grow in the jungle.

But late last year, with help from Congress' Amerasian Homecoming Act, Kieu's American roots finally rescued her. Since December, she, her mother and two sisters have lived in Silver Spring, and Kieu, now 22, is planning a new life.

"In Vietnam, I could not get a job," Kieu said through an interpreter. "Now I have hope in the future. I would like to be a manicurist and hair stylist."

Like Kieu, an estimated 10,000 Amerasians—called "half-breeds" in their own country—will arrive in the United States in the next year. These new immigrants, ages 13 to 27, are the offspring of American military and civilian men who left Vietnam more than a decade ago. The Homecoming Act gives them until March 1990 to apply for visas and provides for refugee benefits for themselves and an estimated 10,000 to 20,000 accompanying family members.

After leaving Vietnam, Amerasians and their relatives spend six months in the Philippines, where they study English and receive cultural orientation.

Next, in the United States, they go to one of 28 "cluster" or relocation sites—including one in the Washington region, which is preparing to welcome nearly 600 Vietnam natives in the next five months. The sites are intended to ease the transition by keeping Amerasians and their families in groups to foster mutual support.

The Washington area is slated to receive the largest number of new arrivals, according to refugee assistance groups, because of its good reputation for resettling refugees.

"Most other refugees... have relatives here to help them adjust," said Joanie Chase, project coordinator for a group of voluntary agencies helping the local resettlement effort. "But the majority of Amerasians don't have that."

Her group—which includes Associated Catholic Charities, the International Rescue Committee, Lutheran Social Services, Traveler's Aid, World Relief Refugee Service and Christian Relief Outreach Inc.—is to provide social service assistance to new arrivals. They also recruit volunteers to befriend and tutor Amerasians and to plan social activities, such as a recent Tet party to celebrate the new year.

Amerasians often have an unrealistic view of what awaits them in the United States, Chase and others said. In Vietnam, many have been victims of discrimination and cruel treatment. In the United States, they expect to be welcomed enthusiastically, to prosper, to see their fathers.

"Some of the children feel they will be greeted by their fathers with open arms," said Hien Vu, deputy director of the International Rescue Committee for the Washington area. "But we have resettled a lot of Amerasians, and there have only been two or three cases where the fathers have wanted to see the children."

Usually, Vu said, the fathers are married, with families of their own, and are not too happy when children—clutching an old address or photograph—come looking for them.

"The war's been over 14 years now," Vu said.

For many, life here is not much of an improvement at first. They have trouble learning the language and adapting to a new culture. They struggle with their identity, an even more complicated struggle for Amerasians whose fathers were black. Often they can't find good jobs or afford decent housing.

Nga Nguyen, 36, another recent arrival, came here with her husband and her 14-year-old daughter, who was fathered by an American contractor in 1974. The couple are looking for work and living in a D.C. apartment. They arrived with virtually nothing, uprooting their lives for the daughter's welfare.

"Her future is the most important," said Nguyen, who is studying English at night school. "In Vietnam, she would never have had the chance to go to college."

Nguyen would like her daughter to meet her American father someday, but doubts she will ever find him. For now, she believes hard work will mean security for her daughter and any future children—"at least I have hope."

Sometimes hope isn't enough.

Amerasian refugees are eligible for federal cash assistance during the first six months of their resettlement. Later, if necessary, they get assistance through local agencies.

Son Thi Nguyen, 45, brought her daughter, now 16, to the United States in 1986. They arrived from Da Hang, leaving behind the beatings and tauntings the child had known from schoolmates—but also leaving behind loving relatives.

After two years, Nguyen has not been able to learn English or find permanent work. She is on welfare. Her daughter attends school in Arlington but is shy and has few friends, her mother said, "because she is embarrassed.... Everybody knows she has no father."

Nguyen's daughter, who asked that her name not be used in this article, said she was "very excited at first" about coming to the United States, "but now I feel that I like it better there."

Thu Kieu, the Amerasian newcomer who dreams of becoming a beautician, said she knows success will take more than dreams. She works as a hotel housekeeper by day and meets with a volunteer English tutor at night. One day, she will enroll in beauty school.

"It's been a hard adjustment," said Kieu. "But I am getting help, and I know it is a good thing that I came here."

March 20, 1989

To Be Young, Gifted, Black ... and Preppie: Author Lorene Cary Recalls Life at a Posh Boarding School

Jacqueline Trescott

Lorene Cary is anxious to become "part of that unruly conversation" of what it means to grow up black in America.

"Black Ice," a memoir of her two years in one of the country's most exclusive boarding schools, is her offering. "I did write it to be part of a tradition that starts with the slave narratives. Who am I as a black American in America? There's that question," she says.

Her purpose stated, Cary hesitates. In a refreshing turn for an author in the throes of promotion, she is practicing some humble backpedaling. She is agonizing over just how to say where her book might fit into the long line from Frederick Douglass, Ida B. Wells, Richard Wright, Gwendolyn Brooks, Ann Moody and John A. Williams.

Her light brown eyes are trained on some spot on the table. Her beaded bracelets are motionless. Finally, she points a long, thin finger adorned with garnet rings at her book jacket, on which biographer Arnold Rampersad has compared her book to Maya Angelou's classic, "I Know Why the Caged Bird Sings."

"I just wrote one book," Cary says, steadily. "I want to throw my penny in the pot. At the same time these are books that I have respected for so long that I am not even thinking 'I am in this category with ...' "

"Black Ice" is not "Womanchild in the Promised Land." It couldn't be. It is truly a different world. It is Cary's lovely and painful look at her life inside St. Paul's School in Concord, N.H., from 1972 to 1974. "It is not a book about St. Paul's. It is about the growing up of a black girl who went away to a boarding school," she says.

It is definitely in the vanguard of firsthand looks at the doors that were opened by the 1960s civil rights movement and a welcome addition to the slim collection of black women's autobiography. "We are finally hearing from the internal immigrants, a new generation of Americans who walked through doors that had been opened a crack but led into an emotional maze," noted columnist Ellen Goodman.

Yet Cary, who hasn't lost her Philadelphia street sense in her 34 years, is worried about another question, the one raised by some callers to talk shows who have challenged the validity of a work that revolves around subtle racism and internal dramas. Is she the harbinger of a generation of affirmative action crybabies who have access to an experience minority people have dreamed about and then disparaged it while getting over on the same credentials?

"Sometimes I feel people are saying 'if it is not overt, then it is not bad.' It is not true. That's very important for our generation. Slowly, slowly you can lose belief in yourself until you are paralyzed and you can't do it," she says. She imagines some in her audience are thinking she is "saying, wow, I went through this prep school and everybody ought to integrate because it is great to do, guys."

That out of the way, delivered in a delightful mimic of the wispy voice and pinched nose of privileged white television teens, she talks about the false starts for the book, how she herself was trapped by stereotypes. "I didn't consider it a story worth telling really," she says. "It just wasn't a good enough black experience. So who cares? Who cares? So you went to this school. You had all these funny feelings. You didn't do anything particularly special. But there is also the fact that old-timers say it's your story and it's the only one you have to tell." And, she says quite candidly, it was the most accessible story she had to write as she was starting her freelance career and wanted to be at home with her husband, R.C. Smith, a former magazine editor, and her daughter, Laura, 6.

Her links to St. Paul's began when she heard of the school and its efforts to recruit girls and blacks from a neighbor in Philadelphia and eventually accepted a generous scholarship. She was then 15 and had definite ideas about race and class. "My assumptions were that wealthy people are degenerate. They don't have character. They got wealthy by oppressing or by scaling somebody. Clearly those were not their ideas about their class. They had ideas about me and just as I never said the ideas I had, they never said the ideas they had. ... There was only a little buffer zone of curiosity," she says. She also had strong ideas about her own blackness. She recalls being brought alive by such books as Sam Greenlee's "The Spook Who Sat by the Door" and Kristen Hunter's "Soul Brothers and Sister Lou," and she chafed at the word "minority."

When Cary arrived in New Hampshire, she was submerged in a white world. The classes were newly integrated and newly coed. The curriculum was tough. And the culture tougher. In chapel for the first time, Cary mused, "My music would not fit here. Neither would my god ... ."

She knew she was part of a historic time. "I was there in spite, despite, TO spite it. I was there because of sit-ins and marches and riots. I was there—and this I felt with extraordinary and bitter certainty—as a sort of liberal-minded experiment. And hey, I did not intend to fail," she says. The Third World Coalition, the organization of blacks, Asians and Hispanics at St. Paul's, felt some group bravado: "How we got there, how we found our way to their secret hideout, was not the point; the point was that we had been bred for it just as surely as they, the point was that we were there to turn it out."

But instead of even a modest militancy, Cary adopted a brisk silence. "Everywhere I went I felt out of place," she says. She stayed walled up, and would get in the bathtub and pretend St. Paul's didn't exist or walk through muddy fields chanting lines from "The Little Engine That Could." Yet she was "frightened" because the last thing a teenager wants is to be an outsider. She found a few friends, lost her virginity through a date rape, tried some drugs and briefly cruised the dorms taking change and jewelry.

She writes about the "inevitable" racial discussions in classes. "I took the offensive and bore my fights proudly. ... I do recall hearing the same old Greek-centered, European-centered assumptions of superiority. Might made right. I had my stories about Chaka Zulu from my Harvard evening course (and I knew they worshiped Harvard!). Nothing mattered. I was like a child again, trying to argue that I was still somebody."

Despite her own interior turbulence, Cary never abandoned her bottom line. She was there for the education. "I wanted it. You go there to steal education from the upper class and bring it back. I did assume there was an education that I wouldn't get with the resources I had," she says, now 17 years removed from the intensity.

She had a number of fears. One was that her blackness would be tainted. "What we were afraid of was that we would change in some way that would betray our people. We were afraid we would turn into Toms. It was hard to know ways to allow yourself to change."

During those times she looked to her personal history for solace, bits and pieces of the British poems that her grandfather learned in Barbados in his youth or the folk tales he recited to her. One seemed to fit the ambiguity she felt about immersion in white culture. A woman took off her skin every night and flew around feeling free. To keep her home, her husband salted the skin one night. It burned when she put it back on and she screamed, "Skin, skin. Ya na know me?"

For her book title, Cary adopted the term used by hockey players to describe a campus pond. That pond became one of her retreats. After a humiliating failure at calculus, she sat by the black ice and thought about her facade of never quite letting go. "I would be well-mannered, big-hearted, defiant, and, because a pose cannot resist great intimacy, at the center of all my posing, I would remain alone," she says. The title was also adopted as a metaphor for her adopted personality.

Now she says she's sorry she took that approach. "You cannot go through life not trusting anybody without enormous psychic harm. You cannot do that pose. The pose is not a life," says Cary. She writes of how she felt at graduation: "I would not admit how profoundly St. Paul's had shaken me, or how damaged and fraudulent and traitorous I felt." Now, as she talks about wanting to share her story, she says she regretted her fears. "I have been busy doing this little job, getting these little grades, trying to be politically correct. But I have been so afraid. I have been holding myself, jacked up against the wall," she says. At the same time, she congratulates herself for being adult enough to develop regrets.

After St. Paul's, Cary attended the University of Pennsylvania, where she earned a joint bachelor's and master's degree In English. She intentionally chose Penn for what St. Paul's was not—large, close to home, diverse. "I was not as involved. It was like coming out of a marriage that has been traumatic," she says. She spent a year at the University of Sussex in England, studying Victorian

Religious Faith and Doubt—"heavy on the doubt," she quips —— and a year at Time magazine and two years at TV Guide. For one year she taught at St. Paul's and served on the board of trustees. Years after she left the boarding school, Cary would tell students to "try and think of St. Paul's as their school too, not as a white place where they were trespassing."

In writing the book, she found it hard to write about her family. yet those descriptions have been cited by reviewers as insightful. "They are just as vigorous today as they seem in the book," she says of her parents. And you get the feeling her father, a teacher, and her mother, a "woman who did hair in the kitchen," would be her first critics, as well as supporters. In a way they went to St. Paul's also. She writes, "Neither my parents nor I really knew what we were getting into. Once you've made the journey, you can't pretend it didn't happen, that everything's like it was before except now you play lacrosse."

Again, she hedges her contribution with a sigh. "This is the story of a life."

April 25, 1991

Japan Discovers the Jews: Is the Surge in Interest Rooted in Admiration or Anti-Semitism?

John Burgess

The Jews, it seems, are to blame. The Japanese are casting about for explanations for their country's current economic troubles, and this one—the Jews—has drawn enough attention to make a best-seller (400,000 copies in 12 months) of a book entitled "If You Understand the Jews, You Can Understand the World."

"International Jewish capital" has been secretly battering Japan for years, writes author Masami Uno. The bribery indictment of former prime minister Kakuei Tanaka in 1976, the softening up of Japanese young people and the rise of South Korea as a competitor were all part of the plot. Now comes the strong yen, which Uno tells us Jewish bankers have created to subvert and subjugate the Japanese economy.

Uno's book was so successful that last fall he brought out a sequel that has sold 250,000 copies. Other Japanese authors have joined in with such works as "Miracles of the Torah Which Control the World," "Understanding the Protocols of the Elders of Zion," and "Make Money with Stocks Targeted by the Jews."

The books by Uno and the others are just one part of a boom in Japanese interest in all things Jewish. Tokyo's Kinokuniya book store recently held a "Jewish fair" that assembled 150 titles on the subject. Most are intended as paens of praise, depicting Jews as dynamic models of success in business, the arts and human relations.

The few Jews (around 1,000) who live in Japan report no sense of personal danger despite the anti-semitic tone of some of the books. "Ninety-nine percent of the Japanese population doesn't know what Judaism or people of Jewish origin are," says Walter J. Citrin, a businessman who is chairman of Tokyo's Jewish Community Center. "They just consider them foreigners."

Still, he is worried. "We feel the contents of these books will create a wrong impression among Japanese young people," possibly leading to anti-semitism, says Citrin.

A few foreigners believe it is already here and that the books are a new sign that nationalist extremism is on the rise in Japan.

"Anti-semitism has greater intellectual currency and respectability in Japan than in perhaps any other industrialized society," wrote David G. Goodman, a University of Illinois specialist on Japan, in a recent letter to The New York Times.

Japanese commentators tend to see the books as generally benign, a passing fad that shows how ignorant the Japanese remain of the world beyond their shores and the sensitivities of people there. "The books sell well because of the Japanese' feelings of isolation," says Jewish-studies specialist Shichihei Yamamoto. "Japanese are being criticized from all over the world and they want to know who is doing it and why." (There are also books alleging an American conspiracy.)

Jews have evoked fascination in parts of the Japanese intellectual world for decades. By some accounts, it began in the late 19th century, when Japan was exposed to anti-semitism in the flood of western ideas it imported for moderniza- tion. "The Merchant of Venice" was the first of Shakespeare's plays to be trans- lated. Pejorative terms applied to Jews remain in many Japanese-English dictionaries.

In the 1930s, the Japanese military came up with an idea to populate occupied Manchuria with a million European Jews seeking refuge from Naziism. Had it gone anywhere, it might have saved many lives. The plan's motivating factor, however, seems to have been a belief the newcomers would draw capital and learn- ing from the United States to that impoverished area.

There is evidence, too, of feelings here of a special affinity with Jews. Perhaps it is due to perceptions that Jews have the same sense of purpose and group loyalty that the Japanese admire in themselves. Tiny religious sects have even sprung up here preaching that the Japanese are one of the lost tribes of Israel.

In Israel there is a forest named in honor of Chiune Sugihara, a Japanese diplomat stationed in Lithuania during the war, who ignored his government's reg- ulations and issued visas that enabled an estimated 4,500 Jews to escape to Japan. As the war progressed, the Japanese interned certain European Jews in a Shanghai ghetto but otherwise generally resisted demands by Nazi Germany for wholesale persecution.

After the war, some Japanese saw a spiritual brotherhood with the Jews as innocent victims of war. One side had Hiroshima; the other had Auschwitz. Anne Frank's story has always sounded a strong chord with the Japanese. Over a recent two-week period, 35,000 of them paid the equivalent of $2 and $3 to see a Tokyo exhibit of objects from the girl's life.

Proud of their "one-race society," the Japanese are forever treading unaware on the toes of other people's ethnic pride. Japanese television frequently depicts Africans as amusing savages. Prime Minister Yasuhiro Nakasone last year remarked in a speech that blacks and Hispanics have dragged down the United States' educational level, and many people here still can't figure out why his com- ments caused such a fuss across the Pacific.

Most Japanese who buy conspiracy books probably have no notion that they present warmed—over versions of theories that the Nazis used to justify the mur- der of millions. Many might think twice if they knew how abhorrent the ideas are considered overseas.

"People buy the books thinking it will give them an international outlook," says Akira Mizuguchi of the Middle East Institute of Japan. "Unfortunately, it makes a very strong impression on those with little knowledge.

Perhaps the supreme irony is that the Jews depicted in the books bear remarkable resemblance to the stereotypical Japanese denizens of "Japan Inc."—rich, treacherous, manipulating, secretly conspiring with every member of their kind to control the world.

Meanwhile, Jewish leaders in Japan are trying bring foreign pressure to bear on the issue. Members of the Anti-Defamation League of B'nai B'rith have met with Japanese Ambassador Nobuo Matsunaga in Washington to express concern. Two members of the U.S. Congress recently demanded that Nakasone take a stand against the books. In response, they got a letter from Matsunaga affirming that Japan opposes discrimination of any kind but also upholds freedom of expression.

The Jewish Community Center's Citrin hopes that Japanese intellectual leaders, and perhaps even politicians, will at some point speak out publicly against the books' ideas. For now, however, the idea is to play down the issue in Japan. "The more it appears in the press here," he says, "the more books it sells."

May 17, 1987

The Empire of Ethnic Russians Retrenches: Return to Soviet Heartland Reverses Six Centuries of Expansion

Michael Dobbs

Every week, hundreds of ethnic Russian families in this remote region along the Mongolian border pack their belongings and join an exodus north, across the Sayan mountain range that separates the autonomous republic of Tuva from Russia proper.

Russian settlers first reached the once feudal state of Tuva in the late 19th century. Tens of thousands more came this century, colonizing the barren plains and inhospitable mountains and bringing Slavic civilization to the indigenous nomadic, Mongoloid people who live in this geographical center of Asia.

Now the Russians are beginning to go home, reversing six centuries of steady expansion. They are fleeing the Soviet Union's latest outburst of ethnic turmoil.

"Some Russians are leaving because of the lack of economic opportunities. But others are leaving because they are afraid, for themselves and for their children," said Altai Piche-Ool, a Tuvinian deputy in the Russian legislature, describing a dramatic increase in anti-Russian incidents in this autonomous republic of 300,000 people over the last year.

A similar trend of Russian emigration can be observed all around the fringes of what was once the Russian empire—from the Baltic republics to Azerbaijan in the Transcaucasus to Tajikistan and Kirghizia in Central Asia. With the collapse of Communist ideology as an integrating force, the Soviet Union is breaking down into the separate nations that populate the vast Eurasian landmass.

Over the last year, many Russians have begun to face the thought that the Soviet Union might fall apart. President Mikhail Gorbachev spoke last month of the possibility of the world's second superpower disintegrating into "15 nuclear states." He aims to keep this from happening by persuading the republics to cede some of their sovereignty—over defense and foreign policy, for example—to the central government under a new union treaty.

In a manifesto published in the Soviet press, exiled Russian writer Alexander Solzhenitsyn called for the peaceful secession of the Baltic, Central Asian and Transcaucasian republics. He suggested that the traditional Slavic heartland of Russia, the Ukraine and Byelorussia, plus Russian-populated parts of Kazakhstan, form a "Russian Union." "We have to make a decisive choice: between the empire which is destroying us and the moral and physical survival of our nation," declared the Nobel Prize laureate.

Many Russian politicians and intellectuals appear to share Solzhenitsyn's belief that the Soviet Union in its present form is doomed. The main political divide here is not over whether to preserve the centralized Soviet state built by Vladimir Lenin and Joseph Stalin, but how to ensure a peaceful transition to a looser confederation of sovereign republics. There is a widespread feeling that, at the very least, the three Baltic states will go their own way.

If the Soviet Union were an empire in the traditional sense, the process of decolonization might be relatively clear-cut. In fact, it is the product of many centuries of Russian expansion culminating in revolution, civil war and a blood-soaked attempt to build the world's first socialist society.

In the process, colonizers and colonized became hopelessly mixed up. All Soviet citizens, Russians and non-Russians alike, have legitimate historical grievances.

The present administrative boundaries of the Soviet Union are almost arbitrary, reflecting neither historic nor demographic reality. One out of every four Soviet citizens—including about 24 million ethnic Russians—live outside their titular republic. Any attempt to unscramble this multinational community into individual nation states could provoke uncontrollable ethnic violence.

Ethnic disturbances have already created a huge and growing refugee problem. According to official estimates, there are now nearly 750,000 refugees in the Soviet Union, half of them Russians. Uprooted from their homes, frequently unemployed and living in appalling conditions, the refugees are easy prey for political demagogues. The anti-Armenian and anti-Russian pogroms that took place in Azerbaijan last January were largely the work of Azerbaijani refugees from Armenia.

"It's quite easy to imagine a chain reaction," said Viktor Rezunenko, who was forced to flee the Azerbaijani capital, Baku, and now heads a Russian refugee center in Moscow. "Many refugees have lost faith and patience. There are some who might resort to the same violence against people they consider foreigners in Russia as was used against us in Azerbaijan. The situation is quite unpredictable."

The Russian exodus from Tuva began late last year, following an alarming rise in the crime rate that affected Russians and Tuvinians alike. But it has quickened over the last few months as relations between the two communities have deteriorated. Leaflets with slogans like "Go back to Russia, otherwise you'll pay" have begun to appear in the streets of Kizil, the capital. Gangs of Tuvinian youths have roamed through remote villages, setting Russian homes on fire, smashing windows and stoning cars.

In one recent incident, reported in the central Soviet press, a young Russian was murdered in Kizil after failing to reply in Tuvinian to the question, "Do you have a smoke?" At about the same time, two Russian fishermen and a 14-year-old boy were murdered near a lake, their bodies charred in an attempt to prevent recognition.

"As soon as I can find another job back in Russia, I will leave as well," said Oleg, a Russian collective farm worker who did not want to give his last name. "Why stick around? I fear they could start taking our children hostage."

About 2,700 Russians over age 16 are officially reported to have left Tuva over the last two months, compared to 6,000 for all of last year. The departing Russians include many doctors and skilled technicians whose presence is vital for the Tuvinian economy. There is already talk of closing local factories, including a major asbestos plant, because of a shortage of trained experts.

Tuva was the last chunk of Asia to be absorbed into the Soviet Union, becoming an autonomous republic within the Russian federation in 1944. Bordering on Mongolia, it marks the outward limit of Russia's territorial expansion.

The Russian march to the east began in the 15th century after the defeat of the Mongolian Golden Horde by czar Ivan the Terrible. Siberia was colonized in the 16th and 17th centuries. Russian armies reached the borders of Afghanistan in the 19th century, alarming the British who felt that their hold over India was threatened.

Educated Tuvinians concede that the Russian colonization of their country had many positive aspects. The Russian immigrants introduced European culture, technology, clothes, even bathrooms to a formerly nomadic people. But they also undermined the Buddhist religion, the respect of the young for the old and the Tuvinian language. Tuvinians say that the curse of alcoholism dates from the Soviet period.

"The Russians raised our living standards, but they destroyed our traditions," said Vyacheslav Solchak, a commentator for Kizil television and an ethnic Tuvinian. "They said there was just one nationality, the Soviet nationality. They forgot that we had our own culture and language. My boy is 7 years old, but he does not speak Tuvinian. That is my great misfortune."

At the Kizil coffee bar in the center of this typical Soviet provincial town, the rival ethnic groups eye each other warily from separate tables. The tension jumps appreciably when a group of Russian Special Forces or spetznaz troops, flown to Tuva to keep order, swagger into the restaurant, swinging their nightsticks.

"If a Russian picks a fight with us, the spetznaz will always take it out on us. They always assume that we start the trouble," hissed a Tuvinian student, who asked not to be named. "The Russians take everything we have: our forests, our gold, our temples, even our asbestos."

It is possible to sense a different kind of anger—a quiet, burning frustration—at the Russian refugee center in Moscow, just behind Red Square.

Russians forced to leave the outlying republics because of ethnic violence crowd into the center in search of jobs and places to stay. Frequently refugees are told that there is nothing for them in Moscow and they will have to move somewhere else.

"We believed in the slogan of friendship between peoples. We did our internationalist duty for 32 years," said Nikolai Trubavin, a Russian oil worker who fled the Central Asian republic of Tajikistan earlier this year after ethnic riots. "Now we find ourselves without a home and without a homeland. Nobody seems to want us."

Some conservatives accuse Gorbachev of irresponsibly frittering away the gains of a millennium of Russian expansion.

In a recent interview, nationalist writer Alexander Prokhonov described the disintegration of the Soviet Union as "a horrifying misfortune, unacceptable to the Russian mind."

Prokhonov predicted that the continued unraveling of the empire could lead to civil war.

Although he claims to speak for sections of the military as well as conservatives in the Communist Party, Prokhonov seems to be in a minority. A more common reaction, even among avowed Russian nationalists, is that Mother Russia may be better off without the non-Russian republics that have been taking advantage of her for far too long.

"Most of these countries asked to become part of Russia in the first place. We have treated them as our guests," said Ilya Glazunov, a Russian painter attracted by nationalist themes. "If a guest does not want to stay in my house, he has a perfect right to leave. But he should not think I will let him take my candleholders along with him."

Even if Russia was reduced to the Slavic heartland envisaged by Solzhenitsyn, it would still be the world's largest country, geographically. The combined population of Russia, the Ukraine and Byelorussia is 210 million people. Together, these three republics produce more than 92 percent of the Soviet Union's oil and gas, 80 percent of its industrial output and about 80 percent of its food.

Opposition to Baltic independence has come mainly from Russians living in the Baltic states who fear that they could become second-class citizens in the event of secession. It is these so-called "aliens"—people living outside their own republics—who constitute the most powerful social and political force for the preservation of the Soviet Union in its present form.

As the Baltic states press ahead with their plans for independence, conservative journals such as Literaturnaya Rossiya have been running articles suggesting that Russia will be better off without them. The argument is based on the fact that Russian raw materials are sold at grossly subsidized prices to the non-Russian republics. In return, Russia is obliged to buy expensive finished products from the republics at above world prices.

The "patriots" do express worries about the fate of the nearly 2 million Russians living in the Baltic republics. But their main concern is the future of Russia as a strong, centralized state.

In a recent article for Literaturnaya Rossiya, commentator Eduard Volodin called for the return of Russian soldiers and officers to Russia. Describing the Russian officer corps as "the gold reserve of our country," he said it risks becoming bogged down in irresolvable local conflicts. "When we stand at the edge of national catastrophe, we cannot continue to take part in the ambitious games of outlying nationalist groups, allowing our army to rot.

"Russia will be alone, but this does not mean that it will become a second-rate state, left out of the orchestra of world politics. Russia still controls the Eurasian continent, with all its raw materials and industrial potential, intellectual power, nuclear missiles and modern army. All this taken together will still leave us among the leading powers," said Volodin.

At the other end of the political spectrum, the progressives openly support the national aspirations of the Baltic states, but draw the line at the defection of the Ukraine and Byelorussia.

"It's in my own interests for Lithuania to become independent," said Alexander Ogorodnikov of the newly formed Christian Democratic Union. "If both Lithuania and Russia were free, we would be able to sell our oil for real currency, not just bits of paper. I cannot think of this empire as a Russian empire, my empire. It is the empire of an alien ideology, Marxism."

October 7, 1990

Chapter Seven

Gender

Patterns of sex and gender stratification differ greatly among societies, from those that severely oppress one sex in favor of another to those that are more egalitarian. The status of being female is changing worldwide, but the pace varies widely. Each of the articles in this section peer into the experience of being female in different parts of the world.

In the first article, author Michiko Yamamoto writes about the forces that caused her to leave Japan and seek her professional and personal life in the United States. Following this, "The Despair of Pakistan's Women" chronicles the ongoing oppression of women in that society. "Female Media Workers Discuss Career-Home Conflicts" reports on a conference of women from 38 countries who have gathered to compare the experience of being both women and journalists.

The conflict experienced by the Japanese vis-a-vis birth control, abortion, and religion is the subject of an intriguing report entitled "Japan's Abortion Agony." The final two articles, one on Tunisia and one on Saudi Arabia, describe life for women "behind the veil."

Single Professional Woman Flees to America for Work and Freedom

Michiko Yamamoto

As immigrant Asian and Third World workers flood into Japan, attracted by the dynamic economy, a steady stream of young Japanese, many of them women, are moving to the United States. Abandoning dead-end jobs, they go abroad in search of a new identity free from the constraints of this highly conformist, status-conscious society.

Rigid social norms govern every aspect of Japanese life. A woman is expected to marry, preferably in her early or mid-twenties, have children and run the household. Around the age of 30, "Miss" assumes a negative connotation. Of course, this is sexual stereotyping, but the real problem is a society that categorizes everyone by social role.

Why do you have to be like everyone else in this society? Who wants to marry just anyone? Still, if you wait for Mr. Right, you're in a quandary.

For many years, I worked in an office, but lacking professional training, I was relegated to perfunctory tasks. There was little chance of promotion or personal fulfillment. Other employees, especially those younger than myself, wondered why I stayed on, making me feel self-conscious and out of place.

In the 1980s, many women rejected the narrow choice of marriage or a career, left Japan and struck out on their own. Most went to the United States, where, unhampered by role stereotyping, they could acquire a working knowledge of English and find challenging work and maybe even a spouse.

After several years of hesitation, I made a break. In 1981, at age 31, I headed for the greener pastures of San Francisco.

I went to the United States on a tourist visa and soon ran out of money and had to look for work. One day I saw a poster advertising the Nobirukai (Japanese Newcomers' Services), a group of Japanese expatriates who counsel recent arrivals about visas, work, housing, school, legal aid and medical care. The Nobirukai was just what I needed. Most of the association's members were women about my age. Impressed by their devotion and efficiency, I, too, later volunteered.

One of the members told me, "Japan is a hard place for women. Those of us who don't think marriage is the answer, or who don't want to spend the rest of our lives as drones, have a third choice: leaving the country."

"Most Japanese women who end up here," Emiko said, "are past 30. They don't have definite goals when they arrive, but they are determined to find their own lifestyle—something that's difficult to do in Japan. They are social refugees."

The intriguing expression "social refugees" seemed an apt term for misfits like myself. Unlike political or economic refugees, Japan's runaways are fleeing an oppressive conformism.

Women join the Nobirukai because they are subjected to greater psychological stress than males. Not bound by a management position or status considerations, they are also freer to drop out and start over.

Japanese society has always generated square pegs. Before the age of foreign travel, they suffered in silence, resigned to their fate.

For nearly two decades after World War II, overseas travel was restricted because of a foreign exchange shortage. In 1964 the curbs were lifted, enabling ordinary citizens to visit other countries.

In the 1970s and 1980s, young people took short group tours and package excursions to the United States. The trend accelerated after 1980, when the strong yen made travel cheap and America a tourist bargain. Last year, about 10 million Japanese were abroad. Many are staying and putting down roots.

Every year, between 4,000 and 5,000 Japanese apply to reside permanently in the United States. Today, there is a sizeable expatriate community in most major American cities.

But not everyone succeeds in acquiring the coveted green card. I spent 20 months in the United States, 15 of them working illegally. In the mid-1980s, there were 10 million undocumented foreigners in the United States; about 17,000 were Japanese.

I applied for immigrant status but was turned down. Threatened with imprisonment for overstaying my visa, I had no choice but to come home. I wrote a book about my experiences and became a freelance journalist. Since then many single women have told me that they, too, longed to leave Japan. It is distressing to think that nothing has changed in the 10 years since my American sojourn. If anything, today more women are looking for a way out.

The mass media deride them for wanting to live abroad, labelling the phenomenon the "spinsters syndrome." Even in the United States, hostile commentators say, "They'll never master English."

The male-dominated media, of course, miss the point. What kind of society makes life so difficult for young women that they prefer to live elsewhere?

Few men realize how liberating the decision to act on one's deepest feelings can be. Taking responsibility for your destiny requires courage and determination, but the rewards more than compensate for any hardship. Women discover an inner strength that enables them to shape a more self-reliant, satisfying existence.

Being an outsider in your own country is no fun. Sexism leads to alienation, which can exact a heavy psychological toll. But despite the risks, we are staking out new territory, creating an alternative lifestyle and pluralistic value system that respects individuality and diversity. The search for a new identity transforms our personal relationships.

Social refugees inhabit an exciting world beyond the Establishment's imagination. It's time Japan heeded these quiet voices.

December 30, 1990

The Despair of Pakistan's Women: Not Even Benazir Bhutto Could Stop the Oppression

Kurt Schork

The woman behind the desk in Islamabad's best hotel was in tears. She had just been suspended for 10 days for shaking hands with a man. "I am being punished for doing my job," she complained. "To be a woman in Pakistan is a terrible thing."

Indeed, Pakistan's 50 million women are trapped in a patriarchal society, victimized by a complex web of social, religious and legal forces that deprive them of their basic human rights. "I wouldn't want to be a horse, a dog or a woman in Pakistan," said one Western diplomat there recently. Or a prime minister for that matter.

When Benazir Bhutto, Pakistan's recently ousted prime minister, swept into office in December 1988 as a champion of democracy and reform, it looked as though women in Pakistan finally would move out of the dark ages. But in spite of her high profile as the only woman to lead a Muslim nation in modern times, Bhutto ventured little and gained even less on behalf of her country's women before she was abruptly dismissed by presidential decree earlier this month on charges of corruption and abuse of power.

The continuing plight of Pakistan's women is vividly illustrated by these accounts, as reported in the Pakistani media: A woman and her two daughters are stripped naked and beaten in public in the town of Macharwali in the Punjab, and the two girls are gang-raped. Police refuse to register a case against the assailants. Two young sisters, seriously ill, are taken to a hospital. The diagnosis: an infection of the bones caused by a lack of sunlight. The girls have not been allowed to set foot out of their father's house for years. There is no prosecution. A 13-year-old girl is abducted and raped by a "family friend." Her father files charges, but the girl—not the rapist—is incarcerated. Faced with the prospect of years of expensive litigation, the father ends up bribing the police to drop the charges. The girl is beaten by her uncle and elder brother and made to apologize to the entire family for disgracing them.

The U.S. Department of State's most recent human-rights report for Pakistan expresses concern over a disturbing increase in the number of newlywed wives being burned to death in kitchen accidents. Many of these deaths are believed to be murders perpetrated by husbands who are dissatisfied with the size of their wives' dowries. The report concludes that "few such cases are seriously investigated... ."
While Pakistani women are likely to find their freedoms even further restricted under a successor regime, other female politicians and activists were outspoken in their criticism of Bhutto while she was in office. "Benazir Bhutto has not demonstrated a commitment to anything other than her own desire to wield power," said

Syeda Amina Hussain, the first woman elected to the National Assembly in 1985 and a bitter critic of Bhutto.

Tehmina Anmed is a dedicated women's activist and an editor of Newsline, a national newsweekly magazine staffed primarily by women. A few months ago she criticized Bhutto for adopting "a permanent wait and see attitude" on women's issues. "In politics, there has to be some risk-taking somewhere."

The ancient tribal customs and feudal traditions that place women at such disadvantage in Pakistan predate the country's creation as an independent Islamic state in 1947. Baluch and Pathan women in the western provinces live according to strict tribal codes that give them no say in their lives, including marriage. They are literally invisible after the onset of puberty, sequestered behind their veils and the four walls of their homes. Any violation of tribal codes—a conversation between a man and a woman who are neither engaged nor married, for instance—is punishable by death.

In the more developed provinces, women often toil in the fields or factories out of economic necessity. But their lives are still severely constrained by rigid tradition, including a dowry system that frequently impoverishes the bride's family and makes daughters an unwanted burden. And while there are successful professional females in Pakistan's urban centers, even their economic and legal rights are seriously abridged.

Women's rights expanded in the early years of the republic, but the advent of martial law under Gen. Mohammed Zia ul-Haq in 1977 slammed shut a door that had just barely been opened. Under Zia's cynical brand of conservative Islamic demagoguery, the lot of women in Pakistan went from bad to worse.

The most egregious example is the Hudood Ordinance, which Zia enacted in 1979 to cover such offenses as adultery, fornication, rape and prostitution. In practice, the law protects rapists, prevents women from testifying on their own behalf and confuses the issues of rape, adultery and fornication. Because the law values the testimony of men over that of women, a woman who complains of rape frequently is prosecuted for adultery while the rapist goes free. Pregnancy in the absence of marriage is prima facie evidence of adultery, not rape. Punishments under the ordinance can include death by stoning and public whippings of up to a hundred lashes.

But perhaps the most insidious effect of Hudood has been to make notoriously corrupt local police forces the guardians of morality. These all-male bastions frequently use Hudood to harass innocent parties on the basis of personal and political animosities. Women have suffered grievously. When the ordinance was enacted there were only 70 women in prison in Pakistan. Today, more than 3,000 women are incarcerated, most of them charged under Hudood. Upon coming to power in 1988, Bhutto pledged to get rid of laws discriminating against women as soon as possible. In fact, Bhutto's legislative record on this, and virtually every other matter, was nil. Her determination to keep conservative interpreters of Islam at bay, especially the Jamaat Islami, an extreme right wing political party, forced Bhutto to postpone action on the women's agenda. Although the Jamaat Islami has never fared well at the polls, its ability to energize parliamentary opposition and foment unrest in the streets of Pakistan is considerable. Earlier this summer, fundamentalist forces in parliament embarrassed Bhutto by proposing a measure reimposing radical Islamic law, including punitive amputations and a requirement that rape victims produce four male witnesses.

To a certain extent, Bhutto may have fallen victim to unrealistic expectations engendered by the Western media's image of her as a thoroughly modern woman. As she made clear in her autobiography, she is a daughter of the East. Harvard and Oxford are nothing in her life compared to the concrete realities of tradition and Islam in Pakistan. She acknowledged as much in agreeing to an arranged marriage with a man she had known for just seven days.

Bhutto's decision to wear the scarf traditionally draped over the head and upper body by Pakistani women, was viewed by many as symbolic of a disappointing willingness to compromise with right-wing religious forces. In Tehmina Ahmed's view, Bhutto was "projecting a false image." Said Ahmed, "If that is what it takes for a woman in Pakistan to strike an attitude of respectability, what does the future hold for us?"

But Amina Piracha, a female member of the National Assembly and hard-core Bhutto supporter, felt that "there has been progress for women under {Bhutto}. Under Zia it was nothing for someone to come up to you in the street and slap you in the face because you were not wearing the dupatta. Today, I am not afraid of being assaulted because my head is uncovered."

There were some other improvements under Bhutto. Pakistani women once again competed in international sports events, something banned under martial law. A cabinet-level office for women's development was created, and a number of women were appointed to senior positions within the government and diplomatic service. Women in prison have enjoyed somewhat better access to legal advice and representation.

But on the critical issue of Hudood, there was no progress. No doubt that was due in large part to Bhutto's distraction by other matters—an endless holy war in Afghanistan, a dispute with India in Kashmir that has nuclear potential, sectarian violence in Sind province. And persistent rumors of widespread corruption within her administration and within her husband's family eroded her once formidable support among the people of Pakistan. "We thought we elected a Cory," said one disaffected member of the National Assembly, "but it looks like we got Imelda instead."

August 19, 1990

Female Media Workers from 38 Nations Discuss Career-Home Conflicts

Eleanor Randolph

Lesley Stahl of CBS News remembers that some of the best advice she ever got about how to juggle family life and work was imparted by a male.

"He said the secret was to... never forget which are the rubber balls and which are the glass balls," she told an audience of about 150 women at the International Women's Media Conference Friday. "Obviously, the glass balls are your family and your health, and some of the rubber balls have to do with the job, let's face it."

In this first gathering of women in the media from 38 countries, participants seemed oddly willing to reveal their frailties and problems.

The conference included the requisite complaints about the male-dominated news business, but the most riveting moment came when these high-powered women talked about managing their hectic and interesting lives—and their feelings about their profession.

They revealed what could be surmised but seldom admitted in the past, when professional women often felt they would have to be superhuman in order to be equal. Now these women want to be able to be as weak as the "stronger" sex—i.e. to take time off for the life outside work.

When a West German journalist complained that she would lose her job if she took time off to have a family, Charlayne Hunter-Gault of the "MacNeil/Lehrer NewsHour" told her and others to look at those who have made similar sacrifices to stay at work.

"If they are miserable, you have to choose whether that's the life you want or you have to tell your editor to stuff it," said Hunter-Gault, who was substituting on one panel because Judy Woodruff of "MacNeil/Lehrer" had a baby boy Thursday.

NBC White Rouse correspondent Andrea Mitchell, known in the business as one of the best and toughest reporters covering the Reagan administration, said that "if there is a way that I have compromised myself, it is to work harder, whether it is self-imposed or not, to always be available for assignments."

Mitchell, who has been single for 11 years, said that when she started covering the White House for NBC she was assigned to weekend newscasts and quickly found that she needed to work all the weekdays to be ready for Saturday and Sunday duty.

But it was not always that way, she said. For seven years, Mitchell was married to a man with a child and "in a funny way that balanced and tempered the demands of my career. Even though logistically it was more difficult, having a child in the house and having a husband made all of the other sacrifices worthwhile because there was a way of sharing and of somehow compensating for a lot of the difficulties of the profession."

Now, she says, the choices are "more trivial" and an assignment competes only with a date or dinner with a friend.

One of her first assignments with NBC was to go to the site of the Jonestown massacre in Guyana because "I was the only person dumb enough to answer their phone on Thanksgiving." Christmas that year was spent in Plains, Ga.—so Mitchell could meet the parents of her future husband, The Wall Street Journal's Albert Hunt.

"My generation has not handled these things very well," Mitchell said. "Those of us who are single have probably made the choices in terms of career and not in terms of our personal [needs]... I am just hoping that we can start holding back something, and not being so available."

There seemed to be less agreement as to whether females are different from males as journalists.

Georgie Anne Geyer, co-chair of the conference and a syndicated columnist, argued that men talk power politics when they interview someone, while women talk about what she called soft geopolitical issues—cultural problems, overpopulation, environmental issues. Women also listen better, she said.

Another participant said that when she was covering the wars in Lebanon, "I was much less sensitive than some of my male colleagues" about the war and found it strangely exciting in a way that troubled her later.

Panelist Nora Boustany, who works in Lebanon for The Washington Post and the Financial Times of London, said women journalists in the Middle East have fared well in recent years because "male journalists are the ones who get kidnaped" in the male-dominated society.

"We begin to see terrible risks as opportunities for career enhancement," she told the group meeting at the Capital Hilton.

But the price is having male journalists believe that she enjoys covering the tragedies in her country:

"They say things like 'You can't get enough, Nora, can you?' and I'm trying very hard to keep down my breakfast from what I have seen."

She added: "I have seen many able men journalists break down and cry covering a story. When I cry, I go into the bathroom.

"I hope one day we can cry together."

November 15, 1989

Japan's Abortion Agony: In a Country That Prohibits the Pill, Reality Collides with Religion

Elisabeth Bumiller

Hiroshi Hihara is a harried gynecologist with a small clinic wedged between the bars and neon signs of Shinjuku, the neighborhood that four generations of doctors in his family saw transformed from rice paddies to skyscrapers. Hihara's great-grandfather practiced Chinese herbal medicine in Shinjuku at the end of the 19th century, and his grandfather and father were both obstetricians who delivered babies in the family clinic before and after the Second World War.

Today, Tokyo women are too affluent and sophisticated to have their babies in such small clinics, much preferring the big city hospitals. Hihara, in a sign of the times, does not even deliver babies. Instead, he makes his living on his infertility work and abortions, many of them for married women whose method of contraception, typically condoms and rhythm, has failed.

Although Hihara, 42, is a member of a Buddhist temple, he considers himself, like most Japanese, not at all religious. But he says he is not comfortable with abortion. "Abortion is legal and approved by the government, and if a patient wants it, I can't turn her down," he says. "She's entitled to it. But I am not happy to do it." And yet, he performs some 200 abortions a year, and quietly admits, when asked, that his fees from abortion represent "a large portion of my income."

Caught in this moral and economic trap, he resolves his feelings in a uniquely Japanese way. First, he tells each abortion patient to make an offering after the operation at any of the Buddhist temples selling miniature stone statues, or mizuko-jizo, which women can buy in memory of an aborted fetus.

Thousands of such statues stand on display at temples these days, and although some are for miscarriages and stillborn children, the vast majority are for abortions. Many of the statues are decorated with crocheted hats, plastic bibs and little pinwheels, all put there by women to keep the soul of the aborted fetus warm and amused. At Hase Temple in the seaside town of Kamakura, 3,000 mizuko-jizo are nestled in the hillside. At Zojo-ji Temple in Tokyo, women sometimes bring the mizuko-jizo little stuffed animals, baby bottles of apple juice or pacifiers.

Once a month, Hihara says, he himself also visits a temple, although not the one where he is a member, and makes an offering for the mizuko-jizo. He gives about $100 to the Buddhist priest to chant a prayer over one of the statues. "Perhaps you will think I am a hypocrite," he says. "But I think it's a good thing for me to go. I am the person who performed the abortions."

Japan may be the richest, most technologically advanced nation in the world, but it depends on an antiquated system of birth control that forces women to rely

153

heavily on abortion in a society that at the same time disapproves of it. At its core, the story of abortion and birth control in Japan is also about the low status and passivity of Japanese women, and about a male medical establishment marked by caution, tradition and—critics claim—greed.

Japan's abortion rate, though declining, is still believed by many health officials to be one of the highest among industrialized non-communist nations. One reason is the lack of alternatives. The government bans the use of the birth control pill as a contraceptive, and doctors do not encourage sterilization, IUDs or diaphragms. Nearly 75 percent of Japanese continue to use condoms and rhythm despite their high failure rate. The Japanese, in fact, use condoms more than any other people in the world. They are widely available in drugstores, supermarkets and vending machines; embarrassed housewives can buy them from door-to-door saleswomen. Abortion is the widely used backup for failed contraception. And yet, while abortions have been legal and easily accessible in Japan for more than 40 years, women who have them feel stigmatized because abortion is regarded by many Japanese, even those who accept it, as "killing a baby."

These contradictions have become more apparent in recent months. In July, the Ministry of Health and Welfare began a review process that will most likely lead, in one or two years, to approval of the newer and safer "low-dose" estrogen pill that has been on the market in the United States since the mid-1970s and is taken by 60 million women worldwide. (A higher-dose pill is available in Japan for regulating menstrual cycles and treating other disorders.) But supporters of the pill are nervous about a recent government report showing that Japan's birthrate is at an all-time low. The report prompted some male ruling party politicians, fearful that there will not be enough young Japanese taxpayers to support social services in the future, to call upon women to bear more children.

"Japan is the only country that legalized abortion and approved family planning, but does not use the pill," says Takashi Wagatsuma, a leading obstetrician, who for two decades has lobbied for approval of the pill. "Japan is a unique country. It is almost a crazy country."

The government justifies its ban by citing the danger of side effects, but some Japanese doctors charge that the government is actually trying to protect politically influential private practitioners who depend on abortion fees. Others say the Health Ministry fears that the pill will encourage promiscuity, importing to a chaste island nation the degradation of the American sexual revolution. (In fact, surveys show that premarital sex is the norm in Japan.) Ministry bureaucrats are also known to be concerned about lawsuits, which have proliferated in recent years over the side effects of government-approved drugs.

Japanese feminists, who might have been expected to support the pill as another contraceptive choice for women, are also worried about the health hazards of what one called "an invasion of artificial hormones." They have instead focused their energies on lobbying the government for more abortion rights.

Japan's actual abortion statistics are debatable. The government reports that 498,000 abortions were performed in 1987, or 18.6 for every 1,000 women of childbearing age—similar to the rate of most Western European nations and well below the rate of 27 per 1,000 in the United States. But the widespread belief in the Japanese medical community is that the government figure is too low because many doctors underreport abortions to avoid paying taxes on the fees. A first-trimester abortion in Tokyo costs about $800.

Ten years ago, Minoru Muramatsu, a public health specialist, calculated that Japan's abortion rate was three times the government figure, comparable to rates in Eastern Europe. Other doctors question these calculations, and Muramatsu himself, now retired, admits his numbers may be high. But even more conservative experts calculate the abortion rate at 1/2 to two times the government figure.

Takayo's Story

Takayo has had three abortions. "I am not ashamed of them," she says. "But they are something to keep private, in my heart." At her request, only her first name has been used for this article.

Her story, like so many others in Japan, is that of a woman who left the birth control decisions to her husband, and who knew only the condom as a form of contraception. For Takayo, abortion was legal and common, the reason she says she does not feel ashamed. But society also told her it was killing a baby. She says she is not a religious person, but today she is filled with guilt and regrets. "I should have had those children," she says. "Now I want to bring them back. When I was young, I thought only of myself."

Married women like Takayo account for the great majority of abortions in Japan. Teenage abortions are increasing, but their number remains small.

Takayo is 42, the mother of a 17-year-old daughter and the wife of a businessman who owns a company that makes women's clothes. He has been successful, so the family lives in a house, not the usual apartment, in Akabane, a suburb of Tokyo. Takayo has a high school education and is a patient of Kiyoshi Omura, a well-known obstetrician and gynecologist in Akabane, who called her and asked if she would talk about her abortions. She reluctantly agreed, but said she preferred to tell her story over the phone.

Takayo first met her husband in the late 1960s when she was a clerk at a cosmetics firm and he was a leader of the company's labor union. Soon they were living together. He quit his job, determined to become a songwriter; they decided to delay marriage until they were more secure financially. But within a year she was pregnant. "Except for the very safe days, he always used a condom," she says.

The pregnancy was a dilemma for her. Although she wanted to have the baby, she and her husband had no money and decided they couldn't possibly afford to raise a child. "I really suffered, worrying about whether to have the abortion," she says. By the time she made her decision, she was at the end of her first trimester. Or as she puts it: "The baby was three months old."

Takayo, like most Japanese, draws little distinction between a fetus and an infant. According to Samuel Coleman, the author of "Family Planning in Japanese Society," a 1968 survey of 1,500 Japanese women found that two-thirds believed the fetus is a human life at conception. Even Japanese feminists who have lobbied for more abortion rights sometimes refer to "killing the baby."

Coleman finds that the reasons lie at least partially in Shinto and Buddhism, Japan's two major religions. Although neither religion promotes active opposition to abortion, Buddhism is based on the ideal of overcoming one's sense of ego. In this context, a woman who aborts wrongly puts her own ego before her fetus. Shinto, an ancient religion based on ancestor and nature worship, holds that an aborted fetus can place a curse on the woman who aborts. One marginal religious sect in Japan, the Seicho no Ie, which draws on Christian, Buddhist and Shinto beliefs, does actively oppose abortion, but it does not have as much influence as American antiabortion groups.

Abortion was legalized after World War II, when the devastated country could barely support the people who survived. The prospect of more Japanese children to feed—as well as mixed children fathered by the American occupation troops—inspired the 1948 Eugenic Protection Law.

Takayo was pregnant again almost immediately after her first abortion. "I was very upset," she says, beginning to cry into the phone. "Even more upset than the first time. When my husband started the songwriting business, we only had money for food. We had no extra money. My husband's parents used to send us rice. We didn't know what to do. But my husband didn't feel that he could raise children because of our finances."

She had a second abortion, then became pregnant again. This time she miscarried. In 1971, she and her husband married, and two years later she was pregnant for the fourth time. By then, her husband had quit the music business and took a job in the company he now owns, and they decided they could finally afford a family. "I was very tired of abortions," she says. The baby, now her 17-year-old daughter, was born in 1973; two years later, she was pregnant for the fifth time. But after a bout with German measles during her pregnancy, her doctor warned of severe damage to the fetus and recommended abortion.

"Now I regret all the abortions," she says. "To look at my own daughter—now I really feel sad to lose those children. If I had known a better way of birth control, maybe I could have avoided that kind of tragedy. I regret I didn't have that kind of information when I was young." She never questioned her husband's use of the condom. "I never saw it as either a good or a bad thing," she says. "I didn't know about anything else."

Although the condom is popular again because of the "safe sex" era in the United States, it has a contraceptive failure rate, in actual use, of 15 percent. Doctors in Japan tell their women patients that the condom is effective only if it is used at all times of the month, and from the beginning to the end of intercourse. But doctors say that Japanese couples do not often use condoms during a woman's so-called "safe" period. This combination condom-rhythm method of birth control is said to have a failure rate of 30 percent. Both feminists and doctors say that the condom would be used more effectively if Japanese women were not afraid to speak up and take the initiative on birth control during sex.

"In actual intercourse, women feel they can't tell their partners to use condoms," says Megumi Tanaka, the editor of More, a popular women's magazine and the publisher of the More Report, a respected survey of Japanese sexual attitudes. "Men do whatever they want to do. And also, men say, 'It's okay, I can put it on in the middle.'"

Kiyoshi Omura, Takayo's doctor, feels equally exasperated. "I don't know about America, but in Japan I think that women rely on men too much," he says. "In my experience, 99 out of 100 women will say that they have to ask their husband's permission before using the pill or an IUD. But I tell them, 'It's the woman's responsibility to think about it. This isn't determined by your husband.'"

Takayo has only recently heard of oral contraceptives, through an article in a women's magazine. "I understand that the pill is the easiest way," she says. And yet, if the pill were made available in Japan, Takayo says she most likely would not take it. "I've never heard anything about the pill from my friends in the neighborhood, and besides"—she begins to laugh a little—"my husband and I don't make love as often as we used to. He is very busy with his own work, and I don't have the energy anymore. So the pill isn't really necessary."

At the end of the conversation, she agrees to meet in person. A week later, she is serving tea at her dining room table, in front of large glass doors that open onto a small garden of vegetables and chrysanthemums. Dressed casually in a cotton sweater and a long print skirt with her hair pulled back neatly in a navy blue ribbon, Takayo has the look of a well-to-do and organized Japanese housewife. Her daughter, who knows nothing of her mother's abortions, is at home, so for an hour there is awkward chitchat about cooking, gardening and children.

But afterward, in the car on the way to the train station, Takayo immediately speaks up. "I thought abortion was easy," she says. "That's why I did it. My husband and I thought because we were poor we had no choice. Why was I so stupid?"

She relieves her guilt in the Japanese way. "Very recently, I felt very sad for what I had done," she says. "So I went to a temple and made an offering to the mizuko-jizo."

'Abortion First, Contraception Second'

Yumiko Jansson is a rare breed of Japanese woman: a feminist. There is only a minor women's movement here, mostly comprising small groups that organize around specific issues, such as sexual harassment.

"I give lectures to both Swedish women and Japanese women," says Jansson, who is married to a Swedish businessman. "Both groups are educated, both are well informed. The only difference I can see is that Swedish women can fight because they are not afraid. But we cannot fight, because we are still afraid. Japanese women are still totally dependent on men. We are raised not to confront. We are raised to be harmonious."

Jannson is 46, the author of several books, the mother of two and the translator into Japanese of Alice Walker. She is also part of a group that promotes reproductive freedom and lobbies the government on health issues.

"The basic attitude of the government is abortion first, contraception second," she says. But she thinks the government's ban of oral contraceptives "has been a wise decision" because of the potential side effects of the pill's synthetic hormones. Like other feminists, she takes a laissez-faire position on the pill: She and her group will not oppose the pill if it is permitted in Japan, but neither will she push for its approval.

Other women take the same attitude, although the scientific basis for their fears is questionable. Tazuko Makitsubo is the director of an unusually frank sex education film for high school students. Yet it features a teacher who tells his classroom that birth control pills "are not designed for youth, because of your hormone imbalances." Asked about the teacher's statement, Amy Pollack, a physician and the associate medical director for the Planned Parenthood Federation of America, says she is "unaware of a scientific basis" for his comment. "I would say just the opposite," she adds. "The pill is an excellent form of contraceptive, particularly for teenagers, because it creates a regular hormonal state which leads to regular menstrual cycles."

Makitsubo's sex education film has been approved by the Ministry of Health and Welfare, but she asserts that she did not feel any government pressure to include the teacher's warning about the pill. "The government says the pill has side effects," she adds. "I say, and other doctors say, that introducing the pill for young girls is not good."

Those Japanese doctors in favor of the pill frequently complain that the Japanese press sensationalizes news of studies about the pill's side effects.

"Whenever I ask a woman why she would not want to use the pill, she will say, 'The pill has bad side effects,' " says Kiyoshi Omura, Takayo's doctor. "And then I will ask her, 'What kind of side effects?' But she won't know. She just has the idea that the pill is a bad thing."

Doctors say the pill's minor side effects include possible headaches, weight gain or loss, spotting and amenorrhea, the failure to menstruate. Major studies do not show any definite cause and effect between the pill and breast cancer, but more research is underway. The pill is currently used by 32 percent of American women in their childbearing years, and is the second most popular form of birth control in the United States. Sterilization of men and women, used by 38 percent of couples, is the most popular method. Condoms are used by 16 percent of U.S. couples. About 4 percent of American women use diaphragms and 3 percent use IUDs.

'It Depends on the Ladies'

If the pill is approved in Japan, and the consensus among doctors is that it most likely will be, will Japanese women use it? In June, a survey released by one of Japan's largest newspapers showed that fewer than 10 percent of Japanese women said they would use the pill if it were made available. Doctors say that at the least, oral contraceptives will take a long time to catch on.

"It's the $64,000 question," admits Douglas Ross, the president of Nippon Syntex KK, the Japanese subsidiary of a major American oral contraceptive maker that has applied with its Japanese distributor for permission to market the pill in Japan. "We've obviously got lots of estimates, but it depends on the ladies here. We don't know if the women are going to take this on and say, 'I want to control this.' I guess we're back where we were in other countries 15 years ago."

October 25, 1990

Sexual Politics, Islamic Style

Jim Hoagland

Here in a Moslem land where the miniskirt long ago replaced the veil, the men have started arguing again about the women. A long and beneficial moratorium on sexual politics, Islamic style, is coming to an end.

This is not the familiar American battle of the sexes over dividing up rewards and responsibilities at work and at home. Here cultures that use woman-as-symbol in different ways and for different purposes are sliding into conflict.

As a meeting ground for oriental and western cultures, Tunisia has always been an unusually tolerant and open Arab society. It juts out into the Mediterranean at the northern tip of Africa as if it were trying to reach across to Sicily and the rest of Italy, to which it is linked in fact by a natural gas pipeline that starts in Algeria.

But the Mediterranean imprint left by Phoenician, Roman, French and other settlements along the coast through two millennia is now fading rapidly. The exodus from the rural interior of the 1970s has given Tunis a strong Arab character that was not visible even 15 years ago, when smartly dressed young Tunisian women frequented the French-style sidewalk cafes on the boulevards.

Souhair Belhassan, a Tunisian writer, remembers clearly when she and many other Tunisian women stopped going into cafes in downtown Tunis in 1978. There was no prohibition, but it gradually became uncomfortable to endure the comments and stares of the unemployed young men who crowded all the available tables.

Drawn from the countryside by jobs that did not exist, the cafe-sitters have in a sense reclaimed Tunis culturally. Arab cities are the property and habitat of men, whose mastery of the streets is still symbolized in many places by women having to don the veil in public.

Islamic traditionalists frequently justify such restrictions as protecting or honoring women. The reverse is true, of course, as Tunisia's modern founder, Habib Bourguiba, repeatedly said throughout most of his career.

Western societies attempt to repress the psychic force of shame and humiliation. Arab culture is much more aware of these emotions and attempts to channel them. Women not only have to carry the burden of discharging these emotions for society as a whole; they also have to be seen to do so. The veil is only the most obvious symbol of this intimidation.

For 20 years, Bourguiba relentlessly pushed his small country (now 8 million population) to westernize and to leave behind the misogynistic tendencies of Islam. He abolished polygamy, he broke with the Koran by making adoption legal and he fought to guarantee women equal rights before the law.

Bourguiba and his equally strong-willed wife, Wassila, preached modernity together. Pictures of the First Couple blanketed Tunisia.

In his fading years, as he drifted into senility, Bourguiba abandoned the cause of feminism. He divorced his wife and renounced an adopted daughter. He continued his obsessive efforts to eradicate Islamic influences, but created a strong backlash that the fundamentalists exploited.

This is the unhappy legacy that Bourguiba's successor, Sine Abidine Ben Ali, inherited when he took power from the incapacitated Bourguiba Nov. 7. To stem the backlash, Ben Ali has emphasized in general terms that Bourguiba's war on Islam is over.

The changes in government have encouraged the Islamic movement here to demand political rights and to begin exerting pressure for a total review of the civil protections that Bourguiba enacted for women.

Ben Ali says that he will safeguard "certain advances" that Bourguiba made for women but he is vague on which ones qualify and which ones might not. He has emphasized the need for "good manners" in public.

Spokesmen for the Islamic movement assert that they have nothing in common with Khomeini's Iran and do not want to take Tunisia backward. They are persuasive to some extent on the broad outlines of their attachment to western financial and strategic realities, but they waffle furiously when asked what they would do about women.

They are reopening a debate that will produce only losers. A country that needs to concentrate on a dramatic economic decline could instead waste its energies in fighting social battles that belong to another century. A people whose geography, culture and economic well-being dictate openness does not need to waste time in rediscovering this fact of modern life.

February 13, 1988

Evolution and Revolution Change Lives of Islamic Women: Saudi Feminists Emerge from behind the Veil

Samira Kawar

An attractive middle-aged woman wearing fashionable western clothes sits with her teen-aged daughter in the first-class section of a plane bound for Riyadh. As the plane enters Saudi airspace, they are handed long, black cloaks which they wrap over their clothes, covering their figures from head to foot.

The few women who can be seen in public places here are all in wide black cloaks and head veils which, in some cases, are drawn over the lower part of their faces leaving only the eyes visible.

In a cloth shop, two women can be seen sampling various materials that a male shop attendant is showing them through a hole in a glass partition.

Saudi Arabia's national laws—drawn from Islam's holy book, the Koran—forbid women to drive and mandate segregation of the sexes in all public places. Social traditions permit men to have as many as four wives. Such realities make Saudi Arabia seem at first glance like one of the remotest places on Earth in terms of the women's liberation movement.

But a slow yet determined feminist revolution is emerging here.

Saudi women, even the toughest feminists among them, are devout Moslems, and many are resorting to the Koran—and society's meticulous efforts to do everything by the book—to gain their rights.

Many women feel that opposition to higher education and work for women, laws preventing women from driving and male demands that women cover their faces are a mixture of Islamic traditions and customs as well as misinterpretations of Islamic doctrine.

Pointing out that Islam merely enjoins women to dress modestly, Saudi sociologist Aisha al Mani stressed that "there is nothing in Islam that says we have to wear a black veil—not only over the face, but also all over us.... It's never mentioned in Islam."

"Islam decrees that it is the duty of every Moslem man and woman to seek an education," said Hind Khutheila, dean of the King Saud University for Women.

Khutheila, a member of one of the kingdom's most prominent tribes, said that some members of the tribe vehemently opposed her decision in the 1970s to go to the United States for graduate studies. Her father, who was chief of the tribe, had to send her to the airport with a bodyguard.

"They opposed me because they didn't believe in education for women. They thought I should be getting married. They were afraid of this new life and that I might get westernized and give up my traditions," she said.

But Saudi women, who make up 4.7 percent of the native work force, are making strides as doctors, engineers, university professors and deans, businesswomen, managers, radio broadcasters and newspaper editors.

The pioneering generation of university-educated Saudi women, now in their thirties and forties, got their training outside Saudi Arabia—in Lebanon, the United States and Western Europe. Now, women can receive degrees in many fields, including medicine and dentistry, at universities in Saudi Arabia.

Regarding Saudi Arabia's prohibition of female drivers, Mani said she believed the law would eventually change. "I don't see anything in Islam that prohibits a woman from driving," she added.

Polygamy, Khuteila said, is another example of this nation's misinterpretation—and occasional violation—of Islamic teachings. Although it is estimated to have dropped by about 50 percent over the last two decades, she said, it still remains prevalent.

"Islam describes polygamy as the least-favored practice allowed by God and stipulates that a man must treat all his wives equally," Khutheila said. "What many people overlook is that the Koran says that it is not possible to treat wives equally, and therefore a man should have one wife except in cases where the couple cannot have children or there are other extenuating circumstances."

She said women were equally to blame for the practice because they fail to exercise their right to reject marriage offers from men who are already married. "It's the fault of the women. If they would cooperate to reject the phenomenon, it would not continue. They must collectively reject it," she said.

Segregation between men and women is another phenomenon that touches on virtually every aspect of Saudi life and results in "separate but equal" facilities for women: Universities have special segregated branches for women. Restaurants have separate sections for women. Banks have women-only branches. And in government offices, women are provided with segregated working spaces that are off limits to men.

In offices where paper work must be passed between departments in which men work, an expatriate woman employe carries the paper work to another area of the building connecting the women's department to the male-occupied offices. There, she is met by a male employee.

Offices in which contact must occur between the sexes are required to employ married couples through whom paper work exchanges are conducted.

Saudi women are not lobbying to desegregate their society, sociologists say, mainly because segregation is a deeply ingrained social custom, and fighting it now could cause women to lose some of the gains they have managed to make so far.

Some women believe that, at least for the time being, segregated employment has provided women with professional advantages because it has allowed them to bypass the male bureaucratic hierarchy and move quickly to the top in parallel female bureaucratic structures.

"Segregation here in Saudi Arabia has to a certain extent helped women when they entered the job market because that gave them the opportunity to take leadership positions which wouldn't have been possible if the workplace had not been segregated," sociologist Mani said.

June 16, 1987

Chapter 8

Crime and Deviance

E ach of the six articles in this section investigate aspects of crime and deviance in various societies around the world. Recall that sociologists use the term "deviance" to describe behavior that violates the norms of conduct and social expectations within a given population. Deviance is not an absolute; rather, it is socially defined. Crime occurs when formal laws (legal norms) are broken.

The first article in this section reports on the status of (still taboo) homosexuality in the Soviet Union. While not a crime, homosexuality is widely considered to be deviant. Following this is a report on how the press has begun to report on "the hidden side of life" in Moscow and Warsaw.

Why is crime so low in Japan compared to the United States? The article "'Shaming Rituals' Keeps Crime low in Japan," explores the thesis that Japanese rituals of shame deter crime in that society.

The final three articles in this section examine one of the world's most pressing social problems—drug abuse. The first of these cites a world health report that estimates at least 5 million people worldwide inject themselves with illegal drugs and that a much greater number otherwise consume them. Teenage guns for hire is the subject of the next article, which paints a horrifying picture of the rise in drug crimes in Columbia, South America. A similar phenomenon is occurring in Belize, a Caribbean port city, as L.A.-style gangs of teenagers traffic in cocaine.

In Age of Glasnost, Homosexuality is Still Taboo in the Soviet Union

David Remnick

Vitya and Pyotr consider themselves married.

Back when they were in their early twenties, both men frequented the Sadko Cafe off Gorki Street and the bus stops near the Bolshoi Theater, looking for one-night stands. But for the past six years they have settled down—sharing a two-room apartment on the fringe of Moscow, pooling their rubles and trying to live a reasonably normal life in a country where homosexuality can still bring consenting adults up to five years in a labor camp.

"We're the lucky few," Vitya said recently at the apartment. "For the most part, there is no 'gay life' in the Soviet Union. Mostly there is just sadness and living a lie."

Lawyers and scientists who have read drafts of a forthcoming revision of the Soviet criminal code say that Article 121, banning sex between men, will be eliminated. There are no laws against lesbianism.

But even in the age of glasnost, when the press is filled with everything from the details of the Gulag Archipelago to the horrors of Soviet abortion clinics, homosexuality is still a taboo that is considered, variously, a perversion, a regrettable illness and, according to one edition of the Great Soviet Encyclopedia, "a manifestation of western decadence." The chief sexual pathologist of Leningrad hospitals, Boris Malenkov, recently told the evening newspaper Vecherni Leningrad that he thought all homosexuals should be registered by the state so that "they can be treated."

"So you see, even the so-called experts know next to nothing about homosexuality. I'm afraid it's quite pathetic," said Igor Kon, a prominent sociologist here whose book, "Introduction to Sexology," was published in massive printings this year after a decade of censorship.

"People here think gays are depraved and want nothing more than rough sex or to seduce children," Ron said. "To change such attitudes would take a lot of time. Just to begin the discussion is dangerous."

"If you write an article, you are seen as defending an abominable phenomenon, and it automatically means you yourself are homosexual or devilish or part of a foreign conspiracy," he said.

In some ways, gays here believe, their situation has gotten worse, not better. In the "bad old days," Vitya said, when homosexuality was "never, ever" mentioned, he and dozens of other "light blues"—the slang term here for homosexuals—could visit the "Blue Ring" near the Bolshoi in relative peace. Usually police would arrest them only when they were seen as a threat to underage boys.

"In those days, it was like we were a disease that people would prefer to ignore," Vitya said. But now young gangs called remonti—literally, repairmen—seek out gays, beat them up and rob them.

"Maybe we'll get a new law, but I sometimes fear life here for us is going to get a lot worse before it gets better," Pyotr said. "I'm scared that people are already responding to our 'sudden appearance' with anger."

"From all I've read about gay life in the West," Vitya added, "living here now must be something like what was happening in the United States in the '50s. We're pariahs."

Vitya and Pyotr, who are in their early thirties, are well aware of the painful consequences of exposure. Their request for anonymity, they said, "is still an unfortunate necessity." For the most part, homosexual men and women in the Soviet Union lead furtive lives, marrying, even having children, as a kind of cover. Vitya and Pyotr know many gay friends who marry but withhold the truth from their spouses and content themselves with an occasional clandestine homosexual liaison.

"The overwhelming emotion for me, when I'm around my Soviet friends, is profound sadness," said a homosexual student from the West who is studying this year in Leningrad. "For their entire lives they are forced to live a terrible secret. The few gay couples I do meet seem to cling to each other, whether they are happy or not, because they see no other possibilities in their lives. They are absolutely stunned that at home I live with my lover and have an ordinary life."

Had it not been for the specter of AIDS, the silence surrounding homosexuality here might have continued indefinitely.

The first article on AIDS to appear here was in the relatively liberal weekly journal, Literaturnaya Gazeta, which announced to its readers three years ago that there was a new virus in the West that affected drug addicts and homosexuals. A vice minister of health at the time, Nikolai Burgasov, confirmed that the virus existed but said there was "nothing to fear" because in the Soviet Union narcotics and homosexuality were illegal. A later article in the same paper accused the CIA of creating the AIDS virus in a biological research laboratory at Ft. Detrick, Md. That charge eventually was retracted.

Over the past two years, the level of discussion about AIDS has grown considerably more sophisticated, and the government has become more willing to publicize the spread of the disease. Still, the accompanying discussion of homosexuality remains largely crude and fearful.

[In an article printed by the government newspaper Izvestia on Tuesday, Health Minister Yevgeny Chazov was quoted as saying that the AIDS "threat that we face is no less than the ecological 'bomb' or nuclear weapons," The Associated Press reported. The article said that the number of persons infected with the AIDS virus now exceeds 140, and it is expected that there will be "1,342 sick people" next year.]

Only recently has the Soviet press printed statistics about the extent of homosexuality in the country. According to pathologist Dr. Victor Zhdanov, between 2 percent and 5 percent of Soviet males and 1 to 3 percent of females are "purely" homosexual, while 48 percent of all men and 37 percent of all women have had some kind of homosexual experience or episode in their lifetime. The figures are roughly parallel to statistics on homosexuality in other urbanized industrial nations.

Recently, the Soviet youth journal Molodoi Kommunist printed a long article quoting letters sent by homosexual readers furious about the way the public and the press treat them.

"Our lives are hard even without AIDS," wrote a 27-year-old homosexual man who identified himself as Volodya D. "I've been homosexual since I was 12 years old. I was expelled from the Young Communist League for that, and I spent a year and a half in prison and was given 'medicine' there. After your terrible article (about AIDS), the number of suicides will surely go up. And if I ever get infected with AIDS, I'll get my revenge on people by infecting as many of them as I can. I've already suffered so much at the hands of the Soviet police, who won't touch murderers but prosecute homosexuals."

Another reader described how homosexuals resort to meeting in public toilets at railway and bus stations and how they avoid going to physicians for AIDS check-ups because they fear being turned in to the police.

At the Sadko Cafe, a cavernous place near the Kremlin that offers classically surly waitresses, sweet Georgian wine and unpalatable food, the tables are packed with young men who appear, in dress, language and mannerism, little different from their straight counterparts. It takes experience, as Vitya said, "to know who is blue."

"The same faces night after night," he said as he scanned the room. "There are thousands and thousands who are too scared to even think about coming to a place like this."

In the early days of the Bolshevik Revolution, there was a great deal of talk about exploding the "bourgeois mystification" of sex. Although Lenin was a puritan, many early Bolsheviks were relatively liberal about homosexuality and sex in general. Alexandra Kollantai, one of the few women in the revolutionary elite, shocked the world with her comment that sex was "like a glass of water," a momentary satisfaction of a kind of thirst.

But as the level of repression in the Soviet Union rose, so did suspicion of all sorts of minorities. Joseph Stalin introduced the first law against homosexuals in the 1930s. And since then, sex has been a subject mainly for private discussion.

For now, sex and sexual images, which are so pervasive in western advertising and popular culture, are almost absent here. Serious Soviet literature with sexual themes, such as some of Mikhail Kuzmin's poetry and the famous "Afanasyev's Tales," a compilation of erotic stories, have been published only abroad. When actors in films such as "Little Vera" are glimpsed naked for just a moment, the audience is taken aback. In schools there is no sex education.

Muscovites still remember with horror the night a few years ago, during one of the first "tele-bridges" between the United States and the Soviet Union, when the Americans began asking the Soviets about sexual issues. One Soviet woman, reddened with embarrassment and fury, rose from her chair and cried, "We in the Soviet Union do not have sex!" Since then, ironic buttons have appeared around town bearing a picture of the Kremlin and the logo, "We Have No Sex!"

There is little serious scholarship on sexual behavior in the Soviet Union. When one of Kon's graduate students at Leningrad State University, Sergei Golod, tried to conduct opinion polls on such subjects as premarital sex, the city's Communist Party committee refused to allow him to defend his resulting dissertation. The Central Committee of the Young Communist League declared Golod's report "ideologically subversive against Soviet youth."

On the way out of the Sadko cafe, Vitya seemed struck by what he called "the poverty of our lives." The meetings in public toilets, the "marriages for cover," the remonti who terrorize his friends—all of it seemed to weigh on him.

"I've known I was gay since I was 14 years old," he said, "and I am tired of being made to feel strange or sick or illegal. All I want is a normal life."

March 9, 1989

In Moscow and Warsaw, the Press Begins to Report on the Hidden Side of Life

Celestine Bohlen

Readers of the Moscow press were surprised recently by an article about the growing number of homosexuals in the Soviet Union. Before that, the big sensation was prostitution in one of the city's neighborhoods where, one newspaper reported, a policeman collected the names of about 3,500 "professionals" over a period of 15 years.

Revelations about the hidden side of Soviet society have been rolling off the presses at a regular pace lately. Drug addicts, whose existence was denied until a year ago, are now shown on the evening news. One magazine ran an article about homeless people who have no identification papers and are believed to number in the thousands. Youth gangs are another popular topic.

Backing up the feature articles, ministers, chief prosecutors and police are now interviewed regularly in the press about the causes of criminal behavior, from official corruption to factory thefts to murder.

"We have everything here, it is just that we kept it all hidden for so long," noted one young woman recently. "My generation knew about it, but for the older people, this has come as a shock."

The avalanche of bad news has exposed the gap between pretense and reality in this country. The admission that all is not as it was portrayed in the workers' paradise comes as both a jolt and a relief.

"What are we going on about?" asked another young Muscovite. "So we have prostitutes. Isn't that normal?"

Yet it was only five months ago that the chairman of a medical commission on drug and alcohol addiction, using the classic Soviet formulation, told the weekly magazine New Times: "We have eliminated such social phenomena as prostitution, pauperism and vagrancy."

Like the new reporting about accidents and natural disasters, the sociological revelations are the result of Communist Party leader Mikhail Gorbachev's policy of openness, or glasnost. In some cases they are accompanied by statistics that until recently were considered state secrets.

Thus, in a series of interviews, Alexander Vlasov, minister of internal affairs, has told the press the annual number of traffic deaths in the Soviet Union (40,000), the number of drug addicts (46,000), the number of moonshiners prosecuted last year (130,000) and the number of people disciplined last year for abusing their positions (200,000).

Still, some figures are held back. In a recent article on household robberies, a journalist complained that readers are told the number of thefts committed hourly, daily, weekly and yearly in North America, but nothing about their own country.

When the journalist put the question to authorities, he got a pre-glasnost response. In 1986, he was told, the number of apartment thefts "went down remarkably."

The failure to publish complete and reliable statistics—on crime, on the economy, on sociological developments—has been sternly criticized in the press by such leading advisers to Gorbachev as Tamara Zaslavskaya. "It is impossible to expect people to be active in political and industrial spheres if one hides generalized data about their living conditions from them," she wrote. Experts have argued publicly that the tendency to be tight-lipped and defensive has encouraged problems. For instance, they say, reticence about sex education has led to syphilis, unwanted pregnancies and other social problems.

In other cases, statistics are advanced, and countered with quick ideological rejoinders. A professor, commenting on recently released mental health statistics, noted that they confirmed the biological, rather than social, origins of psychiatric disorders since they are found in the Soviet Union, as well as the United States.

In some cases, the disclosures in the press mark the launching of a campaign. The first articles about drug abuse last spring led to a major crackdown by police and health officials. Many of the recent articles on prostitution point out the lack of laws against prostitution in the Soviet criminal code. Most consider it a safe bet that after the publicity, such a law will be enacted.

The most daring articles have also come in for criticism. The newspaper Romsomolskaya Pravda recently criticized the article on homosexuality as an exercise in "sensationalism" rather than an attempt to examine the issue.

The most recent article on prostitution hit like a bombshell. According to passers-by, on the day it came out in Sovietskaya Rossiya, readers clustered around the newspaper's display board to read it.

The article described the area in Moscow known as the "three-station" neighborhood for the railroad stations built around one square. According to the reporter, prostitutes of all sorts gather there: Muscovites, fresh arrivals from the provinces, call girls from downtown who have fallen on hard times, even a three-generation prostitution "dynasty." Prices vary, but the minimum is a glass of cheap wine.

Prostitution in the Soviet Union was officially acknowledged last fall in articles that dealt mainly with Moscow's high-class prostitutes who work the tourist hotels and get paid in hard currency.

Readers were stunned to learn that some of these call girls earn the equivalent of $150,000 in five years. But for the most part, the disclosures about "hard currency" prostitutes took few people here by surprise. The inside of tourist hotels is foreign territory to most Soviet citizens, who assume that prostitutes who cater to foreigners are under the control of authorities.

But the Sovietskaya Rossiya article was different.

"This is about us," said one Muscovite who was surprised only by the extent of degradation described in the piece. The details conjured up the kind of lower depths found in the novels of Feodor Dostoevsky, and never—until now—in the Soviet press.

The article pointed out the conflict between the reality of the three-station neighborhood and decades of denials. An older prostitute was detained by police for the eighth time, and the client expressed astonishment.

"There is no prostitution in our country, so maybe I'll write down 'a lady of loose morals,' " the policeman said.

April 4, 1987

'Shaming Rituals' Keep Crime Low in Japan: Why Not Here in America?

Russell Mokhiber

It's Willie Horton time again. President George Bush and Attorney General Dick Thornburgh have recently been pressuring Congress to pass the president's "tough" anti-crime bill that would, among other things, ensure that politicians can execute more criminals at a faster pace. Congress, in a panic over increased homicide rates from around the country, has responded enthusiastically: The House recently gave the president almost every item he wanted in passing a comprehensive crime bill.

Don't be surprised if these tactics prove useless. "Getting tough" on criminals—hiring more police to arrest them, building more prisons to warehouse them and passing laws that make it easier to execute more of them—has been tried before and has demonstrably failed to check the upward spiral of crime.

Crime rates in America and most Western countries have been on a steady climb since World War II. This year, according to FBI statistics, an estimated 23,000 people will be murdered in this country—a new record. Worse yet, it is becoming clear to experts that our conventional theories—chiefly rehabilitation, incapacitation and deterrence—have failed miserably. So have many of our familiar assumptions about what causes crime.

In the past few years, however, a new theory originating in Australia, that former penal colony, has kindled enthusiasm among scholars and policymakers alike. Based on the concept of public shame, it promises to shed new light on the causes and prevention of crime.

A New Old Idea

Over the past decade, John Braithwaite, a professor of social science at the Australian National University in Canberra, has turned from pathfinding studies of corporate crime to the broader question of crime and crime control. His recent works promise to shake the field. He and fellow Australian scholar Philip Pettit argue for a system of "reintegrative shaming."

In this conception, an individual is related to his community by rituals of shame and affirmation: the former provides both a disincentive for antisocial behavior and a means of public atonement; the latter offers the possibility of reintegrating the repentant criminal into the larger society. It is not a new notion. Many so-called "primitive" societies deter and punish crime through rites of ostracization. In ancient Rome, criminals had the doors of their houses burned. In Puritan New England, the stocks had a similar function; Hawthorne's Hester Prynne wore a scarlet letter. In modern-day societies which emphasize collective responsibility—such as China and Cuba—citizens publicly denounce wrongdoing as a part of the trial process.

Yet contemporary Western societies have forsaken this venerable apparatus. Our punishments take place out of the public eye, with no method whereby the criminal can express shame and atonement to victims or his community. Conversely, we have no system for restoring a punished criminal's place in his society or for removing the indelible stigma of the convict. Instead, Braithwaite says, we need a system that "sharply terminates disapproval with forgiveness, instead of amplifying deviance by progressively casting the deviant out," a system in which expressions of community disapproval are followed by "gestures of reacceptance into the community of law-abiding citizens."

Such a concept involves rethinking the entire nature of social disapproval and the forms it can take. Ideally, Braithwaite says, reintegrative shaming is a preventive strategy rather then a punitive one, entailing changes at the family, school and community level. Shaming methods can be as informal as frowns, shunning and gossip, or as stylized as public confrontation and humiliation. The important thing is that the opprobrium be intense and visible, followed by the opportunity for future readmission.

"When a parent punishes a child," Braithwaite says, "both parent and child know that afterward they will go on living together as before. The child gets his punishment as a matter of course—but within a continuum of love, rather than as a distinct and dangerous outsider."

In the larger social family, the theory implies that "punishment need be no more severe than is required to communicate the degree of community disapproval appropriate to the offense." The punishment should be visible and newsworthy "so that consciences can be molded by the unambiguous communication of the abhorrence that society extends toward criminal acts."

Braithwaite and his colleagues acknowledge that some criminals will have to be incarcerated. But if shaming and reintegration can truly control crime, then, as Braithwaite puts it, "contemporary imprisonment would seem a terribly misguided institution." Braithwaite and Pettit call for "less criminal law, less police surveillance, less prosecution and less punishment—until evidence emerges that crime increases as a result." Looking East ... and West Public shaming is gaining recognition in the United States. Last week, the U.S. Sentencing Commission approved an "adverse publicity" penalty (also known as the "Hester Prynne" sanction) for institutional crimes. Under the proposal, a judge would require a convicted corporation to publicize its conviction in newspapers or on TV. One shipbuilding corporation, convicted of toxic-waste dumping, recently was ordered to run an ad in The Wall Street Journal, and many judges around the nation have already ordered similar sanctions.

Traditionally, however, criminal justice systems in the West have moved to "uncouple" punishment from shaming. "The public visibility of the pillory and the chain-gang were replaced by penal practices to warehouse offenders away from public view," write Braithwaite and Pettit. "Public executions and flogging became private executions and floggings." While Braithwaite and Pettit applaud the demise of public flogging, they argue that "the uncoupling of shame and punishment. in many Western countries is an important factor in explaining the rising crime rates in those countries."

In contrast, Japan, which has seen a downward trend in crime rates since World War II, saw a "re-establishment of cultural traditions of shaming wrongdoers, including an effective coupling of shame and punishment." Braithwaite points out that while it is exceptionally rare in the United States for a corporate executive implicated in wrongdoing to publicly adopt a repentant role, in Japan "the public is regularly plied with media coverage of repentant executives pleading public forgiveness and promising corporate rehabilitation."

To be sure, Japanese society is much more rigid and ethnically homogeneous than many Westerners could tolerate. "Given the choice between living in Tokyo with its safe streets and its stultification of diversity, and living in New York with its dangerous streets, its high crime rate but its tolerance for diversity and its artistic and intellectual ferment, I would choose New York," says Braithwaite. "But I don't think that's the choice we have to make. We can choose to struggle for a society that is strong on toleration of diversity outside the constraints of the criminal law, but that is also very strong on disapproval of violation of the criminal law—that's both strong on rights and strong on duties to comply with the criminal law."

But could rituals of public shaming actually work in the United States, with its vastly heterogeneous population and wide variety of cultural values?

There is reason to doubt. Sociologist Thomas Scheff, of the University of California at Santa Barbara, says that in our civilization, shame is ignored: "Except under extreme circumstances, we deny its existence." Braithwaite concedes that it would be a mistake to "assume that Japanese cultural traditions of repentance can readily be transplanted to the West."

He cites two examples. In the first, two American servicemen were accused of raping a Japanese woman. They hired a Japanese lawyer who secured private reconciliation with the victim. A letter was presented to the court stating that the victim had been fully compensated and that she absolved the Americans completely. At a subsequent hearing, the judge asked the Americans if they had anything to say. "We are not guilty," the servicemen said. The Japanese lawyer cringed; it had not occurred to him that they would fail to assume the proper repentant role. The judge sentenced both men to a maximum term of imprisonment.

By contrast, the second example involves a Japanese woman who arrived in the United States with a large amount of U.S. dollars which she had not accurately declared on the entry form. It was not a case that would normally have been prosecuted: There was doubt that the woman understood the form; moreover, the law was designed to catch proceeds of illicit activity, and there was no suggestion that that was the case. After leaving the airport, the woman voluntarily wrote to the

Customs Service, acknowledged her violation and asked forgiveness. She raised no defense. The Justice Department prosecuted the case.

Those considerable cultural differences notwithstanding, Braithwaite believes that a fundamental social consensus can make shaming practices viable even among the most radically dissimilar cultures. After all, in Australia, he writes, "Aboriginals might reject the white man's criminal justice system, might believe that it discriminates viciously against blacks, might have a different view of the punishment appropriate, might view their traditional justice system as superior, but at least there is general agreement between Aboriginals and whites in Australia that the behavior criminalized by white man's law should be criminalized."

Of course, shaming is no panacea, and Braithwaite is conscious of the broader social forces that affect the crime rate. He acknowledges that societies with more unequal distribution of wealth and power will have greater crime problems at both ends: Inequality causes crimes of poverty motivated by need and crimes of wealth motivated by greed.

This problem is exacerbated by criminal-justice systems which encourage "disintegrative shaming," thus dividing the community by "creating a class of outcasts" and pushing offenders "toward criminal subcultures." The problem becomes particularly acute in societies in which large numbers of people are prone to humiliation. In a recent book, UCLA Sociologist Jack Katz puts forth his view that violence and rage are "livid with the awareness of humiliation." Humiliation directly provokes violence. "It is not by chance that homicides among mates so often spring from complaints about sexual performance and acknowledgments of sexual infidelity," writes Katz, who regards humiliation as a driving force in much violent crime.

October 28, 1990

World Health Report Cites Growth in Drug Abuse

Susan Okie

Abuse of heroin and other potent drugs is a growing global problem, affecting both industrialized and developing countries, according to World Health Organization (WHO) officials who will address a special United Nations session on the problem next week.

They said more prevention and treatment programs are urgently needed both to combat the medical and social consequences of drug use and to prevent the spread of AIDS, since most of the world's drug addicts are not yet infected with the virus that causes the disease.

Worldwide, the WHO estimates that at least 5 million people inject themselves with illegal drugs and that a much greater number eat, smoke, drink or chew them, according to Marcus Grant, senior scientist of the WHO Mental Health program.

He said the estimate for abusers of injectable drugs, based on individual countries' reports to the U.N. Division of Narcotic Drugs in Vienna, is conservative. There are 1.1 million to 1.3 million intravenous drug abusers in the United States alone, according to the National Institute on Drug Abuse.

Grant said several kinds of evidence indicate that drug abuse is on the increase worldwide.

"Many countries that have previously not been reporting that they have drug-abuse problems are now saying they do," he said. For example, in Nigeria, Kenya and Zimbabwe, which have large international airports, illicit drugs like heroin are showing up in nearby large cities. Until recently, he said, the only drugs commonly abused in Africa were alcohol and marijuana.

In West European countries, where drug abuse is an acknowledged problem, recent data show an upward trend in the use of heroin and other drugs, he said. Little information is available on Eastern Europe, but in Poland, where social and political change began several years earlier than in neighboring countries, "rates of drug abuse have increased quite dramatically over the last 10 years," he said.

In addition, data from regions of the world where use of certain drugs has long been common suggest that people are switching to new, more dangerous way of using the drugs. For example, chewing coca leaves—the natural source of cocaine—is a common and relatively innocuous habit among the peasants in the Andes Mountains of South America. But inhabitants of the region are increasingly using processed cocaine, a stronger and more dangerous form of the drug, Grant said.

Until recently, most heroin users in Southeast Asia smoked rather than injected the drug, but heroin injection is now becoming more common, he said.

Because of news media attention devoted to cocaine use in the United States, it is the drug causing the greatest concern worldwide, Grant said. But he added that so far, there is little evidence that cocaine abuse is widespread in other industrialized countries, although its use is becoming more frequent in Western Europe and Australia.

The AIDS epidemic lends added urgency to efforts to stem drug abuse, because blood-testing surveys indicate that the human immunodeficiency virus (HIV) that causes the fatal disorder has not yet infected the majority of the world's drug addicts, said Jonathan Mann, director of the WHO special program on AIDS.

He said rates of infection are highest in cities such as New York, Milan, Madrid and Buenos Aires, where more than 40 percent of addicts are infected. Infection rates are somewhat lower, from 10 to 40 percent, in San Francisco, Rome, Athens, Sao Paolo, Brazil, and Rio de Janeiro. The lowest infection rates among addicts, under 10 percent, prevail in many cities, such as Los Angeles, Montreal, and Hong Kong.

Mann said programs to prevent spread of the AIDS virus among drug abusers appear to be succeeding in several cities, contradicting a common view that addicts are "unreachable" with public health efforts.

February 17, 1990

In Medellin, Teenagers on Front Lines of Violence: 'We Have No Jobs, Nothing to Do...'

Douglas Farah

High in the slums that climb the steep hills surrounding the city known as the cocaine capital of the world, where houses are built almost on top of each other, 17-year-old Jimy tried to explain why boys in his neighborhood hired themselves out as assassins.

In Villa del Socorro, one of the most violent slums of the city with the highest murder rate in the world, he said there is little choice.

"We have no jobs and nothing to do, but we have to bring money home," he said. "We hear that they will pay so much to kill so and so, and more than one of us has had to do that."

"With the money you can buy motorcycles and the clothes with the right labels," Jimy said, staring at the ground. "Then girls will look at you. Without that, you are nothing." Like others in his group, Jimy wore braided necklaces and bracelets with hanging plastic images of the Virgin Mary for protection.

Sociologists call it "the culture of death," the combination of economic and social factors that, when mixed with the fast money of cocaine trafficking, turned Medellin into the cocaine and murder capital of the world, with teenage boys as the foot soldiers.

At the height of the drug war, from March to June, Medellin, a city of 1.6 million people 140 miles northwest of the capital, Bogota, averaged 40 murders a day. Since July 27, when the cocaine barons, who call themselves the "Extraditables," declared a unilateral truce, Medellin has been living in relative, but deceptive, peace.

The murder rate has dropped to about 12 a day, still chilling but about what it was before the war began 13 months ago.

Most of the dead are unidentified males 15 to 24 years old—killed by rival drug gangs, police seeking revenge for the killing of other policemen or in personal vendettas. Victims include more than 200 policemen, a senator, judges, journalists and other public figures.

The phenomenon of teenage guns for hire, called sicarios, has spawned a whole new academic field of study, "violentology."

Gen. Harold Bedoya, military commander for the Medellin area, said in an interview that by January, authorities had identified 120 bands of sicarios and had the names of about 2,000 hit men.

In exchange for assassinations, the boys get motorcycles, guns and money—keys to prestige and power for their normally short lives.

"These boys ... are people without a future, which makes them completely skeptical about life," says a soon-to-be-published study written by two Catholic priests who have worked in the slums for years. "The fear of dying young does not exist in these people."

People from the region have developed a reputation as the hardest working in the country. They often measure their worth in terms of material possessions. While they are extremely religious, their prayers to the Virgin Mary are often for material, not spiritual, well-being.

"People are taught to make money, legally if they can, but illegally if they have to," said a sociologist at a local university. "This helps explain why people are willing to work in a business where you kill people. The cultural conditions allowed it."

In the 1950s and 1960s, Medellin grew into the booming industrial center of the nation, producing textiles, construction materials and other goods. With the boom came massive migration from rural areas. But in the late 19705, the textile industry crashed, while the flood of rural migrants continued to expand the slums ringing the city, plunging Medellin into crisis.

At the same time, large-scale cocaine trafficking was just beginning; it needed a work force and a way to recycle the money flowing in.

Drug cartel leader Pablo Escobar and others poured money into the city by building luxury apartments as well as disco and entertainment centers. They became role models as hard-working entrepreneurs, the study said.

"Within drug trafficking, it became necessary to kill anyone who got in the way of the business," the study said.

In the slums, it is difficult to convince the people that there is a viable alternative.

Jimy and others from the neighborhood met in a bullet-pocked church recently with Maria Emma Mejia, the presidential counselor for Medellin, a job recently created by President Cesar Gavira, to discuss ways to end the violence.

With the help of a local priest and social worker, some had taken the first step on their own several months ago, working out an informal cease-fire among the three main gangs in the area, involving about 300 boys. The daily appearance of bodies on the streets stopped. But after several months of effort, the only progress toward creating legitimate work for the young men was a donation of two machines for making cement blocks—and the machines do not work.

While the government talked of the necessity of feasibility studies, the youths wanted to lodge complaints of police brutality and demanded immediate aid.

"The boys are losing interest, and more than 100 have already gone back to their old lives," said Elkin Ramirez, a social worker in Villa del Socorro. "We have a momentary peace, but without jobs and education, we will lose them all. We need help now, not studies."

October 7, 1990

Crack, L.A.-Style Gangs Trouble Torpid Belize: Cocaine Traffic Is Replacing Marijuana Industry

William Branigin

"Big Russian" leaned against a street-corner lamp post as his fellow gang members surveyed the passing traffic. Behind him, on the graffiti-covered walls of a shuttered pool hall, appeared the word "Blood," the aliases of some of his 25 "homeboys" and the name of their chapter, "Ghetto Child."

"We gonna die for our color, man," said Big Russian, 18, a self-avowed former drug runner in Los Angeles. "Blood not scared to die. Police don't sweat me, man. If they mess with me, it be like messin' with a ants' nest."

The accent, the jargon, the mixture of bravado and nihilism, the talk of gangs, street fights, drugs and muggings—all recalled the mean streets and troubled neighborhoods of Los Angeles. But the scene was this sleepy Caribbean port city in a country that has been a bastion of tranquility through years of war, economic dislocation and social unrest in the rest of Central America.

"Bloods," "Crips" and crack cocaine have come to Belize, and authorities seem powerless to do much about it.

Many Belizeans, including police and government officials, tend to dismiss the rival gangs as imitators who do little more than spray-paint walls with graffiti—the result, they say, of too much American television here and too many impressionable young Belizeans in Los Angeles and other U.S. cities. One youth, himself recently returned from Los Angeles aboard the two-stop flight that connects it with this city, summed up the gangs here as "Wanna Be's."

Yet, while the local Crips and Bloods may be pale shadows of their violent U.S. counterparts, they appear to be more numerous than authorities claim. And they apparently are linked with a growing problem of cocaine use here—the offshoot of increasing transshipment of the drug through Belize on its way from South America to the United States. Along with gang graffiti, crack houses have sprung up all over Belize City in the last year or so, a phenomenon unique in Central America.

A former British crown colony known as British Honduras, this sparsely populated land of swamp and jungle became self-governing in 1964, changed its name to Belize in 1973 and achieved full independence in September 1981. About half the Belizean population of 180,000 is of African descent, and about a third live in Belize City, the former capital.

The only English-speaking country in Central America, Belize has developed a peaceful two-party democracy and a budding tourist industry centered on its many cays, the longest barrier reef in the Western Hemisphere and jungle excursions to wildlife reserves and ancient Mayan ruins.

With its small population, Belize is an informal, easygoing country whose citizens can drop in on the prime minister and where no one seems in much of a rush. Watching American baseball on television is a national pasttime.

And, it is a country that, until a few years ago, ranked as the fourth leading foreign supplier of marijuana to the United States. In the mid-1980s "Belize Breeze," as the marijuana here was dubbed, was the country's leading cash crop, with a yield in 1985 of 645 metric tons, most of it exported to the United States. But a massive U.S.-sponsored eradication campaign whittled the crop down, leading to an estimated yield this year of about 73 metric tons.

Marijuana still is being smuggled from Belize, diplomatic sources say, but most of it now comes from the neighboring Peten region of northern Guatemala. The marijuana fields that remain in remote parts of Belize are largely tended by some of the country's estimated 60,000 illegal aliens from elsewhere in Central America—mainly Guatemalans, Salvadorans and Nicaraguans. Belizeans themselves disdain field work, diplomats and Belizean sources said.

Of greater concern, according to diplomats here and U.S. law-enforcement officials in the region, is the increasing use of the established marijuana-smuggling routes in the last couple of years by cocaine traffickers who use boats and light airplanes to take advantage of uninhabited cays and little-traveled highways. Some stretches of road were used so often to land and refuel drug flights that Belizean authorities erected steel poles along the roadsides to clip the planes' wings. But most of these have since been bent back out of harm's way.

Nevertheless, several drug flights have crashed here in the past two years, with the salvaged cocaine then finding its way onto the local market and "giving people a taste for it," one diplomat said. In addition, he said, drug dealers have started to pay for services with cocaine, adding to the local supply. Some of that is turned into crack in Belize, authorities believe.

"Three or four years ago, crack was nonexistent," said Arturo Gallego, a furniture upholsterer in a drug-ridden neighborhood. "It became a problem when marijuana was closed down. People say they can't get a decent joint anymore. Mr. Reagan burned it all down."

The new government here, elected Sept. 4 when the populist People's United Party of former prime minister George Price upset the more conservative United Democratic Party, denies as "total nonsense" opposition charges that local "drug barons" helped fund its campaign. "We're going to intensify the war against drugs in Belize," said Said Musa, the new deputy prime minister. "We consider that marijuana pales by comparison with crack and cocaine, which pose a deadly threat to the health and security of the country."

Authorities appear to take the gangs less seriously, however. "These young fellows, they copy everything off American television," said Police Commissioner Bernard Bevans. "We haven't really looked at it as a real law and order problem."

"It's not a problem now, but it's becoming one," said former home affairs minister Curl Thompson, who was in charge of internal security in the outgoing government. The gangs are "becoming more dangerous because of drugs."

Thompson said he knows of five crack houses in his own district in Belize City. "The cocaine is prevalent all over the country right now," he said. "It has superseded marijuana." He estimated, however, that Belize has no more than 75 Crips and Bloods, who he said are not real gang members but "only use the name."

A few blocks away, "Big Russian" told a different story. He said Belizeans who were members of the gangs in Los Angeles introduced them here, and that membership swelled after the movie "Colors" played to packed theaters. Now there are about 300 Bloods and 1,000 Crips in Belize City, said Big Russian, who refused to give his real name.

Speaking with a ghetto drawl and a permanent sneer, Big Russian said an older cousin brought him into the Bloods in Los Angeles and that he spent two years "selling dope" before returning to Belize in 1987. "Yeah, I got a job: - - - - people off," he said, using a slang term for mugging. "I'm my own boss. I get paid for doin' my job." He pulled out a half-inch wad of 100-Belizean-dollar notes, each worth $50.

Although Big Russian denied selling crack in Belize, an activity he attributed to the Crips, area residents said the two-story building he calls his base is a crack house. At one point, a woman driving a large American car with tinted windows pulled up, spoke briefly with gang members and drove off.

"We don't destroy our people," said Big Russian in explaining his denial. "We destroy the American side. We don't like the Americans. They two-faced." Besides, he said, the U.S. consulate here refused to give him a visa.

Nevertheless, he said, he planned to return to Los Angeles soon through Mexico, crossing the border illegally at Tijuana. "I want to go back now and make big money," he said.

Asked why he calls himself Big Russian, he looked around through half-closed eyes and said: "I'm like a young rebel star."

September 19, 1989

Chapter Nine

Social Institutions

S ocial institutions are orderly, enduring, and established ways of arranging behavior and doing things. Social relationships in institutions are structured for the purpose of performing tasks and accomplishing specific goals. A parent cares for his or her child. A government organizes and allocates scarce resources. A priest enacts religious rituals and provides leadership and comfort. Schools prepare students to be citizens and workers. Doctors and hospitals care for the sick. In the following sections, we examine, in turn, the institutions of Marriage and the Family, Politics, Religion, Education, and Health and Medicine. Each institution, in whatever form it takes within and among societies, has a profound influence on human existence.

Social Institutions: Marriage and Family

A Bride in India

Richard M. Weintraub

Like most weddings in India, it was a bittersweet occasion.

Rinku Roy, The Washington Post's New Delhi bureau assistant, an independent young woman with a winning personality and an occasional sharp word for recalcitrant bureaucrats, walked with the man chosen to be her husband seven times around the sacred fire as millions of Hindu brides have done for centuries.

The first hint of the impending event had come early last summer from Rinku's cousin, met during an assignment in Dubai to cover the Gulf war.

"They are looking for someone for Rinku, you know," she said.

At the time, Rinku herself said nothing. However, one day in late fall, she came into the office and sat silently at her desk, shuffling papers. Suddenly she turned and said, "I'm getting married."

The groom, found through an ad placed by his family in the marriage columns of the Sunday papers, was to be Debashish Ray Choudhry, a 36-year-old entrepreneur making his way in India's nascent computer industry.

From then it was only a matter of weeks until the families' priests determined that Feb. 8 was an auspicious date according to the horoscopes and family traditions.

Although it was Rinku's wish to marry, she grew apprehensive as the wedding day approached. "When all is said and done, it's going to be totally new, no matter what people say," she said. "For me, after 28 years, it will be all new."

Not only would she move abruptly from single to married life, she would be making the move most difficult of all for the Hindu bride—from the home in which she has grown up and been nurtured to becoming a member of her husband's family.

Nowhere is the separation between the Western world for which Rinku works and the Hindu world in which she lives more evident than in the customs surrounding a wedding. In India, it is the families that most often make a match, perhaps with a nod of agreement from the couple, perhaps not. The fact that the young woman is marrying not only a young man but also his family often weighs heavily in the decision.

In Rinku's case, her family had looked for a professional man, someone who had roots in Delhi as Rinku had, and a family that was socially progressive. As Bengalis, they naturally were looking for another Bengali. One ad looked particularly promising.

Rinku's mother and her brother Niloy, a doctor and a newlywed himself, contacted the Choudhry family and went to see them for the first time last April.

185

"We liked them," said Niloy, who had taken on new family responsibilities since the death of his father more than a year ago. "They also liked us. It turned out that one of their main goals was to find a professional woman who could be economically independent. This is a big change in the last 10 or 20 years."

Once the families had agreed, the prospective groom and his family came to visit Rinku at her home.

"They talked and had good vibes right away," said Niloy. The two families went ahead with the wedding plans, consulting priests and family horoscopes for the best day. While dowries play a major and often contentious role in negotiations for many marriages in India, they were not an issue in this marriage; a reformist movement among Bengalis in the early part of this century all but eliminated monetary dowries.

Rinku and Debashish met often and got to know each other, but for the most part it was tradition that took over.

In ritual and custom, much that followed, and especially the wedding itself, underscored the importance of Hindu life and of the shift for the woman from her own household to that of her husband.

After the wedding ceremonies the couple stays one night at the bride's house, a night of teasing for the newlyweds, and especially the husband. "A last reminder from us married girls to take care of her," said a cousin as she plotted the night's pranks.

Then, at dusk the following night, the bride and groom go to the husband's home, where she is welcomed formally by her new family and acknowledges her place within the household. It is all done symbolically at a dinner that follows ancient custom. The groom first serves food to his wife, symbolizing his pledge to support and provide for her, and she serves the other members of the groom's family, symbolizing her entry into the new household. She then spends the first night in the house not with her new husband, but with her mother-in-law.

It is only a day later, after these rituals, that the marriage is consummated.

The role as a new member of a different family weighs heavily on a bride-to-be.

"Here, we marry an entire family," explained a cousin of Rinku's. "A daughter-in-law is never everything that is expected. At home, you were everything. Here, you have to prove yourself. It takes a long time for them to accept you for what you are, not what they expect you to be."

Rinku and her fiance' had discussed this at length. Still, as the hours counted down, she admitted to being a bit ill at ease.

"I'm worried to some extent about acceptance by his family—in the sense of being treated like a daughter rather than a daughter-in-law," she said. "He is always very reassuring that there won't be a problem."

Rinku's family had anticipated this when they began the search for a husband. "Rinku has a mind of her own," said her brother. "Some time after Dad died, she thought about it and said she was ready for marriage, that she was ready to start life with someone else."

More than once Rinku would come into the office and grumble in jest about being put under "Section 144," a reference to a virtual martial law provision in India's internal security regulations.

By the day of the wedding, life was in the hands of aunts, cousins, sister-in-law and all-pervasive tradition. From early morning to late at night, ritual ruled the day—and Rinku.

During the ceremony, Rinku clutched a symbol of Laxmi, the Hindu goddess of abundance and fortune. Why? "I don't really know," she said, "but I'm to hold it until they tell me I don't have to anymore."

The big day began with each family holding a ceremony at its own house during which the family priest invoked the blessings of the family's ancestors on the new marriage, a linkage of past to present. Then, the women of the groom's family brought gifts of saris, clothing and other symbols of welcome to the home of the bride, a ritual that was reversed later in the day when the young men of the bride's family went to fetch the groom to begin the marriage ceremony itself. Each offering was accompanied by a fish, either real or symbolic, in a reminder of that great source of sustenance for the Bengali.

Later, the couple sat under the marriage canopy, built with the limbs of the banana tree and decorated with coconuts, symbols of richness and fertility. They walked seven times around the sacred fire, as couples have done since Vedic times thousands of years ago. As the rites ended, Rinku fed a sweet to a young boy who sat on her lap, invoking her society's emphasis on male children, and then she and Debashish gave sweets to each other in a common hope for the future shared by brides and grooms everywhere.

For the elders in the families, there is reason for all this, reason that says much about the essentially conservative and family-centered nature of Indian society.

All the use of symbols and rituals has "one concept behind it: to wish them happiness for their new life. It is mental preparation," said one of Rinku's uncles. "Our marriages are arranged, so the boy and the girl do not know each other. Convention and ritual take the place of getting to know."

More than a week and a half after the ceremonies, Rinku and Debashish were seeing off the last of the relatives and trying to get themselves settled in a small apartment. The place was very close to Debashish's family house, where they visited much of the day.

And they had begun to build a life together. Debashish has encouraged Rinku in her discussions with Indian newspapers about her career. But more to her liking, linking up her interest in journalism and his in computers, he also has spoken of a computerized news feature service that she might run, an idea that would be a technological leap for India.

And they were beginning to work on "getting to know."

February 28, 1988

A Case of Divided Loyalty for a Returning Native Son: Ghanaian Is Torn Between Wives, Cultures (PART 2)

Blaine Harden

Kwasi Oduro's face went slack with shock.

He had come home to his village in the Ghanaian forest for just three days to pay his respects to his family and to help out with medical bills. He had brought along Stella Adgei, his longtime girlfriend, to introduce her to his kin. He had expected nothing more trying out of the long weekend than his usual guilty discomfort over being unable to afford more than a fraction of his family's demands for money.

Certainly the last thing he expected was for his wife, Margaret, the mother of his five children, to follow him here from the capital, confront him publicly and accuse him of adultery.

Yet there Margaret was, standing defiantly in the middle of Dawu's one dirt street, with her baby boy, Yaw, strapped to her back. Shouting at the top of her lungs, she threatened Stella with physical violence and her husband of 15 years with divorce.

Oduro, 38, a lecturer in sociology at the University of Ghana in Accra, had approached Stella's parents in the traditional way last year, asking for her hand. He had been accepted and had told a few friends that Stella was his second wife. He always had been reluctant, however, to have a public wedding or to inform Margaret about the marriage.

He said he knew she wouldn't like it.

Oduro is like many village-born Africans whose education and career have catapulted them into a modern urban existence that is largely incomprehensible to the folks back home. His life essentially straddles several sets of incompatible values. "Several norms are competing for governance," is how Oduro, the sociologist, puts it.

As a boy here in the village, he used to race on Sunday mornings from mass at the Catholic church to sacrificial ceremonies at the fetish house, where a pagan priestess sometimes allowed him to eat freshly slaughtered meat.

An outstanding student, he was—and remains—the only person from his village to obtain a post-graduate university degree. His education has distanced him, he says, from the tribal rituals, land jealousies and witchcraft that color daily life in his village. Yet, he admits that he often worries about what his relatives and villagers are saying about him behind his back.

His three-bedroom house in Accra always is crowded with distant village kin—11 at present—who show up on his doorstep and whom Oduro is reluctant to turn away. He says he fears they will return home and poison his good name.

188

Polygamy is an accepted and honorable institution in his village and among his tribe, the Ashanti, as it is across much of Africa. But still, Oduro has not made up his mind about it. As a born-again Christian, he says he has "moral problems" with having two wives.

In any case, here in front of his father and assorted villagers, Margaret breathed fire into the issue of polygamy. She transformed it from an ethical dilemma to, as Oduro later called it, "a public embarrassment."

He grabbed Margaret's wrist to prevent her from hitting Stella. He told Stella to take a walk. His father, who witnessed the confrontation from the stoop of his house, called the unhappy couple to come inside to talk.

Once they were inside, Margaret told Oduro, "I followed you home because I wanted to make sure we were not seen in Accra again as man and wife."

Divorce in the Ashanti tribe is a simple affair. A wife need only take a bottle of schnapps to the elders in her husband's family and explain why the marriage cannot work. The husband is then invited by the elders to give an account of himself. If everyone agrees the marriage is hopeless, it is dissolved.

What makes divorce relatively easy is that the Ashanti, like many tribal groups in west and central Africa, are matrilineal.

Property is inherited from the mother's side of the family. Man and wife often live in separate houses: the man in his mother's house, the wife and children in her mother's house.

Even when they are happily married, the future security of their children is the responsibility of the wife's brothers.

By the complex rules of this system, Oduro later explained, his wife was not in a strong financial position to take schnapps to the elders.

She would, of course, have custody of their five children. But Margaret's mother is dead, and she does not have a maternal family house to retreat to with her children. Nor does she have a job.

"She has a wealthy half-brother, but he is her father's son and not a product of her mother's womb, so she has no claim to his wealth," Oduro said. "My wife's options are limited. It took a while, but she came to her senses."

The next morning, a Sunday, Margaret appeared to have calmed down. Several village women had advised her that she had overplayed her cards. At midday, she walked into Oduro's mother's house to say good-bye. Stella was there, sucking on an orange, and Margaret pointedly ignored her.

Instead, she peeled several oranges for her husband, whose polygamy she had been forced to accept. She gossiped with her mother-in-law and then left. With her baby again on her back, she caught a minibus for the six-hour ride back to Accra.

With his first wife gone, Oduro was free to attend to the family responsibilities that, after a year's absence, had brought him back to his village. His parents, aunt and sister needed money. He made the rounds, going first to his father's house.

He gave his father $42 for a badly needed blood test. His sister then received $10 for school fees for her five children, while $10 went to his aunt so a dentist could mend her splayed and badly decayed front teeth.

Government programs such as medicare, social security, unemployment insurance and court-ordered child support do not exist or do not work in Africa. So the social safety net is, by default, the extended family.

In the case of Oduro's family, the safety net is, by default, Oduro—the eldest son and the only person in his family with a higher education and regular salary in the city.

As Africa has grown poorer, with incomes from farm commodities declining steadily, many rural Africans have come to depend on remittances from wage-earning kin in cities. For decades, the convoluted priorities of independent African governments, including Ghana's, reinforced these expectations.

To keep urban constituents happy, governments subsidized the housing, transport and food bills of many city dwellers. They also dished out tens of thousands of government jobs. This was a policy of self-preservation: unhappy city people in Africa have a habit of toppling governments.

Governments funded urban subsidies by creaming off most of the foreign exchange earnings of farm exports. Farmers were paid only a fraction of what their crops were worth on the world market. This inequitable system collapsed in Ghana, as elsewhere, as demoralized farmers neglected their cocoa trees, changed to growing crops they could eat or smuggled their cocoa out of the country.

Five years ago, after a quarter century of bleeding the countryside to pump money into the city—which the extended family, in turn, pumped back out to the countryside—the government of Ghana decided to reverse the flow of resources. It passed along a much higher percentage of world cocoa prices to growers and started firing government employees.

The free-market strategy worked, up to a point. For the first time, farmers had a real incentive to work hard. Cocoa production rose, and the economy grew. The point at which the magic of the marketplace fizzled, however, was when the world price for cocoa fizzled. That was last year. Since then Ghana's economy has been reeling.

For a university lecturer such as Oduro, the effect of this macro-economic flip-flop has been a guilt-soured mixture of hardship for his urban family and unrelenting demands from the folks back home.

Because of frequent devaluations of Ghana's currency, the dollar value of his monthly check has been cut by two-thirds since 1983 as food prices have soared.

"My monthly salary (when it was worth about $300) used to cover us for about a month. Now my wife and I realize that it is now between seven and 10 days before the money is gone," said Oduro.

At the same time, however, the needs of Oduro's extended family have not lessened.

The price of the cocoa they grow is at a 23-year low.

Oduro says that he goes home these days as infrequently as his conscience will allow him to.

He recently received an academic research grant of $160 and said he felt quite compelled, after ignoring his family for a year, to travel and spread it around.

"I am an economic exile," Oduro said. "The extended family for me is a way of spreading poverty."

Ghana's macro-economic mess does not register with Oduro's mother.

Nana Adwoa Achaah, 60, needs drugs to treat her ulcer, wants $400 to have electricity installed in her house and would like some capital to buy goods for trading. As a "queen mother," an Ashanti title making her the principle female guardian of tribal traditions in this village, she also needs extra money for ceremonial regalia, including new clothes and alcohol for the many funerals she attends.

"Now that he is working, I expect Oduro should help me to get on. It was a form of investment to help him in his education. I am the queen mother, and Oduro is the one who should help me to perform my public duties by raising my standards," she said.

It was his mother who made sure that Oduro finished school. To pay his school fees, she sold two valuable garments of hand-woven kente cloth—the multicolored apparel of Ashanti royalty. When, at age 16, Oduro fathered an illegitimate child, she took care of the baby until the mother—whom Oduro did not marry—was out of school.

"If it had not been for my mother," Oduro said, "that scrape would have cost me my education."

For these reasons, Oduro said he has a hard time refusing his mother's requests for money. He gave her all he had left of the money he brought home. "A drop in the ocean of her needs," Oduro said. His grateful mother made him a nice lunch of fufu, a dish made of pounded plantain and cassava in peanut soup.

Demands for money are only one of the burdens that fall on the shoulders of those Africans whose educations have allowed them to escape the village.

Recognized for their supposed expertise in the ways of the modern world, "learned men" such as Oduro are called upon by their kin to resolve conflicts that arise as the late 20th century continues to steamroll the medieval agrarian culture of the African village.

Whenever Oduro goes home, he is asked to wrestle with family land disputes. This trip was no exception.

Land fights, on a continent with the highest population growth rate in the history of the world, are a worsening curse. The World Bank predicts the population of sub-Saharan Africa will nearly quadruple in the next 60 years, to 1.8 billion. In that time, Ghana's population is expected to swell from 14 million to about 53 million. Already, population pressures are forcing changes in centuries-old patterns of land inheritance.

"Certainly new members of the family will not have land," said Oduro. "For the first time in the history of the village, a landless class is being created. It is an unfolding process. Right now, I must admit I am landless."

Tribal traditions that had made property an indivisible, communal holding of the extended family are giving way to new national laws that allow a father to divide up his holdings among his wife and children.

The value of land itself has changed with extensive planting of cash crops rather than food crops. Cocoa trees are a long-term investment, requiring years of expert care. The land on which the trees grow has been transformed from a communal resource that feeds a large extended family to one that puts money into an individual farmer's pocket.

One of Oduro's maternal uncles seized the occasion of his nephew's weekend visit to argue for a radical division of family property. When Oduro finished his meal, his uncle, Peter Amoakahene, invited him for a walk in the cocoa farm that borders the village.

Amoakahene has a reputation in the village as a man with spiritual powers. He was once forced by a village council to confess to being a wizard. He also has a reputation for knowing how to make money. He manages the family's cocoa farm, a large communal holding that in a good year can earn up to $15,000.

As they walked through the rolling and heavily forested land, he explained to his nephew how the farm should be carved up five ways—a fifth for himself and the rest to each of his two brothers and two sisters.

The uncle argued that only Oduro's mother—the uncle's sister—opposed the division. He claimed she was standing in the way of progress and that the farm could be better managed if it were divided into smaller pieces.

After the walk, Oduro's mother buttonholed her son for rebuttal. She sat him down in her house to explain why her brother's scheme was evil. She said she was not afraid of her brother's reputation as a wizard.

If the land were divided five ways, she said, then her brothers could decide to invoke a 1985 Ghanaian law that would allow them to pass on their land to their own children. This would violate the matrilineal Ashanti system. Tribal law mandates that family land may only be passed down along the maternal side of a family.

His mother said that her brothers were intent on destroying the family's most valuable resource—its communal land. She begged Oduro to use his education to make her brothers leave the land alone.

Oduro, as he explained it later, refused to take sides. He had left his village, he said, and sought an education in order to escape endless disputes about land—not to acquire expertise in arbitrating them.

Since he no longer lives in the village, does not know how to farm cocoa and does not want to learn—he said he wanted nothing to do with the dispute. He told his mother and his uncle it was their problem.

Quarrels about land, like incessant requests for money, make Oduro despair of his family.

"I want out of the extended family trap, and when my mother dies, I don't think I will go back to the village anymore," he said.

Late Sunday afternoon, Oduro ended his visit home. He and Stella impatiently ate another dish of his mother's fufu. His sister presented him with 50 pounds of plantains and cassava that she had spent much of the weekend gathering in nearby fields.

Anxious to leave, Oduro quickly loaded the produce into a minibus that was making an evening run back to Accra. Yes, he promised his mother, before the bus roared away, he would be back.

"The fact that they are quarreling shows the strains rural people live under in this country," he said on the ride back to Accra.

"At one level, they are arguing on a customary level, invoking traditions and making threats about witchcraft. At another, they are working according to the norms of the commercial economy and their desire to control as much land for themselves as possible."

He slipped easily, eagerly, into the jargon of sociology. His mood improved. The impersonal language of his city profession seemed to give Oduro a comforting distance from the demands of his village and his family—and from that part of himself that remains tied to both.

November 21, 1988

Therapists Rethink Attitudes on Divorce: New Movement to Save Marriages Focuses on Impact on Children

Paul Taylor

When Cathy Hicks was drifting toward her third divorce last year, she kept telling herself it would be best for the kids.

"I've always thought that if parents can't bring a child up in a happy home, everyone is better off if there's a divorce," said Hicks, 40, who has a 19-year-old daughter by her first husband and 12-year-old son by her second.

Until recently, she wouldn't have gotten much argument from psychologists, sociologists, marriage counselors, family scholars. The United States always has been the most divorce-prone society in the world, and as rates started to soar in the mid-1960s, a good deal of elite opinion focused more on the expansion in freedom for adults than on the possible harm to children of broken marriages.

"I think we were all real naive for a while in thinking that divorce did not have a serious impact on kids," said Anna Beth Benningfield, president-elect of the American Association for Marriage and Family Therapy (AAMFT), which has been debating whether counselors should bring a more anti-divorce bias to therapy. "But I'd say the bloom is off the rose."

The second look has been triggered by new studies that show that the harmful effects of divorce on children are longer-lasting than once had been thought. Children of divorce perform less well in school, have more behavioral and psychological problems and a greater tendency (once they become adults) to divorce than children raised by both biological parents.

To be sure, domestic violence and other problems of high-conflict marriages are damaging to children, and even experts intent on saving marriages acknowledge that divorce is sometimes the best alternative. "We want to be careful not to say that every child who has been through a divorce will be scarred for life ... or that every child raised in a traditional two-parent family will turn out fine," said Nicholas Sill, executive director of Child Trends Inc., a Washington-based firm that does research on children's issues.

"But if you looked at the kind of long-term risk factors that divorce creates for kids and translated them to, say, heart disease, people would be startled," he said.

"For years experts said, 'Once the initial trauma wears off, kids make adjustments.' Well, so do people in prisons and mental institutions," said John Guidubaldi, a psychology professor at Kent State University and past president of the National Association of School Psychologists. "The pertinent question is: Are those adjustments healthy? The weight of the evidence has become overwhelming on the side that they aren't."

Guidubaldi argues that laws and mores have gone too far in sanctioning no-fault, no-guilt divorce. "People simply aren't putting enough effort into saving their marriages," he said. "I think the old argument of staying together for the sake of the kids is still the best argument."

Such views are still controversial. But in the past few years, a rally-'round-marriage movement has begun to stir among psychologists who worry about the impact of divorce on children, legal scholars who argue that a children-first policy should be written into divorce law, and marriage counselors who have come to believe that divorce is a cure worse than the disease.

One sign of the times was the the title of the keynote address at the annual meeting of the 17,000 member AAMFT last fall: "Divorce-Buster."

"I'm passionate about saving marriages," said Michele Weiner-Davis, a Woodstock, Ill., family therapist who delivered the address. Her modus operandi, she explained, is to "concentrate on what works in a couple's marriage rather than on what doesn't."

When Cathy and Jerry Hicks came in to see her last fall, Weiner-Davis instructed them to draw up a list of the things they did together that made them happiest, then rearrange their daily routines so they did those things as often as possible. She told them to negotiate a specific number of hours each weekend that Jerry would do housework, which had been a source of friction.

And she suggested that if Cathy felt she needed to ask questions about past conflicts that had led to her to brink of divorce, such conversations should have a strict half-hour time limit.

"A lot of her homework exercises seemed sort of silly, but it turned out to be exactly what we needed," said Jerry, an executive with a telecommunications company. "I feel more committed to our marriage than I ever have," said Cathy.

Not all cases have such happy endings; nor is there any guarantee that there aren't rough patches ahead for the Hicks. But Weiner-Davis is convinced that counselors can—and should—make a difference in keeping marriages together.

This is causing conflict within the therapeutic community. Classical clinical training teaches counselors to be bias-free; to help clients do whatever seems most appropriate given their particular circumstances. "The trouble with therapists trying to impose their values on clients is that it's the clients who have to live with the consequences," noted Benningfield, the AAMFT president-elect.

"Divorce has become a scapegoat, the easy sacrificial institution on which to lay blame for many of society's problems," said Constance Ahrons, a California therapist who spoke at the AAMFT conference in response to Weiner-Davis. She said that divorce is "often a pathway to a happier life."

Weiner-Davis counters that there is no such thing as value-free counseling. "We declare our biases by the questions we choose to ask," she said. "For a therapist to be neutral when someone is about to jump off a building—that's not neutrality," added Frank Pittman, a therapist from Atlanta and another staunch marriage-saver. "I have always felt that people who are in crisis make bad decisions. It is foolhardy to expect otherwise. It's our job to give them a reality check."

These "reality checks" may already be rippling through the culture. After doubling from 1965 to 1980, divorce rates have plateaued at a level about 10 percent below their peak of a decade ago. Some analysts attribute the decline to the fear of AIDS; others to the aging of much of the Baby-Room generation out of their twenties—the high-risk divorce years.

But some speculate that the research on the long-term consequences of divorce has led to social learning. "I've had family therapists all over the country tell me they have couples coming in for counseling with my book tucked under their arm and a look of concern on their faces," said Judith S. Wallerstein, whose best-selling 1989 book, "Second Chances: Men, Women and Children a Decade After Divorce," popularized the alarmist view of the impact of divorce on children.

Among other findings, the study by Wallerstein and Sandra Blakeslee of 60 middle-class divorced families in Marin County, Calif., showed that while boys are apt to experience the greatest trauma at the time of divorce and suffer most from the father-absence that typically follows divorce, girls are more prone to a "sleeper effect" that makes it difficult for them to establish stable male-female relationships once they become adults.

An ongoing decade-long study by Guidubaldi of 699 families in 38 states has shown that children of divorce are more likely than children in traditional intact families to engage in drug abuse, violent behavior, suicide and out-of-wedlock child bearing. A study by Sill for the National Institute of Mental Health showed that, once they become adolescents, children who were under age 7 when their parents were divorced were three times more likely to be receiving psychological counseling and five times more likely to have been suspended or expelled from school than children of intact families.

Critics of these studies note that when one compares children of divorce to children of conflict-ridden families, the results are murkier. Sill counters that only about 15 percent of marriages involve violence or high levels of conflict, but roughly 50 percent of marriages end in divorce. "There is no question that persistent conflict in marriage is bad for children, but a lot of divorces don't fall in that category," he said.

Marriage counselors aren't the only professionals who are reappraising divorce. Harvard law professor Mary Ann Glendon has proposed an overhaul of divorce laws to assure that, in the 60 percent of all divorces involving minor children, "a judge's main task would be to piece together, from property and income and in-kind personal care, the best possible package to meet the needs of children and their physical custodian."

No state has language like that in its divorce code. Studies show that following a divorce, children and their custodial parent—typically their mother—see their standard of living drop sharply, while non-custodial parents see theirs rise.

Others have called for a cooling-off period to be built into divorce proceedings when children are involved, and—in the most draconian proposal of the burgeoning divorce-buster movement—historian and author Christopher Lasch has called for a constitutional amendment that would forbid parents with minor children from divorcing.

Will the new activism on the anti-divorce front change people's behavior?

"I may be wildly and foolishly optimistic," said Sill, "but as more information gets out that we have yet to find a good substitute for the traditional two-parent family, I think a change is bound to occur."

"Divorce is here to stay," countered Ahrons, a marriage counselor who looks askance at the divorce-buster movement. "We ought to help people learn how to manage it, which is not an easy thing."

January 29, 1991

Refugee Family Builds World-Class Empire: Adversity Met by Hard Work, Risk Taking

Fred Hiatt

In 1946, 8-year-old Kim Young Chull stuffed his ice skates into a knapsack and, leaving everything else behind, fled with his family from communist North Korea to the U.S.-occupied South.

After hiking across mountains through the night, the family reached the narrow trench that marked the border.

"Somebody said, 'This is the 38th parallel, now you are free,' " Kim recently recalled. "Then a big GI appeared out of a white tent, lifted our arms and sprayed each of us with DDT. We all looked like white rabbits."

From that modest beginning, Kim, his parents and seven siblings began an odyssey that would parallel the remarkable shaping of their nation. In the next four decades, the Kims would be turned into refugees twice, rendered bankrupt three times, shot at, bombed out and kicked around by their American patrons.

They also, like many of their compatriots, would rise above every adversity. Today, the five Kim brothers are among South Korea's most successful businessmen, founders of Jindo Industries Ltd., the world's largest manufacturer of fur garments and, like many South Korean companies, a growing power on the world economic scene. They have bought sports car factories in Britain and opened stores on West 57th Street in Manhattan. They drive Mercedes cars in Seoul, own homes outside London, go marlin fishing in Guam and swing deals in Moscow.

In a nation where the average per capita income is only now reaching $3,000 a year, the Kim brothers' wealth is not typical. The workers who sew Jindo furs, many of them teen-age girls, work six days a week for $300 a month.

And in a culture marked by Confucian deference to hierarchy, the five brothers' easygoing, wisecracking friendship also sets them apart.

Yet, the Kims' success and South Korea's success are not easily separated. Hard work, a gambling instinct, fierce self-confidence and more hard work shaped the Kims and helped South Korea overcome the split from the North, the ruin of a civil war, the absence of natural resources, the cramming of 40 million people into a craggy peninsula of rock no bigger than Virginia and the worldwide perception that South Korea was, not so long ago, close to being another Third World basket case.

The Kims, too, despite their informal style, share a traditional Korean respect for family. The five brothers have always stuck together. The No. 1 son, Kim Yung Won, is chairman of the firm and treated with respect by his brothers. A bust of their late father holds center place in the head office, facing a painting of his Pyongyang home.

The extended Kim family reflects the generational changes now affecting the society as a whole. While the brothers painfully remember the long climb from division, war and poverty and accept the halting pace of reform, their children, with no such memories, are impatient for democracy.

The family also reflects the preeminence Korean society accords its males. The Kim sisters married and moved away to make their lives with their husbands' families, unconnected to Jindo.

And since the moment they were sprayed with U.S. delousing powder, the Kims have shared the South Korean ambivalence toward "big brother," the United States. Like South Korea itself, the Kims could not have succeeded without America—without the U.S. military that was long their only customer, the U.S. technology that got them started or the American generosity that prompted Arkansas City Junior College to give the eldest two brothers full scholarships in the 1950s. But the Kims share with the nation a memory of what they view as past insults and a determination to shed the role of "little brother."

"The saddest thing was, nobody knew anything about Korea," Young Chull, 50, recalled of his college days in Kansas. "They all thought I must be an orphan, or my mother must run a laundry shop. I tried to tell them that Korea also has a culture, also has good people. I never could succeed.

"That's why now, when Korea is booming, cars are being exported, VCRs, we have a certain pride, at least my generation," he said. "'Like with the Olympic Games. I mean, when I told these people in Kansas, 'Korea,' they kept asking, 'Where do you live? Do you live in trees?' So I'm glad now they'll understand what Korea is all about."

An Entrepreneurial Flair

Kim Sung Shik was born on a farm in northern Korea shortly after the turn of the century. The eldest of three sons, he was 19 when his father died, and the responsibility of supporting the family fell to him.

In about 1923, he moved to Pyongyang, then a provincial capital in the budding Japanese empire, and began driving the streetcars installed by the Japanese.

"Streetcar drivers were treated like a big deal, they wore uniforms, the Japanese paid them well," son Young Chull said. "These were high-tech things."

Kim had an aptitude for new technology, and he realized that automobiles were the coming thing, even though precious few rode the streets of Pyongyang in those days. He traveled to Japan, learned to drive and returned to establish the Automobile Technical Training School—in short, a driving school.

"In those days, getting a driver's license was like getting a pass to Harvard," Young Chull said. "You were sure to have a job."

Kim prospered with the school, and then with a taxi company and a garage. With the profits, he bought land—acres and acres of apple orchards. Unlike some Koreans—including his father-in-law, who was killed in an anti-Japanese uprising in 1919—Kim made peace with the colonial masters. As with many Koreans, it is a legacy that troubles the fiercely nationalistic younger generation.

"We were never, never told, 'Japan is not really your country,' " said Young Chull, who remembers a teacher once chalking his tongue for speaking Korean in school, where only Japanese was permitted.

"I asked him once, 'Dad, what did you do in the March 1st {anti-Japanese} movement? What did you do?' He said, 'Oh, we hid on a mountainside behind the house.' ... I was so disappointed." When the Soviet Union occupied northern Korea in 1945 after the Japanese defeat in World War II, Kim was in trouble.

"Of course, the North Koreans said, 'You are landlords, you are capitalists, you must be punished,' " Young Chull said. "These guys kept putting my father into jail."

Two Soviet generals of Korean descent had moved into the Kim house, one of the few in Pyongyang with flush toilets, and had befriended the family. But one night, the generals told Kim they could no longer protect him.

Kim's mother-in-law packed the heavy lid to the rice cooker she had polished every day. Kim took the deeds to his apple orchards, worthless documents the family still preserves. Kim's wife put a baby on her back and a bundle on her head, and the family headed south.

"It had nothing to do with democracy, or Yankee side or Russky side. It had nothing to do with that," Young Chull said. "We knew exactly why we had to leave everything and come down, because my father kept being arrested."

With a little gold smuggled from Pyongyang, Kim started again in the U.S.-controlled South, opening an auto-parts store and gradually rebuilding. But in 1950 the North invaded, and everything was lost again. As tanks rumbled into the capital, the family joined thousands of other Koreans walking south, dragging carts loaded with their possessions through the mud.

"I remember it was drizzling, and my daddy carried me on his back," said Kim Young Jin, 47. "But just as we reached the Han River, we saw the bridge explode."

Today, 18 bridges connect north and south Seoul across the Han. But in 1950, when a panicked South Korean Army in retreat blew up the only bridge, the Kims and thousands of others were trapped. During the next three months of North Korean occupation, many accused of being capitalists were shot.

Kim, however, was protected by a former driving student, by then a major in North Korea's Transportation Battalion 485, who set up a motor pool in the Kims' backyard. Living part of the time in a storm sewer, scrounging rice, the Kims were among the lucky ones; they all survived until Gen. Douglas MacArthur's forces arrived.

"I went out to see the Marines coming in," Kim Young Chull recalled of September 1950. "These GIs, they were so big, chewing gum, throwing us candy. One of them stood up in his tank, in the middle of this battle, and threw me a baseball. They were, well, we didn't know what gods were then, but that's what they were."

The Kims moved to a refugee center in Pusan, where the 10th and final child was born (five boys and five girls, two of whom died in infancy). And when the war ended in 1953, they moved back to Seoul and started yet again, in a nation that had lost 350,000 people and most of its roads, railroads and factories.

"There was no business in Korea in those days. Industry then was a noodle shop, a cake shop," Young Chull said. "The only way to have a business was to deal with the Americans. They were the only ones with money."

So Kim went to the Americans and won a contract to rebuild Jeep engines. He ran a gasoline station on the U.S. Army base and a motor pool in the U.S. Embassy. Eventually, in the mid-1960s, he won a contract to build city buses from U.S. Army scrap. "The buses sort of moved sideways, like crabs," one son recalled.

Through it all, he was motivated by a love of cars, a loyalty to his family and the universal Korean desire to send his sons to college. Kim also believed that doing well in business was the best way to do good for others. Young Chull remembers once asking his father to contribute to a charity. "Giving money like that isn't going to help anybody," Kim told his son. "The way to help people is by creating jobs."

In 1967, Kim's business—then known as the Korea General Corp.—went bankrupt. The government would not allow imports of materials for buses, the U.S. Army was not discarding scrap fast enough and the company could not fill its orders.

By then, Kim's five sons were ready to step in and, once again, begin rebuilding. As a new company took shape, Kim played the patriarch, less active day-to-day but determined to keep his sons united, until he died in 1981 at the age of 77.

"My parents never told us about nationalism, Korea, patriotism; nothing, except brothers have to stick together," Young Chull recalled. "In the hospital, one by one he called us in and told us, stick together, stick together."

Rebuilding From Bankruptcy

When the business faltered, it fell to Kim Young Jin, the third son, to help pick up the pieces. The first two boys went to Kansas for college; the two younger boys, now Jindo executives too, weren't old enough. Young Jin stayed home, attending Yonsei University's business school.

Today, with his crisp white shirts and narrow ties, Young Jin, 47, is as fashionable as his brothers, and he travels overseas every month. But he remains in some ways the inside man, quick with figures, reluctant to speak with reporters, good-natured and guileless.

"Many people in Korea have grown up the way we did: 20 years ago, nothing—and then export, export, export," Young Jin said, recalling the Japanese model that Koreans hoped would lead to their own prosperity.

But in the mid-1960s, it was far from clear what the Kims could export. They tried marketing brassware to Sears, miniature Dutch wooden shoes to the

Netherlands and paper parasols to "Polynesian" restaurants—all without much success.

Then Young Jin lugged his Smith-Corona typewriter to the U.S. Embassy library and copied the address of every Manhattan furrier from the telephone directory. "We have inexpensive labor," he wrote to hundreds of them. "Why don't you send us your scrap, and we'll make hats for you?"

Today, as thousands of sleek minks hang in the Jindo factory and Jindo representatives dominate fur auctions from Finland to San Francisco, the audacity of Young Jin's dream is hard to recall. "When the furriers came in, they thought it was crazy," brother Young Chull said. " 'It takes a whole generation to learn the fur business,' they said. 'How can you learn it? Just forget about it.' "

At the time, South Korea was still desperately poor. Average income per person had recently passed $100. At a time when Japan was still known for shoddy goods, South Korea was hardly on the map. But in 1966, Young Jin won a contract—a $1,030 order to make 10,000 pompons, he recalls. Young Chull then flew to London to win a second order for $20,000.

New York furriers began sending scraps—fox paws, muskrat heads, rabbit tails. Teen-age girls, sitting on the floor and sewing by hand, working 365 days a year for about $20 per month, would turn the scraps into hats, hoods and "$29 coats for Broadway hookers," Young Chull recalled.

By the mid-1970s, Young Jin had an even more radical idea: to demystify fur-buying and create a mass market. Jindo would buy and treat pelts and turn them into coats that could be sold for half the normal price.

Again, the New York furriers laughed. "No one would believe we could make mink," Young Jin recalled. "That was a privilege of the New York furriers."

By then, though, Kim had seen the New York workshops. "I thought they would be beautiful factories. Every American, we thought he was a millionaire. When I finally got to New York, they were like garbage disposals. I was very disappointed."

Over the years, many New York furriers dropped out of the business as their children became doctors or lawyers. The Kims kept plowing profits back into Jindo.

Today, Jindo has 44 stores of its own around the world, with plans for 200. Buyers from Japan, Europe and the United States cycle through Jindo's Seoul showroom. Jindo, which now raises its own minks, is expected to sells $150 million worth of fur garments this year, three times South Korea's entire export bill in 1962. A joint venture with the Soviet Union is in the works. A parallel business financed with fur profits, producing metal shipping containers, will gross $200 million this year. Jindo's U.S. operation will soon go public on the New York stock exchange. And, like other South Korean businesses, Jindo is now trying to move from being the cheapest to being the best. "Now we're going to concentrate on quality, like Louis Vuitton," said Kim Young Jin. "We think we can build that kind of name."

The Kim clan was gathered in the backyard of their 76-year-old mother's house. All five sons were there. The younger members of the third generation were there, too, trampling their grandmother's rose bushes and crawling under her persimmon tree. The only fourth-generation Kim so far toddled across the lawn, oblivious to the soccer ball careening past him.

"My children are very spoiled," Young Jin sighed. "It's a big problem. My wife likes to give them things."

The stone house was pleasant, on a hillside above Seoul's smog, but not ostentatious. In South Korea, it is not wise to flaunt one's wealth grossly; Young Chull said he prefers to sit next to his driver rather than in the back of his car.

In traditional Korea, merchants ranked well below scholars, bureaucrats and farmers in social esteem. Since the Korean War, businessmen's association with, and dependence on, unpopular authoritarian rulers has not improved their reputations.

Thus, South Korea today mixes the conspicuous spending of newly prosperous, status-conscious people anywhere with a deeply rooted distaste for wealth and profit. Jindo, with its focus on export and the United States, has been less involved in domestic politics than the big conglomerates, but even Jindo's chairman—No. 1 son Yung Won, 54—spends much of his time lunching with government ministers, playing golf with top officials and otherwise smoothing the relations that underlie business.

"After all, I don't mind saying that without the Korean government and Korean banks, we wouldn't be where we are," Young Chull said. "Five years ago, if you showed your balance sheet to an overseas bank, they wouldn't give you a penny. You needed government guarantees.... At the same time, Korean businessmen worked very hard to be where they are. Some people, even if you gave them all the money in the world, wouldn't be able to do what Koreans did."

The family had eaten its bulkogi—Korean-style marinated and barbecued meat—and the drivers helped themselves near the barbecue.

On the porch, one of two lightbulbs was out; grandmother Kim Myung Hyun, always a refugee in her mind, insisted that using two bulbs was unnecessary.

"I had to leave everything, our land, our belongings," she said, stepping outside to watch her grandchildren. "In Seoul, I would cry every day. And just as my tears dried, the war started, and we had to move again."

As with many South Koreans, religion is not an important part of life for the Kim sons. But their mother visits temples every day, ignoring her children's good-natured complaints as she gives away their money to the temples and their priests.

When asked how she produced such a fine family, she replied, "Praying to Buddha."

"When something good happens, she says, 'You see, it's from my prayers,' " Young Chull said. "And when I ask her about the bad news, she says, 'Well, it could have been worse.' "

A Lesson About Making Money

Kim Young Chull is the ideas man, the philosopher, the creative one. His thoughts spill out faster than he can talk, and he loves to talk. He is fluent in English, and he relishes the feel of the language. To an Englishman, he talks about "blokes;" To an American, "guys."

He is a long way from the gawky student on his way to Arkansas City Junior College in 1957 who found himself baffled by the pay toilets in the San Francisco airport.

"Some guy said, 'Money, money,' " Kim recalled. "I said, what, money? I'm just trying to use the damn toilet. He said, 'No, you need money'.... And while I sat there, I thought, this is a great country, eh? This is a money country."

In Kansas, despite his frustrations at American ignorance of his country, he was struck by people's kindness and generosity.

"They never let me spend a holiday alone," he said.

But when he returned to South Korea and had to deal with U.S. Army officers on his father's behalf, "all of these good feelings ... just disappeared."

"They didn't treat us like businessmen, they always treated us like house-boys," he said. "After all, they were the kings then.... If they didn't like the way you looked, they cut you off like that.... And I started, you know, my God, some-day I'm going to make money and I'll show them, I'll show them what we can do. And it wasn't just me who felt that way.

Kim said his generation today disapproves intellectually of militant students who stage anti-American protests, but it sympathizes nonetheless.

"Koreans had to bow and scrape, as drivers and maids, and the kids who are demonstrating now grew up hearing their fathers come home talking about that," he said. "They watch the kids, and they feel guilty that they didn't have the guts to stand up."

Kim's own children and those of his brothers attend Boston University and the Rhode Island School of Design, Harvard Business School and Stanford Law School. Like Kim questioning his father about his relations with the Japanese, the children criticize their fathers for not having fought for democracy and against the authoritarian, unpopular and recently retired president Chun Doo Hwan.

"They say, dad, you're a businessman, so you're chicken," Kim said. "And I say, no, not at all. At least he led the country to a point where it could survive. We're a country with no resources.... But the kids, oh, yes, they give me hard time."

Kim said he believes South Korea will evolve successfully into a democracy, but he said the country must mature beyond its preoccupation with survival, exports and money.

"In the past, our philosophy was materialism," he said. "From material success came confidence, and now that we have confidence, what the hell are we going to do with it? It's an identity problem."

More prosaically, Kim said his company, like all of Korean industry, remains far behind Japan and the West—in technology, in management skills, in resources. Can the nation ever catch up?

"It will take a long, long time," he said. "But I'm sure we will get there."

September 5, 1988

Social Institutions: Politics

In Face of Francophone Nationalists, Quebec's English-Speakers Looking toward Exits

William Claiborne

As predominantly French-speaking Quebec heads toward a separation referendum next year, a malaise has gripped the province's English-speaking minority that could lead to an exodus greater even than after a Parti Quebecois election victory in 1976, say politicians and demographers.

In the nine years following that last surge of Quebec nationalism, personified by the election of separatist premier Rene Levesque, more than 200,000 Anglophones fled the province. Most went to neighboring Ontario.

Recent polls suggest that nearly a third of the remaining 800,000 Anglophones in Quebec plan to leave within five years because of what they perceive as growing restrictions on the use of their language. The same surveys indicate that if Quebec separated from Canada, 44 percent would leave. The province's total population is about 6.6 million.

Pollsters say the majority of the Anglophones who would shift to Ontario and other predominantly English-speaking provinces are aged 18 to 24 and well-educated.

Partly as a result of the trend, some strident French-Canadian nationalists here have begun to tone down their rhetoric on the need to preserve the French culture at all costs, and even to reexamine some of the language laws that Anglophones regard as mist onerous.

"The Francophones are beginning to realize that they would be unable to occupy that permanently lost space that English speakers would leave if there is an exodus. We're not talking about a few hundred thousand peasants here. These people have a role to play in Quebec's future," said Robert Keaton, president of Alliance Quebec, a Montreal-based Anglophone rights group.

Richard Bolden, a member of the provincial parliament from the English-speaking enclave of Westmount, near Montreal, said that of his three children, one plans to leave Quebec, one is uncertain and the third thinks he will stay.

"If there's a separate Quebec, and God knows I hope it won't happen, I'm not leaving. But the young people are much more mobile, and they don't necessarily listen when we say that we can't have a viable community here if it's a monolithic community," said Holden, a member of the Equality Party, which holds four of the 125 seats in the provincial assembly.

Most frequently cited as the cause of the current Anglophone malaise is the Quebec government's decision to hold a sovereignty referendum next year if the central government and nine predominantly English-speaking provinces fail to come up with constitutional changes to give Quebec more autonomy.

A similar referendum on "sovereignty association," advanced by the then-governing Parti Quebecois in 1980, narrowly failed. The impetus for another plebiscite was the collapse last June of proposals that would have recognized Quebec's distinct character.

But Anglophones here and in Montreal said their discontent stems from an accumulation of other grievances that began with the adoption in 1988 of a law banning English on outdoor commercial signs here. Although Canada's Supreme Court ruled later the law was unconstitutional, the Liberal Party government of Quebec Premier Robert Bourassa used a constitutional provision that allows provinces to override such rulings.

Gordon Atkinson, an Equality Party member of the provincial parliament, said adoption of the signboard law is analogous to a state legislature in the United States abrogating the First Amendment, and said that even after three years, many Anglophones still are rankled over the issue.

"They [the French speakers] say, 'Well, it's only signs.' But where does it stop? Maybe some day they'll want to ban English radio stations, or English newspapers. They keep moving the goalposts," Atkinson said.

Anglophone leaders said that many non-French Quebecers also became alarmed when the Montreal Catholic School Commission last year proposed a ban on the use of any language but French by its students, even outside the classrooms. The plan was dropped after it generated widespread criticism.

A current proposal would tighten the 1977 French-Language Charter that requires all non-Anglophone immigrants to attend French—language schools. The proposal would close a loophole under which some non-Francophone immigrants can avoid sending their children to French—language schools by claiming temporary residence.

Referring to the polls predicting an Anglophone exodus from Quebec, David P. Birnbaum, executive director of Alliance Quebec, said, "They reflect what we've known for a long time. There's a profound level of frustration, anxiety and anger out there among the English-speaking community. People who stuck out some very difficult times in the past are saying, 'I'm not sure this is home anymore.' "

Both Bolden and Atkinson noted that since the publication of public polls suggesting an exodus of English speakers, some militant French-Canadians have begun to modify their positions on banning the use of English in the province. These include even Jacques Parizeau, leader of the Parti Quebecois, who recently declared that "they are us," and suggested that protection of the French culture should not be enforced at the expense of minority rights.

Moreover, provincial Education Minister Claude Ryan recently proposed a means of reopening debate on the signboard law and possibly amending it to the satisfaction of Anglophones.

Ryan, a Francophone, again raised eyebrows among Quebec nationalists when he defended a newly appointed adviser on the province's French-only language law who had called the law "utterly ridiculous." Ryan rejected calls from the Parti Quebecois to fire the adviser, McGill University political science professor Charles Taylor, and said Taylor had a right to express divergent opinions on the language issue.

And Lucien Bouchard, leader of the separatist Bloc Quebecois in the federal parliament in Ottawa, also has suggested that Quebec cannot justify giving one language dominance to the detriment of the rights of a minority.

The leader of the federal Liberal Party, Jean Chretian, said in an interview in Ottawa that restoring political stability in Quebec and Canada as a whole would go a long way to assuaging the fears of Quebec English speakers.

June 11, 1991

War Takes Toll on Serbo-Croatian Couples: Former School Friends, Lovers, Spouses Now Look at Each Other as Enemies

Blaine Harden

They were married four years ago, paying no attention to his being a Serb and her being a Croat.

She is in camouflage uniform now as a medic with the Croatian National Guard, posted here in a village on the front lines of a war between Serbs and Croats. Mirjana Vojnovic, 24, has been trained to give shots and patch wounds, and also to fire a machine gun and fight with a knife.

He is now fighting on the Serbian side. Zeljko Vojnovic, 28, is reported by his neighbors to have joined up with a guerrilla unit operating within 10 miles of this village. For the past month, Serbian guerrillas have been using sniper fire and mortar attacks to terrify local Croats and seize their villages.

Nearly everyone has already fled this tiny village, which is about 35 miles southeast of Zagreb, the Croatian capital, and an assault on it is expected any day.

"If I have to, I will shoot him," said Mirjana, referring to her ex-husband and the father of her 13-month-old son. "It is better that I shoot him than he shoots me."

The collapsed marriage of Mirjana and Zeljko Vojnovic, and the possibility that they may soon fight against each other, is a nightmarish example of tensions that are tearing at mixed marriages across the Yugoslav republics of Croatia and Serbia.

Worsening civil war is rapidly laying waste to the ethnic tolerance that took temporary root here after the World War II era of fratricidal butchery between Croats and Serbs.

In Zagreb, where there are about 200,000 ethnic Serbs, and in Belgrade, the capital of the country as well as of the republic of Serbia, where there are tens of thousands of Croats, there is as yet no fighting. But Serbs and Croats in mixed marriages in both cities have spoken in recent weeks of an insidious and inescapable turmoil in their domestic lives.

Those married people do not speak for the record, for fear of upsetting their spouses and infuriating their in-laws. But Mirjana Vojnovic, now divorced and living in makeshift barracks at a primary school here in Komarevo, is free to speak about domestic life in a multi-ethnic nation where tolerance has evaporated.

"When we were teenagers, we played together, went to school together, drank and danced together. There was no question in the minds of people in my generation about marrying a Serb or a Croat. Our parents thought about it, but we didn't," she said.

What the parents remember, she said, is World War II. Historians estimate that of the 1.7 million Yugoslavs who died between 1941 and 1945, about 1 million were killed in inter-ethnic fighting, most of it Croat against Serb.

But when the war ended, Tito, the guerrilla leader most responsible for the Yugoslav victory over Germany, made a concerted effort to replace ancient nationalist hatreds with communist ideals.

As a war hero and a charismatic dictator who did not hesitate to use force when idealism did not suffice, Tito managed to turn down the volume on nationalist hatred in Yugoslavia for most of the 35 years he held power.

In parts of rural Croatia where Croats and Serbs had killed each other during World War II, they began to work together bringing in crops. By the 1960s, mixed marriages between Serbs and Croats became common.

Many of the children of those marriages declared themselves to be Yugoslavs, rather than Croats or Serbs.

When Tito died in 1980, old hatreds were unchained. Communism had merely repressed ethnic differences; little had been resolved.

Serbian nationalism exploded in the late 1980s with the rise to power of Communist strongman Slobodan Milosevic. He used the state-owned media to remind Serbs of Croatian war crimes.

As a response to threats from Serbia, a similar ethnic eruption occurred here in Croatia last year. A free election brought to power an ardent Croatian nationalist, former Yugoslav general Franjo Tudjman. His government dressed itself up in old Croatian crests and symbols that terrified many of Croatia's 600,000-strong Serbian minority.

Those Serbs, goaded by distortions and exaggerations in Serbian newspapers and radio, were reminded of Croatia's Nazi puppet government, the Ustashi, which during the war killed hundreds of thousands of Serbs.

When Tudjman's government declared Croatia independent at the end of June, Serbs and Croats were primed for violence. More than 200 people, most of them Croats, have since been killed in fighting that shows no signs of stopping.

Mirjana Vojnovic's marriage fell apart shortly after Nilosevic rose to power in Serbia. She was living at the time with her husband's family in Vrginmost, a town in Croatia with a large population of ethnic Serbs.

"I didn't have a name in that house. They called me 'she.' But my husband wanted me to stay there, so I did, for two years," she recalled. "I thought it would get better, but they hated me all the time."

She said she left that house in 1989 and went to live with her mother in the town of Sisak, about four miles north of here. After two months, she said her husband came to live with her and her mother. Yet the marriage quickly collapsed. Two weeks after her husband left for the final time, Mirjana discovered she was pregnant.

The child is now staying with his Croatian grandmother.

And Mirjana sleeps here on a mattress on the floor of the principal's office in the primary school that has been commandeered by the National Guard. A sign on a bulletin board reads: "Our Croatian Homeland."

Mirjana said she almost never talks to Serbs anymore.

"People I played with and went to school with, we look at each other as enemies. It is really hard for us," she said.

Asked if she would ever consider marrying a Serb again, she laughed and shook her head grimly.

"I don't think it will be possible to have mixed marriages again. Croat people hate Serbs," she said. "For this generation, for two or three more generations, it is finished."

August 4, 1991

Rural Bangladesh Almost Untouched by Changes; Democracy Drive That Ousted President Is Viewed with Apathy, Distrust Outside Cities

Steve Coll

The worldwide wave of democratic revolution splashed into Bangladesh last week as thousands of students and professionals took to city streets and toppled President Hussein Mohammed Ershad's authoritarian government.

But the wave was not powerful enough to reach the countryside, where a majority of Bangladeshis struggle not for civil liberties but for survival.

To many of the rural poor in whose name the democracy movement was launched, Bangladesh's recent upheaval appears at best an irrelevancy and at worst a frightening harbinger of civil turmoil. In interviews, landless laborers and subsistence farmers expressed relief that the agitation was over, distrust of those behind it and conviction that democracy would not make their lives any better.

They have reason to be pessimistic, since the opposition parties that brought down Ershad have governed Bangladesh before and have done little to break the cycle of poverty, malnutrition, disease, natural disaster, political violence and government corruption that for two decades has shaped daily life in one of the world's poorest countries.

In a thatched hut here this morning, at the weekly meeting of the Shahipratap Landless Women's Society, a private banking cooperative organized to assist the rural poor, 30 women spoke animatedly about their pressing concerns: children and relatives who are sick and dying, rising food prices, cattle theft and an acute shortage of drinkable water.

Ershad was brought down by weeks of protests, strikes and violence in Bangladesh's cities. But the rural women did not mention the democracy movement except to complain that the stir contributed to growing violence and theft in the countryside and disrupted their lives by generating higher prices as well as isolated strikes and curfews.

"We were frightened," said Musammet Majeda. "We were afraid there would be war—we heard that people were being killed, buses and houses set on fire."

Following Ershad's resignation last Tuesday, a caretaker government headed by a Supreme Court justice has promised to hold parliamentary elections within 90 days.

"We don't care about all these changes. Since the government doesn't do anything for us, we don't much care for" those who ousted Ershad, said Sharifa, who goes by only one name. Sharifa said she has lost her house to floods and two young daughters to disease during the past 18 months.

Her themes were echoed at a second women's cooperative meeting in a nearby village, by farmers in the area and by laborers at a rural brick factory who earn about 90 cents a day by squatting in an open field and molding clay mud into blocks.

Pessimism in the countryside, where there was little significant protest during the student-led movement against Ershad, reflects the daunting challenges faced by anyone promising meaningful change in densely populated and deeply impoverished Bangladesh, a flood-prone country struggling to keep its head above water— literally and figuratively.

The attitudes in rural areas also suggest that Bangladesh's unresolved fight for democracy is being contested almost entirely by sections of the country's relatively small middle and upper classes: university students, professionals, traders, businessmen, bureaucrats, career politicians, and the military.

The temporary alliances among these groups that forced out Ershad, a retired general and former martial-law administrator seen by urbanites as corrupt and autocratic, were forged by a surge of democratic aspirations in the capital of Dhaka and several other large cities. But since the democracy movement lacks mass support among the rural majority and involves leaders who have fought each other for two decades, even city dwellers sympathetic to the movement worry about what will come next.

While some military officers and democracy movement leaders want to try Ershad on corruption charges, the former president appears to believe he can stage a political comeback. From his heavily guarded compound, he told the BBC in a telephone interview on Sunday that he was working on his golf, writing poetry and planning a public rally for Dec. 16.

Some anticipate violence if Ershad presses his candidacy; officials of his Jatiya Dal (National Party) are in hiding or under police protection, wary of angry mobs. But if Ershad is not allowed to seek office, "There won't be peace," said Jatiya officeholder Iran Mesbauddin. Renewed unrest could spark military intervention. Some urbanites see the army's hand manipulating events.

While in power, Ershad enjoyed support from industrialized countries in the West, which contribute about $2 billion to Bangladesh annually and fund 86 percent of the country's development budget. Ershad's fervor for free markets, export industries and infrastructure projects pleased donors such as the United States and the World Bank. In August, he dispatched several thousand troops to Saudi Arabia in support of U.S. policy in the Persian Gulf.

But the United States and other Western donors grew weary of corruption and inefficiency in Ershad's government according to Western aid officials in Dhaka. Opposition leaders and urban Bangladeshis locked out of Ershad's small circle of ministers and advisers resented his government's disregard for civil rights and its eager solicitation of Western aid dollars, which they said were funnelled to corrupt industrialists and cronies.

Apart from their dislike of Ershad, however, the opposition groups that came together in city streets last week appear to have little else in common. The leftist

Awami League-led alliance, favored to win any new election, has advocated nationalization of industry and more government spending on the poor. The rightist Bangladesh Nationalist Party-led alliance leans toward Islam and free markets.

University students chanted for democracy during their protest movement but are split on the issues. Some acknowledged that they have a long way to go to gain the confidence of the rural majority whose cause they have championed.

"In the past, different parties talked about poverty, particularly women and children, but they were never able to deliver," said a Bangladesh Nationalist Party student leader in the rural town of Narsindi. "This time, we will try to do something."

December 11, 1990

Inside Stalin's 'Marble Gulag;' Soviets Allow Rare Visit to Siberian Camp for Uranium Miners

Michael Dobbs

Stark granite mountains rising to a height of 8,000 feet surround this Stalinist-era labor camp, forming a natural prison more awesome than anything man could possibly invent. In winter, the temperature drops to 60 degrees below zero.

Visiting this desolate Siberian camp, it is difficult to conceive of anybody trying to escape. The only natural exit—down the mountain valley to the nearest village, about 35 miles away—is blocked by guardhouses and machine-gun posts.

And yet, according to Soviet secret police documents, 83 prisoners did try to escape during the years 1949 to 1951 when the camp was in operation. Most tried to scramble up the almost vertical rock face—a daunting route even for well-equipped mountaineers. No one got away.

Part of a vast network of Stalinist labor camps stretching across Siberia, never before accessible to Western journalists, the Marble Gulag provides a point of departure for a journey through Soviet history. The camp symbolizes a totalitarian economic and political system that continues to mold in significant ways the everyday lives of ordinary Soviet citizens, more than 35 years after Stalin's death.

A land of appalling hardships and huge natural resources, Siberia encapsulates the challenge facing President Mikhail Gorbachev as he attempts to steer the Soviet Union into the 21st century. This article, based on a week-long trip across an area as large as the United States, compares modern-day Siberia with the Siberia of Joseph Stalin.

Until a few months ago, the existence of the Marble Gulag was a closely guarded secret. It was here, in the taiga, or forest region, of eastern Siberia, that uranium was mined to produce the first Soviet atomic bombs. The Soviet Union's rise to superpower status rested on the merciless exploitation of tens of thousands of slave laborers.

Today, the Marble Gulag is being turned into a museum commemorating the victims of Stalinism, the Soviet equivalent of Auschwitz or Buchenwald. The decision to allow Westerners to visit the camp (the word "gulag" derives from the Russian acronym for Stalin's prison system) represents a further step in Gorbachev's drive to shed light on the "blank spots" of Soviet history, especially the quarter century of Stalin's rule from the late 1920s to 1953.

The liberal Soviet journal Novy Mir has begun serializing excerpts from "Gulag Archipelago," Alexander Solzhenitsyn's landmark exposure of the Stalinist camps, more than 15 years after its publication in the West. A competition is now underway in Moscow to erect an anti-Stalinist monument in the Soviet capital.

"Richard III and Ivan the Terrible were innocents compared to Stalin. This kind of murderer never existed before the 20th century," said Evgenii Tokar, a young Soviet director making a documentary film about Marble Gulag. "In my opinion, Stalin was even worse than Hitler. Hitler did not destroy his own people."

Soviet and Western historians estimate that up to 50 million people were "repressed" by Stalin. The greatest bloodletting took place before World War II with the destruction of the kulaks, or rich peasants, and the "Great Terror" of 1937. But several million people were sent to camps after the war, including many Soviet soldiers captured by the Nazis.

'Death Valley'

Even today, the Marble Gulag is difficult to reach. From the nearest village, Chara, you drive three hours by four-wheel-drive vehicle along forest trails that meander into a rocky river bed. Then there is a two-hour hike up to the camp itself.

As you climb above the tree line, at 6,000 feet, the luxuriant taiga becomes suddenly barren. The play of light on the mountain sometimes gives the granite rocks a marble hue, explaining the name of the camp. The mountains form a gigantic soundbox, mixing the moans of the wind with the gurgling of running water.

A line of unused electricity pylons leads past a row of single-story wooden guardhouses to the labor camp. About 200 yards long and 200 yards wide, it is surrounded by two parallel barbed-wire fences and four corner posts. Most of the buildings in the camp have been largely destroyed by the elements, but the outlines remain: a long barracks where about 500 prisoners huddled around a stove, the punishment cell where it was easy to freeze to death, the kitchen.

Attached to one of the buildings, a flimsy one-log thick, is a sign erected by members of the local Komsomol, the Communist youth league. "Comrades!" it announces. "Here will be created a historic monument. We ask you to leave everything as it is."

There is not much to pilfer. Some scraps of clothing and leather sandals worn by the zeks, Russian slang for inhabitants of the gulag, and crude kitchen utensils. Rolls of rusty barbed wire. The carcass of an American Studebaker truck donated to the Soviet Union in World War II under lend-lease. A piece of cardboard containing instructions to the guard.

Local residents were well aware of the existence of the camp but, until very recently, were reluctant to talk about it. Fantastic legends circulate in Chara about a "Death Valley" in the mountains that no living creature or plant can possibly survive.

"You're crazy to go up there. Your hair will fall out. The entire valley is radioactive," said one Chara resident, on being asked directions. Soviet geologists who scour the mountains for minerals, and regularly visit the camp, insist there is no danger.

The secrets of the Marble Gulag began to unravel at the beginning of this year when Komsomolskaya Pravda carried a photo of the camp on its front page. It had been taken more than 10 years earlier by the paper's correspondent in the region, Vladimir Sungorkin, who came across the camp by chance.

"I never thought that I would be able to publish such a picture," Sungorkin said. "This was the first photo of a Stalinist labor camp ever to appear in the Soviet press. Until very recently, it would have been dangerous to have told anybody that I even had such a picture. The whole subject was taboo."

Even today, under glasnost, or Gorbachev's policy of greater openness, Komsomolskaya Pravda felt itself unable to fully describe the historical background to the establishment of the Marble Gulag. That history goes back to the Potsdam conference in July 1945 when Stalin learned about the development of the American atomic bomb from President Truman.

After returning to Moscow, Stalin decided to give top priority to the development of a Soviet bomb. Teams of geologists were sent to scour the country for deposits of uranium, the radioactive chemical element whose nuclear fission sets off a chain reaction that results in the explosive force of an atomic bomb. One of the sites they discovered was the Udokan mountains near Chara, deep in the Siberian taiga and accessible only by plane.

To extract uranium from this desolate spot, a huge human investment was required. About 600 zeks stationed year-round at the Marble Gulag were responsible for mining the ore. But this was just the tip of the slave-labor pyramid servicing the camp.

Sungorkin estimates that at least 1,000 prisoners worked on constructing a road from the Marble Gulag to a base camp and airport about 25 miles away at a place called Sinelga. Tens of thousands more zeks worked on a road that stretched 500 miles across the mountainous taiga to the town of Mogocha on the Trans-Siberian Railroad. Another 100,000 prisoners were assigned to build a northern branch of the Trans-Siberian, known as BAM, that is only now being completed.

'Kill Me, Kill Me'

Mikhail Shinkin was a 22-year-old sergeant in the Soviet army when he was sent to the Marble Gulag. Without his knowledge, his soldiers had sold a sheep to some starving civilians. A military tribunal sentenced him to 10 years in a labor camp for the crime of abetting the theft of state property.

The journey to the gulag was like a trip through hell. In September 1948, just as winter was setting in, a party of 500 prisoners set off by foot from Mogocha. For the first 60 miles, to the village of Tupik (which means "Dead End" in Russian), there was a rudimentary forest road. Beyond Tupik, they had to cut their way through 200 miles of Siberian wilderness, building their own road.

"We lived like animals, sleeping out at night. Dozens and dozens of prisoners simply froze to death along the road. At night, we would light a fire, then clear away the embers and sleep on the warm ground," recalled Shinkin, a retired metalworker who now lives in the Moscow region.

As punishment for petty offenses, the prisoners were forced to spend the night lashed to wooden stakes away from the fire. Shinkin still bears scars on his wrist from being placed in handcuffs that restricted the circulation of the blood. He says he only survived because he was young and strong.

Throughout the five-month ordeal, the prisoners had practically nothing to eat. Sometimes they would be given a handful of uncooked grain. The guards would often throw meat to their dogs rather than give it to the prisoners.

"I remember one night we were sitting around the fire. The dogs were howling all around us. The person next to me was showing us pictures of his family when he collapsed into the fire, dead from hunger, cold and exhaustion," Shinkin said.

After the horrors of the journey, it was almost a relief to get to the Marble Gulag. The flimsy huts provided at least some protection against the harsh Siberian winter. And since the extraction of uranium had been declared a top-priority project, the zeks were relatively well fed.

Shinkin said he never thought of escaping from the camp, knowing that it would be impossible. But he remembers an escape attempt by three of his friends. Two of the zeks were shot as they tried to scramble across the rocks. The third was caught and viciously beaten by the guards.

"They left him out all night underneath the watchtower. I can still remember him crying, 'Kill me, kill me,' all night," said Shinkin.

Komsomolskaya Pravda's revelations about the Marble Gulag triggered a flood of letters, including some from former zeks. At least half the letters were in support of Stalin. Many accused the paper of defaming the late dictator and grossly exaggerating the hardships of the camps.

"You are blackening Stalin's times and Stalin himself. There should have been more such camps so that all the kulaks could have been annihilated," wrote an inhabitant of Irkutsk named Ivanova.

Some readers attacked Komsomolskaya Pravda for printing "absurd rumors." A regional prosecutor, V.P. Balyaba, said secret police archives showed that the inmates of the Marble Gulag were either common criminals or Nazi collaborators. No shootings ever took place at the camp, he claimed.

It is difficult to calculate how many of the inmates of the Marble Gulag were serving terms for political offenses. Political prisoners and hardened criminals were mixed together. Many of the zeks were like Shinkin—serving long sentences for offenses that would not be considered crimes in a civilized country.

"The only people who can say such things in defense of Stalin are those who never experienced the gulags themselves. If you lived through this, you are bound to have a completely different attitude," said Shinkin, who was a front-line soldier in World War II and remembers going into battle shouting "For Stalin, for the Motherland." The Power of Repression

A Westerner visiting the Marble Gulag is struck by a paradox. The camp provides dramatic evidence of the penury and backwardness of Stalin's Soviet Union.

The people who produced the atomic bomb and transformed their country into a superpower lived in conditions of appalling misery and political repression.

It is contradiction that goes to the heart of the difference between the United States and the Soviet Union. The United States became a superpower by releasing the individual energies of its people. In pursuing a dream of a better life, Americans also contributed to the overall strength of the nation.

The Soviet Union has traditionally taken the opposite path. By keeping the living standards of the population as low as possible, Stalin was able to concentrate resources on priority projects such as development of the atomic bomb. The Soviet Union achieved superpower status through merciless repression and the creation of a vast network of slave labor.

The Stalinist system worked for a time—despite the huge cost in human lives. Repression was an effective instrument during the early stages of industrialization, when economic progress could be achieved by mobilizing vast resources. But during the information revolution, which is driven by the free flow of ideas, repression is counterproductive.

Gorbachev is the first Soviet leader to recognize that economic modernization cannot be achieved through force. The implications of this lesson are particularly important for Siberia, a place that has almost become a symbol of Stalinist brutality and extensive economic development.

Czars and Communist Party general secretaries alike have sought to tap Siberia's great natural wealth through the system of political exile and grandiose projects such as the Trans-Siberian Railway. But Gorbachev is trying to use different methods—and Siberia is finding it difficult to adapt.

October 1, 1989

A Crucible of Conscience: Protester Claims, 'I Never Knew There Were So Many Kind People in My Country'

David Remnick

The barracks of the Kantimirovskaya tank division were dark and still, and Pvt. Vitaly Chugunov was in the middle of a deep, untroubled sleep. It was two hours before Monday reveille, the last moments of quiet before another week of training.

Chugunov had thought he would be among the first generation of Soviet soldiers blessed by the rise of a peaceable kingdom, a country in which a policy of "new thinking" ensured against another Afghanistan, another occupation of Eastern Europe.

Suddenly, an officer burst into Chugunov's darkened barracks, shouting his charges out of bed. There were no complicated explanations, no inkling that hundreds of miles to the south, on the Crimean peninsula, Soviet President Mikhail Gorbachev and his family were under house arrest and that the ministers of defense, the secret police and the interior had engineered a state of emergency and a military coup.

"We all thought it was one of those training alerts, and we quickly got everything ready to go," Chugunov later recalled.

Soon, the young man with wheat-blond hair and blue eyes from the city of Ulyanovsk was inside his armored personnel carrier in a huge convoy headed for Moscow. Chuganov and his friends were confused, not quite sure why they were taking the Kiev highway at a fast clip.

All over Moscow, people were waking up and hearing the news of a military coup. Soon all of them would be faced with moral decisions: to accept or resist, to pretend nothing had happened or risk everything. These were days that would change everyone, and everything.

Soon word filtered down to the young troops that they were headed straight for the center of the city. And then, as the first few people at the side of the road waved at the tanks and the armored personnel carriers, as they began shouting at them to turn around, to go back home, the young soldiers slowly understood.

"My father was in the tanks when the Soviet Union invaded Prague in '68," Chugunov said. "He's always told me how scared he was. They were told the Czechs would give them boxes of chocolate and the chocolate would have poison inside. They were looking out for poison wine. He was humiliated when the Czechs shouted insults at him."

Looking out at the people on the road, Vitaly Chugunov began to think that he was headed for something worse than his father had ever known.

Later that morning, Nadezhda Kudinova, a 44-year-old seamstress at a parachute factory on the edge of Moscow, arrived at work. On the way, she had heard some vague rumors on the bus that newscasters were announcing that Gorbachev had resigned for "health reasons" and that the vice president, Gennady Yanayev, and some "unpronounceable" committee had taken power.

It all seemed so vague and unreal. But when she arrived at the factory, the place was abuzz. The factory director immediately declared that everyone should stand by the State of Emergency Committee, that what the country needed now was stability and discipline at the workplace.

"The situation was so strange," Kudinova said. "Just looking out the window, we could hear nothing, we could see nothing. And on the radio there was nothing but these wonderful decrees of the committee. So all of us, we started sitting around talking as we do. I only talked with the people I could trust, and I thought about what I should do."

At the factory, opinions were split down the middle. Half were outraged about the news, and half thought that maybe life without Gorbachev would be a change for the better. Maybe there would be food in the stores for a change.

"This was nothing new. It was a long-standing division between us in the factory," Kudinova said. "People were divided politically and morally. The people that stood up for the coup, they were not that stupid. They realized what they were doing. They knew what they had to lose in the situation. But fortunately, Yanayev miscalculated. He didn't realize, even though he was a Komsomol {Communist Youth League} leader, that most people in this country are not what they once were. He never learned from the Komsomol song, 'Today, I am not what I was yesterday.'

Kudinova thought she might write up some leaflets. In the afternoon, when it was clear that Russian republic President Boris Yeltsin was in the Russian parliament building organizing the resistance, she was relieved.

"At that point, my friends and I realized we will not give in that easily," she said. "We knew we would get organized, that there would be a struggle."

In the early evening, as she headed for home, she saw what had happened to her city, how it had become "an armed camp." Walking along Kutuzovsky Prospect on the way to the barricaded Russian parliament building, she made a quick decision. She would stay all night, or as long as it took, to help the resistance.

"Gorbachev was the last man we wanted to protect. We were there to protect the legally elected president of Russia, Boris Nikolayevich," she said of Yeltsin. "Unlike the Americans on the radio, none of us was talking about Gorbachev. All our questions were about Yeltsin: 'Where is Yeltsin?' And 'Where is (Moscow Mayor) Gavril Popov?' Those were the questions that worried us. Not about Gorbachev. Gorbachev got what he deserved."

At the Ostankino television studios, the staff reporters, script writers and producers of the official news program "Vremya" were in shock. For the most part, these were conservatives—"screws in the machine" as Stalin once said—people who were ready to shift with the wind and broadcast without question the decrees of those in power.

Around 6 a.m., two announcers took turns reading the proclamations of the State of Emergency Committee. They seemed shocked, nervous. They stuttered and gulped. Between repetitions, television played music by Tchaikovsky and other Russian classics.

Ruben Oganesov, a 27-year-old reporter for "Vremya," rolled out of bed and watched the screen with confusion. At work, at the program's third-floor studios, he got his assignment.

"They told me, 'Go out and report a story called "Calm Moscow." ' I couldn't do that exactly, because there were tanks in town," he said. "But, still, I made the story about people wandering around, eating ice cream, the children. I did say there was peace in the streets, which was true. Even the demonstrations were not that big. After all, what's 150,000 people in a city of 9 million?"

The order for Oganesov's report came from his boss, but obviously that editor was getting his orders from on high. Leonid Kravchenko, the head of state television, had been criticized for months as a reactionary—one willing to stifle anything controversial, anything critical of the government. He had canceled the most popular show in the country, the magazine program "View," and then canceled a late-night news program called "TSN," which dared to report critically on last January's failed Soviet coup in the breakaway Baltic republic of Lithuania.

"My feeling is, 'Judge not and ye shall not be judged,' " said Oganesov. "Maybe Kravchenko should have shown more resolve. But there are tanks in town. And power hadn't been seized by some 'black colonels' or lieutenants. It was the minister of defense, other ministers, the ruling oligarchy. I imagine it was hard for Kravchenko. I don't support him for letting the junta use the airwaves as their tribune, but I can't judge him either."

"After all, we work at state television. We report to the president of the Soviet Union. We never just make things up. We try to report on the news, but we always act in the framework of the president's wishes," he added.

On the same program, Oganesov's friend, Vladimir Stepanov, read a long commentary asking that the people of Moscow stop considering the new leaders a bloodthirsty "junta." After all, Stepanov said, these men were "legitimate" ministers and officials.

"Vladimir spoke like a man who has children. He was afraid for the lives of his four kids," Oganesov said. "He was really begging people not to fight with one another. My view is that he spoke from the heart."

In the meantime, the leaders of the coup took "Vremya's" ideological and journalistic competitor—the Russian news program "Vesti"—off the air.

Another young reporter at "Vremya," Sergei Lysenko, avoided coming to work. But he said he too sympathized with the people at "Vremya."

"Some people are weaker, some are stronger," he said. "Not everyone is a hero. Sure, we'd love to work in the kind of conditions they have at CNN, with great cameras and all the rest. It is not easy living in this country when you don't know what will happen from one day to the next. You have to find a life for yourself."

In the Lenin Hills, just down the street from Gorbachev's Moscow city residence, Pvt. Chugunov sat in his armored personnel carrier dreading his next order.

As night fell, he still was stunned from his arrival in Moscow. "There was real fear," he said. People had shaken their fists at the tanks and the long convoy. They'd cried out to the young soldiers, "Don't shoot your own people! Turn against your officers!"

"I saw women crying along the road," he said. Some met the soldiers with kindness and gave them food to eat, flowers to stick in their gun turrets. Some gave the soldiers leaflets to read, copies of Boris Yeltsin's order to the Russian people to obey the law of the republic and not the "anti-constitutional" junta. All of the soldiers had AK-47 assault rifles, but they kept them unloaded and out of sight of the crowds around them.

"We guys were saying to each other, 'Why don't we just make a U-turn and go home?' " Chugunov said. "Everyone wanted to go back home. We felt ashamed before our people and our government. We told the people we would not disgrace the names of our fathers, and we will not turn against the people."

Somehow, Monday night passed, but now the leaders of the resistance inside the Russian parliament building were getting reports from intelligence and military informants that the attack was planned for sometime Tuesday night or before dawn Wednesday.

A retired senior lieutenant from the Tamanskaya tank division—"Baskakov is my name, here is my tattoo," he said—took command of Russian civil defense unit No. 34. His old tank division was the first to come over to the side of the resistance.

Baskakov quit the Communist Party only last year and felt that "as a Christian, I had to be on the barricades. I had to come protect our government. I never even told my family I was going. I just knew my place was there."

Baskakov's men were assigned to guard entrance 22 of the parliament building, where many of the most important figures—Popov, former foreign minister Eduard Shevardnadze—were coming and going. The troops' weapons were pathetic, and they called themselves "suicide soldiers."

"The most terrible period was 1 to 5 a.m. Wednesday. With just 10 tanks and our defenseless people all around, we were just cannon fodder," he recalled.

Baskakov's people spotted snipers taking positions in windows across the street from the crowd. They were convinced that the KGB was using the Hotel Mir, across the street from the U.S. Embassy, as their base. But while the danger was extreme and the constant rumors of attack from all parts of Moscow—including from the air—were putting everyone on the streets in a state of excruciating anxiety, Baskakov was deeply moved at the sight of his own ragtag troops:

"I used to be critical of young people. There were bikers, the rockers, going on reconnaissance missions on their motorcycles across the barricades, giving us news about the troop movements. The young girls people call prostitutes, they were there giving us food and drink."

Just down the street, on Kutuzovsky Prospect, the sense of tension and emotion was just as profound. Nadezhda Kudinova was soaked from the rain. But someone gave her new shoes and socks. The usually surly administrators of the Ukraine Hotel across the street opened their rooms for the women on the barricades to stay overnight. Those who could slept in two- or three-hour shifts.

All the while, the women listened to a portable radio tuned to the independent station Echo of Moscow, where Russian Vice President Alexander Rutskoi and the parliament chairman, Ruslan Khasbulatov, were urging vigilance, civil disobedience and calm. Every few minutes there were bulletins about troop movements, the possibility that reconnaissance planes would signal the final attack.

"We always felt they were with us. They spoke with us in a special sort of language, in a heightened tone, like the words a man would speak before his death," Kudinova said. "I remember Rutskoi and Khasbulatov. They spoke to us very candidly, creating a feeling of unity beyond description. We heard them and they heard us."

The women insisted on forming the front line of the barricade on Kutuzovsky Prospect, and they carried signs that read, "Soviet Soldiers Don't Shoot Your Mothers." They were as ready to die as any hero of war.

"The people in the White House (the Russian parliament building) ordered us to step aside, not to jump under the tanks," Kudinova said. "But we knew that if the tanks came, we would step in front of them. We talked about where should we put the tanks that had defected over to our side, in front of or behind the barricades. We put them behind the barricades, because if they had been captured, the coup loyalists would have shot them dead. They are just young kids, after all."

A miracle happened. For some reason—timidity, fear of failure or sheer incompetence—the leaders of the coup backed off. Before dawn Wednesday, Vladimir Kryuchkov, the former KGB chief, called one of Yeltsin's chief aides and said, "O.K., you can go to sleep."

"God saved Russia," said the patriarch of the Russian Orthodox Church. Others added Yeltsin and the people of the republic to the list.

Like a man who has just learned from his doctor that a disease he once thought mortal was now benign, the city's mood shifted quickly. Suddenly the atmosphere was one of celebration. After Gorbachev finally was back in Moscow early Thursday, there was a fireworks display over the Russian parliament. Echo of Moscow began playing American rock-and-roll, and "The Hotel California" was booming from every radio.

Suddenly people realized not only that the political danger was over, that they had entered a new world of possibility. They also learned something about how deeply they had changed and what was inside of them.

"We would never have filled that order. Every soldier understands that they should not shoot at their own mothers and fathers," Chugunov said. "These were insane people who did this. We are dealing with a power struggle, and they're just a bunch of people who wanted to turn the world upside down. And if someone tries it again, they will fail."

Baskakov, the senior lieutenant at entrance 22, said he was moved that no one, not even those with everything to lose, betrayed his hopes. Just the opposite. His closest friend, a Jew who is planning to emigrate to the United States, was there at the barricades with him. "He left his family and joined us even though he was expecting attacks and repression against the Jews," Baskakov said at the funeral of the three young men who were killed on the barricades.

Kudinova, still weary from her three days spent on Kutuzovsky Prospect waiting for the tanks, also came to the funeral today. And she wept, both in grief and happiness, about all she had seen in so short a time.

"On the barricades," she said, "there was this incredible feeling of fellowship, which you will never get on a queue or on a trolley where men will never give you a seat. In everyday life, I guess you just don't notice it. But these were extreme circumstances, and somehow this week I saw the profound aspects of human nature. I never knew there were so many kind people in my country."

August 25, 1991

Glasnost Unstills Antisemitic Voices; Russian Nationalism Seen Reviving Currents of Prejudice

David Remnick

Glasnost, the Kremlin policy of free discussion that has opened up a world of literature and information, also has revealed what critics here see as an abiding, ominous tendency in Russian culture—"intellectual antisemitism."

No essay has drawn more attention among the Soviet intelligentsia this year than Igor Shafarevich's "Russophobia," which argues that "The Little People"—mainly Jewish writers and emigres—have ruined the self-respect of native Russians—"The Big People"—by describing them as a nation of slaves who worship power and intolerance.

Such journals as Nash Sovremenik (Our Contemporary), Molodaya Gvardiya (Young Guard) and Literaturnaya Rossiya (Literary Russia) regularly run articles and letters that many Jews here say echo the resentful themes of "Russophobia." But Shafarevich, a mathematician and a prominent political dissident in the 1970s, denied in an interview that he is antisemitic, calling such accusations the result of Jewish "persecution mania."

"There is only one nation about whose needs we hear about almost every day," Shafarevich wrote in Nash Sovremenik. "Jewish national emotions are the fever of the whole country and the whole world. They are a negative influence on disarmament, trade agreements and international relations of scientists. They provoke demonstrations and strikes and emerge in almost every conversation.

"The Jewish issue has acquired an incomprehensible power over people's minds and has overshadowed the problems of Ukranians, Estonians and Crimean Tatars. And as for the Russian issue, that is evidently not to be acknowledged at all."

Shafarevich says that certain Jewish authors and other members of "The Little People" hold inordinate power in Soviet society and head off all potential criticism through "the powerful Jewish lobby" and with hasty complaints of antisemitism.

"The term antisemitism is like an atom bomb in our heads," he declared. Of reports and rumors of attacks on Jews, Shafarevich said: "Against the background [of anti-Armenian and anti-Russian violence] it is impossible to speak of antisemitism. I haven't heard about a single quarrel or of people being beaten in the face because of antisemitism. It is absolutely incompatible with the real problems present now. I am just amazed to hear such things."

What frightens Jews most about Shafarevich and a number of other prominent figures here who agree with him is their intellectual and social stature. Unlike most members of the stridently antisemitic Organization Pamyat (Memory), a group often represented by close-cropped youths in black T-shirts waving neo-fascist banners, Shafarevich is a world-class mathematician with a reputation as a former political dissident of great intelligence and daring.

His essays on the need to restore Russian culture and values were included in "From Under the Rubble," an anti-socialist collection edited by dissident novelist Alexander Solzhenitsyn in the early 1970s. During that period, he found himself fired from teaching jobs, but now he is calling for government pressure on journals that publish the work of writers he identifies as Jewish "Russophobes."

"A couple of years ago there was just Pamyat, but they are on the lowest intellectual level, just the most lumpen people you can imagine," said Alexander Shmuckler, a leader of the Confederation of Jewish Organizations in the Soviet Union. "But now you have the rise of people like Shafarevich, and they are much more dangerous. They represent a merging of old anti-Zionist, anti-Jewish theory and practice. And all of it is under the guise of a return to a notion of the Great Russian empire."

Similar concern is voiced about Valentin Rasputin, a Siberian novelist who recently was appointed to President Mikhail Gorbachev's powerful advisory council. In recent years, Rasputin has spoken of Pamyat with sympathy and has pronounced Jews responsible for both the killing of Jesus and the terror of the first decades of the Soviet state.

Gorbachev has shown no sign of antisemitism. He has done a great deal to ease restrictions on religious believers. But some Jewish leaders and liberal-minded political figures here have conjectured that the Soviet leader may have been trying to use the Rasputin appointment as a conciliatory gesture to Russian nationalism—a strong, if politically disorganized, stream of contemporary political life.

Physicist Yuri Osipiyan, another member of the council, seemed slightly embarrassed by the subject.

"So-called ordinary, everyday antisemitism exists in the Soviet Union, probably to a greater extent than elsewhere in Europe," Osipiyan said. "There are two reasons for that. The first is that under glasnost a lot of things have cropped up once again. Second, economic differences among the groups in the less advantaged part of society cause resentment, much as they did in {pre-World War II} Germany."

An intellectual ally of Rasputin, historian Valentin Pikul, has taken the argument of Jewish revolutionary culpability even further, all but excusing Soviet dictator Joseph Stalin as a "product of his epoch" but labeling Jewish leaders of the Bolshevik period as "fanatics of mass murder" who were responsible for the "genocide of the Russians and other peoples." Pikul, writing in Nash Sovremenik, says that those same "fanatics" are now "being elevated to the ranks of the saints and want a memorial built to themselves."

While such voices are strident, they do not represent a coherent political movement. Candidates running for national or local office with the endorsement of Pamyat or similar groups almost invariably lost in recent open elections. In Moscow, not one of the 200 candidates running as Russian nationalists won in last month's balloting for local offices. "That's the good news about all this," Osipiyan said.

But neither is the viewpoint of Shafarevich and other like-minded intellectuals in want of an audience. He appears frequently on television and radio, and his theory of politics and cultural conflict in Russia is treated with great seriousness. Nash Sovremenik, the journal that best represents his views on "The Little People," has doubled its circulation recently to nearly 1 million, while other publications seem to have abandoned any semblance of restraint.

Last month, 72 Russian writers published a letter in Literaturnaya Rossiya saying that "a Zionist organization Beitar legalized in the U.S.S.R. is responsible for slogans of Jewish national supremacy and hundreds of bloody crimes and acts of terror that make the world community shudder.... It is precisely Zionism that is responsible for many things, including Jewish pogroms, for cutting off dry branches of their own people in Auschwitz and Dachau..."

In the interview, Shafarevich did not defend such views, but he did not dispute them either. Instead, he sought to defend Russian nationalism generally, saying: "Isn't it strange that when, say, French nationalists like Charles de Gaulle were at the head of government, there was no danger in that? But with us it's different? These are the myths created by this movement of 'The Little People.'"

Over the last two years, Soviet Jews have been leaving the country for Israel and the West in record numbers. About 100,000 left in 1989, and Jewish sources here estimate that a half-million have applied for exit visas out of a population of about 1.3 million. "It seems that in 10 years you might have just 500,000 Jews left in the Soviet Union, and most of them older people," Shmuckler said.

As reasons for migrating, they cite the great uncertainties of Soviet life in a period of political rupture. They say that as the economy grows worse, the likelihood of people turning on the ancient scapegoat, the Jews, grows more likely. In a recent poll conducted by Soviet sociologist Tatyana Zaslavskaya, 72 percent of Moscow's Jewish leaders said they could envisage an explosion of antisemitic emotions in the "nearest future." Among prominent Jews in Leningrad, the figure was 94 percent.

Such anxieties have led to frequent rumors of outbreaks of anti-Jewish violence. Although they support the new free-speech climate here, Jewish leaders say it is nearly impossible to bear what they read in the pages of Nash Sovremenik and Molodaya Gvardiya, much less the cruder pamphlets put out by Pamyat.

"We live frightened lives," said Natalya Rappaport, a chemist whose daughter Vika recently left for Israel. "In dangerous times, eyes always seem to turn to the Jews. When Vika left, it was the first time in weeks that I had a good night's sleep.

April 12, 1990

Social Institutions: Religion

Chinese Students Turn to Churches; Curiosity, Desire for Change Stimulate Interest in Religion

Daniel Southerland

Hundreds of Chinese young people, including elite university students, crowded into Beijing churches this Christmas season with an eagerness not seen since students demonstrated in the streets a year ago.

The students' attendance at Christian churches seems to reflect a desire to escape the dullness of life here and a growing curiosity about the culture and traditions of the West. In some cases, it also appears to show an upsurge in genuine religious feeling.

Whatever the motivations for this new interest, the Chinese Communist Party has one more reason to worry.

"People don't want to join the Communist Party," said a scholar who joined the party many years ago. "They want to go to church."

Another academic related the churchgoing to a continuing "crisis of confidence" in the Communist Party and its ideology and to the party's decision to suppress student demonstrations in early 1987.

"They were so disappointed by the party that they've been searching for something else," the scholar said. "They've tried dancing, card playing and premarital sex. Now they go to church."

Yet most seem attracted to the services out of curiosity.

"I asked my daughter why she went to church, and she said she found it interesting—she said it was just for fun," said another Chinese intellectual who has never attended church.

A student at Beijing University said that his generation never had a chance to believe in anything except what the party preached. He said he was envious of people who believe in something, particularly those who believe in the concept of life after death.

Another student said, "We feel Christianity is more closely tied to human nature than orthodox Marxism. Students are trying to find something that is more connected with their daily life."

The increase in the number of young people attending church this Christmas was evident in other Chinese cities as well.

The South China Morning Post newspaper reported that in Guangzhou, formerly Canton, in the south of China, the crowd entering the Sacred Heart of Jesus Cathedral for a midnight mass was so large that priests tried to control admission.

"If you are not Catholic you should not come in," one church assistant was quoted as saying.

He refused admission to a young man who could not provide his Christian name.

Other church officials tried issuing tickets to keep out curious spectators.

The party is now much more tolerant of religion than it was during the Cultural Revolution (1966-76) when churches were destroyed and believers were driven underground.

The Communist Party has banned proselytizing by Christians in China.

It is widely known, however, that a number of foreign teachers come to China hoping to spread their faith.

Christians still constitute a small minority of the population, but church officials and others say the number is growing.

As one university dean who is a party member commented, "It is a child of the open policy," referring to the government's tolerance of different beliefs.

Roman Catholic Bishop Michael Fu Tieshan of Beijing estimated that China now has 3.3 million practicing Catholics in the state-approved Catholic Church, which has no ties to the Vatican, according to a recent New China News Agency report.

Fu said 30,000 people join the church each year.

Bishop K.H. Ting, principal of the Nanjing Union Theological Seminary, said recently that China has 3 million to 4 million Protestants.

For some city youths, going to church is part of an exploration of things western. One practice that has become popular for city people of all ages is buying and exchanging Christmas cards.

According to the official New China News Agency, it is not uncommon for a Chinese in Beijing to spend $2 to $4 on Christmas cards, a large expenditure by Chinese standards.

The manager of a foreign language bookstore said the store had sold more than 400,000 cards.

"I've never gotten so many Christmas cards as I've gotten in China," said a Jewish foreign teacher who lives here.

"I like Christmas cards with the Virgin Mary and little angels on them," said Zhao Huanhong, a high school girl who is a nonbeliever. "They give me a holy feeling."

Students' growing interest in Christianity comes despite last winter's Communist Party campaign against western democratic influences and western-style consumerism.

This campaign against "bourgeois liberalism," launched after students began calling for democracy and freedom in street demonstrations, appears to have failed, based on interviews with several students in Beijing.

While they have muted their views on the need for democracy, the students have not changed their minds nor have they abandoned their desire to acquire consumer goods.

It sometimes takes the form of a "money is everything" attitude.

In some ways, therefore, the Communist Party may be grateful that the churches are teaching a form of morality. Indeed, for some years now, Communist scholars have said Christians can make a constructive contribution to Chinese society.

The officially approved Chinese Catholic Church broke with the Vatican 30 years ago and refuses to defer to Rome. But church sources outside China said that a large number of Catholics in China quietly recognize the authority of the pope and worship in secret.

This November reports circulated that Pope John Paul II might visit China following Filipino Cardinal Jaime Sin's visit to Beijing and behind-the-scenes negotiations. The Vatican subsequently denied any plans for a papal trip.

But at this point, the young people of China are still not likely to fervently welcome the pope. As one student put it, "Most students don't understand Christmas or Christianity. They are more interested in the holiday atmosphere of Christmas."

January 2, 1988

Soviets End Controls on Religion; New Law Abolishes Atheist Education in Public Schools

David Remnick

The Soviet legislature today adopted a historic new measure that puts an end to the Bolshevik policy of atheist education and state control of religious institutions and permits organized religious instruction for the first time in the memory of most Soviet citizens.

The legislature, or Supreme Soviet, voted 341 to 1 with one abstention to adopt the new law, but it will continue to debate on a number of particular issues covered by it, including the concept of religious education in public schools and religious services in Soviet military units.

After decades of official persecution, the practice of religion in the Soviet Union has been allowed far greater freedom in the past five years, a development that was illustrated perhaps most vividly last Sunday when Russian Orthodox Patriarch Alexei II celebrated the first full Mass in the Kremlin's Uspensky Cathedral since 1918.

Soviet President Mikhail Gorbachev, who was baptized into the Orthodox faith as a child, has met frequently with religious leaders since he assumed power in 1985 and had promised publicly to do away with harsh restrictions on religion.

Since the founding of the Soviet state by Lenin and the brutal dictatorship of Joseph Stalin that followed, the Kremlin has confiscated or destroyed thousands of churches and synagogues, executed or otherwise persecuted countless members of the clergy and infiltrated religious organizations with KGB agents.

The new law on "Freedom of Conscience and Religious Organizations" declares that all religions are equal under the law and bars the state henceforth from interfering in religious affairs.

Over the course of seven decades of Communist rule, the state outlawed most religious education and kept iron control over what little remained. The new measure forbids such interference and declares that religious institutions are free to set up classes, send students abroad for training and receive exchange students. It also allows religious groups to establish "societies, brotherhoods, associations" and other organizations for the public profession of their faiths.

Patriarch Alexei told the Soviet legislature today that the church is generally satisfied with the new law, but he added that he hopes state-run schools also would allow religious instruction. He was supported by Armenian legislator Genrikh Igitian, who said that traditional atheist instruction had worked to help "destroy" the country. "I believe every educated person should be instructed in religion," he said.

But another lawmaker, scientist Sergei Ryabachenko of the Ukraine, said that divisions between Russian Orthodox believers and Ukrainian Catholics—who unlike Orthodox adherents acknowledge the authority of the pope—are so heated that religious education in public schools in the Ukraine could turn the republic into "another Beirut."

"Given current conditions," he said, "we cannot allow our schools to be turned into scenes of battle between conflicting confessions."

The law maintains existing policy of exempting charitable donations from taxes and cuts the tax rate on profits of enterprises run by religious organizations from 69 percent to 35 percent. The most common enterprise is the publication of copies of the Bible and Koran.

Alexei also proposed establishment of an Orthodox Church publishing house to earn money to help restore the churches that were ruined or used as warehouses or factories under previous Soviet regimes.

Since Gorbachev came to power five years ago, many key religious centers, such as the Orthodox Pechorski Monastery in Kiev, have been returned to the religious organizations that founded them. The state also has allowed many more Soviet Moslems to make their required pilgrimages to Mecca and allowed importation and domestic publication of books sacred to various faiths. Jews have been allowed to emigrate in greater numbers than ever before, and a rabbinical school has opened in Moscow.

Christian and Islamic religious leaders now hold seats in the Soviet legislature, and even dissident Orthodox priest Gleb Yakunin, who had been jailed and exiled in the Brezhnev era, has won election to that body. Yakunin is also the leader of one of a number of Chriatian Democratic political parties.

September 27, 1990

Islam, Secular Life Pull at Pakistan; Many Back Laws Promoting Piety But Profit from Illicit Pursuits

Steve Coll

At an open-air stand across from this city's largest mosque, a trader named Yusuf does a brisk business selling illegal sex accessories: aphrodisiacs, pornography, love potions and the best-selling Stud, advertised as the "world-famous delay chewing gum for men."

A spirited entrepreneur who speaks in enthusiastic bursts about the benefits of his products, Yusuf also considers himself a committed Moslem. He supports Pakistan's new government of political and religious conservatives and welcomes its proposal for tough Islamic laws that, if implemented, would likely push him into bankruptcy, jail or both.

Yusuf's seemingly irreconcilable attitudes illustrate the quandary faced by Pakistan's new leaders as they try to fulfill their pledge to create a more pious Islamic society by enforcing strict interpretations of the Moslem legal code, known as Sharia. The new laws are expected to prescribe amputation for thieves and imprisonment or death for fornicators.

Many Pakistanis, tired of crime, corruption and the breakdown of civil institutions, support the idea of tough new laws and punishments. But at the same time, millions of citizens prosper from booming and well-organized trade in pornography, prostitution, drugs, smuggling, kidnapping and petty extortion. Neither the powerful proprietors nor the numerous customers of these businesses show any enthusiasm about changing their ways.

For months this year, Pakistan's prime minister, Nawas Sharif, and his supporters delivered fiery Islamic exhortations in their campaign to defeat the secularist former prime minister, Benazir Bhutto. But Sharif's government, which faces a panoply of economic and foreign policy problems, already has indicated that it does not want to alienate Pakistanis by pushing too suddenly for a strict Islamic order.

Several weeks ago, the government promulgated a law derived from the Koran, Islam's holy book, requiring bus and taxi drivers to pay the equivalent of 100 camels—just under $10,000—to the family of any pedestrian killed in a highway traffic accident. Bus drivers promptly went on strike, saying the fine was too stiff, and the law was quickly suspended to settle the protest.

For at least a decade, rightist Pakistani politicians and generals frequently have mouthed fundamentalist Islamic slogans but rarely have put them into practice. In the broadest terms, that is because 43 years after Pakistan was founded as a homeland for Moslems on the Indian subcontinent, neither the country's leaders nor its citizens have been able to forge a comfortable marriage of religion and politics.

234

The reasons are many and complex. As an institution, Islam in Pakistan is weakened by a diversity of sects. And while many ordinary Pakistanis profess a strong sense of Islamic identity, they have consistently rejected the most radical Moslem clerics, who are widely seen as power-hungry, opportunistic or financially corrupt. Particularly among the country's urban elite, there is a wide gap between frequent, pious, public pronouncements about Islam and private social mores that have been heavily influenced by the West. "There's a lot of hypocrisy in this society," said Razia Bhatti, editor of Newsline, a Karachi-based magazine. "People try to pretend that they are what they are not."

The country's tiny secular elite feels pressure to toe a religious line in public because Pakistan's small cadres of organized fundamentalists have proven that they can quickly stir up popular frenzy against anyone branded as anti-Islamic.

Bhutto, for one, appeared intimidated during her 20 months as prime minister by the cultural veto power of the fundamentalists. Although vocal in her support for women's rights, she cultivated a demure and traditional public manner and never sought secularist laws challenging the widespread discrimination against women engendered by Islamic practices.

Stuck between the country's Westernized elite and its Islamic radicals are tens of millions of peasant farmers, urban laborers and small-time traders, whose personal lives are steeped in Moslem traditions, but whose livelihoods depend on a deeply corrupt economy. These ordinary Pakistanis sometimes voice a yearning for credible religious leadership even as they prosper and revel In its absence.

At Karachi's Smugglers' Market, where Yusuf and dozens of other traders offer a dazzling variety of illegally imported sex accessories, Indian and pornographic films, Western cosmetics and luxury goods, the contradictory forces shaping modern Pakistan are obvious.

Across from the sex market looms the Meman Mosque, a towering edifice of red sandstone with cool marble floors and an aura of solemn beauty. A number of the Smugglers' Market traders lamented in interviews that they cannot leave their shops to pray at the mosque because they fear they will be robbed while gone. It is a reduction in Pakistan's crime and chaos, rather than any evident enthusiasm for an austere religious life, that leads the traders to say they favor strict Islamic laws. When an Islamic system is achieved, "ours will be a peaceful and strict society," said shopkeeper Muhammad Sayeed.

In a back office of the Meman Mosque, the chief mullah, Razaul Mustafa Azmi, his shirt buttoned with jewelled studs, pored over the mosque's accounts. A burning cigarette dangled from his lips. He paused to discuss negotiations over a construction project with an assistant, stuffed a wad of chewing tobacco in his mouth and settled back to explain why Islam has been slow to take hold as an organizing principle in Pakistani society.

"Until religious leaders like us are in the government, it won't be possible to have proper Islam," he said. "People lack Islamic education.... They are only interested in rituals and prayers."

While Azmi dismissed the sex market across the street as "wildness," he said it occurs in all Moslem countries. Besides, he noted, since Islamic law allows a man to take four wives, he may require some help to please them.

Next to the mosque is one of Karachi's police stations, where officers lounged one afternoon reading newspapers. Traders at the Smugglers' Market say they bribe the police not to interfere with their business. The police say that is not true, but they concede that if they arrested any of the traders for selling sex objects, local residents would mutiny—as happened recently in the city of Lahore after police raided a popular brothel.

One senior officer said that the basic problem was that "sex mania" from the West had corrupted Pakistan's women, causing them to lose their minds and seduce men in an accelerating cycle of decadence. Strict Islamic laws might eventually solve this problem, he said, "but it will take some time."

December 23, 1990

Islamic Resurgence in Malaysia: Singapore, Indonesia Worried about Leader's Control

Keith B. Richburg

Malaysia is in the midst of a growing Islamization movement, and the country's Southeast Asian neighbors are worried about the government's ability to control it.

In Singapore and Indonesia, government officials, diplomats and political analysts have voiced concern in recent weeks that the Islamic resurgence here in Malaysia may embolden Moslem extremists in those two countries.

Singapore is home to a Malay-Moslem minority that maintains close links to Malaysia; Indonesia is the world's largest Moslem country.

Increasingly, officials in those two countries are raising questions about Malaysian Prime Minister Mahathir Mohamad's approach to the Islamic movement here. Mahathir has tried to outmaneuver the Moslem extremists by embracing the Islamization drive as his own.

Malaysia is a multiracial society of 16 million with a slight Moslem majority. About 48 percent of the population are ethnic Malay, and almost all the Malays are Moslem.

Begun as a student-led movement in the 1970s, the Islamic resurgence has rapidly gained respectability here as many of those Moslem student leaders graduated and entered the political mainstream, including the ruling party.

Although Malay Moslems are almost entirely Sunnis, many of those involved in the Islamic resurgence say that one of the driving influences has been the Shiite revolution in Iran.

Ayatollah Khomeini's revolutionary brand of antiwestern Islam apparently has a strong appeal among young Malays, and many of them have traveled to Iran to study the revolution on trips arranged by Tehran or by an extremist group in Malaysia.

Over the past decade, more students have enrolled in Moslem religious schools, many new mosques have been erected around the country, and many more women walk the streets of the capital wearing traditional Islamic veils, according to longtime residents. The government has also established an Islamic bank to operate on Islamic financial principles, such as not charging interest on loans.

"Before we sent our students abroad and we were afraid they would come back and be hippies," said Rosna Majid, a journalist for the Utesan Malaysia newspaper. "Now we are afraid they will come back and be dakwah {a proselytizing Moslem} Now the way people are covering themselves is different. The older people just use scarves, but younger women are covering themselves like the Iranians."

Although most analysts here seem unconcerned about the spread of Iranian influence because of Iran's policy of confrontation, the government is treading delicately. Certainly in the eyes of its neighbors, Malaysia appears to be accommodating the Islamization movement.

That policy so far appears to be succeeding. In the last national elections, in 1986, the government held the Parti Islam Se Malaysia, or Pas, a Moslem opposition party that wants to make Malaysia an Islamic state, to a single seat in the 177-seat parliament.

But many analysts, and officials from Singapore and Indonesia, are wondering whether the Malay government, by accommodating the movement, is encouraging the fundamentalists to escalate their demands.

"Mahatir appears to be kowtowing to the fundamentalists," said one western diplomat in Singapore. "There is a feeling that Mahathir is riding the tiger of Islamic fundamentalism, but not really controlling it."

This diplomat and others cited a series of recent incidents that have raised questions about where the movement is headed. In Johore Bahru state, across the causeway from Singapore, officials have proposed changing a state law so non-Moslems as well as Moslems could be flogged publicly with a cane if caught committing khalwat, or "close proximity" between the sexes.

A few weeks ago in Kuala Lumpur, a respected Islamic scholar proposed changing the constitution to have Islamic law, or sharia, prevail when it comes into conflict with Malaysia's adopted English common law code.

"From a Singaporean perspective, they are very concerned about what's happening in Malaysia," said another western diplomat in Singapore. "Almost weekly some state is announcing tougher Islamic measures."

The Malaysian government's response has been the mirror image of the reaction of officials in Indonesia, which with 160 million people is the world's largest Moslem country.

Indonesia has pursued a tough campaign to depoliticize Islam. In recent years, the government of President Suharto enacted a series of restrictions, such as forcing the major Moslem-based party to adopt the national secular ideology of Pancasila, while building up moderate Moslem leaders. Suharto also launched a crackdown on the extremists, many of whom were arrested after a series of bombings.

As a result, Indonesia has won widespread praise in the region for successfully defusing Islam as a factor in Indonesian politics.

But on Oct. 5, an Indonesian Justice Ministry official was quoted as saying Indonesia will incorporate far more Islamic law into future legislation because almost 90 percent of the population is Moslem.

Baharuddin Lopa, quoted in the Jakarta Post, said future penal codes would be based more on Islamic law than in the past to make them more acceptable to the people. Such a change would mean tougher punishment for adultery and murder, he said.

"We face difficulties with Malaysia," said Abdurrahman Wahid, the head of Nahdatul Ulama, a conservative council of Islamic teachers in Jakarta. "I ask them, don't follow the appeasement policy too much. The fundamentalists will demand more and more. Now they demand caning, and after 10 years they will demand cutting off hands."

Malaysian officials in Kuala Lumpur said the fears are misguided.

"The government has delved more into Islamic matters because it feels the people want these things," said Kamarudim Mohamad Nor, an official of the ruling United Malays National Organization, known as UMNO, and a member of the World Assembly of Moslem Youth. "If they do not counter this sentiment, then people will swing to Pas. Rather than lose to Pas, you might as well become more Islamic yourself.

"This is what UMNO wants the non-Moslems to understand—you are better off having moderates like us institute the Islamization," he said.

Political analysts and religious leaders said the resurgence was born mainly of a youthful desire to preserve some of the trappings of traditional rural Malay life in the face of rapid growth and development.

"The resurgence of Islam here started long before anyone knew Khomeini was in the world," said Subky Latif, a spokesman for Pas.

"But of course their victory [in Iran] gave us new spirit that Islam can achieve victory." He said the party has helped "a few" young people travel to Iran.

October 24, 1987

Singapore Fears Surge in Command Tension: Race, Religion Issues Simmer Below Surface

Keith B. Richburg

From the outside, this prosperous island city-state is Asia's model melting pot: "A Nation For All," as this year's Independence Day slogan proudly proclaims.

But a series of incidents here has forced Singaporeans to confront issues of race and religion, and officials have voiced unusually candid concerns in recent weeks that internal and external pressures could disrupt the appearance of ethnic harmony.

The latest controversy surrounds the government's fear that the involvement of Catholic lay workers in leftist Organizing might politicize other groups, notably the predominantly Moslem Malays, who make up 15 percent of the population. Amid a surge of Islamic fundamentalism in neighboring Malaysia, the government here has publicly questioned the loyalties of Singapore's ethnic Malays.

Such issues are old here. But the intensity of discussion in the press and in interviews with government officials, diplomats and dissidents suggests a new urgency and a recognition that after 22 years of independence Singapore remains more ethnically divided than the government would like.

"We are seemingly prosperous and peaceful, but let us not forget the ultimate vulnerability of Singapore," said one government official close to Prime Minister Lee Kuan Yew. "Any concerted effort can spark racial tension."

"You look at Singapore and see a western-style democracy. We dress western, we act western," said another high-ranking minister. "But there are some deep, emotive pools that can never be wiped out—race, language and, in the case of the Malays, religion. These are very deep and abiding loyalties."

In an Aug. 9 Independence Day message, Lee warned that "once religion crosses the line and goes into what they call social action, liberation theology, then we are opening up Pandora's box in Singapore."

Lee's message was most specifically directed to the Catholic church, which saw several of its lay workers arrested in May for involvement in what the government claims was a Marxist conspiracy.

But Lee also aimed his remarks at Islamic clerics and at a recent influx of American-influenced Christian fundamentalists, who have angered some Malays here by trying to convert Singaporean Moslems, according to diplomats and Singaporean officials.

As part of his concern about the politicization of religion, Lee said he recently barred four Moslem preachers from entering Singapore because they had incited Malays here to militancy during earlier visits.

Government officials privately said they are worried about a growing Moslem resurgence in Malaysia and about the Malaysian government's ability to control Islamic extremism.

As an island city-state of 2.6 million people—three-quarters of them Chinese—Singapore is sensitive to its potentially vulnerable position between two large Malay-Moslem nations, Malaysia to the north and Indonesia to the south. Singapore's population is about 58 percent Buddhist, 16 percent Moslem, 12 percent Christian and 4 percent Hindu.

The country's racial mix stems from 100 years as a British colony.

Britain encouraged massive Chinese and Indian immigration. Now, 22 years after Singapore became independent from Malaysia, the government still grapples to maintain peaceful relations among its races and prevent a repeat of racially motivated rioting here in the 1950s and early 1960s.

The recent warnings about the dangers of mixing religion with politics have followed two controversies involving the Malay community.

The first was sparked by an official visit here last November by Israeli President Chaim Herzog. That visit prompted huge protests from outraged Moslems in neighboring Malaysia, who saw the visit by the leader of the Jewish state as an affront to Islam. They demonstrated at the narrow causeway linking the two countries. When Singaporean Malays also protested, Lee questioned whether they were loyal to Singapore or took their cues from Malaysia.

Earlier this year, Lee's son and trade minister, Brig. Gen. Lee Hsien Loong, opened an emotional debate here by saying Malays played a limited role in the Singaporean armed forces because "we don't want to put any of our soldiers in a difficult position, where his emotions for the nation may come into conflict with his emotions for his religion."

Such statements have rankled many Singaporean Malays, most of whom were born here. "All we ask is that we be treated like Singaporeans," said an outspoken Malay lawyer, a Moslem.

To demonstrate their loyalty, more than 200 Malay community leaders and others went last month to Orchard Road, the central downtown thoroughfare, to sign their names in a ceremonial pledge book set up for Independence Day.

The government had already raised some suspicions among Malays by the prime minister's new campaign to boost the country's population by using tax incentives and other measures to encourage people—particularly better educated and more affluent people—to have more children.

Some Malays and Indians interviewed said they believed that the policy was aimed at encouraging the Chinese, who tend to have the country's highest education and income levels, to boost their population.

Race relations have been helped by the country's dynamic economic growth and some constitutional guarantees for the country's Malays, such as free education.

At the same time, the government is using the race issue to justify tight restrictions on expression and dissent and tough controls on the foreign and local press.

Even though the situation here is far different from that in Sri Lanka, government officials invariably raise the ethnic violence in that island nation as an example of what they fear most for Singapore.

September 16, 1987

Social Institutions : Education

New Focus Sought in National High School Exams: NEH Backs Approach Used in Europe and Japan to Assess Knowledge Rather Than Aptitude

Kenneth J. Cooper

In a report on national testing of high school students, the National Endowment for the Humanities has called for U.S. schools to give examinations similar to European and Japanese tests that assess knowledge of history and the other humanities rather than college aptitude.

Several official and private groups have been working to develop or promote national exams that measure achievement, which they say could spur improvements in education and the work force by setting tougher standards for high school curricula and higher expectations for students.

Last month, President Bush endorsed a national system of voluntary "American achievement tests" as part of his administration's education strategy.

In the introduction to the report by the federal agency, endowment chairman Lynne V. Cheney endorsed content-oriented national testing and concluded that exams given in the other nations surveyed reflect "very high standards for the humanities," including U.S. history. She questioned whether American students know as much about their own history.

"Could American students answer the questions that the French ask about the foreign policy of the U.S.? That the British ask about American progressivism? That European schools ask about South Carolina's secession?" Cheney asked. "Do we expect our students to know American history as well as other countries expect their students to know it? Do we expect our students to know the history of other nations in anything approaching the detail with which they are expected to know ours?"

Cheney does not respond directly, but indicates the answers are hard to know because the major college entrance exams, the Scholastic Aptitude Test (SAT) and American College Testing Program (ACT), are designed to assess English and mathematics skills, not knowledge of specific subjects.

"Our most common, high-stakes examinations are divorced from the classroom study of subjects like history. They do little to advance the notion that hard work in school matters," she said.

The College Board, which sponsors the SAT, also offers Achievement Tests in specific subjects that some colleges require their applicants to take. But in an interview Cheney criticized Achievement Tests in two humanities, English and history, as "loosely related" to what students learn in high school because they demand little specific knowledge of literature and events.

Her introduction praised the academic standards contained in Advanced Placement exams, another group of College Board tests, but noted that only 7 percent of U.S. students take them.

"Many educators in the United States are coming to believe that it is a great mistake to limit achievement testing to a small group," she said. "A system that now benefits a few of our students should be put to work for all."

Bush's plan calls for more than one exam, all calibrated to the same national standards, that states and school districts could choose to administer to every student in grades 4, 8 and 12. Students would be tested in English, math, science, history and geography.

The endowment's report examines national tests from Japan, Germany, France, Britain and the European Community, which has established "European Schools" in Italy, Belgium, the Netherlands, Luxembourg, Germany and Britain, primarily for children of diplomats posted in those nations.

The National Center for Fair and Open Testing, which has opposed national tests as a costly diversion from school improvement efforts, charged that the endowment's report holds "little relevance" to Bush's proposal because the other nations cited do not test all of their students.

"The truth is, no other country has national exams like those the administration proposes—not Germany, not Japan, not Great Britain, not France," said Monty Neill, associate director of FairTest, based in Cambridge, Mass. "They don't test every child, and they don't use the tests to compare teachers and schools."

Britain plans to give all 16-year-old students basic standardized exams, while about a third of French students took the baccalaureate exam and 15 percent of Japanese took the college entrance exam last year, according to the report.

Cheney said the endowment's survey determined that national testing need not depend on a multiple-choice format or a national curriculum—two criticisms leveled by various U.S. education and civil rights groups. Japan and France tie their exams to a uniform curriculum, she said, but noted that each German state develops its own version of the college entrance exam. She said only the Japanese rely heavily on multiple-choice items, which are easily graded, while the other nations commonly require test-takers to produce written answers.

Among test items about U.S. history reproduced in the report are a French question on "the president and presidential power in the Constitution and domestic and foreign policy of the United States since 1945," a British question on "why were so many of the victories of progressivism won at city and state, rather than at federal, level" and a European Community passage, requiring oral responses, on South Carolina's reasons for seceding from the United States in December 1860.

May 20, 1991

National Test for High School Seniors Gains Backing

Kenneth J. Cooper

A new education group chaired by former New Jersey governor Thomas H. Kean yesterday proposed that all high school seniors be required to take a national examination of their knowledge and skills.

The proposal for a comprehensive system of national testing, which does not now exist, came as other groups have endorsed the idea as a way to measure progress on national education goals and to push schools to produce better results. The proponents have included a presidential advisory panel and the National Alliance for Business.

But the notion of a national test remains controversial among many educators, who fear it would undermine state and local control of schools by leading to a national curriculum. Other critics have argued against another standardized test by saying U.S. students already spend too much time taking multiple-choice tests that have limited educational value.

Whether the debate will lead to a national test may depend on governors, who as a group have appeared unwilling to relinquish state authority, and President Bush, who has not publicly addressed the subject.

Kean's nonprofit group, Educate America Inc., proposed that high school seniors each November spend nine hours taking tests in reading, writing, mathematics, history, geography and science. Graduation would not hinge on the results, but scores could be sent to prospective employers and colleges.

Many states already require high school students to pass basic skills tests, and nearly all college-bound students take the Scholastic Aptitude Test or the American College Testing program. But there is no single test required of all students.

Kean, now president of Drew University in Madison, N.J., said that such testing would "add meaning to that (high school) diploma. encourage student achievement and instill higher standards."

Average state and school results would be published, he said, to strengthen accountability for learning. National figures could be used to track progress on the national goals of improving student achievement and reaching universal literacy among adults.

Saul Cooperman, Educate America's president and New Jersey's education commissioner under Kean, urged Congress to mandate the testing and pay costs estimated at $90 million a year. A possible approach would be to mandate the testing in school districts that receive federal funding, as most do.

A spokesman described Rep. William D. Ford (D-Mich.), the new chairman of the House Education and Labor Committee, as being skeptical of a national test because of the cost, potential for teaching only those subjects covered by the examination and possible creation of a national curriculum.

Chester Finn, an education professor at Vanderbilt University in Nashville and Educate America board member, said a national test would "sort of" lead to a uniform curriculum, but he argued that one created partly by textbook publishers already exists. "We ought to acknowledge that we have a national curriculum that is doing us no good at all," he said.

The prospect of a national curriculum has been a sensitive one for a panel of governors and Bush administration officials charged with figuring out how to measure progress on national education goals. The panel, chaired by Colorado Gov. Roy Romer (D), appears to be leaning toward adopting a single set of achievement standards that could be used to "calibrate" several tests. Those tests could then be adopted by regional groupings of states.

"We modestly think our proposal is a little better," said Cooperman, suggesting results of a single test would be more easily understood.

Bush's advisory panel on education policy also favors national testing in grades 4, 8 and 12. Kean is a member of that panel. So too is former Tennessee governor Lamar Alexander, Bush's nominee to be education secretary.

January 31, 1991

Shrugging Off the Burden of a Brainy Image, Asian American Students Say Stereotype of 'Model Minority' Achievers Is Unfair

Stephen Buckley

The stereotype says they're overachievers, gifted in math and science. It says they study harder, get better grades and consistently outscore other students on standardized tests. Yet some Asian American students regard their status as America's "model minority" as both a blessing and a burden.

They say they grow weary of unreasonable expectations from peers and teachers, and harbor a sense that their accomplishments are rarely appreciated because everyone expects them to succeed.

"Everybody thinks you're smart, everybody thinks you know everything," said Rowena Flores, 17, a junior at Howard High School who emigrated from the Philippines in 1986. "One girl said to me, 'I wish I was from the Philippines so I could be smart.' "

During the past decade, as Asian Americans have flocked to the Washington area, their numbers have risen significantly in some area school systems. Fairfax County schools are now 11.7 percent Asian American, compared with 5 percent in 1980. In Montgomery County, the Asian student population has leaped to 12.5 percent from 5.7 percent a decade ago.

Asian Americans are well represented in advanced placement classes and gifted and talented programs, and are often a strong presence in magnet schools, school officials said. In Alexandria, for example, 30 percent of that system's Asian students are enrolled in gifted and talented programs. In Fairfax County, the Thomas Jefferson High School for Science and Technology, which draws students from all over Northern Virginia, has a student enrollment that is 22.6 percent Asian.

But with such success have come high standards and extraordinary pressures, school officials, students and teachers say.

Alan Cheung, who last November became the first Asian American elected to Montgomery County's school board, worries especially about newer immigrants. He fears they will be pushed too hard by a school system that "automatically assumes they will do well. [Administrators and teachers] perceive that if a child is Asian, they don't need what other students need."

"The stereotypes may be positive, but they are not always for the benefit of the kids," said Lily Wong-Fillmore, a professor of linguistics at the University of California at Berkeley, who has studied how immigrant children adjust to American schools. "God was operating with a normal curve when he produced Asian kids. Some are remarkably bright. Some are not."

Stereotypes and parental pressure often lead to insecurity among Asian American young people, particularly middle-of-the-road students, Wong-Fillmore said. "It's a real hardship for kids who're ordinary Joe Wongs," she said.

Stan Cheung (no relation to Alan Cheung), a sophomore at Wilde Lake High School in Columbia, learned in grade school that his friends saw Asian students as workaholics who spent all their free time studying and never having fun.

Cheung didn't like that perception, so he worked at being socially accepted. "I didn't want people to laugh. I didn't want people to tease me," said Cheung, 16, whose family moved here from China about 20 years ago. "So I screwed around, basically."

Cheung said that teachers and classmates who know him aren't surprised by his C-average grades. But, he said, students unfamiliar with him see his marks and say, " 'Hold up here for a moment.' They expect you to do really good."

Asian students said they are rarely confronted directly by fellow students or instructors who expect that all Asians will be academic success stories. Instead, pressure often comes in more indirect ways.

Jeff Wang, a sophomore at Montgomery Blair High School in Silver Spring, remembers attending a math camp last summer. "They tended to expect people like me to do well," Wang said. "They didn't say it, but you could feel it in their attitudes."

When Asian Americans do well, Wang added, "people will say, 'He's just a normal Asian.' They expect me to achieve a lot, but they don't notice it when I do."

Myung Park, a junior at Wilde Lake High, recalls earning a mark of 78 on a social studies test this year, which tied for the highest mark in the class. His teacher "asked me what happened. She asked me if I was slacking off. I wouldn't have minded if she had talked to everybody, but she didn't."

Area school officials say that teachers' attitudes toward Asian American students have changed in recent years, as systems have placed greater emphasis on sensitivity workshops and training.

"Teachers used to think Asians were all superachievers, and I think that's changing," said Carol Chen, who works with students and their parents in Montgomery's English for Speakers of Other Languages program.

Instructors acknowledge that they're aware of the stereotypes and battle—usually successfully, they say—to resist prejudgment. However, they add, they know that some teachers stumble.

Friederika Hoppes, a teacher at Montgomery Blair who sponsors the Chinese Club, said that stereotyping occurs because "when some teachers see a pattern emerge where Asian Americans are succeeding in their intellectual pursuits, they conclude that it has something to do with race."

Asian students say that some stereotypes are reinforced by their parents, who often balk when their children express a desire to pursue professions that are not related to math or science.

"I want to work with animals, but my dad wants me to go into medicine," said Cori Liv, a junior at Howard High, whose family moved here from Cambodia in 1977. "He wants me to go back to Cambodia and help the people there. That's great, but it's just not for me."

Some Asian parents say they do push their children. And Asian cultures traditionally prize education highly.

"In China, we had worse teachers and bigger classes—maybe 50, 60 students—and I was able to learn," said Annie Chien, of Potomac, a computer scientist whose son, Steve, is a 10th-grader at Blair. "It's not the environment, it's expectations. If we put higher expectations on children, they meet those expectations."

If Steve gets a B, his mother said, "He will have to explain. If he makes a B, it means he didn't work hard enough. I think he can do better." She would prefer that he go into a science-related field, although "I probably ultimately will accept whatever he becomes." But, she said, "If he decided to become a carpenter or a mechanic, I would have a hard time. I don't think he would contribute as much to society if he did those things."

Some students say they don't mind being typecast, as long as Asian Americans are seen in a positive light. "If people want to think I'm smart, let them," said Cindy Yi, a junior at Howard High. "That's fine with me."

June 17, 1991

Studious Teenager Shows How Education Opens Doors; South Koreans View Schooling as Vital to Nation

Fred Hiatt

Streaming out of Saturday morning classes in a shabby neighborhood of this port city of Pusan, the high school students at first overlooked their local hero standing quietly at the gate.

Chung Seong Tae, age 18 and back for the first time since his graduation six months earlier, watched the familiar scene. Boys in chinos and running shoes played stickball and soccer at crazy angles across the cramped dirt schoolyard, built four years earlier atop a trash landfill.

Then, gradually, students began to notice Chung, who had just completed his first semester at South Korea's premier university. In twos and threes, seniors approached to welcome him, as if some of Chung's magic might rub off, and soon younger boys were clapping and yelling from second-floor classroom windows. Chung, son of an unschooled factory worker, future theoretical physicist, bowed shyly and hurried indoors.

In South Korea, through war and destitution and foreign occupation, education has been revered as the source of moral virtue, social advancement and progress. It is the engine that has driven this nation's phenomenal growth from seemingly hopeless poverty 35 years ago to the "miracle" economy of today.

It is also the engine of social and ideological ferment. Long viewed as moral exemplars, university students have helped bring down one military ruler and affected the means of succession of a second since 1960. Last year, their street protests for the first time put South Korea on the path toward democracy.

Now, as Chung found in his first semester at Seoul National University, a generation of students is searching for a new philosophy to replace the pro-American, anticommunist dogma that had suffused South Korean life since a civil war against the communist North ended in a standoff in 1953. Far from a radical by South Korean standards, Chung nonetheless discovered that the explosion of new ideas and feelings he found in Seoul was quickly changing his world view.

"When I entered university, I thought the United States was a friendly ally," said Chung, who had been sheltered in a cocoon of studying during high school. "But after six months of hearing this and that, I found the United States is not all friendly."

Squarely built, curly-haired and unflappably good-natured, Chung in many ways symbolizes both the possibilities and uncertainties facing South Korea as the next generation matures.

As a child, he lived with his mother and two sisters in a Seoul house the size of an American front hall, without water or electricity. He grew up on rice and pickled vegetables, never tasting milk until he reached high school.

While his widowed mother worked—as a tenant farmer, as a street vendor in Seoul, and today, as a seamstress sewing size labels into 2,000 pairs of running shoes each 10-hour day in a Pusan factory for $200 per month—Chung studied, every evening, every Sunday, every day of every summer vacation.

Last December, he came to embody the South Korean dream when he scored first among 700,000 high school seniors who attempted the national university entrance examination, showing that even the poorest can succeed in this fast-changing society. The boy who never tasted milk, who had neither time nor money for movies or dates or sports, who had never spoken with a foreigner before being interviewed for this article, now plays tennis every morning and speaks of doing graduate work at UCLA, Berkeley or Harvard.

Yet Chung belongs to a very different generation from the South Korean businessmen who made the country's economic miracle and who remember the help they received from the United States along the way. Chung said that as he grew up, he never heard talk of the Korean War, the defining event of an older generation during which Americans and South Koreans fought side by side.

At Seoul National, Chung encountered the bitter political and generational divisions that charge daily life here with tension. How he comes to handle those tensions in the coming years, how he balances his filial piety and love of science with his new political awareness, and how similar choices are made by others in his generation, will help set South Korea's future.

Unusual Student

"He was a soft and mild baby," his mother recently recalled. "I could just leave him alone and go up into the hills to gather firewood."

Ann Ok Soon, Chung's mother, sat on the floor of the small cement room that is the family home in Pusan. (In South Korea, women keep their names when they marry, while children take their fathers' names.) She looked younger than 41, despite years of back-wrenching labor, and she was clearly the source of Chung's round cheeks, shy smile and wide grin.

The house, about 6 feet by 9 feet, was one of seven tiny one-room abodes—each occupied by a different family—surrounding a small courtyard with a faucet. A desk and chair, piled with books, were the only furniture. Strings of onions and garlic, staples for the pungent national dish called kimchi, hung next to the door.

Ann said she had been wed by a match-maker at age 18 to a tenant farmer in a village near her childhood home. She had little education, she lived in South Korea's traditionally most backward province and she had never traveled beyond Kangjin City, the county seat of her home near the southwest coast of South Korea.

But when she was 27, with three children, she decided life might be better in the big city. When Chung was six, the family moved to a hakobang, a "matchbox" house where they could barely stretch out on the floor to sleep, in one of the Seoul slums that fill and refill with emigrants from the countryside.

Ann did not know what to do with transfer forms, so her oldest daughter simply stopped going to school. While Ahn worked from 6 am. to 9 pm., the girl cared for her two younger siblings; she now works in the same shoe factory as her mother.

At first, Ahn earned a few won, the South Korean currency, by buying apples or fish or cabbage at the big market and reselling the produce from a street cart. In winter, when Seoul was too cold for street vending, she scavenged cardboard, paper and anything else the junk merchants might buy. "Somehow, I managed," she said.

Her husband joined the family in Seoul after the first winter and found work on construction sites but soon died of a liver ailment, she said. Through a neighbor in her "moon village"—so called because Seoul slums tend to perch on high hills, a long climb from public wells—Ann found regular work on a farm outside Seoul. The labor was still wearing, longer than the daylight, seven days a week.

Throughout, Chung was a well-behaved and studious child, who borrowed his classmates' books. He loved math and science; on rare clear nights in Seoul, he stared at the stars. He was so studious, in fact, that Ann began to fret about paying for his education.

In South Korea, only elementary school is free. Junior high seemed out of reach of Ahn's income, and college, unthinkable.

"He had good marks, but I didn't know how I could support him," she said. "I worried very much."

The family moved to Pusan, where a few cousins lived, and life grew a bit easier. Work in the factory paid about $200 per month—an improvement—and Ahn had Sundays off. Chung won a citywide math competition and a scholarship for junior and senior high.

For Chung, high school started at 8:30 am., six days a week, and lasted until 6 pm. After a bowl of noodles, he would return to a quiet classroom and study until midnight. On Sundays, he studied at home 15 1/2 hours, working for two, resting for 30 minutes, working for two more; during month-long summer breaks, he would take the bus to school and study some more.

Chung studied harder than most, but serious study is commonplace in South Korea. "When two housewives gather, what they discuss is their children's schooling, marks, test scores," he said. "Education is everything, and going to university means success. It is the only way to improve your social position, so we must study religiously."

By his junior year, Chung's teachers knew he was unusual, and they urged him to apply to Seoul National University. It was a high-risk strategy; the South Korean system allows students to apply only to one school, and at Seoul National, the most competitive, only excelling on the exam would win the scholarship that Chung needed.

Other relatives urged Chung to apply to a safer school, and to aim for medicine or the law, careers that could enrich the family. Seo Byeon Do, his home-room teacher, urged Chung to follow his heart—for the good of South Korea.

"I said to his mother, don't think of this as just your son," Seo said. "He's a resource for the country, he can contribute to the Korean people.... In Korea, there are no natural resources, we are depending only on manpower, and we are weak in basic science."

Chung agreed, and Ahn, more hesitantly, followed. When he placed first, guaranteeing a scholarship, "I didn't know how to express my happiness," Ann said. "I just went out into the courtyard and yelled and yelled and yelled."

The local newspapers heralded the results, which made Chung as much a fig-ure of respect as a Heisman Trophy-winning college quarterback in America. "Mother, Thank You for Enduring Hardship," the headlines read, and, "Early Morning Study the Key to Success."

To an outsider, Chung seemed a tribute to the South Korean educational sys-tem: conversant in two foreign languages, skilled in modern and classical Korean, politically aware, brilliant in science, modest and curious.

But Chung sees a dark side to the South Korean studiousness. Just in the past two months, he said, more than two dozen high school students had killed them-selves, citing their dread of taking, or failing, the all-important entrance exam.

"The competition is terrible," he said. "The pressure is terrible."

Moreover, the curriculum of 15 courses, in classes of 60 or more, with exams every month, discouraged independent and creative thought, he said.

"The teacher would lecture, we would fill our notebooks and memorize," he said. "I think school should be a somewhat pleasant place, but in Korea it is different."

Perhaps as a result, the independence of life at the university was all the more shocking.

"In high school, there's no time to talk about anything but studying," Chung said. "In college, we stay up late into the night, talking—about politics, about girls, about our feelings. It's the first time, and many students feel a lot of confusion."

Chung hung a calligraphy from his high school headmaster over his narrow dorm bed. "One Hundred Lessons, One Thousand Polishings," it said, urging Chung on to further study.

And Chung continued to study hard. But for the first time, he did more than study.

He went to his first meeting, Korean for a kind of group blind date, during which seven boys and seven girls met at a bar for what often turns out to be stilted conversation with the opposite sex.

The meeting, Chung's first real date, didn't go anywhere, but Chung found a girlfriend, a biology major, on campus; there is a woman's dormitory not far from his. Chung said he finds arranged dating "unnatural" and will not marry someone selected by a match-maker, as his mother did. Asked about sex on campus, he replied, "From what I read, Korean students are catching up to American students in that department."

Chung, whose mother visits a Buddhist temple monthly to pray for her children's health, also turned to Christianity. "I expect it to give me something fundamental and permanent, when everything else is changing so fast," he said. About one-fourth of South Koreans are Christian, including many of its fighters for democracy.

Perhaps most disquieting, Chung discovered politics. From the moment he arrived last February, the university's central plaza buzzed with political meetings, debates and indoctrination sessions about something vaguely referred to as "MT," or membership training.

One year ago, such training, in which well-organized leftist student leaders instill their dogmatic world view in the freshman class, would have been largely covert, but in South Korea's liberalizing atmosphere this spring, almost anything could be discussed. Yet despite the new open discussion, students who have demonstrated this year for reunification with the North and against the presence of the 43,000 U.S. troops stationed in the South have failed to win over significant public support as they did in years past when they spearheaded demonstrations against the nation's authoritarian rulers.

"I've heard that in the U.S., you have to watch television, or you don't have anything to talk about," he said, smiling. "Here, I have to read the political books and pamphlets, or I won't be able to talk with my classmates."

Chung and his fellow freshmen soon heard and read things they had never imagined, things that conflicted with what they had learned from retired military officers in their high school anticommunism classes. They watched videotapes of the Kwangju incident of 1980, when Army troops in the southwestern city gunned down at least 200 civilians protesting a military coup. They read revisionist histories that charged the United States with dividing the Korean peninsula 43 years ago and propping up a series of military dictators ever since. And they heard militants label President Roh Tae Woo a fascist, his election fraudulent, his administration a gang of military thugs.

Chung, like many around him, found much of this persuasive. "There are no conservatives here," he said. "Only those who are interested in politics, and those who are not."

He came to believe that the United States must have played some role at Kwangju, despite U.S. denials of involvement; that Roh probably stole last December's election, despite independent observers who said he won because of a split in the opposition; that Washington plays the bully on trade and military issues. He began talking about what "we" believe, meaning the students, in opposition to the government and the official truth he had learned. And he came to question the fundamental principle of South Korean ideology of the past four decades, that communist North Korea is the root of all evil.

"We believe that, before being our enemy, North Korea is part of the Korean race, and unification is a most urgent problem," he said. "We believe many other problems stem from the division of our land."

On the last Saturday of the term, Chung slowly walked from his last exam, in physics, to the nearly empty dormitory in Seoul. It was a rare day in the capital, bright and clear, and the university—moved to this suburban one-time golf course by an earlier president-general who wanted the troublesome students out of town—seemed calm and pastoral.

In the central plaza, though, Chung had to pick his way through the debris of a recent occupation of the university president's office: a leather chair, a clock and some files had been hurled from the president's fourth-floor office. Students had been protesting the university's refusal to fund their summertime trek to the countryside, where they traditionally help farmers transplant rice seedlings and, less traditionally, try to sow their leftist philosophy as well.

Chung, who did not participate in the demonstrations that are almost a daily feature of Seoul life, sympathized with some of the protesters' goals, but said he disapproved of violence. Besides, Chung said, he had other plans: a month of summer school to study German and a month in the library with his physics textbooks.

'Something for My Country'

On the train from Seoul to Pusan, through the heart of the South Korean countryside, Chung pointed out the vineyards and the ginseng farms. The rice was lush and soft, bunches of black-eyed susans brightened the roadsides, and green hills framed meandering pathways for rushing streams.

It was easy to understand the intense love of country that informs almost every South Korean, from leftist student to wealthy businessman, and their drive to win respect after centuries of poverty and foreign domination.

Musing about his future, Chung spoke of his desire to study in the United States. The country has its dark, imperialist side, he said, but it also is "the land of opportunity." Still, without question, he said, he will return to South Korea with his degree.

"Of course, it's very difficult to tackle advanced research in Korea, but I'd like to do something for my country," he said.

And, he said, his mother would want him to help other Koreans as well. "She didn't want her children to have the hardship she had," he said. "So education is the best way, the only way.

September 6, 1988

Black Suburbanites' Tough Choice: Shift From Public Schools Spurred by Parents' Frustrations

Zita Arocha

When Lena and Bill Lockett purchased a home two years ago in Riverway, a Bethesda, Maryland, neighborhood of spacious houses and manicured lawns a major reason was to move into one of the best public school systems in the country.

Their high expectations quickly turned to disenchantment with the Montgomery County public schools, they said, when their 11-year-old son began having discipline and academic problems at Bannockburn Elementary School and their 16-year-old son started talking about dropping out of Walt Whitman High, a demanding school with a high rate of college placements.

The Locketts now spend about $11,000 a year to send their sons to private schools in Kensington, where they are doing better academically.

"I wanted to be able to tell my children that I gave them the opportunity to do the best they could do and to get a good education," said Lena Lockett, a 47-year-old legal secretary who works in the District.

"I think it's important for their survival."

As more high-achieving, well-educated black families, such as the Locketts, reach a comfortable level of economic security in suburban areas such as Montgomery, they are facing a difficult choice: Do they stick with public education or opt for private schools as a way of ensuring the high expectations they have for their children's financial and professional success?

The number of blacks in private school has risen steadily over the past 15 years, and the reasons black families give for forsaking public school often mirror the reasons whites have for going the route of private education: They want smaller classes, better academics and stricter discipline.

But some blacks say they are making the switch because of the subtle but disturbing perception that some public schoolteachers have lower expectations for black children and do not challenge them to succeed academically.

Paul Vance, an associate superintendent of the county public schools, said he has "rarely come across a case where I can say a person is dead set against black student achievement, and if there is an error it's not of commission but of omission."

Whatever the reasons, the decision to switch to private school does not come easily for many families in the black community, where education traditionally has been seen as a major path to advancement, and public schooling has played the dominant role.

"When [blacks] move to the suburbs, they think they have it all wrapped up," said Alberta Vallis, a D.C.-based child psychiatrist who has helped many black families in the Washington area find the most appropriate school placement for their children.

"But if they become disenchanted [with the public school system], then they say, 'Here I am in this expensive environment and my needs still are not being met, so I will go to the private system,' " added Vallis.

Black families acknowledge that private schools do not necessarily satisfy all of their needs. Two common complaints are that class selections in private high schools tend to be more limited than in public high schools and that the opportunity to socialize with other black students is minimal in predominantly white private schools.

The parent of an 11-year-old boy who attends a private, all-boys school in the District said she makes sure her son does not lose touch with his racial identity by having her family attend an all-black church and belonging to an organization of black families.

But despite the tradeoffs, black families interviewed said they believe that private schools will be more demanding on their children and more responsive to what parents want.

Clarence Featherson, a lawyer for the federal government, and Olivia Featherson moved in 1971 from the District to Quaint Acres, a predominantly white neighborhood near Rte. 29 and New Hampshire Avenue, because of "its good, progressive educational system."

This year, however, they pulled their 11-year-old son Troy from Jackson Road Elementary School and placed him in a private, all-boys school in the District.

A yearlong paper battle over Troy's grades was a major factor in the Feathersons' decision to move him to a private school, the couple said.

Also, Olivia Featherson said she believed that her son needed more discipline and supervision because he skipped a grade in school and is younger than most of his classmates.

"We want to see he has a small, strict setting where he can make some progress," said Featherson, a speech pathologist, who added that Troy already says he wants to attend Princeton, Yale or Harvard.

"I don't want people to think private school is a panacea. But my son has already decided he's going to be somebody, and we are concerned about his grades and credentials for college."

Nationally and regionally, the number of blacks who attend private school has been on the rise in the past 15 years.

The number of blacks enrolled in nonreligious private schools throughout the country rose 49 percent from 1971-72 to 1984-85, during a period of decline in overall student population. Black enrollment also rose 22 percent in Catholic schools from 1970 to 1983.

White enrollment rose 31 percent in nonreligious private schools during the same time, but fell sharply, by 39 percent, in Catholic schools.

In the Washington area last year, blacks made up about 9.5 percent of the enrollments at 47 area private schools, compared with about 1 percent of the enrollment in five local private schools in 1964, according to Barbara Patterson, executive director of the Black Student Fund, a D.C.-based organization that provides scholarships and referrals to blacks who want to attend private school.

Montgomery County, where black student enrollment has risen from 9 percent to 15 percent in the past 10 years, does not keep statistics on how many black students leave for private school. Such statistics are not kept by Prince George's, Fairfax County and D.C. schools either.

An issue that sometimes motivates black parents to switch to private school is the troubling belief that their children are not challenged to achieve academically because of their race.

James Robinson, a black parent who heads a citizens committee that monitors issues pertaining to minority students in the Montgomery County public schools, said that in the past four to five years he has talked to dozens of black families who have pulled their children out of Montgomery County public schools and placed them in private schools.

"What I hear is that black youngsters are not getting the kind of encouragement and enhancement they feel they need in order to make it, and there's dual treatment for black youngsters and white youngsters," he said.

Robinson said middle-class blacks also are concerned about school system statistics showing that black students lag far behind whites on achievement tests, are suspended more often than whites, are underrepresented in gifted and talented programs and are overrepresented in classes for the learning disabled, handicapped and emotionally impaired.

Olivia Featherson, however, said that one of her son's public school teachers "was attempting to program him for failure. My child did not fit the stereotype of a black male, and [the teacher] decided he couldn't be as bright as his record indicated...

Lawrence Gary, a professor at Howard University, lives in Springbrook Manor, a racially and culturally mixed neighborhood in Silver Spring. He sends his three children to private schools in the Washington area, saying that his daughter Lisa, now 14, encountered low expectations for her in public schools.

He said he had to appeal to Montgomery County school officials to have Lisa placed in a program for gifted and talented students. Gary said his daughter was qualified because of her high scores on achievement tests, but was not initially placed in the program because her teacher felt she was not ready for the program.

"The people in the regional office could not believe that she didn't qualify," said Gary, whose wife Robenia is a professor at George Mason University in Fairfax County.

The Garys' decision to place Lisa at Newport Preparatory School in Kensington was based on several factors, including what they termed negative experiences and a drop in Lisa's grades.

Also, she was having problems fitting in with her classmates and felt rejected by the blacks, who were not as academically motivated as she was, and the whites in her class, her father said.

When Lisa's hair started to fall out because of a nervous condition that a doctor said was stress-related, the Garys decided to move her to Newport Prep.

At the new school, classes are smaller and there is a strong emphasis on academics as well as racial and ethnic diversity. One-third of the students there are minorities.

"I like the philosophy of the school that... it's all right to be a minority," Lawrence Gary said.

"We wanted her to be in a school with high-achieving black girls so she'd learn that it was all right to be smart and black."

Another factor motivating black parents to choose private schools is the expectation that their children will attend college and that a private school background will help attain that goal, several educators said.

According to Patterson, 98 percent of the students in private schools are college-bound.

Barbara Schneider, a professor at Northwestern University who helped conduct a three-year study on why black families choose private education for their children, said most black parents do not think that public schools are terrible. "What is happening is that black parents have an expectation and aspirations for their children, and they want them fulfilled."

Lena Lockett said she and her husband Bill, an executive for the United Stations Network, decided to put both sons in private schools because we got scared that our children were not going to learn enough and not get into college and not be able to survive out there.

The Locketts, who moved to Montgomery County from Connecticut two years ago, became alarmed last year when their 11-year-old son began getting in trouble with his teachers by not finishing his assignments on time and by socializing too much in class.

His grades, previously As and Bs, were declining.

Meanwhile, the Locketts' 16-year-old son, a 10th grader at Whitman, also was having academic problems. Though he had been a B and C student, his grades began to drop to the C and D range, his teachers were threatening to remove him from several honors classes, and he was talking about dropping out of high school. "He didn't even want to go to college, Lena Lockett said.

"Whitman deals with one kind of student.... That is the highly motivated, highly aggressive smart student.... But if you fall in the smart range but you are not highly aggressive, you get lost in the shuffle.

"Basically, I think he never got a mentor. Students like that need a mentor, and there was nobody there to give him a push."

In this, their first year in private school, both sons are doing better academically, and her older son has indicated he plans to attend college, Lena Lockett said.

"So far [private school] has not disappointed me," she said. "Everything I thought I would be getting, I'm getting."

Lawrence Gary said his family could afford to buy a more expensive house in Potomac were it not for the high tuition bills. Even so, he said, the move to private school has been worth the sacrifices.

"When you are paying $16,000 a year, there's the assumption that a child can learn and that your child will be a winner.

"What it's costing is killing me. But if education is a priority, I guess you just have to change your budget."

November 23, 1986

Social Institutions: Health and Medicine

Tracing Medical Costs to Social Problems: U.S. is Paying Dearly in Comparison

Spencer Rich

The nation's health system has been sharply criticized as the most expensive in the world.

But at least some of the extra billions are not the fault of the system or of waste and over-lavish care, argues Leroy L. Schwartz, physician and president of the nonprofit think tank Health Policy International in Princeton, N.J.

Rather, he says, they result from social problems that are more widespread in the United States than in Europe or Japan and cause huge added health outlays.

"Social pathologies such as the breakdown of the family structure, chronic unemployment, poverty, homelessness, substance abuse, violence and despair wind up in the emergency rooms, intensive care units and morgues of our hospitals," Schwartz and associate Mark Stanton say in a sugary of their findings.

"The United States, more than any other developed country, is paying dearly for its social problems once they become medical problems."

Schwartz says he believes the existence of these problems—in a degree unmatched in other industrial nations—helps explain why health care in the United States in 1989 consumed almost 12 percent of gross domestic product, compared with 8.8 percent for Sweden and 8.7 percent for Canada and France, the next highest.

Schwartz has not completed a comprehensive review of all health costs to test his thesis, but he cites a number of problem areas where he has looked at comparative numbers:

Violence in the United States is far greater, with more than 20,000 homicides annually. The U.S. male homicide rate, for example, is 10 times that of Britain or Germany and four times that of Canada.

Schwartz says one study estimates there are as many as 100 assaults reported by U.S. emergency rooms for every homicide. At any given time, there are about 177,000 people with spinal cord injuries, about 45,000 of which result from an assault. When an injury results in quadriplegia, as many do, it normally costs $600,000 over the person's lifetime for care.

As of January 1990, there were about 118,000 AIDS cases in the United States, about four times the Canadian rate based on population—resulting, in many cases, from drug abuse and unsafe sex and "costing some $75,000 {each} for lifetime treatment or about $8 billion plus large research outlays."

The United States has about 375,000 drug-exposed babies, an enormously higher proportion than in Canada, according to information provided to Stanton by Canadian authorities. Estimated five-year costs of treatment are $63,000 per child.

Liver disease, sometimes treated with a $250,000 transplant, can be caused by alcohol abuse. An estimated 18.5 million people in the United States abuse alcohol.

Poverty and drug abuse are associated with low birthweight, and the United States, more than other countries such as Britain or Sweden, uses expensive high technology to keep many low-birthweight babies alive. The cost of this technology is about $2.6 billion annually and does not include added health costs over the life of the child resulting from residual disabilities.

A 1988 study by the Urban Institute found that U.S. child poverty rates at the start of the 1980s were higher than in most other developed countries—triple those of Switzerland and Sweden and double those of West Germany and Canada.

Schwartz says these findings do not mean that the U.S. health care system should not be improved, that universal coverage for Americans should not be a goal, or that administrative and paperwork inefficiency and a costly malpractice insurance system should not be corrected.

But he says it is advisable to determine which health costs are a result of faults in the system—such as excessive use of high technology in cases where less costly care is usually effective—and which are a result of social problems and population differences not paralleled in other countries often favorably compared with the United States.

A similar plea for more research on how social problems affect health costs was made by George J. Schieber, director of the research office at the federal agency that runs Medicare and Medicaid, and Jean-Pierre Poullier of the Organization for Economic Cooperation and Development in Paris.

Writing in the magazine Health Affairs on health-cost differences among the world's developed nations, they say substantially more information is needed on the extent to which "health systems costs really reflect social costs (such as teenage pregnancy, substance abuse and violence), as opposed to waste and inefficiency in the health system."

Schwartz says the U.S. health system may not look so costly compared with those of other developed nations once health costs that are really the fallout of social problems are taken into account.

In any case, he says, the United States must make a "commitment to resolve our social problems before they become medical problems."

August 28, 1991

Health Care in Canada a Model with Limits: AMA Tries to Discredit System as U.S. Grapples with Soaring Costs

Michael Specter

Stella Lacroix's death started as a suicide. But most people here think it ended as something else.

Moments after she swallowed a quart of cleaning fluid, she changed her mind and raced to the nearest emergency room. The hospital wasn't equipped to perform the surgery she needed to stop internal bleeding, so her doctor began a frantic search for an available bed elsewhere in the Toronto area.

"She was turned away from 14 hospitals," the doctor, Derek Nesdoly, said after his three-hour search had failed. "There was no space anywhere and she just bled to death. This woman needed immediate care and we couldn't get it for her."

The death caused outrage in Canada, where the government guarantees its citizens universal access to competent health care at no charge. But it may have made an even bigger impression in the United States, where officials of the American Medical Association have launched a well-financed and highly public campaign to discredit Canada's health care program, which is often presented in the United States as a model of compassion and coherence.

The U.S. health care system is staggering under costs that are rising faster than any other segment of the nation's economy, while 37 million Americans have no health insurance. Congress has just passed the first sweeping controls on doctors' fees for Medicare patients, a move seen by many specialists as an omen of more government controls. The entire system has come under such steady and violent attack that legislators, policy-makers and industrialists concerned about global competition have begun to search the world for a new model.

Canada is almost always the first place Americans look for an example of a different approach that seems to work. By almost any standard, the Canadian system keeps its citizens at least as healthy as Americans, and sometimes healthier, but at a cost U.S. officials can only envy. In 1986, for example, Canada spent $1,370 (U.S.) per person on health care, while the U.S. figure was $1,926.

The Canadian approach is an insurance system financed largely by taxes. Patients choose their own doctors, whose bills are then paid by the provincial government. Unlike Britain's system of socialized medicine, Canadian doctors are not employed by the state, and patients can seek medical care from any professional willing to treat them. Most Canadians never see a hospital bill.

Because the government holds all the funds for health care and limits the amount it will spend each year, it has a mighty leverage over doctors' fees and hospital costs that cannot be matched by the uneven and often irrational U.S. system, in which federal, state and local insurance programs overlap and compete with 1,500 private insurers—often paying different rates.

Still, critics say that because the Canadian government is the single source of income for doctors and hospitals here, it improperly interferes in decisions that should remain between patients and their doctors, that state-of-the-art technology is scanty and that waits for hospital beds can be appalling. Some U.S. doctors complain that the Canadian government spends far too little on such important advances as magnetic resonance imaging machines and organ transplants.

Setting limits on service has never been acceptable to the people who control U.S. health care. Until recently, simply suggesting that choices could be curtailed, or invoking the word "rationing," would have been enough to convince U.S. legislators that other countries' health systems were morally flawed.

But old views are disappearing fast. With millions of Americans becoming impoverished by illness, or failing to get care at all, approaches once completely ignored are now taken seriously.

"As a society, Canada chooses what it can afford to spend on health care," said A. Eugene LeBlanc, executive director of policy development for the Ontario Ministry of Health. "So do you. The fact that rare Americans have access to distinguished medical services, so that millions have none, seems like rationing to me. I have never understood why Americans stand for it."

Few people think the United States will ever adopt the entire Canadian system, based as it is on strict government control over fees that doctors can charge. But clearly overwhelmed by runaway costs, Congress and the Bush administration have agreed to put a cap on what the government pays doctors to treat the elderly under Medicare. Health experts predict that private insurers will adopt it as well.

"The American health care system has always offered an open checkbook to doctors, hospitals and nursing homes," said William Hsiao, an economist with the Harvard School of Public Health, who has developed a highly regarded plan to reallocate doctors' fees so they are more equitable. "I don't see how it can possibly go on this way."

From any financial vantage point, the sense of urgency has never been greater. While the United States spends nearly 12 percent of its gross national product on a health care system that serves a smaller percentage of the population every year, Canada spends less than 9 percent of its GNP and delivers care to virtually all who seek it. By comparison, the average industrial country spends slightly more than 7 percent; Japan spends 6.6 percent.

Every year for the past decade, the United States has devoted a larger share of its resources to health care, while other industrialized countries have mostly managed to keep costs from rising sharply.

In a country frightened by the prospect of waning competitiveness, that means one of the most expensive parts of a product like an American-made car is often the cost of health care for the employees who made it. Proponents of change, including conservative business leaders chastened by the costly bottom line, have begun to doubt old assumptions—including the widespread belief that more is better when it comes to expensive medical technology.

The opposition to change has been strong from the medical establishment, insurers and many in the nation's massive health care industry. Increasingly, defenders of American medicine seize on rare but well-publicized Canadian medical nightmares like Lacroix's death as powerful symptoms of a system that they claim does not work. They say the waiting lists for spaces in hospitals and the often-limited surgical facilities in Canada would never be acceptable in the United States. And most important, they decry the total dependence of doctors in Canada on government allocations for their fees.

"We know our own health care system has severe problems" said James Todd, AMA deputy executive director. "But there is no question that it is the best in the world. People who think that the Canadian approach is a magic solution need to think harder. Americans want choice. I don't believe for a minute that they would settle for that kind of rationed care and limited access."

There is a growing debate in the United States over what constitutes outstanding medical care. Many experts agree that Canada has held its costs down in part by limiting the number of certain expensive procedures such as coronary bypass surgery and angiograms—procedures that a growing number of public health experts say are used unnecessarily in the United States. Instead, the Canadians devote more money to prenatal care for pregnant women and more frequent doctor visits for sick people.

That has led the AMA to charge that Canada constrains costs at a large sacrifice in medical care. A pamphlet the AMA has distributed to thousands of American doctors compares the number of open-heart surgery and organ transplant hospitals available per patient in the two countries. The United States wins by leagues. For example, Canada has only 11 heart surgery facilities, one for every 2.3 million residents, according to the AMA. In the U.S. there are 793, one for every 300,000 people.

"Big deal," said Jonathan Lomas, a leading Canadian health policy analyst at McMaster University in Hamilton. "High-quality care has to be judged on achieving the best possible results with the least possible intervention. To say you have better medicine because you spend more on high technology or fancy specialties than we do is crass, gross and untrue."

Because the United States has 10 times the population of Canada, and because its inner cities are poorer and more heterogeneous, direct comparison with Canada is imperfect. However, statistics make it clear in general that Canada does a good job of keeping its people healthy. Life expectancy is almost two years longer for Canadians, and their infant mortality rate is 24 percent lower. Heart disease, the focus of much advanced U.S. medical technology, kills Canadians at a rate 20 percent lower than that for Americans, despite similar dietary habits.

A growing number of physicians and policy-makers in the United States fear that equal access to health care has become a largely unattainable vision.

Emergency rooms are sagging under the burden of patients with routine problems but nowhere else to go. Family physicians have become the worst-paid doctors in a society that has invested billions of dollars and much of its faith in fancy technology that serves only a sliver of the population.

For doctors, often unable to prescribe essential but expensive drugs because they know their patients are unable to buy them, the dreaded concept of "rationing" has been an American de facto standard that many have practiced for years.

"On a daily basis I give people different levels of care according to what they can afford," said Robert A. Berenson, a Washington internist and former federal health policy official under President Jimmy Carter. "The best drugs in the world don't work too well if you can't buy them. These patients don't talk about choice or access. They take what they can get."

The most important difference between Canadian and U.S. medicine can be found in one slender book, issued annually by every Canadian province. It is the "Schedule of Benefits"—the fees doctors are permitted to charge the government for treating their patients. Every known ailment or operation is listed, along with its price. Those prices can vary from province to province.

For example, in Ontario, the nation's largest province where more than one-third of the 27 million Canadians live, a routine physical brings a family doctor $33.66 (U.S.), a Caesarean section costs $243 and a complicated procedure involving replacement of the aortic heart valve and repair of connecting arteries can cost as much as $1,557.37.

These procedures cannot cost a penny more, however, because once the province doles out the money doctors can earn each year, and once the local medical association divvies it up, the discussion ends. There are more than 14,000 practicing physicians in Ontario, and it is illegal for them to charge more than the government allows.

In the United States, on the other hand, fees vary according to locale, hospital and doctor. Two comparable surgeons, performing heart surgery in parts of the country where other costs are similar, could charge vastly different fees. Payments often are distorted by specialty, too. The average thoracic surgeon makes at least seven or eight times what a family physician makes, despite spending less time with patients.

The set fee structure does not mean the Canadian system works without fail. Each year the provinces decide on one total budget for doctors' fees, and then they essentially say to the local medical associations: Here is the money. Do what you want with it.

"It gets ugly very fast," said Daniel J. Weinkauf, director of economics for the Ontario Medical Association (OMA), speaking of the brutal sessions, called the "Bear Pit," where doctors decide how much each of their specialties should earn. "We get them all in one room and ask them to state their case, one by one."

If obstetricians get a 10 percent raise, and the budget allows only a 7 percent increase, as in 1988, then some other specialty has to take a cut.

Doctors nevertheless remain among the highest-paid professionals in Canada. According to the OMA, the lowest-paid doctors, family practitioners, average an annual salary of $77,900 in U.S. currency. Surgeons can make much more.

Although comparable incomes are significantly higher for self-employed U.S. physicians, doctors in Canada do not have to pay the cost of handling insurance forms, billing clients or writing off bad debts.

Most important perhaps, Canadian doctors devote only a small fraction of their income each year to malpractice insurance. In the United States, the premiums have become steep enough—tens of thousands of dollars a year, sometimes more—to drive many doctors away from specialties, like obstetrics, that are particularly prone to lawsuits.

While Canadian doctors sometimes complain that they don't make enough money and point to long waits for elective surgery and occasional shortages of beds, as in the case of Stella Lacroix, few say they would exchange their health care system for that of the United States.

"I don't think you would find too many of my colleagues saying they find the American way more attractive than ours," said Michael Wyman, a Toronto family practice physician once active in the medical association. "But the increasing government control of what we can earn is very frustrating. If I see a patient with the flu in my office, I can't charge more than $20," he said.

Few U.S. physicians charge so little for an office visit. When the Ontario government first prohibited doctors from charging patients more than the government would pay, doctors in Ontario struck and many others fled to the United States. But the strike failed and most doctors accepted their roles in the health system.

Like the pay of their American counterparts, the income of Canadian doctors remains in the top one percent of all professional workers. Still, the power of the Canadian government scares many south of the border. In efforts to control health care spending, which has risen from 26 percent of the Ontario budget in 1978 to more than one-third this year, hospital spending has been contained.

That has led to occasional shortages of beds, and in September it caused officials of Princess Margaret Hospital, one of the nation's best cancer facilities, to announce that they would take no new patients for six weeks. The political outcry that followed forced the hospital to reverse its position.

"How is that different than having 40 children in a classroom?" said Lomas, the Canadian health policy analyst, who has argued that the hospital brought on its own problems by wasting its resources. "It would be better to have fewer kids in a class, and it would be nice to have an empty hospital bed waiting nearby for anybody who needs it. But that isn't the world we live in and it never will be."

December 18, 1989

Health Status of Hispanics: Nation's Fastest-Growing Minority Lacks Access to Medical Care

Larry Thompson

The nation's 20.5 million Hispanics face major barriers to getting health care and have higher rates of some diseases such as diabetes and AIDS.

In the first comprehensive health survey of the country's fastest-growing minority group, researchers found that Hispanics tend to go to the doctor less often than non-Hispanic whites and blacks largely because they are poor and lack health insurance. Cultural factors ranging from difficulty speaking English to fear of medical technology plus; for illegal aliens, fear of deportation, also play a role.

Many of the District's estimated 85,000 Hispanics, who recently emigrated to the U.S., are living in poverty without their families.

"Within the first six months {of arriving}, they will face problems of conduct, such as looking for alcohol, and develop psychosomatic symptoms, such as insomnia, headaches, gastritis, problems of weakness, lack of appetite and a desire to cry," said Juan Romagoza, director of Clinica del Pueblo, a Hispanic health clinic in Adams-Morgan, through an interpreter.

Even though the public clinic with a Spanish-speaking staff sees patients free of charge, many Hispanics still do not seek medical assistance unless they are critically ill, Romagoza said.

To examine the health status of Hispanics, the federal government conducted a major survey—called the Hispanic Health and Nutrition Examination Survey, or HHANES—of 11,000 Hispanics between 1982 and 1984. The first comprehensive analysis of this data was published in last week's Journal of the American Medical Association and as a special supplement to December's Journal of the American Public Health Association.

By the year 2000, the Hispanic population is expected to reach 31 million, making it America's largest minority group. Yet there are several distinct Hispanic populations in the U.S. Most of the estimated 250,000 Hispanics in the Washington area are from Central America. In New York City, most are from Puerto Rico; in Florida, they are largely of Cuban ancestry; and in Texas and California, the majority were born in Mexico.

In general, Hispanics are less likely to have medical insurance than any other group. In 1988, the latest year for which statistics are available, 13 percent of the population lacked health insurance overall: 10.2 percent of whites; 20 percent of blacks and 32 percent of Hispanics.

"The uninsured are the less educated, the poor and the sicker Hispanics," said Fernando M. Trevino, director of the Center for Cross-Cultural Research at the University of Texas Medical Branch in Galveston.

Non-Hispanic whites and blacks also go to the doctor more often—an average of 4.8 times per person per year—compared to Mexican Americans, who visit a physician 3.7 times a year.

Experts once believed that Hispanics don't go to doctors because they choose instead to go to a curandero or a herbalista, who are folk medicine practitioners, but the HAANES survey found that only 4.2 percent of Mexican Americans had seen a folk healer in the previous year.

Even with the lack of medical care, Hispanics appear to live about as long as whites, said Olivia Carter-Pokras, a statistician with the National Center for Health Statistics. In a 1980 Texas study, the only year for which estimates are available, Hispanic men lived an average of 69.6 years and white men lived 70.2 years; Hispanic women lived 77.1 years and white women lived 78.1.

But "looking at how long we live is not enough," said Jane L. Delgado, president of the National Coalition of Hispanic Health and Human Service Organizations. "You have to look at the quality of that life."

While Hispanics get cancer less frequently, they are three to five times more likely than non-Hispanic whites and blacks to develop adult-onset diabetes and to suffer complications from the disease.

Lack of financial resources to pay for care is one reason. A 21-year-old Hispanic woman in the District recently developed a form of diabetes that requires her to take insulin, said Sister Maria Ceballos, medical clinic coordinator of the Spanish Catholic Center Medical Clinic in Mount Pleasant. But the woman can't afford to buy the insulin she needs, and she is afraid to apply for medical assistance because she is an illegal alien and does not want to be picked up by immigration officials. "Her biggest concern is that she is going to end up in a coma," from her uncontrolled diabetes, Ceballos said.

A 1986 University of Texas study of 17 Texas border counties found that uncontrolled diabetes in the Hispanic community led to a number of preventable complications. Of all the cases of diabetes-caused blindness identified in the study, researchers concluded that 60 percent could have been prevented with proper treatment, as could 51 percent of kidney failures and 67 percent of diabetes-related amputations of feet and legs. Preventable amputations alone cost $40 million, Delgado said.

The problems seen with diabetes extend to other diseases as well. Ceballos described a woman with breast cancer who delayed treatment so long, the cancer spread, seriously reducing her chances of survival.

The survey also measured infant health. For non-Hispanic whites, the infant mortality rate was 8.3 per 1,000 births, 17.2 for blacks, and 8.7 for Hispanics overall, a statistically significant difference when compared to whites.

Pregnancy is a particularly stressful time for mothers, said Maria Gomez, director of Mary's Center for Maternal and Child Care, a clinic run by midwives in Adams-Morgan that delivers 240 babies a year. Employers tend to fire women from their low-paying jobs around the sixth month when they can no longer hide the pregnancy, she said.

AIDS, too, is beginning to have an impact. While Hispanics only make up 7.9 percent of the population, they account for 14 percent of the AIDS cases nationwide, according to the Centers for Disease Control, including 21 percent of AIDS cases among women and 22 percent among children.

AIDS is not yet a major problem among the District's Hispanic population, accounting for only 3 percent, or 71 of the 2,537 cases reported to the D.C. Commission of Public Health as of October 1990.

The HIV testing program at Clinica del Pueblo actually showed a decline. In 1989, 5.8 percent of the 121 people tested at the clinic were positive; that dropped to 3 percent of the 289 people tested in 1990. Romagoza, however, worries that those tested are not among those at highest risk of contracting the disease, including gay men, intravenous drug users and prostitutes.

Several federal studies examined the changes in behavior as Hispanics moved from poor, rural communities in South and Central America to urban areas in the U.S. Researchers found that as Hispanics learned English and became assimilated into North American culture, they picked up some of its worst health habits, such as increasing their use of illegal drugs—up to 25 times greater for cocaine. Cigarette and alcohol consumption also increased for some groups.

"The longer people are here," Delgado said, "the more likely they are to drink and smoke. The more they speak English, the worse they behave."

January 15, 1991

Devising a Cure for High Costs of Health Care: Support Grows for Concept of National Medical Insurance

Frank Swoboda

As a single mother of two children, Brenda Holstine brought home a little more than $160 a week from her assembly-line job at Louisville Manufacturing Co. So when her health insurance premiums were increased to $59.30 a week a little more than two years ago, she felt she had no choice but to cancel her insurance.

"There was no way I could make ends meet and pay for insurance for my kids," Holstine told an AFL-CIO health care hearing last October. "I've just kept my fingers crossed that my kids don't get sick."

Priscilla Brewer, a co-worker on Louisville Manufacturing's baseball cap production line, gave up coverage for her family after her daughter's leukemia had gone into remission because rising health insurance premiums had cut her take-home pay to $77 a week.

Since then, the two women have taken an additional cut in pay as the slumping economy forced the company to adopt a four-day workweek. Holstine said she now brings home $120 a week.

But medical costs continue to climb. Louisville Manufacturing, reflecting an increase in its own costs, now wants to charge employees $78 a week for family medical coverage.

Holstine and Brewer have become front-line troops in a growing political campaign for some form of government-imposed universal health care that would provide quality coverage for everyone. The idea, in various forms, is gaining the support of groups ranging on the political spectrum from the AFL-CIO and the American Association of Retired Persons to the National Association of Manufacturers and the American Medical Association.

For the first time since the mid-1970s, supporters of national health insurance believe they have a legitimate chance of winning congressional approval for a universal health care bill, if not this Congress, then next. "This is the best shot we've had in 15 years," said a key congressional aide.

With health care costs climbing more than 20 percent a year for major corporations and even more for many small businesses, disparate political groups are beginning to form a coalition for reform.

Although there is a growing coalition pushing for some form of universal health coverage, ideas vary widely on how to implement such a plan, particularly on the question of how best to contain costs.

Walter Maher, director of federal relations for Chrysler Corp., which has been a strong advocate of national health insurance, said the goal of any new program should be to "spread the cost of this {health care} throughout the economy" to avoid cost shifting from one segment of society to another.

Maher said that as major corporations have been putting pressure on doctors and hospitals to control costs, the medical community has simply been raising the costs they charge small companies or individuals who do not have the economic clout to fight back.

The major vehicle for any congressional debate is expected to be the product of negotiations among Democratic leaders on the Senate labor and finance committees. The negotiators, who include Sen. Edward M. Kennedy (D-Mass.) and Senate Majority Leader George J. Mitchell (D-Maine), are working on a bill patterned after the recommendations of the U.S. Bipartisan Commission on Comprehensive Health Care, the so-called Pepper Commission.

The commission recommendations, issued last fall, call for a plan that combines employer-backed insurance with a public insurance plan. The so-called "play or pay" approach would require companies to either provide minimum health coverage for their employees according to standards set by the government or pay a tax that would go into a public fund to provide health coverage for their employees.

Sources close to the committee negotiations said they expect agreement on a bill by mid-March. Although there are some Republicans involved in the negotiations, sources said they did not expect any Republicans to endorse the bill. "This will be a Democratic leadership bill," a congressional source said.

Once agreement is reached on legislation in the Senate, Democrats will introduce a comparable bill in the House.

So far, the White House has indicated it would oppose any national health legislation, but supporters of health care reform hope to make it enough of an issue in Congress to at least force it to become part of the debate in the next presidential elections.

Changing Positions

Perhaps the best example of the changing political positions in the health care debate is the scheduled appearance today of AFL-CIO President Lane Kirkland at the leadership conference of the American Medical Association in Miami Beach to discuss labor's views on the need for national health insurance. It's the first time the president of the labor federation has ever been invited to address an AMA gathering.

Four months earlier, AMA President C. John Tupper made what he called an "historic first" appearance before an AFL-CIO panel in San Francisco investigating problems in the nation's health care system. Tupper used his appearance to outline the AMA's plan for universal health care and to urge the two organizations to join political forces to push for reform.

With health care costs increasingly taking center stage as labor contracts come due around the country, several major unions have banded together with influential members of the business community in a search for consensus on a way to address rising costs.

Last year, 55 unions, corporations, medical groups and public interest lobbying groups formed the National Leadership Coalition for Health Care Reform to develop a proposal to overhaul the nation's health care system. Among the 35 corporations in the coalition are American Telephone & Telegraph Co., Ford Motor Co., Time Warner Inc., Xerox Corp., Lockheed Corp., Du Pont Co., Eastman Kodak Co., Minnesota Mining and Manufacturing Co. and General Electric Co.

Peggy Rhoades, executive director of the Washington-based coalition, said the group hopes to have a proposal by spring. "The purpose is to develop a systematic reform plan, not patch it anymore," Rhoades said. But she said, "I don't have a sense yet of where everybody's going to go."

The leadership coalition also includes the American Association of Retired Persons (AIP), which has become a strong advocate of broad universal health care coverage as a way to protect the benefits of the elderly. Writing in the current AIP Bulletin, Executive Director Horace Deets said the message to political candidates is simple: "We need health care reform."

Lack of Consensus

So far, general business support of legislation that would "mandate" companies to provide health care has been less than enthusiastic. Groups like the U.S. Chamber of Commerce and the National Federation of Independent Business, which primarily represent smaller businesses, oppose such legislation on the grounds that many small employers can't afford such coverage.

But a number of large corporations, particularly in the auto and steel industries, appear supportive of some form of national health legislation that would either shift their costs onto the government or spread the economic burden around by forcing all employers to pay the health care costs of their workers.

Large corporations figure that they end up paying more than their fair share of medical coverage. They argue that if a spouse has an inferior health plan or none at all, the couple's dependents get shifted to the plan of the larger company. Dependent care, even though some of it is usually paid by the employee, is one of the fastest-rising health care costs.

The lack of consensus on health care reform extends to even the most ardent advocates of national health insurance.

The AFL-CIO, for example, opens its annual midwinter leadership meeting in Florida this week unanimous on the need for national health care reform but bitterly divided over how to achieve it.

After a year of study, a special 16-member AFL-CIO Health Care Committee is split 8 to 8 over which approach to take toward national health insurance. The union leadership had hoped to use this week's meeting of the federation's Executive Council to outline its legislative position in the upcoming debate. There is now a better-than-even chance the union's leadership will not be able to reach a consensus position and will go their separate ways in the congressional debate.

Congressional supporters of health care reform are keeping a close eye on labor. "We can't pass a bill without them," said a congressional source close to the negotiations between the two Senate committees. "We're very hopeful that they can come together."

Which Approach?

The split within the labor ranks centers on whether to have a national health insurance plan patterned after the Canadian system, where the government is the single payer, or an approach similar to the Pepper Commission recommendations, where the majority of the population receives health insurance coverage through their employers under a private, nonprofit insurance system regulated by the federal government.

Kirkland is reported to favor the Pepper Commission approach, which is being backed by Kennedy and Mitchell. Failure to reach a consensus this week could significantly weaken labor's lobbying power in the upcoming debate.

The unions have already spent several million dollars on a campaign aimed at stirring up grass-roots support for national health insurance. Over the past six months, the AFL-CIO has held hearings in eight cities on the health care issue, and it is about to embark on an initial $3 million television campaign with a half-hour program being offered to 300 stations on the Public Broadcasting System.

"We hope to influence the bidding," said Robert McGlotten, legislative director of the AFL-CIO. "All of us have a great stake in this."

McGlotten said he was hopeful the unions would be able to work out a consensus legislative position rather than have individual unions lobbying Congress for a number of different bills.

But even McGlotten concedes final passage of health care legislation this Congress is unlikely.

"Maybe lightning will strike and it will happen before the presidential debates," McGlotten said. "But I don't believe it."

February 17, 1991

France Wants Me to Have This Baby; The Story of a Pregnant American in Paris

Robin Herman

The French government found out I was pregnant before my mother got the news. My gynecologist looked over the laboratory results, congratulated me and then took out a sheaf of official papers. She signed and stamped the forms; I added my signature at the bottom, and thus I was registered in France's system of pregnancy surveillance.

The health of my baby-to-be was now a matter for the state.

Contrast my experience here with the U.S. system, which leaves expectant mothers to look after themselves according to their income, education, motivation and ability to obtain care. It is a system, health experts say, that is riddled with contradictions. While American medicine is regarded as the most technologically sophisticated in the world—capable of saving the lives of desperately ill 1.5 pound premature babies—it cannot guarantee adequate care for pregnant women or their infants.

A few weeks after the positive pregnancy test, I received by mail from the government a booklet of instructions and coupons that looked like an automobile care manual. It was my carnet de maternité, literally a maternity notebook, marked with my pregnancy registration number. It outlined how I should feed and take care of myself during the next nine months; it listed the dates of what amounted to my 150-mile checkup, 500—mile checkup and so on.

I was to see my obstetrician a minimum of five times—at four months, six months, eight months, nine months and a postnatal visit. The cost of all exams would be fully covered by French social security—the national health insurance financed through payroll deductions. After each exam, the doctor was to sign and stamp the appropriate coupon from my carnet de maternité and send it to the social security office. As an incentive to keep these appointments, the French government would pay me 830 francs (about $160) per month from the fourth month of pregnancy through the third month after the birth. This payment would be made regardless of income.

The carnet de maternité also detailed my rights under French law. If working, I was entitled to six weeks of paid maternity leave before the birth and 10 weeks afterward in addition to two more weeks if the doctor certified it was necessary.

This was my introduction to how a country with socialized medicine approaches maternal care. France would essentially pay me to have a healthy baby, spending money early in an attempt to minimize expensive neonatal and pediatric problems later.

An investment in prenatal care has a direct effect on a nation's infant mortality statistics. France's rate, according to UNICEF, was 7.7 deaths per 1,000 births in

1988, among the lowest in the world. Sweden and Finland did even better—only 5.8 deaths per 1,000. By contrast, the U.S. rate was 9.9 per 1,000.

Compared with the rest of Western Europe, particularly Scandinavia, France's efforts are considered minimal. But to an American—particularly one with a high-risk pregnancy—they seemed impressive. I felt that France really wanted me to have this baby.

Jeopardizing my pregnancy was the fact that my mother, like thousands of other American women in the 1950s (including my mother-in law), had been given diethylstilbestrol, or DES, while she was pregnant with me. DES, a notorious and discredited anti-miscarriage drug, had led to congenital gynecological defects and sometimes even cancer in daughters of the women who took it. Thus, I knew from the start I would have a grossesse a risque, a high-risk pregnancy.

For that reason, I enrolled at a large public teaching hospital—Hospital St. Vincent de Paul—devoted exclusively to maternity and pediatrics. Although there was a waiting list at this particular institution, as a high-risk case I was boosted to the top in what was a matter of public policy. Several slots are always reserved for difficult pregnancies, I learned later.

I had no "connections." I could barely explain my case in French to the secretary who took my initial call. Relying on a dictionary, I relayed the facts that I was 37 years old with a spontaneous first pregnancy after five years of unsuccessful infertility treatment and that my mother had taken DES.

I was placed in the care of a first-rate obstetrician and professor who, it turns out, is in charge of the state's program of obstetrical and gynecological instruction for the entire Paris and suburban region. He had seen hundreds of DES cases and n fact was a specialist in the field. It was obvious from the start that he was up to speed on what could be done to forestall problems.

The doctor, Michel Tournaire, quickly put me on a biweekly schedule of checkups—again free of charge—instead of the more usual monthly checkups. When at three months I needed an operation to reinforce my cervix, he performed the surgery. The operation, plus a three-day hospital stay, was all covered by social security and cost me not one extra franc.

When early contractions started in the sixth month, I was ordered to stay in bed at home and take medication to stop the spasms. Now the French surveillance system really went into high gear.

Each week, the hospital sent to my home a sage-femme—a kind of maternity nurse with four years of medical school—to give me a full checkup. This service was free. She took my blood pressure, a urine sample, measured the growth of the uterus, listened for the baby's heartbeat and checked to see that the cervical stitches were holding. She also inquired about my morale and spent time trying to boost my spirits. Before and after these visits she reported to my doctor.

A second sage-femme came to my home—at a modest charge—to give my husband and me private classes in labor and childbirth. One week I needed a blood test. A local laboratory sent a technician to my bedside to take the sample—covered by social security at no extra charge.

One medical precaution considered routine in the U.S. for women over 35 years old—amniocentesis—was not covered by French social security. In fact, genetic screening by amniocentesis is not available to women in France under the age of 38, except in cases where there is a family history of genetic disease. This policy stems from a shortage of labs that can do the analysis, according to Tournaire, and to the slowness of the health care bureaucracy to realize the increased importance physicians now attach to amniocentesis. The only hospital in Paris that would do the amniocentesis test for someone "underaged" like me was the American Hospital, which is not part of the French social security system. My husband and I paid for the test ourselves.

Further contractions in the seventh month landed me back at Hospital St. Vincent de Paul, where I was obliged to lie quietly for six weeks with an intravenous tube inserted in my arm. The medication again controlled the situation, and I was assiduously monitored by a rotating team of maternity residents who reported to my doctor, Tournaire, who also came to see me frequently. Throughout my stay, without fail, I was visited twice daily by doctors. My contractions were measured several times a week by machine, and I was given the occasional sonogram. Three sonograms are standard for all pregnant women in France—high risk or not.

The nurses were vigilant, peeking in on me at intervals all day and night long. Everyone gave me the feeling that I was safe, in good hands, and that the team would let nothing jeopardize my pregnancy. "Tenez le coup!" the nurses and doctors urged me. Hang in there!

I am grateful to the French government for paying for my long hospital stay and good care. My only costs were for a rental T.V. and private phone line, but this is not to say I spent weeks in the lap of luxury. Hospital St. Vincent de Paul has the tired look of an institution operated for years on an inadequate budget. The ceiling paint is peeling. The beds are old—fashioned, springy and soft with no electric mechanism for raising the head or feet. There are occasional shortages of equipment and amenities. Patients are asked to provide their own towels, soap and other toiletries. Hospital gowns are made of paper so everyone wears T-shirts or nightgowns brought from home. Supportive husbands shuttle back and forth with laundry.

On the other hand, this being France, the food at St. Vincent de Paul was quite good for a hospital. Two hot meals a day included such dishes as veau bourginon, veal burgundy, and lapin sauce moutarde, rabbit with mustard sauce. But the typical French breakfast, café au lait and a roll, leaves something to be desired. "C'est tout?" I asked the nurses incredulously—"That's it?" They laughed. Another hungry American. I was offered an extra roll.

I soon got wise and had my husband bring me cereal from home while I hoarded fruit from lunch and dinner to eat instead at breakfast time. I also got the hospital dietitian to give me a special order of juice and skim milk in the morning. The nurses laughed at the "enormous" breakfast I laid out for myself to start each day.

As the weeks progressed, I saw next-door neighbors with greater problems than mine go home cuddling premature babies of robust size and good health. With each birth, the team of doctors and nurses burst with a sense of pride and accomplishment.

When I reached 35 weeks of pregnancy (a full-term pregnancy is 40 weeks), Tournaire was all smiles and congratulated me. He confided that initially he had had his doubts about my case. A DES daughter with my problems, he said, had only about a 20 percent chance of getting to the 35-week mark. From this point on, he assured me, I could basically count on a healthy birth. "Bravo," he added as he left my room.

I later thought to myself that perhaps my chances had been better than twenty percent because of the meticulous care I'd received under the French health care system.

My hard-kicking fetus and I hung on until 37 weeks. At that point my doctor removed the cervical stitches, because the baby would no longer be considered premature. Three days later, as predicted, I went into labor.

Blood tests had been performed weeks before to make sure I could safely have an epidural anesthetic. The epidural is the childbirth approach of preference in France, where anesthesiologists have worked hard to refine the technique. It involves the insertion of a needle into the spinal column and the introduction of a chemical that deadens feeling in the lower half of the body. "Natural" childbirth is not in vogue among French women. At Hospital St. Vincent de Paul, 75 percent of deliveries are done under epidural.

Alas for me, labor began so suddenly and proceeded so swiftly that there wasn't enough time to set up the epidural and benefit from it until the very end of the birth.

At first, I was attended by a duo of sages-femmes. They perform about half of the deliveries in France. But if a case gets complicated or if there is a problem or forceps are needed, a doctor is called in. When my baby began to suffer some distress from my strong contractions, two doctors immediately appeared at my feet and took over. With the anesthesiologist on my left, my husband on my right and two sages-femmes and two doctors attending I felt protected and tried to concentrate on my job: breathing and pushing.

Our son Zachary popped out after 2 1/2 hours of labor. He was immediately laid across my stomach, and, in a matter of seconds, reassured us with a good strong cry. Then he was whisked away to be cleaned up and reappeared, dressed in one of the little outfits we'd brought for him, sleeping contentedly in a clear plastic crib. No incubator was necessary. I was still on the labor table when a sage-femme proposed to me that I might want to start breast-feeding right then. It was the first indication I had that France is quite serious about instructing and supporting mothers who want to breast-feed. In fact, many French companies, in contract agreements with their unions, give an extra three months' paid maternity leave to women who breast-feed—a total of six months paid leave after the birth.

People always talk about the trials and tribulations of giving birth, but you don't hear much about the challenge of recovery afterward. Between bleeding, soreness, stitches, fatigue and postpartum depression, recovery is no easy matter, and French hospitals recognize this fact by advising a minimum five—day postpartum hospital stay. By that time, women on my corridor who started the week as wincing, shuffling zombies, exited the hospital perfumed, coiffed and jeweled, better able to rejoin normal Parisian life. Women in fact have a right under the French system to 12 postpartum days in the hospital free of charge. The average hospital stay for an uncomplicated birth in the U.S. is about three days.

Having been weakened before the birth by so many months in bed, I had a more difficult recovery than most women. When five days were up and I was still wobbly, the sage-femme in charge of my case encouraged me to stay longer and I was happy to, finally leaving the hospital after eight days.

By that time, I felt strong enough to manage our new baby and our 2-year-old daughter Eva, whom we adopted in 1987. Breast-feeding was well established thanks to the attentive sages-femmes and baby nurses who assisted me at every feeding, day and night, until Zachary and I got the hang of it ourselves.

An American friend who had given birth at a different Paris hospital three weeks before I did also remarked on the support for breast-feeding. Her daughter was still losing weight when she left the hospital. A sage-femme appeared at my friend's apartment several times during the following week to see how the breast-feeding was going, to offer advice and to weigh the baby on a scale the hospital provided. A nurse also arrived, unbidden, to check my friend's blood pressure and general health.

Before I left the hospital, I had asked about the availability of baby nurses for the early weeks home. I was referred to a private nursing service, but the hospital also told me about a different kind of help provided free of charge by the city of Paris. Baby specialists, called puericultrices, are employed by the city to make house calls to new mothers and offer practical advice on feeding, hygiene and general baby care. During the first week home, I called twice for help with various aspects of breast-feeding, and a lively French woman knocked at my door the next day, spent 40 minutes or so with me answering questions, shook my hand and then left without charging me a thing.

Following the instructions of the carnet de maternite' and in order to continue getting my monthly stipend and comply with requirements for Zachary's care, I took him to a pediatrician for the prescribed first-month checkup. The doctor entered his measurements of Zachary's length and weight into my son's very own carnet de santé, certificate of health, issued to him at birth, which serves as a permanent record of all his medical care and childhood vaccinations.

The last command of my carnet de maternité was for me to get a checkup six weeks after the birth. French health care is not for babies alone. The hospital also gave me a prescription for 10 sessions of physical therapy, completely covered by social security, part of the postpartum package for all new mothers to get us back in shape. A nod to the French fashion industry? I wondered.

France really wanted me to have a healthy baby, and I did. We Americans tend to think that we have the world's best health care, and in a certain sense we do—the most sophisticated medical technology is to be found in the United States. But when it comes to consistent, general health care for ordinary people, there are other nations that do a far better job. From my experience with maternal and child care here, France seems to be one of those nations, and Zachary and I are lucky we were able to take advantage of it.

May 1, 1990

Some Victims' Wish to Spread AIDS Sparks Fear in Brazil

Bradley Graham

Late one Friday afternoon last month, a 31-year-old homosexual with AIDS visited a local treatment center feeling depressed.

He had murder on his mind. Lonely and distraught, he had been planning a sexual binge to spread the fatal acquired immune deficiency syndrome widely through Campinas, a city of 850,000 about an hour's drive north of Sao Paulo.

Silvia Bellucci, an immunologist at the center, recognized the killer urge. She had seen the same impulse numerous times before in other AIDS victims, this macabre wish to pass the deadly virus to unsuspecting others.

She also knew the visitor from his attendance at group therapy sessions. He is a systems analyst at a data processing firm, the father as well of two daughters. Three years ago, he began having homosexual relations and got AIDS.

Soothingly, Bellucci comforted the would-be murderer and drew him back to his senses.

"He sat right here on the couch," the doctor recalled during an interview in her large outer office. "It was his birthday and he said he was feeling sad and anxious. No one had done anything to celebrate the day. He started crying and said he had been thinking of going out and spreading AIDS to at least 50 people. I cried with him, and then we talked for an hour and a half until he calmed down."

Second to the United States in the number of reported AIDS cases, Brazil is now confronting the threat of willful transmission of the disease. Medical experts here say the desire to spread the incurable virus occurs in victims elsewhere but seems to have received more widespread publicity in Brazil.

Simply identifying the sufferers of AIDS and easing the physical pain of their final days is said to be insufficient both for the victims and for everyone else's protection. The illness demands psychological care. But in developing countries like Brazil, already hard-pressed to provide even basic medical services, the complications and traumas of AIDS go largely untreated.

In one unpublicized case two months ago, according to the center where Bellucci works, a 29-year-old drug addict who knew he was close to dying of AIDS gave a party in Campinas. Without confessing his condition, he passed around a syringe of cocaine diluted with his own infected blood, exposing about 20 people, ranging in age from 15 to 25, to the risk of contamination. They are now being seen at the center.

In the southern city of Florianopolis, residents have been terrorized for two weeks by a police report of a purported pact among a small group of confessed drug addicts to disseminate AIDS. An 18-year-old girl caught stealing furniture from an apartment building where she lived told authorities of the alleged plot. She identified a married couple as the ringleaders.

They were said to have hosted drug parties at which they mixed their AIDS-infected blood with cocaine and used a single syringe to inject the poison into others. Some infected group members also are reported to have taken to prostitution to transmit the virus and raise money.

The accused have denied scheming to spread AIDS. As authorities try to establish the truth, Brazilian newspapers say Florianopolis is in a panic and swirling with wild rumors—that, for instance, up to several hundred people may have fallen prey to the reputed plotters, that members of some prominent families are among those victimized and that schoolchildren were fed contaminated chocolates by the group. The virus is not transmitted through foods.

Behind the urge to inflict AIDS on others lies a combination of sadistic and masochistic impulses, doctors say. Resentment against society merges with loneliness, despair and disgust with oneself.

"It is a mix of wishes to contaminate others and, as a kind of self-punishment, to be re-contaminated," said Margo Mair Marques, a psychologist who treats AIDS victims in Campinas. "It is usually a phase, part of the ups and downs of coming to terms with the disease. The urge may be triggered by a variety of situations related to a person's relationships or personality."

Often, the impulse is not explicitly articulated but exists subconsciously. "Some victims knowing they have AIDS keep behaving as if they were not infected," said the psychologist. "Others say they are not worrying about the consequences of their actions. They say they couldn't care less about passing on the disease. That's really a kind of masking of the intention to infect others."

Public insensitivity to those with AIDS has aggravated the problem, according to medical experts. Along with a growing awareness in Brazil this year to the dangers of AIDS have been reports of infected persons being expelled from jobs, run out of towns or hunted down by police. Recently, health officials ordered clinics to start reporting the names of anyone tested positive for AIDS antibodies.

Such measures are said to drive victims of the illness deeper into depression and emotional backlashes. Some end in suicide. In Sao Paulo, Brazil's largest city and the one where the majority of known AIDS cases are concentrated, 60 AIDS victims killed themselves in the first six months of this year, according to unpublicized statistics kept by a medical law institute.

"Others start to rebel and to spread the virus more than if AIDS were treated with greater sensitivity," said Bellucci, who has been working with AIDS patients since Brazil's first cases surfaced five years ago. She urges more psychological attention for AIDS victims to combat what she calls the "AIDS ghost," an obsession with this disease that so far is considered inevitably fatal.

The Center of Immunology Control and Investigation, which Bellucci helped to establish in Campinas, has become a national model in counseling those afflicted with the virus.

Like other countries, Brazil was slow to react to the rising count of AIDS sufferers. The government took concerted action last February, launching a series of TV ads with instructions on preventive measures.

The effort brought talk of sexual habits into the open. But federal budget cutbacks and pressure from the Roman Catholic Church resulted in a briefer, less explicit campaign than planned. Many of Brazil's poor and illiterate never got the message.

In recent months, responsibility for combatting AIDS has fallen largely to state and local authorities, employers, the media, doctors, religious organizations and volunteer groups. There is a consensus that the country's best defense against the illness rests in expanded education programs. But experts are still searching for effective ways to explain AIDS to a nation where sex education is banned from most public schools and where many people know only crude slang terms for such words as condom, sperm and homosexual.

"Awareness of AIDS has increased dramatically in middle- and upper-income groups, but is still low in large poorer parts of the population," said Evahyr Lyra Jr., head of health-care products at Johnson & Johnson in Brazil, the dominant local manufacturer of condoms. "Some concepts are proving too tricky for mass communications."

By the end of September, the total number of reported AIDS cases in Brazil had risen to 2,102. Current rough estimates of the number of Brazilians thought to be carrying the AIDS virus range from 300,000 to more than 500,000. Nevertheless, Brazilian health officials remain divided over just what priority to assign AIDS in relation to other, older diseases that continue to affect millions of people in Brazil, including malaria, dengue, leprosy and Chagas disease.

Of particular concern nationwide is the contamination of blood supplies. Despite a Health Ministry order in Hay requiring blood banks to test for the AIDS virus, doctors estimate that at least 70 percent of private donor operations are still not screening banks, due to a shortage of imported testing kits and the expense of testing. Some hospitals have stopped accepting blood from private banks and refuse to use nationally manufactured plasma products.

"We know what should be done in education and control against AIDS, but there's neither sufficient intensity nor continuity in official programs," lamented Vicente Amato Netto, superintendent of the Hospital of Clinics in Sao Paulo and a member of the national commission on AIDS.

November 4, 1987

Chapter Ten

Population

S ociologists are particularly interested in the population processes of fertility, mortality, and migration, the size and distribution of a population, and the characteristics of the people who live in a given city, region, or state. Unprecedented population growth over the past 250 years, and the environmental degradation that has accompanied this growth, make sociological inquiry into the dynamics of population change a crucial one, as the following articles attest.

The first article in this section looks at the population explosion from two opposing points of view—an optimistic one and a pessimistic one. Article 2 describes the impact of the developing world on global warming. Next, "New Breeze in Eastern Europe is Fouled by Pollution" shows how pollution has ravaged the environment in Eastern Europe and threatens the health of the people in this region.

Concluding the population section, the status of the "greenhouse effect" is examined in two articles focusing on its effects on the United States. The final article describes the fears of Chinese officials that, despite years of strict population planning, a new baby boom is occurring.

With Twice as Many People, Planet Could Expect Boom or Doom

William Booth

If the population of the Earth doubles as predicted by the middle of the next century, what kind of world will our children see?

The popular image is often nightmarish, a teeming planet covered by megalopolises, the Third World a neo-Malthusian hell where bodies are stacked like cordwood and all but the very richest are reduced to nibbling cakes of bioengineered fish meal.

This is the version of the future in the crystal ball of biologist Paul Ehrlich, the pen behind "The Population Bomb" and "The Population Explosion," who predicts that growing human numbers spell mass starvation and environmental ruin.

Such a future, however, is anything but certain. The popular images obscure a lively debate among researchers, who are fighting over whether population growth is good or bad or irrelevant to the quality of human life.

"I venture to say no one knows," said Carl Raub, a demographer with the Population Reference Bureau here. "But it is a hell of a good fight."

Optimists vs. Pessimists

Squared off in the ring are the optimists and the pessimists, the boomers and the doomers, go-go economists and neo-Malthusian ecologists. The optimistic economists focus on labor and capital. Above all, they value human ingenuity and technological development.

The ecologists look at natural resources, at the finite supplies of land, water and air. As biologists, they speak of carrying capacity and the limits of a closed system. They point to the habitat loss, species extinction and environmental degradation.

"Ecologists are concerned with the natural world. Economists are concerned with what is valued in the marketplace. It is a very different set of approaches," said Sam Preston, a University of Pennsylvania economist with an interest in population.

"Is the world going to be more or less prosperous? That's the real question. And population growth doesn't tell you very much about that," said Duke University economist Allen Kelly, a guarded optimist. "Prosperity depends on market economics and government policies."

The optimists like to point out that, on average, standards of living have improved throughout the world. Between 1960 and 1990, as world population went from 3 billion to 5.3 billion, infant mortality dropped and life expectancy, literacy, per capita income, food production and nutrition all increased on average. Even in

Bangladesh, considered a textbook case on the horrors of population pressure, literacy, infant mortality and life expectancy have all improved.

The ecologists reply that the economists fail to take into account the fact that the world is consuming its natural resources at a furious clip.

"They don't ask, 'Is there enough water? Is there enough land? Is there enough wood? What are people going to cook with? What are they going to eat?'" said Lester Brown of the Worldwatch Institute and author of the popular annual "State of the World" reports.

Debating Earth's Capacity

How many people can the world support? The upper limit of Earth's population has been debated for centuries. Abraham and Lot were concerned about carrying capacity. Chinese scholars in the time of Confucius played the game. So did the ancient Greeks, who worried about overpopulation, overgrazing and the loss of forests. (The barren, rocky landscape of today's Greece was thick with trees in ancient times.)

The United Nations is currently revising its population projections for the next century. U.N. forecasters say that instead of reaching a stable world population of 10.2 billion persons in the year 2085, today's population figure could double by the middle of next century. Almost all of the growth will occur in the cities of the developing world.

Of course, demographers have been wrong before. They missed, for example, the Baby Boom in the United States. In the 1950s, they were predicting that Japan, then a crowded, less-developed country that made rubber sandals, would be worse off than India in the future.

The United Nations now predicts world population will stabilize at 11.6 billion. The reason for stabilization is that as countries grow rich, their birthrates fall. It happened in the United States, Japan and European nations. The Greek government now frets its population growth is "too low." Germany and Hungary are shrinking.

A similar fate may await South Korea, Taiwan, Thailand and other so-called NICs, or Newly Industrialized Countries. NICs are marked by increased use of birth control, falling birthrates, growing affluence and an increased life expectancy. Some optimists see no reason why every country on Earth won't eventually be like South Korea.

But before Bangladesh can become like South Korea, some scholars fear, the planet will run out of natural resources. The traditional candidates for causing limits in population growth have been energy, metals, minerals, arable land and food.

Yet even if all renewable and nuclear energies were ignored, researchers have calculated that there are enough known fossil fuel reserves to sustain population growth for 280 years.

"On the global level, existing energy resources do not appear to constitute a limiting factor for many generations to come," according to Paul Demeny, a scholar at the Population Council in New York. Moreover, minerals and metals will also probably hold out, or as the optimists contend, will be replaced by materials derived from recycling.

Food Supply in Question

Food is the subject of hottest debate. Brown and colleagues contend that the ever-increasing productivity of agriculture, supported by fertilizers and new high-yield plant varieties, is showing signs of exhaustion.

"Developing countries as a whole have suffered a serious decline in food self-sufficiency," according to the U.N. Population Fund, which estimates that about 560 million people are now living in absolute poverty.

Robert Repetto of the World Resources Institute points out that a world population twice the present size, coupled with improved dietary standards in the developing world, would mean that all the world's current cropland would have to produce 2.8 tons of grain per acre per year. This is like saying that all the world's farmers will have to be as productive as an Iowa corn farmer—the most productive in the world.

But the U.N. Food and Agriculture Organization found that in 90 developing countries, less than half the potential cropland is under cultivation. The optimists add that in addition to expanding the area under cultivation, genetic engineering and improved technologies will continue to increase yields.

"In the future, every single measurement of human life will be better than it is now," said Julian Simon of the University of Maryland and perhaps the most optimistic of the optimists. "Why? Because that is the trend."

"You can't assume the future will be an extrapolation of the past," said Brown. "We're entering uncharted territory."

June 10, 1991

Developing World's Role in Global Warming Grows: Population Rise, Technology Spread Cited

Susan Okie

Developing countries, where populations are growing explosively and where personal income and use of technology are also increasing, will surpass industrialized countries in the next few decades as the major source of carbon dioxide and other gases that cause global warming, according to a U.N. report on world population released yesterday.

The report said that by 2025 the countries now comprising the Third World are likely to be spewing four times as much carbon dioxide as the developed world now produces.

The report by the U.N. Population Fund said the number of human beings, currently 5.3 billion, is increasing by a quarter of a million every day. At the current growth rate, the population should reach 11 billion by the end of the next century, but may climb to 14 billion by that time if population-control programs are not as effective as hoped.

The greatest threats posed by such massive increases in population are further global warming, deforestation and soil degradation, according to the report.

Industrialized countries currently account for most fossil fuel consumption and use of chlorofluorocarbons (CFCs), chemicals used in refrigeration and aerosols that contribute to depletion of the stratospheric ozone layer. But population growth and the spread of technology are rapidly changing that pattern.

For instance, the human population has doubled since 1950, but the car population has increased sevenfold, according to the report. Currently 400 million, it is expected to grow to 700 million in the next 20 years, with much of the increase occurring in developing countries.

Carbon dioxide, the gas thought to contribute most to global warming, is released by burning organic materials, especially automobiles and industries burning fossil fuels. Carbon dioxide emissions from industries in developing countries increased almost sixteenfold from 1950 to 1985. They are expected to soar even faster in coming decades.

Even if developed countries stabilize their carbon dioxide emissions at current levels, global emissions will triple by 2025, the report said.

CFCs, besides contributing to global warming, are believed to be the major cause of ozone depletion. Under a treaty signed in Montreal in 1987, industrialized countries agreed to reduce CFC use in an effort to cut worldwide consumption by 50 percent by the year 2000. But under the treaty's current provisions, developing countries, which now account for only a small percentage of global CFC consumption, could increase their emissions 70 percent in the next fifty years, the report said.

The findings were announced just a week after the Bush administration instructed its delegates to an international conference on CFCs held in Geneva to oppose a plan that would provide funds to developing countries to reduce their CFC use.

Population growth causes up to eighty percent of deforestation in the world, and is a major reason for soil degradation caused by erosion and other factors, the report said.

More than 28 million acres of forest are cleared each year—an area larger than Virginia—and more than 17 million acres of farmland become unproductive annually because of soil erosion, according to estimates by the U.N. Food and Agriculture Organization. Erosion reduces farmers' capacity to grow food and forces them to clear more forest, establishing a vicious cycle. Deforestation is believed to contribute significantly to the levels of carbon dioxide in the atmosphere, because trees remove the gas from the air.

The report said control of world population growth must be a major part of any strategy to reduce global warming and halt damage to forests and soils. It said other steps would include improving the efficiency of energy use, shifting from fossil fuels to renewable energy sources such as wind, solar and geothermal energy, and limiting deforestation.

It said that stabilizing the world's population below 10 billion—just short of another doubling from today's level—is still possible, but would require a major increase in funding for population-control programs over the next decade.

May 15, 1990

New Breeze in Eastern Europe Is Fouled by Pollution: Large Areas May Become Uninhabitable

Jackson Diehl

For the last two decades, people in the historic city of Krakow, a former seat of the Polish kings, have watched as corrosive soot from a steel mill slowly destroyed its treasured monuments, blackening the ancient red brick of the Jagiellonian University and rendering medieval carvings at the Wawel Castle into shapeless stumps of stone.

A decade ago, Poland's Communist government did not even allow scientists and journalists in Krakow to mention the pollution in public. Not until 1981 were they allowed to establish an environmental club to study the threat. And until recently, anyone seeking to stage a peaceful demonstration calling attention to the problem was likely to be handed a two-year prison sentence.

The continuing impasse between environmentalists and industrialists here is a sign of one of the most serious conflicts Eastern Europe's Communist governments are likely to face in the 1990s. Even as they seek to rebuild their economies and political life, these countries will be confronted with the necessity of managing some of the world's most serious environmental problems, including water and air pollution, which threaten to render large areas virtually uninhabitable.

Today, some of the specialists whose environmental platforms were once junked or locked in drawers are organizing an environmental political party on the model of the West German Greens. Their followers are staging almost daily demonstrations against pollution in Krakow and around the country. Several leaders of the group have just negotiated a 26-point program of environmental action with the government that declares Krakow a place for "special defense" against "the serious danger of ecological catastrophe."

Still, the huge Lenin steel mill on Krakow's outskirts, built by the Communist regime in the early 1950s and now the country's biggest source of pollution, continues dumping 500,000 tons a year of gaseous pollutants on the only major Polish city to survive World War II. "In one sense the situation has radically changed, and yet in another way nothing has happened," said Zygmunt Fura, a chemist active in the Krakow environmental movement for the past decade. "The authorities now accept us, but the structures that created the environmental crisis have not changed."

Emboldened by Soviet leader Mikhail Gorbachev, Poland and Hungary are preparing to open a new era of change in the Communist world by dismantling their state-run economies and one-party political systems in favor of Western-style market economies and parliamentary democracy. Yet, it remains unclear whether this tricky and possibly tumultuous process will offer answers for the critical problems that helped to prompt it, particularly the environmental ones.

Already, the changes under way in Poland and Hungary have allowed for the rise of active environmental movements and parties pressing for solutions. The news media have been encouraged to publicize extensively the problems of pollution, and governments and parliamentary deputies about to be dependent for the first time on votes have begun to react to public pressure. A host of new environmental regulations have been drawn up, and some of the worst sources of industrial pollution have recently been marked for closure.

Weak Regulators

Yet, despite this obvious improvement, a number of conflicts continue to brake environmental action in these countries, including some caused by the transition itself. Weak regulators have proved unable to enforce new antipollution laws on state factories, which now have strong economic incentives to avoid the controls. Environmental groups intoxicated by the new atmosphere of freedom have drifted toward broader political agendas or split into factions. Governments trying to make drastic cuts in state spending and to pay foreign debts have resisted the massive outlays needed for antipollution equipment.

Meanwhile, the international cooperation essential to resolving environmental problems in Europe is in danger of failure on both sides of the East-West divide. While conservative Communist leaderships in Czechoslovakia and East Germany cling to Stalinist policies of secrecy and obstruction on environmental issues, Western countries waver between lukewarm efforts at assistance and attempts to exploit the region's backwardness by using it as a site for waste and industrial projects no longer tolerated in the West.

"Poland could create a certain model of environmental protection for the Eastern Bloc," said Stefan Kozlowski, a specialist who headed the opposition negotiating team on the environment at the recent "round-table" talks with the Communist leadership. "But to do that, we have to create a way of thinking that in all our countries did not exist until now. If we do that in the next five years then we will have achieved something."

The need for quick action is particularly pressing because environmental hazards in Eastern Europe, particularly in Poland, have reached a crisis stage. As the joint program signed by the Polish government and opposition put it, "The threat to human life in Poland as a result of environmental conditions is one of the greatest in the world."

In Poland, regions covering 13,500 square miles—11 percent of the country's land area—and including one-third of the national population were declared environmentally endangered by a comprehensive study by the National Academy of Science last year. Six million people were said to be living in "environmental disaster areas." More than 125,000 acres of Polish forest already have been destroyed, and half of the country's total forest area is threatened by air pollution.

Contaminated Rivers

Ninety-five percent of the river water in Poland is now unfit for drinking, half of the lakes have been irreversibly contaminated, and more than three-quarters of drinking water sources do not meet official standards of purity, according to Polish scientists. Warsaw and Tirana, Albania are the only capital cities in Europe that do not treat their sewage. Much of the food Poles consume also is contaminated with toxic metals, and milk in some areas of the country has been declared unfit for children under the age of 6.

The environmental problems are particularly severe in the southern industrial region of Silesia, which forms the eastern edge of a vast zone of environmental devastation stretching south into Bohemia in Czechoslovakia and east into East Germany. Lead concentrations in the Silesian soil exceed standards by 150 to 1,900 percent. Concentrations of soot in the air are up to 35 times greater than that judged dangerous to health. Life expectancy in the region is lower than in the rest of Poland and has fallen in recent years, while complications with pregnancies are far above national levels. A report issued last year by the Polish Chemical Society said that air pollution and other kinds of environmental damage appear to have caused substandard health in 30 to 45 percent of schoolchildren.

Although Hungary's environmental problems are not as severe as those of Poland, Czechoslovakia and East Germany, the country still faces severe threats from air and water pollution. Air pollution in Budapest, whose streets are clogged with thousands of cheap East Bloc cars and buses, is so severe in the winter that one study estimated a one-hour walk outdoors causes the same harm to one's lungs as smoking a pack of cigarettes. Hungary's Environment Ministry says one in 17 deaths in the country is related to air pollution. Rivers flowing from the Soviet Union are contaminated even before they reach Hungary.

The catastrophic effect of the socialist economic system on the environment has been a major factor in persuading the elites that change was essential. "We were all convinced that a planned economy created a real chance for effective environmental protection and that socialist countries having that kind of economy would have an advantage over Western countries. But that hope proved totally unfulfilled," said Adam Urbanek, chairman of the Man and Environment Committee in the Polish Academy of Science. "Priorities were neglected, because the only priority under our system turned out to be heavy industry."

At the same time, the alarming growth of the environmental threat during the past decade has played a major role in mobilizing the opposition groups that helped prompt the new process of change. The Polish Environmental Club, founded in Krakow, won legal registration in 1981 in the wake of the revolution in the country led by the Solidarity trade union, but unlike Solidarity it survived the imposition of martial law that year.

As a result, the Environmental Club and a host of related movements both above and below ground soon became an outlet for political activists unable to pursue the broader aims of Solidarity. In particular, youth coming of age in the Poland of the 1980s embraced environmental causes as a field in which to act outside Solidarity's stagnating underground structures. Groups such as the Freedom and Peace Movement began environmental protests, and after the Chernobyl nuclear disaster of 1986, new local organizations sprang up to oppose Poland's nuclear program as well as other projects potentially damaging to the environment.

Polish sociologists studying the environmental movement concluded that more than 60 local and national groups had formed by early this year, while 80 more organizations of various kinds were involved in antipollution causes.

Controversial Dam

In Hungary, an entire social movement grew up after 1985 around a single environmental issue—the construction of a huge hydroelectric dam by the government at Nagymaros, on the Danube River. Government officials, pushed into the project by partners Czechoslovakia and Austria, now largely concede that the dam is ill-conceived and possibly damaging to the delicate environment along the river. But as they have pressed ahead with the construction, the small group of dissidents and environmentalists who formed a committee to stop the dam have seen their ranks swelled by thousands of Hungarians who had never before dared to participate in politics.

After years of slowly gaining strength, the Nagymaros movement touched off the first truly contentious debates in Hungary's once rubber-stamp parliament as a group of deputies defected to the opposition. Even after the parliament voted to go ahead with the project last year, the movement protesting the dam collected more than 100,000 signatures on petitions demanding a national referendum on the issue and prompted the government to suspend work this month pending another parliamentary debate.

"Nagymaros is the first thing that could be called a mass movement in Hungary since the revolution of 1956," said Judit Vasarhelyi, a dissident organizer and environmental activist. "This drew in tens of thousands of intellectuals and working people who gave up the mood of resignation that we had for so long after 1956 and said, 'This is ours and we must try to do something.' "

Throughout the 1980s, the environmental movements frequently suffered from official repression, and authorities refused to grant them formal channels of influence or even admit that their protests were heard. Scientists working on official reports about the environment came under intense pressure to water down their conclusions or keep them secret.

Now the environmental groups in Poland and Hungary stand to be legalized, and in Poland they will be granted substantial influence over policy through membership in various oversight commissions. The Polish party has gone so far as to promise in writing that peaceful environmental protests will not be broken up and organizers of groups will suffer no discrimination.

At least in the short term, however, the new situation presents the environmental movements with a difficult challenge of adjustment to working in a more open political system. In both countries, the relaxation of repression has quickly led to both a proliferation of groups and the eruption of somewhat anarchic competition among them. At the same time, many environmental activists have shifted to other political fields now that open organization is tolerated.

In Krakow, some activists of the original Polish ecological club moved on to found a Polish ecological party last year, only to see it change its name to the Polish Green Party and split in two. One of the two parties has shifted its platform so that its main demand is for Poland to declare neutrality. "The ecological movement did a lot to change the system because it introduced a new style of independent movement and precipitated a lot of conflicts," said Fura, an organizer of the Green Party. "But now I see a certain impasse developing in the movement."

Varied Approaches

"There are a lot of initiatives, not all of them positive or constructive, and a lot of groups, each of which wants to be the leader," Fura said. "This is an inevitable stage in the process of development. Ideally all the groups should form a federation or a Green parliament and work to see that the environmental agreement worked out at the round table is really implemented. But we're simply not ready for that. It could take three years at least."

Under the modified system of centralized political and economic power maintained by Poland and Hungary until now, a handful of environmental activists protesting a source of pollution were often enough to make a difference, even if authorities pretended to ignore their protests. But as political and economic decision-making are greatly decentralized by the coming reforms, a much larger and more organized environmental movement will be needed to monitor events at the local level.

Although it may produce closings of some of the most polluting factories, the market-oriented economic program pursued by Poland and Hungary may thus conflict with the effort to clean up the environment, experts say. "If the economy is centralized, a decision maker can make a big mistake, but the mistake can be corrected. Now those that make mistakes will be counted in the thousands," said Roman Andrzejewski, a biologist leading a comprehensive program of official ecological research.

For factory managers trying to survive in the new era of profits and losses, Andrzejewski said, "the cheapest thing is to throw waste on the pile. The cheapest thing is to push environmental protection outside one's own factory. We must have strong laws and services that enforce them. But we haven't done well on that until now."

For several years, Poland and Hungary have had laws mandating the installation of water and air filters by factories and spelling out fines for non-use. But while Hungary collected $20 million in fines last year, Poland's deputy environment minister, Waclaw Kulczinski, conceded, "I don't know of a case where anyone was punished." Kulczinski added: "There are laws, but they are not always used. There used to be a climate in which prosecutors were not to look too carefully at environmental violations. With the problems of the economic situation, it was felt that this could not be enforced."

Even factories that want to obey the new environmental regulations often are unable to do so because they cannot buy the equipment on the local market. Poland and Hungary have only the beginnings of an industry producing antipollution devices. Government officials say they do not have the money to import the equipment or invest large sums in new factories. Although Poland claims that environmental protection is one of its top three priorities, it has frozen spending for it at about $1 billion annually since 1986.

"There is a general problem for us in that we have great difficulty obtaining technology for environmental protection," said Hungary's environment minister, Laszlo Marothy. "The real solution to our air pollution in Budapest would be 100 billion forints in foreign currency [about $2 billion] to switch to brand new cars that have catalytic converters. But that is not realistic for us."

Governmental officials and environmental activists alike frequently express the hope that some of the financial and technological problems can be overcome with Western assistance, particularly from the Central European and Scandinavian countries most affected by East European pollution. But modest initial efforts at cooperation have been overshadowed in both countries by scandals concerning efforts by Western producers to illegally export hazardous waste to Polish and Hungarian dump sites. In Poland, one of the shipments tracked by customs agents involved a shadow Austrian company that contracted with equally fleeting Polish private agents last year for the import of 9,000 barrels of hazardous chemicals.

Environmentalists are concerned that the Western industrial investors their governments now eagerly seek will use Eastern Europe for environmentally damaging production no longer tolerated in the West. One example is the Nagymaros dam, which has been financed and strongly supported by Austrian power companies that were blocked from constructing a similar Danube dam in Austria by that country's environmental lobby.

Tensions in Bloc

The problem of international cooperation is further complicated by the growing tensions between Hungary and Poland and the hard-line regimes in East Germany and Czechoslovakia. These countries not only have continued to pursue policies that favor heavy industry and minimize environmental protection efforts, their critics say, but also have been slow to cooperate with neighbors seeking to coordinate antipollution efforts.

Poland, which gets 45 percent of its air pollution from Czechoslovakia and East Germany, has been trying for more than a year to negotiate an environmental cooperation agreement with the two countries, but the results have been meager. "In Czechoslovakia and East Germany, nothing changed," charged opposition expert Kozlowski. "There are no structures and no funding. There is only destruction."

Still, the Czechoslovaks and East Germans might answer that even if Poland and Hungary have created new social and political structures, they have neither brought adequate funding for the environment, nor lessened its destruction. Ultimately, "the room for maneuver in our countries is limited," said Andrzejewski. "Our governments are under a lot of internal pressure. Our economies are weak. Our people say housing and food are more important than ecology."

"Europe needs to be dealt with as a single ecological system," he said. "If Poland gets 50 percent of its pollution from abroad, how can we act independently? We can't do anything about it. When it comes to the environment, our sovereignty is limited."

April 18, 1989

Scientist Says Greenhouse Effect Is Setting In

Michael Weisskopf

Man-made gases that trap solar heat, resulting in the so-called greenhouse effect," have left the Earth warmer today than ever before and increase the likelihood of the type of drought now parching U.S. farmland, a NASA scientist told a congressional hearing yesterday.

James E. Hansen, chief of NASA's Goddard Institute for Space Studies, said it is impossible to blame a specific heat wave or drought on the "greenhouse effect." But he said the record-breaking, global warming of the 1980s, hitting hardest in the American Southeast and Midwest, is the first firm evidence that gases emitted by automobiles and coal-burning factories have accumulated in the atmosphere, shrouding the Earth and trapping its heat like a greenhouse.

"The greenhouse effect has been detected and it is changing our climate now," Hansen testified at a hearing of the Senate Committee on Energy and Natural Resources. "We already reached the point where the greenhouse effect is important."

Although scientists have previously theorized about the greenhouse effect and issued vague projections of rising temperatures sometime in the next century, Hansen is the first to concretely link warming and greenhouse gases and to authoritatively proclaim the phenomenon's arrival.

He warned, moreover, of an "increasing tendency" for droughts and heat waves, especially in the Southeast and Midwest, during the balance of this decade and the 1990s.

None of the scientists joining Hansen at the hearing went as far in suggesting a link between current weather patterns and greenhouse gases. But Michael Oppenheimer of the Environmental Defense Fund appeared to express the consensus that the drought "is a warning. Whether or not it's related to global changes, it provides a small taste of the dislocations society will face with increasing frequency if we fail to act."

Syukuro Manabe, a scientist with the National Oceanic and Atmospheric Administration, lent theoretical support to Hansen's position. He said computer models show that with a doubling of carbon dioxide—the most common greenhouse gas—soil becomes drier over "very extensive," mid-continental regions of North America, including the American Great Plains, Southern Europe and Siberia.

Higher temperatures caused by carbon dioxide melt winter snows earlier than normal, increasing the land's absorption of solar energy that evaporates soil moisture, he explained. Moreover, the warmer, moisture-rich air moves north, reducing rainfall.

Manabe said the greenhouse effect probably aggravated the current drought but has not warmed the Earth enough to account solely for the dry conditions.

According to Hansen, a climate specialist at NASA, global temperature in the first five months of 1988 is "substantially warmer" than any previous period since measurements were first taken 100 years ago. This year is expected to be the warmest on record barring a "remarkable, improbable cooling" in later months, he said.

The Earth has warmed at a record pace in the past two decades, Hansen said, noting that the four warmest years of the last 100 years have been in the 1980s. The warming has been matched by increasing emissions of carbon dioxide, mostly from power plants.

Compared to the 30-year mean temperature, the recent warming pattern is three times larger than the standard deviation, giving NASA "99 percent confidence" that current temperatures represent a "real warming trend" rather than chance fluctuation, according to Hansen.

Although global climate models are not sufficiently reliable to predict the effects of greenhouse warming on regional climates, he said, studies projected into the late 1980s and 1990s indicate greater than average warming in the Southeast and Midwest, where high temperatures will be accompanied by less rainfall.

"It is not possible to blame a specific heat wave/drought on the greenhouse effect," he said. "However, there is evidence that the greenhouse effect increases the likelihood of such events."

Projections by as authoritative a figure as Hansen are expected to stimulate debate on the impact of greenhouse gases and fuel efforts in Congress to impose controls on sources of carbon dioxide, nitrous oxides, chlorofluorocarbons (CFCs), methane and other gases that do not easily break down in the atmosphere.

"We have only one planet," said Sen. J. Bennett Johnston (D-La.), committee chairman. "If we screw it up, we have no place to go. The greenhouse effect has ripened beyond theory."

Sen. Dale L. Bumpers (D-Ark.) said Hansen's report "ought to be cause for headlines in every newspaper of the country. What you have is all the economic interests pitted against our very survival."

Oppenheimer listed a number of measures designed to reverse the global warming trends, including a halt to deforestation because trees absorb carbon dioxide. He also recommended energy conservation, strengthening international controls on CFCs, development of alternative fuels and tapping solid waste landfills for methane.

Much of the opposition to such measures is expected to come from coal-producing states. Sen. Wendell L. Ford (D-Ky.) pointedly asked witnesses whether they were ready to endorse nuclear power as an alternative to coal-fired utilities.

June 24, 1988

Greenhouse Effect Foreseen Straining U.S. Society, Resources

Michael Weisskopf

The United States could lose coastline equivalent in size to the state of Massachusetts and suffer crop losses of 25 percent in the Great Plains as the nation is warmed by the "greenhouse effect" in coming decades.

Demand for air conditioning could rise 15 percent in the South and that region could experience a battle between farmers and urban dwellers over scarce water supplies. San Francisco could become much smoggier and the groundwater of the Northeast more riddled with pesticides.

This dire forecast is contained in a draft Environmental Protection Agency report obtained yesterday. The analysis—based on the widely held prediction of a 3- to 9-degree rise in world temperature by the middle of the next century—is the most comprehensive effort to detail the impact for U.S. society and natural resources.

It was prepared for Congress and is being reviewed by the EPA's Science Advisory Board. A companion study nearing completion is supposed to examine options for dealing with the warming trend.

But the jarring dislocations spelled out by the conservative agency and its overall prediction of a "world that is different from the world that exists today" represent the fullest official acknowledgment of the problem and may foreshadow proposals to control the man-made gases, especially carbon dioxide from the burning of coal, which trap solar heat like a greenhouse and warm the Earth.

"Global climate change will have significant implications for natural ecosystems," said the report, "for when, where and how we farm; for the availability of water we drink and water to run our factories; for how we live in our cities; for the wetlands that spawn our fish; for the beaches we use for recreation, and for all levels of government and industry."

An obscure scientific theory for 90 years, the "greenhouse effect" has gained wide scientific acceptance recently as the world has become warmer than at any time in recorded history. The four hottest years of the past century all have fallen in this decade, and 1988 is expected to be the warmest yet.

The EPA report, two years in the making and drawing on the work of leading scientists, was designed to specify the national and regional consequences of drought, ice cap meltings and sea level changes generally predicted during a period of global warming.

Some regions on the globe will benefit from the effects predicted in the report. In northern states, for example, yields of corn and soybeans could double with longer growing seasons assured by warmer temperatures, according to the study. Fish in the Great Lakes may prosper and migrate to new habitats in warmer waters.

But the overall impact for nature is expected to he negative as the climate changes faster than vegetation and wildlife can adapt. As soils dry up in Mississippi and Georgia, trees will die and their seedlings will not grow, said the report, predicting that forests in the Southeast could die back in 30 to 80 years.

Sea level rises due to thermal expansion of the water and melting of glaciers are expected to require spending of up to $111 billion on coastal barriers and even so 7,000 square miles of dry land will be inundated.

Higher temperatures could increase poisonous algae and increase the concentration of pollutants in rivers as the volume of water decreases. The report predicted conflicts over water use that would pit farmers wanting to irrigate their lands against consumers and urban industries.

Agricultural losses could reach 80 percent of corn, wheat and soybeans in a drought-prone South, livestock diseases and pests typical of the South may move north and pesticide use could rise, increasing groundwater pollution.

Electricity demands will increase for summer cooling, especially in the South and Southwest where additional generating capacity would grow up to 30 percent.

Since ozone is produced by the mixture of auto exhausts and sun, hotter days for longer parts of the year would be expected to increase levels of the pollutant, which is the main ingredient of smog. In San Francisco, ozone concentrations could increase 20 percent even if auto emissions did not increase, the study said.

October 20, 1988

Despite Years of Controls, China Fears New Baby Boom

Daniel Southerland

Chen Zhongmin, the Communist Party chief in this model community in Zhejiang Province, was complaining that no matter how hard he tried, he still had difficulty convincing farmers that a girl child was just as good as a boy.

"A male is considered to be stronger than a female," said Chen. "And, traditionally, when a daughter leaves her family to get married, she goes to live with her husband's family. The family loses a farmhand when the daughter leaves."

Farmers also want sons to carry on the family name.

But the party chief stressed that eventually, people would believe in the logic of his argument that the size of families must be limited if the world's most populous nation is to raise living standards for many of its impoverished citizens.

After eight years of a controversial family planning program to limit Chinese couples to one child, this land of 1 billion people is expecting a new baby boom.

The English-language China Daily newspaper reported last month that 1.6 million more babies were born last year than the number set by state planners and that, if current growth trends continue, there will be 100 million more Chinese by the year 2000 than the 1.2 billion in the official plan.

Officials in Beijing have warned that if action is not taken to curb recent "sharp increases" in births, the world's largest national population may grow out of control.

In the provinces, family planning officials and others have mobilized for a new propaganda drive to convince couples that they should limit their families to one child, or to two children under certain circumstances.

Adding to a sense of urgency over the growing number of mouths to feed are indications that during the past year China's grain production has failed to expand as much as expected.

In the United States, critics of China's family planning program are predicting that the new drive to limit births will turn into a crackdown and lead to forced abortions.

Yao Quanjin, deputy director of the family planning committee for Zhejiang Province, said in an interview that the biggest problem facing family planners is that men and women born in the early 1960s, when births reached a high point, have come of child-bearing age. The earlier baby boom is expected to produce another baby boom, or what some experts call an "echo" boom.

"We will do propaganda work among the young people and ask them to pay attention to this problem," said Yao.

Yao insisted that the government plans to use persuasion, not coercion, to limit the number of births. But he acknowledged that there is a system of fines for those who violate the state's guidelines.

If a woman insists on continuing with a pregnancy that goes beyond the one-child guidelines, the woman and her husband would be required to pay a fine amounting to 15 percent of their annual salaries for several years, Yao said. Under the program, those who limit the size of their families would receive extra benefits.

"In some cases, people still want another boy, although they already have several sons," he said. "This is still a problem."

The Chinese press has suggested that another problem is a growing laxity among local officials who have themselves violated one-child guidelines. A radio program on China's remote Hainan island spoke of "leading cadres" who have "contravened" regulations.

"Our current emergency task... must center on stressing energetically remedial measures for unscheduled pregnancies. At the same time, we must pay attention to stressing [tubal] ligatures for those who have already given birth to two children."

Here in Hongshan, Chen and other party officials insist that for several years the family planning program has permitted exceptions to the one-child guideline. Many couples, they say, have been allowed to have a second child, after a wait of several years, without being penalized.

According to the Chinese media, a 1984 Communist Party Central Committee directive allows couples in rural areas who face "real difficulty" to get approval for a second child.

It turns out that the difficulty is often that the first child is a girl.

It is clear that some farmers, such as those in Hongshan, cling to what officials call "feudal ideas" about the need to have many children—preferably male children.

Authorities are embarking on a "major rural campaign," using educational materials to dispel "the old viewpoint" that more sons mean more blessings, an official newspaper reported last month.

But officials such as Chen say that the number of couples who want only one child is increasing, even in rural areas.

Hongshan has succeeded in limiting the size of most of its families, Chen said, but he added that it took much effort to explain to some farmers the reasons behind the family planning program. "Some farmers don't understand the policy, especially the older farmers," Chen said.

Another problem for the family planners is rural prosperity. Many farmers can now afford to pay the fines imposed when they violate guidelines.

The 3,700 people of Hongshan are more prosperous than most Chinese. Although Hongshan is called a farm, most of the farmers here don't work on the land but in small, group-owned factories, known as collectives, that produce tiles, plastics and silk garments.

The farm also has its own reception center with a model of the farm, meeting rooms and a director who acts as a public relations man.

According to Chen, before the Communists took power in 1949, the community was extremely poor and the people lived in huts. Many of the farmers now live in two-story houses.

Chen said that Hongshan has sent a few of its farmers to institutes and universities for short periods to learn more about scientific farming. But he said the educational level among the 800 million people living in China's rural areas is still too low. Most of the farmers, he said, have had only a primary school education.

Chen and experts in Beijing argue that, with more education, farmers in China, as in other countries, will have less need for many hands to work their farms and will be more inclined to accept planning.

In 1985, the United States—reacting to reports that the Chinese were resorting to coercive methods, such as forced abortions, to curb population growth—began to withhold contributions to the U.N. Fund for Population Activities (UNFPA), which supports China's family planning program.

But UNFPA officials insist that the U.N. funds that go to China are devoted to voluntary activities, such as education, training and the provision of contraceptives. They say that none of the money is used to support coercive methods.

Joan Kaufman, a former UNFPA officer now with the Harvard University School of Public Health, said the last thing top Chinese officials in Beijing want is coercion.

"What they want is for people to voluntarily accept a smaller family norm," said Kaufman, who worked for four years in China with UNFPA and is studying the program in rural areas under a Rockefeller Foundation grant.

"Most of the effort goes into publicity and education," said Kaufman. "They send teams out with TV programs, movies and posters."

Other experts said that if coercion occurs, it is likely to come from local officials, many of whom were recruited during the Cultural Revolution years of 1966 to 1976. These officials lack professional training, want to meet the population planning targets they are given and tend to take the law into their own hands, experts said.

Kaufman said she believes that such coercion has diminished over the past few years.

May 24, 1987

Chapter Eleven

Urbanization

In 1910, only 10 percent of the world's population lived in cities. By 1989, that figure had increased to 41 percent. While cities in the developed world are growing at a relatively slow pace, urban populations of developing nations are increasing rapidly. This tremendous growth is a product of two factors: a natural increase because of more births than deaths, and unprecedented rural-to-urban migration. Many cities in both both the developed and developing world confront a wide range of serious problems, including poverty, lack of affordable housing, crime, and pollution.

"Seoul—Dynamic Capital," explores conditions in South Korea's largest city. Rapid modernization has transformed Korea from a country that was predominantly rural in 1955 to a nation that is overwhelmingly rural today. In Brazil, economic growth has been accompanied by a tremendous economic gap between that country's rich and poor. As illustrated in "Living in Brazil's Streets," these inequities are everywhere apparent in cities such as Rio, Sao Paulo, and Brasilia.

Many of the world's urban areas are plagued with a host of environmental hazards, including air pollution. Article number 3 describes how smog is threatening the health and well-being of the residents of Mexico City. "Southern California Battling Smog" reports on the problems of air pollution in Los Angeles and the steps local officials are taking to combat it.

Notwithstanding the myriad of problems threatening many of the world's great urban centers, we should not forget that some of humanity's most notable achievements are to be found in cities. The last article in this section takes us to breathtaking Warsaw, the capital city of a newly democratic Poland.

Seoul— Dynamic Capital; Koreans Energies Always at Full Throttle

Fred Hiatt

It is late Sunday afternoon in South Korea's capital, for most of its residents the close of their one-day weekend.

Several hundred have gathered to play badminton on a dusty patch of Namsan Park, a precious open space in this crowded and noisy city. With characteristic persistence, they play with imaginary nets, on imaginary courts, in a space that five or six Americans might find adequate for Frisbee.

As dusk falls, dozens of shuttlecocks rise and fall in softly whirring confusion, mixing with the moths in the hot summer air. It is a rare gentle moment in this city of hard edges, a product of a hard history, hard politics and hard-charging development.

Here in Seoul, amid the pushing crowds, the blue-suited company workers drinking at outdoor stalls late after work, the no-nonsense market women hawking dried squid and a spicy Korean cabbage dish known as kimchi, the winding alleys of the old city and cement apartment blocks of the new middle class—it is here that one can best sense the pulsating, adaptable, angry, tender, proud, industrious energies of South Korea.

This is where the refugees from the communist North came 40 years ago, bringing with them a zealous attachment to the glories of profit. Here are the universities that attract South Korea's best students, intensely patriotic, single-minded in their studies, preparing to serve their countrymen as they demonstrate against their government.

From here, thousands of Koreans left for the United States to seek a better life during the decades of hunger and poverty. And it is to Seoul's Kimpo International Airport that they or their children return, often weeping as the jet wheels bounce onto the earth of their motherland—what Koreans call uri nara, our country.

This is the dynamic center of power and money in a country acutely aware of its authoritarian past and once-destitute status before it began accumulating wealth at an astonishing rate. Here, since the Americans installed the dictatorial Syngman Rhee as the country's first president in 1948, assassinations and columns of tanks in the streets have brought to power one general after another, to be replaced only this year by a more modest ex-general elected by the people.

This is home to 10 million people, one-quarter of South Korea's population, about 10 times as many as in 1953, when the Korean War laid the city to waste. It is home, too, to thousands of U.S. troops, stationed here since the inconclusive end of that war.

From the air one sees best the Seoul that South Korea would like the world to meet this month, when it hosts the Summer Olympic Games: gleaming skyscrapers

305

crowding each other among jagged, violent peaks, split by the broad and snaking Han River. This is the Seoul of South Korea's economic miracle, of its 100-fold increase in exports in 25 years, of near universal literacy, successful population control, a model for developing nations.

From the ground, the signs of Seoul's rapid development are more visible: occasional caved-in sidewalks, clouds of dust from unceasing construction, a few old ladies still begging on subway landings with babies strapped to their backs. South Korea developed so quickly that many residents of Seoul grew up without cars and won their driver's permits as adults; they now drive through the city's clogged arteries with the aggressive zeal of the converted.

From above or below, the energy is palpable: sometimes self-defeating, occasionally self-pitying, always at full throttle.

Controlling the Future

The 1988 Seoul Olympics are often compared to the 1964 Tokyo games, which provided a similar forum to display economic success, and outsiders often compare the South Koreans to their former colonial masters in Japan. People in both nations live by elaborate systems of courtesy, bow instead of shake hands, and speak a hierarchical language that constantly reinforces the notion that all men are not equal and most women are decidedly less so.

But a visitor to Seoul expecting Japanese-style decorum and reserve will be very much surprised. Koreans look you in the eye, take you by the hand, jostle you and hug you and tell you what they think.

There is, by New York standards, little violent crime in Seoul, but what violence there is seems to erupt passionately, irrationally, volcanically. Shaven Buddhist monks in long robes assault each other with crowbars in sectarian battle. Cattle farmers displeased with beef import regulations fling cow manure at unsympathetic officials. Baseball fans take to the field to beat up the home team after a loss.

Due process, malpractice suits, and appeals to the rule of law have in the past yielded little for Koreans, accustomed to centuries of royal decree and decades of authoritarian fiat, to big men taking and little people staying out of the way. Riot policemen in green fatigues or plainclothes agents carrying rolled-up, unread newspapers still patrol almost every downtown corner.

In the modern era, Seoul's first two authoritarian leaders yielded only to violence. Rhee gave up power after his police gunned down dozens of unarmed schoolchildren marching toward the presidential palace in Seoul. His successor, ex-general Park Chung Hee, was shot at dinner by one of his closest aides. Last year, ex-general Chun Doo Hwan honored a long-held promise to retire voluntarily, but the ruling party agreed to a direct presidential election to choose his successor only after students once again took to the streets with rocks and firebombs, winning the support of people from all walks of life.

The fear of all-encompassing violence, a repeat of the fratricidal Korean War, is never distant. Seoul, for all its new Burger Kings and discotheques, remains in some ways a frontier town on a war footing, 30 miles from the North Korean border, with tank traps and revetments disguised by modern bridges and garages.

Until a few years ago, the city shut down every night at midnight under military curfew. Red neon signs and red passenger cars, redolent of communism, were taboo. Even now, a midday air raid drill sends Seoul residents scurrying into underground passageways once a month, as a shocking stillness blankets the city.

Fitfully, uncertainly, the South Koreans are growing too prosperous, too educated, too self-confident, to accept the old ways. Hyundai and Daewoo build and sell red cars; Seoul's restless tycoons trade with communist China and eagerly eye the coal in North Korea. Just as Seoul residents put handkerchiefs to their mouths and carry on with their lives when tear gas drifts from the campuses, so the city itself rises around and beyond the tank traps and riot police.

After years of hearing that their society was too layered, too Confucian, too militaristic and too autocratic to give root to a foreign plant like democracy, South Koreans are seizing control of their futures. "My parents' chauffeurs won't be talked to the way people used to talk to them," says one young and wealthy South Korean woman visiting from her studies in the United States.

Some of the violence, the sit-ins and marches and clashes, are experiments with new freedoms. And as suddenly as it appears, the violence is often replaced by a stunningly genuine warmth; a university student lambastes the imperialism of America, and then invites you home and shows you pictures of his cousins in New Jersey.

South Korean Style

For centuries, Koreans proudly say, they paid tribute to the emperor of China, lord of East Asia, without sacrificing their independence. Today, Seoul digests imports from Japan and the United States, always stamping them as its own.

At the Pizza Hut in Itaewon, a young Korean woman stands at the automatic door, her only job to welcome customers and thank them as they leave.

Koreans eat Japanese-style sashimi, or raw fish, not with a delicate Japanese-style hint of horseradish and soy—which the Koreans think is pale and flavorless—but with fiery red chili paste and hunks of raw garlic—which the Japanese think is unspeakably crude.

The street stalls of Seoul's teeming marketplaces have not yielded to the gleaming department stores of the middle-class neighborhoods south of the river. Doing business late into steaming nights under a single naked light bulb, they still offer tofu and dumplings, grain alcohol and cane liquor, pig heads and noodles and even, like the Chinese, dog meat.

But in a nod to the modern era, some provide Samsung television sets perched on stands above the stalls. Others sell Spam and M&Ms, which somehow find their way from U.S. Army PXs to the narrow market lanes.

Even the department stores resist homogenization. The pride of Seoul is the Lotte store, opened in January, larger than Tokyo's largest. Hundreds of thousands of Seoul residents filed through the store to see the Tokyo-style Dancing-Doll Clock, the garish chandeliers, the indoor waterfall and atrium.

By this summer, though, no one would have thought the lushly planted atrium was in Tokyo. Squatting at the top of the escalator, an old man tended his fortune-telling birds, which would hop through the bars of their cage and peck at a specially printed fortune paper for a 100-won coin.

'We Never Fall Down'

Pas or Paul Yonggi Cho is a resident of Seoul, born, like so many Seoulites, in a small village. Today he shepherds the largest congregation in the world, the Yoido Full Gospel Church.

Cho is not the kind of Korean minister whom foreigners often meet, the black-suited human rights activists who have led the fight for independence and democracy since early in this century. Like the brash, entrepreneurial founders of Hyundai and Daewoo and Samsung, Cho is an empire-builder, a charismatic leader in a tan leisure suit and white shoes, a man with big accomplishments and big plans.

He was born and raised a Buddhist but converted to Christianity when he was struck down at age 17 with tuberculosis, he says. "By God's miraculous touch, I was healed. Since then, I've been working for the Lord."

In 1958, his first church, in a tent, attracted five followers. Today, his 530,000 church members are tracked by church computers and organized into neighborhoods, blocks and 60,000 "cells" of 10 or so worshipers each.

"Success is measured in faith, not in volume," Cho says, but his aides readily reel off the statistics: seven services each Sunday in the giant round church near the National Assembly building; 25,000 congregants attending each service, with as many watching on closed-circuit television in 15 auxiliary chapels; two more sessions on Saturdays, three on Wednesdays. Then there are magazines, television shows, and plans to go international.

Cho credits the Lord with the remarkable growth of his church, but he also acknowledges that the upheavals of recent history have played a part. "The Korean War, the insecurity of Korean society, the intimidation of impending communist attack, the continuing social upheavals because of changes of government—all of these factors have contributed to the prospering of the church," he says.

And, Cho says, the rapid urbanization of the nation, from three-quarters rural in 1955 to about one-quarter rural today, also encouraged conversions. Traditionally Buddhist and Confucian, South Korea has more than 12 million Christians now, with fundamentalist churches like Cho's attracting most of the converts in recent years. Red neon crosses of storefront churches glow from every Seoul hilltop at night.

"People, once they move to the city, are more or less free of their obligations and traditions, so they can freely come to church," Cho says.

Cho does not involve himself in politics, he says, but he is optimistic about the future of Korea. "If Korean people had not been strong, we would have been a

Chinese province long ago," he says. "Korean people are very tenacious, very strong."

That Korean tenaciousness is everywhere in Seoul: in the women who must carry water up steep slopes to their "moon village" hovels in the dusty slums of outlying hilltops, and in the high school girls who rent desks at commercial study halls because there is no room at home, and who study every night until after midnight.

It is in the mothers of political prisoners who throw themselves, again and again, at lines of stolid riot policeman, and in the suave government bureaucrats with Berkeley and Georgetown Ph.D.s who work late every night charting the nation's course. It is in the dissident lawyer, jailed and disbarred for representing the politically unacceptable, who nonetheless speaks warmly of a prosecutor with whom he went to school, because in Seoul human relations and networks remain paramount. And it is in the businessmen who, never fully accepted in this Confucian society that views the entrepreneurial spirit as something a little unclean, have nonetheless struggled to turn Seoul into a trading capital of the world.

"Many people worry about violence, contention and riots," Pastor Cho says. "This is the way of Korean living throughout the centuries. But when we come to the precipice, we never fall down."

September 4, 1988

Living in Brazil's Streets Imperils Millions of Youths

Eugene Robinson

Tall and angular, with sad eyes and a warm smile, Mario lives by his wits in a seedy commercial zone. He left home when he was 8 because his parents beat him, he says, and now at 15 he is a veteran of the streets, having survived mostly by begging and robbing. Mario has never been to school.

It is not such a bad life, he says, "except that when it rains, I get cold." Pressed further, he allows that there are other dangers as well.

"A friend of mine was robbing all the time, just robbing and robbing," Mario says, in a voice that betrays neither emotion nor alarm, "so they shot him and he died." He shrugs when asked who "they" might be, then looks up with a puzzled expression.

Mario at least has been lucky enough to find a civic shelter, where he can spend the daylight hours. He exemplifies one of Brazil's most critical social problems—the hordes of children who live on the streets of the big cities, uneducated, unwashed, unloved.

Estimates of their number range as high as 7 million in a total population of 150 million. Medium-sized urban areas report seeing a sharp increase in street children, but most still live in the metropolitan centers of Rio de Janeiro, Sao Paulo, Recife, Salvador, Belo Horizonte and Brasilia.

New attention was focused on their plight last month when Amnesty International, the human rights lobby, issued a report saying hundreds of street children are being killed each year in Brazil, many by extermination squads who view the slayings they carry out as what amounts to pest control.

"Death squads—many run by off-duty police officers—kill them to 'clean up the streets,' remove witnesses or guarantee the security of an area," Amnesty International alleged. The report sparked widespread press coverage and embarrassed the administration of President Fernando Collor de Mello, who has vowed that Brazil must never again be cited for human rights abuses.

The report is based on research that for the most part infers, rather than proves, the involvement of organized death squads. But it provides a context for a steady stream of sensational cases that even a society inured to crime, violence and poverty has found shocking.

In Rio earlier this year, for example, a teenage boy died from a bullet in the brain after being arrested by police and allegedly forced to play Russian roulette. In Sao Paulo last month, a 13-year-old boy was accosted by private security guards who thought he was a graffiti vandal—they shot him, beat him senseless and then let him bleed to death before finally calling for medical help.

The problem of homeless children is evident in all of Brazil's big cities. By day, groups of barefoot youths play unsupervised in residential streets or saunter through commercial areas looking for robbery victims. Children as young as 3 or 4 dodge traffic at stoplights to beg from motorists. By night, teenagers cruise the docks of Recife, the red-light strips of Sao Paulo and the beachside hotel zones of Rio de Janeiro, selling their bodies.

Social workers say few of these children are true orphans. Most have families and know more or less how to find them, but have been thrown out of the home or have left of their own accord.

"These children come from extreme poverty, and they leave home because they need money," said Vera Moreira, a sociologist who works with the Children's Crusade, an umbrella agency in Rio that coordinates a variety of programs aimed at helping the street children.

"They earn their way by begging, stealing or prostitution," Moreira said. "At first, they leave home to get money to bring home to their parents. Then they decide there's really no need to give the money to anyone, and so they stay out on the streets, on their own.

Some youths sniff glue or use drugs. Some become involved in the violent drug trade that flourishes in the slums, called favelas, sprinkled throughout the big cities. That connection with the drug world has often been cited as a possible factor in the killings.

However, a study by the Brazilian Institute of Social and Economic Analysis—on which the Amnesty International report was based—casts doubt on that theory. The institute was able to document 457 slayings of children and teenagers last year in Rio, Sao Paulo and Recife, the three cities where the problem was seen as most acute.

"Most of the victims were boys 15 to 17 years old," said Rosana Heringer, one of the two researchers who conducted the study. "From what we could determine, most had no prior police record. In most cases, there was no apparent link to crime."

The study relied heavily on press accounts, at times sketchy. But Heringer said it appeared that most of the youths were alone or with other youths when they were killed—no adults were present, a fact that she said tends to refute the notion of young apprentice drug dealers being caught in the middle of shootouts between rival gangs of traffickers.

"Most of the killings were not the result of fights or domestic violence," she said. "Most, it appeared, were premeditated. It is already well documented that there are groups organized in Brazil to kill, to take justice in their own hands. We believe most of these killings fit that pattern.

Volmer do Nascimento, Rio-area director of the National Movement of Street Children, was more blunt in his criticism of the authorities.

"The politicians and especially the police are as guilty as those who actually pull the trigger," he said. "Everybody knows about the death squads. These kids are begging and robbing in front of businesses, and the businessmen want to get rid of them. Then all of a sudden they turn up dead."

Nascimento, whose five-year-old organization has sponsored two national "congresses" of street children and established itself as a leading children's lobby, also was critical of the Collor administration. "We hear speeches but we see no improvement," he said. "On the contrary, crimes against children seem to be rapidly increasing."

The needs of the street children reflect the more general failure of successive Brazilian governments to translate impressive industrial and technological gains into benefits for the vast poor majority. Only two other countries have income distributions more unequal than that of Brazil, according to a recent World Bank study. Political scientists often describe Brazil as not one nation but two—a small, modern state surrounded by a large preindustrial society; Belgium, say, inside of India.

Most of the homeless children, say social workers, are illiterate. Few have access even to ill-staffed, ill-equipped, state-run health facilities. "The great majority of these children are without opportunities, without a future," said Nascimento.

Activists have begun to try to solve the problem on a local level. The Children's Crusade, for example, coordinates a number of programs in the Rio de Janeiro area where street children are being taught handicrafts. The resultant dolls and wooden toys are sold in upscale shopping centers, with the proceeds going back to the children.

"Perhaps our biggest role is to sensitize the society to the problem," said Children's Crusade director Belmiro Nunes. To that end, the organization is launching programs in Rio's wealthy south zone. The project has the backing of the owners of the major tourist hotels, who have long complained about street children harassing, assaulting and ultimately driving away their clientele.

In the center of the city, Roberto Jose dos Santos heads the Sao Martinho Benevolent Association, where an average of 150 youths—including Mario, the 15-year-old—come each day for a few hours' respite from their razor's-edge existence on the streets.

The center, built partly with municipal funds, offers recreational facilities, limited health and educational programs, counseling, legal help and three meals a day. It closes at 5 p.m., however, and the youths return to the streets. Dos Santos said the center eventually wants to open an overnight shelter but lacks the funds.

As it is, however, few of the older boys take full advantage of the center and most remain suspicious.

"They are hard to reach," dos Santos said. "These children already have discovered the adventure of total liberty. And adults? Adults are just people who try to use them."

October 10, 1990

Environmentalists Say Mexico Just Blowing Smoke on Smog Curbs

William Branigin

Faced with one of the world's worst smog problems, the Mexican government is coming under increased pressure from environmental groups and political opponents to alleviate the capital's air pollution.

After a dense brown haze smothered Mexico City during a thermal inversion Thursday, producing the highest pollution readings so far this winter, the government said it implemented an emergency plan to reduce the operations of 271 major polluting industries by 30 percent.

In a news conference Monday, Secretary of Urban Development and Ecology Manuel Camacho Sol is cited a clearing of the smog during the weekend as evidence of the "great success" of the emergency plan.

Environmental groups, however, said the weather, including a rare dry-season rain, had more to do with the dispersal of the smog than any measures taken by the government. Some critics expressed skepticism that any such measures had actually taken effect.

One group, the Mexican Ecological Movement, yesterday called on the government to apply its plan rigorously and to give top priority to actions to control automobile emissions, the major cause of Mexico City's air pollution.

"Mexico City's problem—living in a chronic state of environmental disaster that surpasses all tolerable limits of human health—must be resolved now," said another environmental organization called the Group of 100.

In addition, four opposition political parties from the left and the right accused the administration of doing little but talk about antipollution plans. The conservation National Action Party and the leftist Mexican Unified Socialist Party, Mexican Workers Party and Popular Socialist Party called for the implementation of more drastic measures to limit factory operations and vehicular traffic during smog alerts.

Sprawling over a huge dry lake bed 7,400 feet above sea level and surrounded by mountains, Mexico City frequently becomes a smoggy basin in which buildings less than half a mile away are practically invisible. Residents, especially children, routinely suffer stinging eyes, sore throats and other cold-like symptoms during smoggy periods.

According to Alfonso Cipres Villarreal, the president of the Mexican Ecological Movement, animal life also suffers. He asserted in a news conference yesterday that "thousands of birds have died" in recent days because of unusually heavy smog.

The Secretariat for Urban Development and Ecology said it implemented phase one of its antismog plan for the first time Friday and Saturday after monitor-

313

ing devices showed air pollution exceeding hazardous levels in parts of the city for the second straight day. The pollution consists largely of carbon monoxide, suspended particles, sulfur dioxide and ozone.

The secretariat recommended Friday that children and the elderly stay indoors during the weekend and that all residents refrain from outdoor exercise.

In announcing implementation of the antismog plan, the secretariat said 271 polluting industries reduced their emissions by 30 percent. But government officials were unable to produce a list of the participating industries and indicated that the plants were under no legal obligation to comply with the program.

In any case, environmental groups have pointed out, the 271 targeted industries, while considered major individual polluters, represent a small fraction of the 30,000 factories in this capital of 18 million people, the largest metropolis in the world. Moreover, according to government statistics, it is Mexico City's 3 million automobiles that account for at least 75 percent of the capital's air pollution, and nothing has yet been done to limit vehicle emissions.

In a list of 100 ecological measures announced last month, the government said that starting in 1988, new cars would be required to have pollution-control devices and that cars made between 1977 and 1982 would be required to undergo inspections starting this year.

Some environmentalists charged that this measure is too little too late and express concern that inspection requirements will fall victim to the widespread custom of bribery.

Some Mexican sources and diplomats suggested that the government may be leery of moving drastically to curb car pollution because of the political consequences of annoying the motoring public and imposing additional costs on car owners, especially during a time of economic crisis.

Western experts said little is known about potentially harmful long-term effects of the city's smog on residents. To date, no monitoring of unburned hydrocarbons released from vehicles or studies on their long-term impact have been carried out here.

However, the sheer volume of pollutants being spewed into Mexico City's thin air has been enough to alarm many environmentalists. According to the Mexican Ecological Movement, the city's automobiles, which have an average age of 12 years, emit 4.5 million tons of toxic particles into the atmosphere every year. Industries and other "fixed sources" account for 728,000 tons a year, and "natural sources" produce 308,000 tons of particles a year, the movement said.

Of greatest concern in the latter category is "fecal dust" that blows across the city during the dry windy season in February and March from areas where raw sewage is dumped or from slums that lack sanitation facilities. In its news conference Monday, the Secretariat for Urban Development and Ecology announced a plan to install 60,000 special solar-powered latrines designed to recycle organic waste into fertilizers.

It has long been rumored that fecal dust makes this capital the only city in the world where it is possible to get hepatitis by breathing the air. But one specialist called this "one of the great Mexico City myths." No research has been done to show that the disease is spread that way, he said.

Fecal dust does cause eye infections, however, the specialist said. He added that the combined effects of air pollution, dry air and dust can wear down people's resistance and make them more prone to various diseases.

February 5, 1987

Southern California Battling Smog with New Sense of Urgency

Jay Mathews

Some days, the smog in this northeast corner of Los Angeles County is so thick it sets off a high, unnerving squeal on the little black radio in the local school headquarters. That signals a first-stage smog alert. Glendora children must come off the basketball courts and baseball diamonds until it passes.

Four decades after southern California became the section of the country with the worst air pollution, there has been a resurgence in the struggle to loosen the toxic grip of yellow-brown haze on America's second-largest metropolitan area.

In recent months a rejuvenated local air pollution agency has revived "smoke patrols" on the area's highways and ordered all large employers to begin offering car-pool incentives or pay as much as $25,000 a day in fines. The area's new anti-smog chief, declaring himself ready to sacrifice some jobs for cleaner air, has been given new powers and has promised that rental and bus companies will soon be required to buy vehicles that burn "clean" fuels such as methanol.

Los Angeles County antipollution officials and even some motorists have begun to realize that population growth and business expansion are about to bury what seemed for years to be modest gains in the war against smog. The unusual initiatives against air pollution are expected to affect clean-air controls through much of the rest of the country, as other cities wait to see whether human behavior in a land so addicted to cars can be changed for the good of the environment.

"There is a new sense of urgency," said James M. Lents, the new South Coast Air Quality Management District (AQMD) executive officer who is credited with much of the new antismog effort.

A physicist, Lents arrived in 1986 after seven years as the chief air pollution official for Colorado. "In 1987 everyone woke out of their sleep," he said. "It came upon folks that we were talking about having clean air by the end of '87 and it was not going to happen.

National experts such as William Becker of the Association of Local Air Pollution Control Officials and Ronald White of the American Lung Association said the new AQMD smog-control measures are unprecedented in style and scope.

They have caused nervousness among local business executives, some of whom worry that if the changes go too far too quickly, there could be a backlash that will retard the clean-air movement. Nonetheless, environmentalists are impressed by Lents, according to Mark Abramowitz, program director for the 1,000-member Coalition for Clean Air.

Lents, Abramowitz and other clean-air activists here acknowledge that a steady if slow decline in some pollutants, particularly lead, has resulted from smokestack restrictions and cleaner cars and fuels.

Even so, the air in Glendora, the worst part of the Los Angeles basin, exceeded the federal ozone standard on 148 days in 1986, three times more than in any other U.S. city. And experts project a 40 percent growth in automobile traffic during the next 20 years.

In one University of Southern California test of lung function, Los Angeles County children scored 15 percent below children in Houston. Research by the Statewide Air Pollution Research Center in Riverside reveals losses of up to 20 percent in the state's three principal crops—cotton, grapes and oranges—because of the aging effects of ozone.

Sporadic efforts to encourage car-pooling have done little to change the single-passenger habits of southern California drivers. ARCO's downtown headquarters, with one of the few successful ride-sharing programs, has raised to 2.15 the average number of commuting employees per car, but the area average remains stuck at 1.1.

In an interview, Lents said he needs federal help to "convince a significant portion of the population to abandon their private automobiles." He said he wants new federal rules encouraging development of cars that use methanol or electricity. He also suggested that defense contractors be required to use less toxic paints and that more limits be placed on smog-producing substances in hair spray and deodorants.

Lents said he developed an acute awareness of the air around him while growing up and starting a family in Knoxville, Tenn. "We had to mop the floors every day because of the soot that flew into the house, and the odor from the rendering plants was enough to make you sick," he said. When, with a doctorate from the University of Tennessee in 1970, he encountered a job slump in the aerospace industry, he turned his attention to air pollution.

He spent eight years in Chattanooga helping rein in an iron industry with few pollution standards. In Colorado, his 1984 effort to encourage Denver commuters to abandon their cars one day a week during the winter smog season received much national publicity, and modest results.

When he arrived in Los Angeles as chief deputy executive officer in February 1986, Lents encountered a district board split by politics and personalities. After being virtually ignored for several years, the AQMD governing board stumbled into an emotional fight over permits for new plants to burn garbage for energy and to save overstuffed landfills.

Public outcry over alleged inattention to the air pollution hazard posed by such plants led to a new state law sponsored by state Sen. Robert Presley (D–Riverside) reducing the size of the board, streamlining its procedures and giving it new powers. The city and county governments in the AQMD area—Los Angeles, Orange, Riverside and San Bernardino counties—were persuaded to send different representatives. The new chairman, veteran Riverside County supervisor Norton Younglove, pushed for drastic action to erase years of political stagnation.

Gladys Meade of the American Lung Association of California said the new board creates the sense "the South Coast district is finally going to achieve the mandate that we thought they had achieved in 1977."

In a blunt warning, the board's latest annual report says "attaining clean air standards in this basin will cut across the fabric of how we live, work and play."

The toughest initiative appears to be Regulation 15. Adopted in December, it will require all companies with more than 100 employees—8,000 firms representing 1.5 million workers—to offer incentives for ride-sharing, such as preferential parking, cash bonuses or subsidized bus passes. Lents, who became executive officer in December 1986, can levy fines of up to $25,000 a day on any company that does not comply.

This month, the board revived the highway "smoke patrol," not seen since 1975. Eight California highway patrolmen plus five AQMD smog inspectors will be dispatched to find and ticket cars, buses and trucks spewing black exhaust, mostly from diesel engines exempt from state smog checks. "It's unfair to ask commuters to car-pool and tell industries to cut their pollution when they see dirty trucks and buses dumping black smoke into the air," Younglove said.

The board tentatively approved a five-year, $30.4 million clean fuels demonstration program that will require car rental firms and bus companies to buy clean-fueled vehicles when they replace current fleets and will initiate a task force to promote the development of electric cars and trucks.

Abramowitz, despite his praise for Lents, is pursuing a lawsuit to force the U.S. Environmental Protection Agency to write a plan for southern California compliance with clean air laws. In January, the AQMD board for the first time voted specific deadlines for reaching state and federal air quality standards — the end of 1996 for nitrogen dioxide, 1997 for carbon monoxide and 2007 for ozone.

Lents said he hopes that Congress, as it writes a new Clean Air Act, will accept those targets.

He said automobile emissions have been aggravated by the economic geography of the basin. Jobs are concentrated in central and western Los Angeles, while affordable housing is most common in Riverside County to the east. Commutes of 40 miles a day become necessary, and common. The board is studying proposals to grant incentives to factories that locate in the east.

Lents has said many times that he would choose blue skies over a surging economy. "I don't see myself as the economic director for the area," he said. "... I have to be the advocate for clean air."

March 14, 1988

Warsaw—Where Everything Old Is New Again

Pat Dowell

Warsaw is a city famed for living its grim and glorious past in the present. Struggles for a future that never seemed to come are a part of the landscape. But today, the city's past—everywhere defiantly evident—is not what impresses. Today, it is the future that dazzles.

The night I packed for a six-week stay in Warsaw, an exhausted Washington was just beginning to agonize over the mayor's arrest. When I arrived in Poland's capital—a city of 1.6 million in the throes not of a degrading public spectacle but of an economic upheaval touching virtually every individual—there was fear matched by unshakable hope, a certainty that Warsaw has everything before it. The Old World had become new again, as anyone from the shell-shocked New World could plainly see.

In fact, Warsaw currently has, in some ways, the air of a booming frontier town, replete with gambling dens in the form of hotel casinos. Visitors are, to some, prospective customers to be welcomed with open arms, but as with all frontiers, it's a case of buyer beware. Shifty-eyed men sidled up to me on the sidewalk promising a pitifully small premium over the new official exchange rate. Waiters brought whispered deals on Russian caviar with the check. Some of this is not new to Eastern Europe, but the open spirit of enterprise is.

And perhaps some Poles' grasp of a decentralized economy is a bit imprecise. A taxi driver who was planning to overcharge me by 600 percent one evening cheerfully explained, when I objected, that this was now a free country where the government no longer told people what to do. Those other cabs, the ones that charged by the meter, were "government taxis," he informed me, by which he meant they obeyed the law. "Now the government no longer runs anything," he said, with more shrewd insight, some would say, than he knew. It was almost his patriotic duty, I gathered, to make as much money as possible. He proffered his business card, hand-lettered, with a flourish, and pointed out that he didn't smoke and he did speak English (a double feat uncommon among Poles, unique among cab drivers). I paid—for the panache.

A Polish friend called such taxis, usually Mercedes-Benzes camped in the prime waiting line at hotels, "Mafia taxis." It was hard to be too angry. Like most Poles, who are famed for their hospitality, the cabbie was friendly and helpful, and he faces a frightening slide down the economic ladder. His fairer fellows follow the semiofficial rule of charging 100 times the meter, since they long ago stopped trying to install updated meters often enough to pace Poland's inflation rate.

Poles of all description need cash. They stand in the many informal sidewalk markets that have sprung up, offering new and old goods for sale. As we walked to work one day, a friend and I passed a flinty old man, silently holding up one pack of American smokes, offered silently for sale. A flicker of regret crossed my friend's face and he said, "You know, there's a lot of poetry in that guy selling one pack of cigarettes on the street. People like us, coming here, we're going to change all that."

During the six weeks 1 was in Warsaw—to work at a United States Information Agency exhibit—a liter container of orange juice tripled in price. Little old ladies would walk into the market I frequented and cluck over the scandalous prices of food. And then walk away without buying anything. Like everyone else in Warsaw this winter, they took to buying their groceries off the backs of trucks parked on the sidewalk (where all Warsaw vehicles park), braving the drizzle and fog to find something affordable.

The Cold War propagandist who fashioned the stereotype of Eastern Europe as gray and monotonous may have been a February visitor to Warsaw. The city itself, dotted with corner florist kiosks sporting vivid and unusual blooms for the sophisticated bouquets required on every social occasion, could hardly be called colorless, but its weather seemed to be. The days are short and, even in this warmest of Polish winters, raw and windy. As in New York, a gray scum collects on the pavement, and rarely (until the end of February) did this wet blanket of a climate lift to find the sun striking the city's baroque churches and classical palaces.

Dozens of such marvelous buildings sit side by side with the genuinely dull, squat apartment blocks that litter the city in too few numbers to house the people of Warsaw. In most cases the palaces are no older than the apartments, because Warsaw was almost entirely reconstructed after World War II, beginning with the medieval walled Old Town, Warsaw's heart and oldest neighborhood.

A product of Warsaw's rapid growth in the 15th century, when the city on the Vistula River became the home of the powerful dukes of Mazovia, the Old Town occupied the high ground above the river crossing. From its bustling cobblestone alleys and stuccoed houses, all ablush with color and ornaments like rows of plump curtsying maidens, the great boulevard called the Royal Way sweeps south in a gentle curve, changing names as it reflects the city's history, past palaces of later design (now embassies and official ministries).

Along its path is Lazienki, the elegant 18th-century park that holds Chopin concerts in the summer under a massive sweep of bronze that celebrates this Warsaw son. In Lazienki too is the delicate Palace on the Water, an island confection on its own little lake, built by the cultured but doomed Stanislaw August Poniatowski, Poland's last king, who was deposed and exiled when Russia, Prussia and Austria partitioned all that was left of the country among themselves in 1795. (Poland did not return to the map until 1918.)

At the end of the Royal Way, in Warsaw's suburbs, is the summer palace of Wilanow, which sits in another pretty park. Its watery frescoes, discovered in restoration, cover wall upon wall—and ceiling—like an unfolding dream. Wilanow, the country home of John III Sobieski—king of Poland's Golden Age in the 17th century, when he stopped the conquering Turks at Vienna and saved Europe—was one of the few Warsaw monuments to survive World War II.

The German army occupied Warsaw but couldn't conquer it, and so eventually destroyed it. A resistance army fought the Nazis continuously, culminating in the two uprisings: the ghetto rising of 1943, which ended in the murder of Warsaw's once large and influential Jewish community; and the uprising of 1944, a valiant attempt to hurry the Germans out of the city before the Soviet army could move in. In reprisal, the German dynamite teams finished off what the bombs of 1939 had left. They systematically blew up block after block, including the sewers and water lines, as they retreated, until only ruins remained. Reporter John Gunther likened downtown Warsaw to a jumble of enormous broken teeth.

There are photographs of Castle Square, at the entrance to the Old Town, which show the only thing standing in 1944 to be the column topped by a bronze statue of Sigismund III Vasa, the king who moved the Polish capital from Krakow to Warsaw in 1598, so that the united kingdom of Poland and Lithuania would be more centrally served.

The Royal Castle, which stands staid and grand in its red brick again in the square, was merely rubble in 1944. The castle was rebuilt later than the Old Town, which was finished in the '50s. And the castle was reconstructed entirely by public subscription, the last work completed only two years ago, according to my English-speaking guide, who was provided for an individual tour that cost only $2 more than the insignificant entrance fee typical of all Warsaw's museums and monuments.

Donning the clownish felt slippers that are the first part of palace visits in Poland, I was led first through the ancient cellars, past the astounding treasure offered up by the Polish people at the start of the war to rebuild an army and then a city. A nation's bounty is heaped on tables and displayed on the walls, gold and silver in every imaginable form, from soup spoons to medals of valor.

Upstairs is a series of grand salons, their details reconstructed from photographs and the famous paintings of Bernardo Bellotto, the younger Canaletto, whose expansive "24 Views of Warsaw" were looted successively by Napoleon, the czar and the Nazis. They hang once again in the Royal Castle, a place so prized by Poles that its heroic caretakers rushed in during the bombardment in 1939 to rescue a gilt plaster pattern here, a grill there, a clock, a chair, a tapestry (spectacular Flemish and Aubisson works collected by Polish kings). They even cut out sections of the ceiling to preserve for the future they knew must come. In the great Knights Hall, the French rotary clock, a globe borne on the shoulders of a larger-than-life figure of Chronis, is stopped at the hour when destruction began on Sept. 17, 1939, at 11:15 a.m.

So perhaps it is understandable that Warsaw, with so many daily reminders catching the eye, seems obsessed with its history. The streets are punctuated by well-tended shrines to martyrs executed on the spot nearly 50 years ago. There are monuments to the uprisings of World War II, including a strong, bleak walled square commemorating the ghetto. Countless statues stand witness to patriots who fought the Russians, Swedes, Prussians, Germans and Austrians who have overrun the country for four centuries. There are unofficial memorials to those who resisted Poland's post-war fate and to the brave struggle for self-determination in the '80s that has ultimately led Eastern Europe out of the Soviet sphere. Czarist jails and Nazi torture chambers are on view, along with an eerie Jewish cemetery, the largest community of Jews remaining in a country where once lived the greatest part of European Jewry. The Warsaw buildings that survived Nazi wrath are still pock-marked with bullet holes, like the national psyche.

Much of this history is collected in the Historical Museum of the City of Warsaw, a fabulously labyrinthine warren made up of several adjoining houses on the north side of the Old Town Market Square. Enter through a slave-trader's door, watch a harrowing movie documenting the destruction of the city, follow winding staircases through reconstructed rooms of the burghers, past cases hoarding mountains of artfully arranged china, guns, clothing, photographs, documents and furniture, from models of the first prehistoric settlements on the Vistula to the triumph of Solidarity in last year's election. I found it the most fascinating museum in Warsaw, a journey through time unexpectedly interrupted by glimpses of the square through small, seemingly ancient windows. Not bad, considering that the city archives perished, like the vista the museum overlooks, in the war.

Each room, as did all the Polish museums I visited, has its own attendant, usually an elderly woman. Only in the Historical Museum were they chipper and friendly, however, jumping up to turn on the lights in each section as I entered on a quiet February day. In other collections, especially at Wilanow, these women were stern and stiff, visibly on the alert for any infraction of the rules. Perhaps they have had to put up with too many schoolchildren, who troop dutifully through all of Warsaw's museums, most of them aching to glide across the fragile rooms in their felt overshoes.

These museum attendants and many shop clerks were the only Poles I met with a down-in-the-mouth attitude toward visitors. Most of Warsaw's store employees stalk their counters with angry resignation and always appear to be on the verge of throwing up their hands and stomping out past the line of customers. The lines are shorter than they used to be, I was told, now that high prices and unofficial distribution systems have been put in place. But most lines result from the fact that most goods are kept out of reach. You must ask to see that Smurf pencil (yes, even in Poland), that crystal bud vase, that book on the history of Warsaw. If you decide to buy it, the clerk writes up a ticket that you take to the cashier and then you return to the clerk for your merchandise, which has been neatly wrapped in paper and string. Such procedures make the lines grow longer, and frazzle nerves.

But polite people are never far away in a country where a visitor wouldn't dream of arriving without flowers for the lady of the house, and where men above the age of 35 generally kiss a woman's hand in greeting—a custom that, try as I might to act grown-up, never failed to make me giggle in embarrassed delight. I felt like an extra in a sparkling Ernest Lubitsch comedy from the '30s, set in some mythical Ruritania.

One afternoon, sitting in a cocktail bar (which serves milkshakes and whipped cream desserts, not alcohol), I was joined by a pert shopper and her little boy. She could speak no English, and I had very little Polish, but with the help of a phrase-book we worked out a conversation. She told me about her raspberry milkshake and inquired about the hotel rates at the Holiday Inn, where the government had put me up. She was properly aghast at the idea that one night there cost a third of her monthly income. I was too. But she was sure that everything would be all right in a few months.

The Poles' courtliness of manner and appetite is charmingly displayed in the way they take their meals. Warsaw is fond of sweets, and cafes for coffee and dessert can be found everywhere. The evening meal, eaten late, is a grand affair, consisting of several courses, elaborately garnished. Due to rising prices, restaurants are not as full as they were six months ago, but to the hard-currency visitor the most sumptuous repast seems embarrassingly cheap. At the city's best-known establishments, where reservations are expected, one dines on several courses among 300-year-old suits of armor and feudal banners for less than $10.

But the memory that stays with me is of a magical afternoon in a fresh,bright room, decorated like a garden with painted vines and white latticework. One cold, sunny day just before I left Warsaw, I led skeptical companions to a spot recommended by a Polish acquaintance. Gessler's is a restaurant that keeps its back to broad Senatorska Street, nuzzling its stone terrace and tall Palladian windows into the greenery of the Saxon Gardens, once the retreat of kings and now a public park. Inside is a serene stopping place just a few blocks off the city's bustle.

As soon as we were seated, waiters hovered, produced a hand-written menu in a heavy album and served elegant food, while the manager sat down to play a few Gershwin tunes on the piano.

The bright sky grew dark and violent in a twinkle and pelted Warsaw with snow and hail. The tempest was a five-minute wonder complete with thunder and then the sky lit up again underneath the clouds for sunset. Now, that's a floor show, and Gessler's capped it with a dessert of celestial excess. A 10-inch footed plate appeared before each diner, with ice cream (made on the premises, as in all top-notch Polish restaurants), meringue cake, marinated fruits and custard fanned out with a generosity that ignored the four courses that had come before.

The Gesslers, it turns out, have only recently regained the restaurant Warsaw has known since before the war; it belonged to the state in post-war Poland, and has come home to them again. That winter afternoon, with its heavenly fireworks and earthly pleasures, makes me wonder—what will Warsaw be like in the spring, so surely making its way through all of Eastern Europe?

April 15, 1990

Chapter Twelve

Modernization

The term *modernization* describes the ongoing process of change that transforms traditional agricultural or pastoral societies into post-industrial nation-states. The process of modernization that took up to two hundred years in Western nations and Japan is proceeding at a much faster pace today in many developing nations. The following articles examine various aspects of the complex process of development, including varying rates of change within and among countries, a widening gulf between rich and poor, and ethnic strife in the Middle East, Mexico, India, Burundi, Africa, and Thailand,

In the astonishingly oil-rich Saudi Arabia, an absolute monarchy continues to rule by divine right. "Saudi Society Faces Hard Choices on Modernization" describes the search for a social formula that will protect the country's traditions while accommodating the inevitable demand for change. The focus of "The Gap Widens" is the gulf between the oil-rich and oil-poor Arab nations and the fears that regional instability will grow as a result of the unequal distribution of wealth in much of the Islamic world. The question of whether a Moslem nation can be a truly modern nation is posed in the next article in this section.

In "Mexican Reforms Unlikely to Change Indians' Lives," the 82 million Indian inhabitants of Mexico are depicted as sharing unequally, if at all, in their country's economic development. "The Legacy of Colonialism" offers an extended look at the complex forces operating in the little-known African nation of Burundi, the eleventh poorest in the world and heir to a terrible history of Western colonial exploitation and internal tribal violence.

"Ghana's Chiefs Cross Cultures" illustrates a rare instance in which traditional rule by tribal chiefs in this country of 75 distinct languages and major ethnic groups successfully coexists with a modern army and judiciary. The final article in this reader describes Bangkok, capital of Thailand and home to 8 million people—one third of the country's population. Poised to be the "next little tiger," Thailand has followed a classic export-led growth strategy to modernization.

Saudi Society Faces Hard Choices on Modernization

Thomas W. Lippman

Shoes off, legs crossed, teacups in motion, six professors from the university here were sitting around after dinner musing about the future of their country.

The Saudi Arabian political system has to be opened up to allow citizens to participate, they said. Some forum must be set up for developing a consensus about the role of women—a forum in which women must participate. Islamic fundamentalists are going to have to be controlled in the universities. Contact with American troops should be encouraged, not restricted, to increase Saudi Arabia's exposure to Western ideas.

These professors were not dissidents or radicals. They were prominent members of the new Saudi Arabian establishment, fluent in English, holders of advanced degrees from American universities, at ease in conversation with foreigners, financially comfortable. They said they think of Saudi Arabia as an island of stability and individual liberty in a regional sea of repression and violence.

But they also said the country is approaching a time of painful, potentially disruptive choices about its future. Transformed in a generation from mud-hut backwater to technologically advanced petro-power, Saudi Arabia is searching for a social formula that will protect its traditions while accommodating the inevitable demand for change.

"We have already made all the easy decisions," one of the professors said. "Now we have to think about where we are going."

In conversations across the country with oil industry executives, business leaders, educators and government officials—all men, of course—the theme recurred. When the country had nothing, the Saudis said, it was easy to know what to do. Everybody agreed on the need to build roads, hospitals and airports, to electrify the villages, to send all the children to school.

Now all that is done. What next? Can this theocratic state accommodate itself to the material well-being and increasing sophistication of its people? The shock of Iraq's invasion of Kuwait, its exposure of Saudi military weakness and the arrival of 200,000 American troops appear to have accelerated a self-evaluation process that was already underway.

"When you have no schools, how can you make a mistake in deciding whether to build 100 or 1,000?" said Hisham Nazer, oil minister and acting planning minister. But now the universities are turning out graduates faster than the economy can provide jobs for them.

This potential sore point is acknowledged in the country's latest five-year development plan, which calls for more vocational and technical education to "reorient the training system toward labor market needs"—that is, make sure the young people have good jobs so they don't become a political liability, as in many other developing countries.

Of the 575,000 Saudis expected to enter the labor force in the next five years, according to Planning Ministry estimates, 68,600 will have university degrees and 30,300 of those will be women.

Some younger Saudis said the political system is open to question because an educated citizenry will no longer accept an absolute monarchy in which the Koran dictates social policy and crucial decisions—such as the invitation to U.S. troops to help defend the country against Iraq—are made behind the closed doors of the royal palaces.

Even some of the young princes, the most privileged of the privileged, said Saudis are restless about the current system of lawmaking in which the ulema, or religious elders, "are like your Supreme Court. The law is what they say it is," as one of them put it.

"People want change, but they want it by evolution. You can't just scrap tradition," said one of the many young princes waiting for generational change to move them into positions of power. "But you have to recognize [that] we, the royal family, have always been an instrument of change."

This is now a highly urbanized society, subject to modern big-city problems. Cities where everyone used to live side by side, regardless of income, in neighborhoods based on family and tribe, are now economically segregated. The very rich live in lavish suburban villas, isolated from their former neighbors. At the same time, restaurants, sports complexes and other diversions, previously unknown, are changing patterns of family life.

In the words of the five-year plan, "The emergence of an urban society has led to changes in the social structure.... Problems associated with anomie, delinquency and substance abuse will continue to be countered with preventive treatment and rehabilitation measures."

In smaller towns and villages, several Saudis said, the traditional authority figures—the imam of the mosque and the local emir, or tribal ruler—have been supplanted by police officers and government officials, usually from elsewhere, who do not play the same role of moral mentor.

A visitor returning to Saudi Arabia after an absence of a decade becomes aware almost immediately of striking social changes and new ideas. Bedouin women herding goats and sheep drive pickup trucks to steer the flocks—exercising a privilege still denied to urban women. In Jiddah, the commercial capital, many women have stopped veiling their faces in public.

Newspapers, controlled by the Ministry of Information, print debates about such topics as whether the rich spend too much money on frivolities and whether the millions of foreign workers in the country are corrupting Saudi traditions. This fall Saudi television showed a documentary about in vitro fertilization, filmed at a hospital in Riyadh. The five-year economic plan suggests development of a tourism industry, a radical proposal in a country that issues no tourist visas except for the annual Moslem pilgrimage to Mecca.

The plan, an official state policy document, also recommends "policies to enhance the participation of Saudi women in the development of the kingdom," including employment in government jobs.

Would that include women in the Saudi diplomatic corps? "Why not?" said one of the professors.

November 7, 1990

Gap Widens between Arab Rich, Poor: Disparity May Add to Mideast Instability

Caryle Murphy

The crisis sparked by Iraq's invasion of Kuwait has widened the gap between wealthy, oil-producing Arab countries and their poorer neighbors, a disparity that is likely to add to regional instability even after the crisis is defused, according to Arab officials and analysts of the region.

Higher oil prices have brought windfall profits to the Persian Gulf states, some of which have already doubled their income over last year. But other Arab countries, such as Egypt, Jordan, Syria, Tunisia and Yemen are reeling under heavy economic losses resulting from the Aug. 2 invasion of Kuwait and U.N.-imposed sanctions on Iraq.

Not only have these countries lost trade with Iraq because of the sanctions, they also have suffered steep drops in tourism and the loss of remittances from migrant workers who once worked in Iraq, Kuwait and Saudi Arabia but have returned home.

With Arab diplomacy swirling anew this week with discussion of an Arab emergency suit aimed at resolving the gulf crisis, the split between rich and poor nations is especially striking. The countries most eager for the suit are the poorer ones—led by the impoverished monarchies, King Hassan II of Morocco and King Hussein of Jordan—while the rich Arab states of the gulf, led by Saudi Arabia, seem reluctant to attend.

This growing disparity between Middle East "haves" and "have-nots," a long-standing cause of conflict among countries in the region, should be addressed by a new regional economic order once the gulf crisis is over, many Arab and Western observers say. But the deep animosity and political rifts in the Arab world brought on by Iraq's actions have made that task extremely difficult.

"The Arabs will have to look into their own eyes and say, 'Is the gap between the haves and have-nots sustainable?'" said a senior British Foreign Office official.

The contrast between the gulf states' petrodollar prosperity and their neighbors' economic stagnation is as visible on the street as it is in the ledgers of their central banks. Gleaming skyscrapers, expressways and heavily perfumed shopping malls catering to new and abundant wealth are hallmarks of most gulf cities. Gas-guzzling, chauffeured luxury cars abound, and the foreign servants who cook, clean and fill the swimming pools are just part of a huge imported work force needed to keep the gulf economies running.

Many of these expatriate workers are from nearby Arab states where finding employment is a never-ending struggle. In Tunisia, the main boulevard's cafes are crowded with men looking for jobs rather than with tourists in search of charm.

In Egypt, government employees work in dingy, dirty offices that look like stage sets for a 1930s movie. Schools are so crowded that students attend in shifts, and taxicabs are often little more than springs on wheels. In the Syrian capital of Damascus, people stand 20 deep in lines waiting to use the few public phones at the central post office. And were it not for the smuggling of merchandise over mountain roads from Lebanon, shelves in Syrian shops would be half-empty.

In all of these states, governments' promises to provide all their citizens with jobs, affordable housing and a decent education are not being kept—or believed by their citizens.

"'Oil envy' is something they are going to have to tackle," observed the British Foreign Office official. "King Hussein is so jealous of those [gulf] sheiks with so much money. That is a driving force for him. Something will have to be done about that."

Saudi Arabia, which has increased its oil production from about 5.8 million to 8 million barrels a day since Iraq invaded Kuwait, will earn $50 billion by the end of this year, almost double its 1989 income, one Riyadh-based Western economist said. If the price of oil remains between $32 and $35 a barrel throughout 1991, Saudi Arabia could earn between $85 billion and $100 billion, he said.

Likewise, the United Arab Emirates, whose central bank has put 1990 oil earnings at $11 billion, could take in $28 billion next year if those prices hold. The price of oil fell slightly more than $2.00 a barrel to $31.87 today on New York futures markets.

To be sure, Saudi Arabia and other gulf states are using most of their petroleum bonanza to finance the U.S.-led multinational military buildup here and to aid states which have sided with them against Iraq.

They are also coping with a large outflow of capital as skittish investors, fearing a war, have moved their money to outside the Middle East. In August alone, between $4 billion and $5 billion was removed from Saudi banks, one economist estimated.

In addition, if there is a war that destroys Kuwait's or Saudi Arabia's oil facilities, reconstruction costs could run into billions. And many analysts are predicting that oil prices will fall back to near $20 a barrel "probably very quickly after the shooting is over," said Philip Verleger, a visiting fellow at the Washington-based Institute for International Economics.

But even if these factors diminish the optimistic projections for the gulf states' oil revenue next year, long-term oil market trends show a growing demand for gulf oil as other world sources dry up, according to some analysts.

U.S. government experts have projected that the gulf states, which earned around $75 billion last year, could receive nearly $250 billion based on current dollar value calculations in the year 2000.

By contrast, Jordan's central bank Deputy Governor Michel Marto recently said his country has almost run out of foreign exchange reserves, and Crown

Prince Hassan predicted Jordan would see a 50 percent drop in its gross national product in 1991.

Jordan, whose economy is closely tied to Iraq's, has suffered huge trade losses during the crisis, and tourism has dried up. Jordanians fleeing Kuwait and Iraq have lost an estimated $8 billion in assets and income, according to Labor Minister Qasim Obeidat. Jordan also spent $55 million to feed refugees from Iraq and Kuwait early after the invasion.

King Hussein's criticism of Saudi Arabia's decision to call in U.S. forces to protect it from Iraq added to his economic woes when Saudi Arabia, in retaliation, cut off oil shipments to Jordan. The Saudis, along with other gulf states, also barred Jordanian goods from their territory.

Egypt, which has had to absorb nearly a quarter of a million workers returning from Kuwait and Iraq since the crisis began, has also been hit hard. Officials there have estimated the crisis will cost Egypt $4 billion.

Unlike Jordan, however, the blow to Egypt's economy has been cushioned by substantial aid from gulf and Western countries because of its political stand against Iraq and its decision to send troops to join the multinational force. The United States is canceling Egypt's $6.7 billion military aid debt.

Some economists argue that Egypt could break even or come out ahead because of the aid and debt relief. But even if that turns out to be true, most of the aid is going directly into Egyptian government coffers. How much will reach the pockets of returning workers who lost everything they owned in Kuwait and Iraq is unclear.

Iraqi President Saddam Hussein, who invaded Kuwait because of his country's dire economic troubles, has used Arab resentment against gulf wealth to try to justify his invasion.

Saddam has accused gulf rulers of being a "tyrannical group that uses [its oil wealth] for vice, corruption and aggression" and has sought to portray himself as a leader who "stands with the Arab poor and not with the wealthy Arabs from whose vision God has been absent as long as poverty has been absent from their lives." Arab oil wealth, he has said, should be used to help all Arabs.

Such rhetoric strikes a chord in poorer countries, whose populations were raised to believe that all Arabs are one nation. But in the gulf, which supported Iraq with about $40 billion during its war with Iran, it draws contempt.

Abdullah Quwaiz, deputy secretary general of the six-nation Gulf Cooperation Council, said Saddam is using such notions as an attempt "to give a moral excuse for the invasion of Kuwait. When [Iraq] had oil money, they did not give it to anybody. What did he do? He went and fought with his neighbor and then began extracting more money" from the gulf states.

According to Western diplomats, the Saudi and Kuwaiti governments have been so stung by what they consider the betrayal of Iraq and those Arab countries that sided with Saddam that their aid policies will never be the same.

Saudi Arabia, which has given out $60 billion in economic assistance to other countries in the past 17 years, is now displaying "a much more cynical attitude to aid," said a senior Western diplomat in Riyadh. "They are going to demand that those who receive their money show their gratitude in concrete ways."

November 13, 1990

Can Moslem Mean Modern?

David Ignatius

The men of this little village on the Asian side of the Bosphorus are doing something on Fridays that would have upset the founder of modern Turkey, Kemal Ataturk. They are listening to the muezzin's call (in Arabic) and going to the local mosque to pray.

Beykoz is typical of the quiet Islamic revival that is taking place in this most secular of Moslem countries. And the spread of worship here raises anew the question that vexed Ataturk 65 years ago—and that lies at the heart of the Salman Rushdie affair today. Can Islam coexist with the cultural and political values of the West? Can a Moslem nation, in short, be a truly modern nation?

Ataturk doubted that it was possible. He viewed Islam as a backward religion and an enemy of progress and civilization. So when he took power in the 1920s, he embarked on a ruthless campaign to sever Turkey's Islamic roots. He closed religious schools and ministries, replaced Islamic sharia law with the Swiss civil code, imposed a new Roman alphabet in place of Arabic script, and required that muezzins chant the call to prayer in Turkish, rather than the Arabic of the Koran.

Ataturk went so far as to decree in 1925 that it would be a criminal offense for Turkish men to wear the traditional Islamic headgear, the fez. He explained: "Gentlemen, it was necessary to abolish the fez, which sat on the heads of our nation as an emblem of ignorance, negligence, fanaticism and hatred of progress and civilization [and] to accept in its place the hat, the headgear used by the whole civilized world...."

Salman Rushdie couldn't have said it more bluntly in "The Satanic Verses."

Ataturk, like Rushdie, was offended by the Islamic elders of his day. The Grand Mufti of Egypt warned in 1926: "He who wears the hat because of an inclination to the religion of another and a contempt for his own is an infidel, according to the unanimous opinion of the Moslems."

But Ataturk persisted. He even denounced the wearing of the veil by women, telling one crowd: "In some places I have seen women who put a piece of cloth or a towel or something like it over their heads to hide their faces, and who turn their backs or huddle themselves on the ground when a man passes by. What are the meaning and sense of this behavior? Gentlemen, can the mothers and daughters of a civilized nation adopt this strange manner, this barbarous posture? It is a spectacle that makes the nation an object of ridicule. It must be remedied at once."

Ataturk's vision of a purely secular Turkey is losing ground these days. Islamic religious expression is on the rise. The men of Beykoz haven't returned to wearing the fez, but a few are wearing knitted Islamic berets. And it's increasingly likely their children are attending religious schools or studying the Koran with special tutors.

"Turkey is rediscovering its Islamic inheritance," says Serif Mardin, a prominent Turkish scholar who is teaching this year at American University. But he argues that an increasingly Islamic Turkey won't necessarily be any less modern or less oriented toward the West.

U.S. officials hope he's right. Turkey is a frontline member of the NATO alliance, and the United States has premised its strategic planning in the region on the expectation that Turkey will remain a strong, pro-Western bulwark against the Soviet Union.

There's no reason, for now, to doubt Turkey's commitment to NATO or the West. (Indeed, Turkey has applied to join the European Community.) But there's a growing sense that the austere secular state that Ataturk created is gradually giving way to something different—and more Islamic. And nobody yet quite knows how this new Turkey will behave.

The Islamic revival in Turkey is clear on various levels:

Education. Religious schools, which were banned by Ataturk, may now account for as much as 40 percent of total school enrollment. Attendance at these "Imam Hatip" schools, as they are called, increased gradually from zero in 1933 to 36,378 in 1973—and then jumped to 212,878 in 1983, according to a study of Turkish Islam by Nicholas Luddington published last year by the American Institute for Islamic Affairs. That study also noted that 120,000 Turks are taking private Koran courses.

Politics. Turkey's current prime minister, Turgut Ozal, is the most openly Islamic prime minister in modern Turkish history. Indeed, when he first ran for parliament in 1977 as an independent, he was supported by an Islamic religious party. Ozal's new ruling party, the Motherland Party, has a strong religious faction that is well represented on its central committee. And Ozal's brother Korkut is widely rumored to be a member of the Naksibendi sect, a Sufi Moslem brotherhood that is officially outlawed.

The Military. The ultimate political force in Turkey remains the military, which has regularly intervened against the civilian government, most recently in 1980. And the military is generally thought to be the ultimate guardian of the Ataturk legacy of secularism and modernization. Reliable information about the military's views on religion—or on any issue, for that matter—is hard to come by. But it's said that mosque attendance is up at Turkish military bases, as in most cities and villages. The issue worries the military enough that two years ago, the authorities expelled several hundred students from military academies because of their links with Islamic Fundamentalists.

The growing visibility of Islam in Turkish life shouldn't necessarily be worrying for westerners. After all, fundamentalist Christianity and Judaism have been experiencing something of a revival in the United States in recent years. And the majority of Turkish Moslems seem to have little interest in creating an avowedly Islamic state. Pollsters report that less than 10 percent of Turks support the imposition of Islamic sharia law. And the largest vote ever won by a Moslem religious party was 11.8 percent, in 1973.

"When you look at the political clout of Islam in Turkey, you see a very limited beast," argues George Harris, a State Department official who has written extensively about Turkey.

Still, there's a vague uneasiness among some Turkey-watchers, a sense that having come so close to being a fully modern nation, Turkey may not quite get there. The reason for doubt, quite simply, is that there is no example in the world of a nation that is both fully Moslem and fully modern and democratic. That awkward gap between Islam and the West was Ataturk's greatest worry. And it's still there in the shadows of Turkey's mosques.

March 5, 1989

Mexican Reforms Unlikely to Change Indians' Lives

Edward Cody

While modernization brings economic and political change to most of Mexico, Juan Aguilar's world remains what it has always been: isolation, poverty and the struggle for enough hillside to grow corn.

Aguilar, who believes he is 38 but is not sure, wears his Cancuc Indian tribe's traditional white toga, leaving his arms and legs bare to the rain. His only concession to modern times is a pair of leather boots, which he wore the other day on the four-hour bus trip from his mountain village to this regional hub in the Indian country of Chiapas State in southern Mexico.

Nearly a tenth of Mexico's 82 million inhabitants speak native Indian languages and, like Aguilar, lead lives that in many respects cut them off from the rest of the country as it moves into the 21st century.

Francisco Hernandez, executive secretary of the Fray Bartolome de Las Casas Human Rights Center here, said the discussions in Mexico City and Washington about the proposed Free Trade Agreement are far removed from the lives of the Indians he deals with. Many of them do not even know of their state capital, Tuxtla Gutierrez, he pointed out, and have no world beyond their remote farming villages and occasional trips to the market here, which is why Aguilar said he had come to San Cristobal de Las Casas.

"All they know is that the prices of beans and sugar, basic products, are going up, because that's what their lives revolve around," he said.

Since colonial times, when they were enslaved by the Spaniards, the copper-skinned Indian population has occupied a second tier in Mexican society.

A recent report from the government's National Program for Development of Indigenous Peoples acknowledged that "a set of relations of inequality for indigenous peoples was formed in the system of colonial domination, which, although transformed, still persists."

The government avoids using the word racism to analyze the plight of Mexico's Indian and mixed-blood population, referring instead to economic and social deprivation and isolation because of language problems. But Jose Agustin Ortiz Pinchetti, a lawyer and government critic, notes that, whatever the reason, Mexico's political ruling class and business elite come largely from among the white-skinned descendants of Spanish colonialists.

"Go to a luxury restaurant and look around at who is serving and who is being served," he advised.

Although many indigenous tribes remain fixed in their ancestral forests, millions of less isolated Indians and mixed-blood Mexicans have migrated to cities in search of jobs and a different life. Often victims of racial discrimination and nearly always victims of their social differences, they have become the servants, waiters and street vendors of Mexico's wealthy.

"The cities have not been generous in receiving indigenous migration," the government report said.

Although reliable information is scarce because of isolation and language difficulties, the Mexican government estimates that substantially more than a million Indians, many of them women, speak no Spanish at all and several million more speak only halting Spanish. This over the years has been a barrier separating indigenous people from their government, Hernandez said, leading to lack of attention and, in some cases, injustices.

Nearly all the 70 percent of Mexico's Indians who live in rural villages are in areas classified by the government as "marginalized." In practical terms, this means that 90 percent of them do not have sewer systems and thus suffer widely from intestinal disease, and only one-third have access to mail or telephones to put them in touch with the rest of the world.

According to government surveys, 80 percent of the babies in remote Indian areas such as the mountains above San Cristobal are born without trained medical doctors. In those communities lucky enough to have bilingual schools to teach children Spanish, more than half are staffed with a single teacher for all six primary grades.

Only one Indian child in five who enters these schools completes the primary program. As a result, according to the National Adult Education Institute, the rate of illiteracy remains above 20 percent in areas where indigenous people are numerous, such as the mountains of Chiapas and Oaxaca states. These rates compare to a national average below 8 percent, the institute pointed out.

But Hernandez said the overwhelming problem facing Mexico's indigenous tribes is lack of land to feed a growing population. Because land ownership was less affected by the Mexican Revolution's reforms in back country such as the Chiapas hills, much acreage remains in the possession of large family estates, he explained, leaving Indian farmers with nothing to cultivate.

"How can modernization affect them if they don't have any land?" Hernandez asked. "What are they going to modernize?"

May 18, 1991

Third World Crossroads: India Faces Questions About Debt, Reform

Steve Coll

Buried in borrowings and short of hard cash, India may become the world's next victim of the debt crisis that already has crippled developing economies in Africa and Latin America, according to a growing number of finance specialists here and abroad.

Even though it is stumbling under the weight of huge internal budget deficits and the world's fourth-largest external debt load—$63 billion and rising—India's economy nevertheless has continued to lurch ahead at an admirable rate of growth. But planners and international financiers are beginning to worry that without politically painful reforms, India's economic bubble could burst during the early 1990s, with devastating consequences for the country's impoverished and rapidly expanding population.

"India is at the crossroads, and its decisions could take it either toward the bankrupt economies of Latin America or the booming economies of East Asia," said Gene Tidrick, chief economist of the World Bank here.

Runaway inflation or a deep recession—the calamities that lurk for economies overloaded with debt—would cause widespread suffering in India, where an estimated half of the country's 820 million people live in poverty. In addition, military planners and diplomats have begun to worry about what would happen in populous and friction-ridden South Asia if India, the bastion of stability in the region, experienced a serious economic crisis.

"It may be three years, it may be five, but an [economic] crisis is going to hit our policy makers in the face," predicted Surjit Bhalla, an economist and political scientist at a private New Delhi research center. "The potential loss to India for inaction now is very high."

Such fears about India's immediate future are based on signs of disturbing imbalances in the economy. The most obvious is the rapid rise of external debt—money owed to international lenders such as the World Bank and International Monetary Fund, commercial banks in Europe and the United States, and to private citizens. Not only has the absolute amount of India's external debt tripled since 1980, but the country's debt-service ratio—a key economic measure that depicts how much available cash is needed each year to pay off existing obligations—is reaching levels comparable to such crippled debtors as Brazil and Nigeria.

India's overseas debt load is exacerbated by two other emerging problems: a spiraling internal budget deficit twice as large as that of the United States relative to the size of the economy, and a cash crunch due to a trade deficit now running between $5 billion and $6 billion annually.

While India used to have a comfortable reserve of foreign exchange with which to pay for necessary imports—products ranging from oil to artillery to industrial machinery—it now has only enough hard cash to cover two months of imports. India's currency, the rupee, isn't convertible on world markets and thus can't be used to pay for imports from abroad.

These complex and difficult problems loom at a time when India is being led by a minority government backed by a unusual array of political parties, ranging from Communists on one side to Hindu conservatives on the other. The new prime minister, V.P. Singh, a former finance minister, is regarded as an informed economic thinker, but his cabinet includes a potpourri of agricultural populists, unbending socialists and political opportunists.

A number of senior economic planners in Singh's administration concede privately that the problems are serious, but most dismiss the fears of an impending crisis. They argue that the country can use its continuing industrial growth to muddle through the early 1990s without undertaking drastic budget reforms and trade liberalization measures recommended by commercial bankers and international agencies such as the IMF.

Some Indian economists also say that comparisons with such debt-laden countries as Mexico and Argentina are not justified because a large amount of India's debt burden is fixed at concessional interest rates by international lenders, meaning that India is less subject to the whims of commercial bankers and is better able to manage repayment schedules.

Since it achieved independence in 1947, India has been a vocal champion among developing nations of economic self-reliance and what Indian politicians call "the middle way" between capitalism and socialism. With a high savings rate and an ancient culture that emphasizes frugality and adaptability, it has maintained remarkable political and social stability despite regular droughts, wars and other catastrophes. While some in Singh's cabinet support a gradual shift toward free markets, none calls for a radical departure from the country's historically cautious path.

India's economic policies of heavy public ownership of industry, centralized planning, big domestic subsidies and some of the world's highest tariff barriers have produced some notable successes, such as the virtual elimination of famine. The country's relative economic stability also has allowed the government to implement an array of poverty-abatement, health and other social programs, while at the same time building a strong defense capability.

Nonetheless, India's economic problems are formidable. Poverty remains deep and widespread. High tariff protection for domestic industry has produced a surfeit of shoddy consumer and industrial goods—nails that bend upon hammering, tape that doesn't stick and cars that belch and rumble at a maximum of 50 miles per hour. Government intervention in the economy, in the form of an impenetrable thicket of regulations and required licenses, has led business to institutionalize payoffs.

India's politicians apparently believe the country can carry on this way indefinitely. But the country's growing debt load, combined with political and economic changes at home and abroad, have led a growing number of Indian economists and international finance specialists to question whether the "middle way" is viable any longer.

For example, India's economic balancing act during the 1970s and 1980s depended in considerable part on its close relationship with the Soviet Union, particularly on a series of trade agreements that allowed India to import Soviet military hardware and export consumer and industrial products without spending any of its precious hard currency. New Delhi's so-called "ruble account" with Moscow permits India to account for all of its Soviet trade in rubles and rupees, currencies that are not recognized on world financial markets.

Soviet President Mikhail Gorbachev is under pressure to change this system, and if he does, India will face a series of major problems during the early 1990s.

Last fall, the Soviets floated a proposal that constitutes an Indian economic nightmare—that India start paying for its huge Soviet military imports in hard currency, not rupees. This would put enormous pressure on New Delhi's balance of payments at a time when its trade deficit is already badly out of whack.

The Indian team that heard the Soviet proposal at a November meeting in Moscow rejected it adamantly, saying it was not part of the two countries' most recent trade agreement. But the Indians came away with a sinking feeling that the change was inevitable, according to S.B. Chavan, the former finance minister who led India's delegation at the talks.

"They are bound to ask for it again. The question is how long can you resist," said Chavan.

Other economic challenges loom at home.

Expectations among the country's growing middle class are rising and there is an increasing awareness that in terms of the quality and availability of most consumer goods, India lags badly behind its Asian neighbors, including China, whose xenophobic Communist leaders have, ironically, done much more to liberalize their economy and to import foreign technology than have democratically elected politicians in India.

Socialist and free-market economic planners alike agree that the best way to keep India out of the international debt trap would be to reduce its massive budget deficits, easing the country's appetite for foreign funds.

But the budget promises made by Singh's new administration, including continuing large agricultural subsidies, waiving loans to small farmers and businessmen and instituting massive public employment schemes, offer the minority government little room for political maneuvering. Analysts say that whatever programs emerge from India's parliamentary budget session this spring, they will be a far cry from the austerity programs recommended by international lending agencies.

March 25, 1990

Legacy of Colonialism, Killing Infects Future of Burundi

Blaine Harden

Daily life in this small nation in the highlands of central Africa is infected with memory.

On main highways there are scores of roadblocks where soldiers of the ruling Tutsi tribe check the zonal residence papers of Hutu farmers. In 1972, the previous Tutsi-controlled government systematically exterminated about 100,000 educated Hutus. Restrictions on travel prevent the Hutus, who outnumber the Tutsi six to one, from gathering to plot vengeance.

On back roads in the mountains above Lake Tanganyika, teen-age girls run in terror at the sight of a car filled with white people. Local people have fled the whites since the Belgian colonial era, from 1916 to 1962, when whites rounded them up for forced labor.

On Radio Burundi there are daily denunciations of the Roman Catholic Church. Catholic priests and "their white racist god... destroyed Burundi culture," claims the radio. That claim is a rationale for vengeance on the church. In the past year, priests have been jailed, Catholic schools have been nationalized and week-day masses have been banned.

Burundi is a little-known nation of 5 million people, a byzantine product of the wrongs of the Belgians and the wrongs of the Africans. It is a place where, as with many African nations, the memory of colonial abuses have a powerful resonance and the legacy of tribalism sways national policy.

This, combined with the good intentions of western countries that prop up a tribal regime with more than $150 million a year in aid, comprises a country where nothing is quite as it appears from the outside.

The Belgian-dominated Catholic Church has too dark a history in this country to be cast as an innocent victim. Nor is the present Tutsi regime an unregenerate villain.

The regime continues to practice its own rigid brand of tribal apartheid, a system that the leaders of black Africa choose to ignore, even as they travel the world to condemn white-minority rule in South Africa.

Yet, by pursuing limited reforms that help the Butu, the government has proved itself to be something more than the complacent heir to a genocidal tradition.

But Burundi's past has not prevented it from becoming a favorite of donor countries and lending institutions such as the World Bank. In part, money flows because Burundi is needy. It is the world's 11th poorest country and one of Africa's most densely populated.

But donors also point out another reason why aid levels have soared here. Burundi's government, they say, is far more efficient than most others in Africa. They say aid projects work in this country: roads are built, electric lines are strung, equipment is well-maintained and theft is not a problem. They say they can send home reports about projects that are on schedule and money that is efficiently spent.

"Tutsis are good managers," said an agriculture specialist here. "When they make a decision, they stick with it."

Donors prefer not to talk about it, Tutsis deny it and Hutus are not even supposed to think about it—but Burundi's future is inextricably tied to its bloody past. African historian Rene Lemarchand describes the legacy of the 1972 killing as "an unprecedented potential for ethnic hatred." Memory of the killing and fear of Hutu revenge help explain both the good works of the Tutsi government and its recent harsh repression of the church.

The possibility of Hutu revenge also raises questions about the long-term value of donor investment in a government whose ruling philosophy echoes that of South Africa. No one in this country is permitted to admit the obvious. The government declared this month that Hutu-Tutsi conflict "is nonexistent in Burundi." Many Burundians and long-time expatriates are reluctant even to say the tribal names "Hutu" and "Tutsi."

Instead, they speak of the Short Ones—the Hutu, who make up 85 percent of the population and who are mostly subsistence farmers of Bantu origin. And they speak of the Tall Ones—the Tutsi, who make up 15 percent of the population and who were once cattle people, probably of Ethiopian origin.

The tall ones—many of whom are taller than six feet, while most Hutus are well under six feet—have been Burundi's elite for four centuries.

The most visible, most publicized recent victims of government repression here are foreign missionaries and members of the Catholic Church. About 65 percent of Burundi's 5 million people are Catholic.

The Tutsi regime has shut down church newspapers, canceled religious radio programs and banned rural prayer meetings. This spring 3,000 Catholic lay catechists were ordered to stop preaching and giving communion in churches. Late last year a Catholic program providing primary schooling for 300,000 rural children was canceled by government decree.

Five years ago there were more than 500 Belgian priests in Burundi. Now there are about 30, and by the end of this year, all of them are expected to be forced out. That will leave 107 Burundi-born priests and 60 nuns for the country's 1,200 churches.

Pope John Paul II last fall said the crackdown "seems to indicate a deliberate attempt to discredit the church and its pastors through accusations, insinuations and threats in order to marginalize the Catholic community."

Catholic leaders and human rights groups have been quick to see a connection between suppression of the church and tribal politics.

In neighboring Rwanda, where majority Hutus were successful in overthrowing a minority Tutsi government in 1961, the Catholic Church played a crucial leadership role. Tutsi leaders are said to be haunted by Rwanda's precedent.

"The church serving Burundi necessarily serves the Hutu majority more than the Tutsi," said one diplomat. "This means the church de facto is a threat."

The Catholic Church in Burundi, however, does not have an impressive record either as a defender of human rights or as an institution committed to improving the life of Hutu peasants.

Before the country's independence in 1962, Belgian Catholic priests conscripted Hutu tribesmen to build churches. Burundian priests were not allowed to sleep or eat in the same rooms with the "white fathers." The church made no attempt to democratize the centuries-old feudal system under which the Tutsi played lords to the Hutu serfs.

Nor were gifted students encouraged to go abroad for education. At independence in 1962, after nearly half a century of Belgian colonial rule, Burundi did not have a single college graduate.

The church made little effort to draw world attention to tribal genocide in 1972. One prominent Burundian businessman here argues that the church was an instrument of Belgian colonial control, both before and after independence. It is a view shared by most western diplomats and many Burundian clerics.

"The Belgian missionaries never accepted the independent government. The church kept too much power over education and health care," said the businessman. "The government could not do anything without asking the church's permission."

A senior western diplomat here, who is critical of the harshness of the government's recent actions against the Catholics, says there is a measure of hypocrisy in the church's complaints.

"The church is rallying the Hutu to defend its own prerogatives, not those of the Hutu," said the diplomat.

The most visible villain of the campaign against the Catholic Church is the military government of President Jean-Baptiste Bagaza, a 41-year-old Army colonel who makes no secret of his anticlerical feelings.

"The president of this country is convinced that the Catholics are trying to kick him out," said a diplomat here who has personal dealings with Bagaza.

Since coming to power in a bloodless coup in 1976, the Tutsi leader has consolidated his power by surrounding himself with senior military officers and security officials who are all Tutsis.

Tutsis dominate Bagaza's Cabinet, the National Assembly and the university system. Thirteen of 15 provincial governors are Tutsi, as are about 96 percent of the country's soldiers. Most businessmen are Tutsis.

Yet, even as Bagaza enforces tribal apartheid in the central government and continues to dismember the Catholic Church, he has insisted on land, economic and educational reforms that offer rural Hutus unprecedented opportunities.

In an attempt to heal the wounds of the tribal massacre, Bagaza has invited home the 150,000 or so Hutus who fled to neighboring countries after 1972. Perhaps 20,000 have returned. Former Tutsi overlords have been forced to give land to Hutu peasants, who now have proprietary rights over what they till. Landlord-tenant relationships were abolished.

In the past year, as part of a $50 million structural adjustment loan by the World Bank, the government eliminated import monopolies held by Tutsi businessmen and raised producer prices for farmers—mostly Hutu—by up to 30 percent. The program last year boosted annual economic growth, which had averaged less than 1.9 percent since 1980, to 3.3 percent.

"What Bagaza has allowed is a program that increases the purchasing power of the farmers, who are mostly Hutu, while limiting the purchasing power of the city people, `who are mostly Tutsi," said a western economist here.

The economist said that Bagaza also has committed his western-oriented government to support an ambitious World Bank program for universal primary education and widespread vocational training.

Bagaza has accepted the bank's argument, the economist said, that Burundi must use financial incentive to encourage 2 million Hutus to give up subsistence agriculture and turn to small-scale manufacturing.

Bagaza's egalitarian reforms have threatening implications for a minority government that apparently has no intention of sharing power.

In an interview here, one highly regarded Tutsi business leader said confidently that "if people have many opportunities, they tend to be more tolerant.... If Hutu farmers get enough income they are happy."

A few minutes later the businessman, without seeing any contradiction, said: "If farmers get more education, if they get rich, they will demand democracy. It is a dynamic of democracy that no one can prevent."

The donor governments and multinational lending agencies that are helping to pay for Bagaza's reforms say they hope economic growth will somehow smooth Burundi's transition to a more democratic government. Specifics about how this transition might occur do not exist.

"The Tutsis realize that the time bomb exists. They are trying to ease the situation by expanding the economic pie," said a diplomat here. "If it works, Bagaza could have an awfully long breathing space before the Hutu demand revenge."

July 27, 1990

Ghana's Chiefs Cross Cultures: Traditional Leaders Seen as Key to Intertribal Calm

Neil Henry

It was with great solemnity that Amakuade Wyete Ajeman Labie II, paramount chief of the Awutu tribe, called his subjects together one day last month to impart some very important news.

"The light is coming," the ruler announced, standing before his people in a robe of green and gold. "The government people say they will bring wires to Awutu Breku and everyone will have power.

Murmurs of surprise and appreciation swept through the crowd of mostly corn and cassava farmers, whose wood-frame shacks in this coastal village 25 miles west of Accra, Ghana's capital, have never had either plumbing or electricity.

Then the chief held up his hand for quiet.

"If you want the light," he said sternly, "you will have to pay for it every month." And with that, leaving his people to ponder their pocketbooks, Amakuade strode back to his palace of painted mortar and stone, his kingly duty done.

In modern Africa, the life of a village chieftain—the king, as he is also known here—is not an easy or simple one.

Once upon a time, a Ghanaian king needed to know only a few things well— how to lead his warriors in battle, punish miscreants, settle disputes between villagers and apportion the richest farmland fairly enough to keep most of the peasants happy. A wise chief also made sure there was enough liquor or fruit juice on hand to pour regular libations to the revered ancestors.

But nowadays, a chief must know how to lobby the state for public works, how to get emergency assistance in times of epidemics or other hardships and how to interpret and explain the government's policies to the people.

"You must not be a drunkard. You must not be a prison convict. You must be sober, wise, fearless and bold," said Amakuade, 55, calmly explaining the essential attributes of a good king as he sat one recent night in his palace in the glow of a kerosene lantern. "You must enforce customary laws of the village, but you also must understand the rules of the government."

He sighed. "As a chief, I have many worries."

This West African nation of 14 million people is one of the few countries in sub-Saharan Africa in which a concerted official effort has been made to integrate traditional methods of local organization and rule with 20th-century notions of statecraft.

On a troubled continent where tribal concerns and ancient practices often clash with the missions of modern government, sometimes with deadly results, this nation stands as a notable exception. Ghana's more than 75 distinct languages and major ethnic groups have been bound peacefully together with the help of some imaginative government policy.

In 1971, 14 years after independence from Britain, the nation's legislature passed the Chieftaincy Act, which constitutionally recognized and protected the powers of village chiefs in local matters, granted them authority to enforce customary tribal laws and established regional and national assemblies where they could discuss and govern their affairs.

In effect, Ghana set up a system of dual authorities—one modern and state-centered, the other traditional and defined by blood ties. One system was responsible for the armed forces, the judiciary, the economy and other national matters. The other handled more customary concerns—divorces, child-custody matters and land disputes—while maintaining Ghana's cultural heritage and identity in the face of progress.

That was one way the newly independent state, acknowledging the powerful influence of old beliefs and values, set about using Ghana's 168 paramount chiefs as partners in development. Those chiefs, chosen by village sub-chiefs, preside over nearly 200 tribal districts in Ghana. More than 5,000 lower-ranking chiefs serve under them.

An added benefit of the Chieftaincy Act was that it unified Ghana's once war-prone ethnic groups in an officially recognized national forum.

"Ghana is a nation of many nations. The people have always recognized that," said J. Max Assimeng, a professor of sociology at the University of Ghana near Accra. "But the state is a pretty new concept. We are still trying to figure it out."

Since 1971, more than a half-dozen Ghanaian governments supported by a shaky, single-party system have been overthrown by the military, but the regional and national houses of chiefs have continued to function under the Chieftaincy Act. While the power of Ghana's governing political authorities has proved ephemeral during the nation's first three decades of independence, the popular influence of village chiefs has never waned. They remain virtually indispensable to the fabric of Ghanaian culture and society.

Although some friction has been inevitable between local government representatives and tribal leaders, Ghana has suffered little of the horrific ethnic strife that continues to afflict many other countries in Africa. "In the developing world, peace is a resource that very few countries enjoy," Assimeng said. "In Ghana, I think we have peace in abundance."

Certainly, many countries in Africa could do worse than to follow Ghana's example of dealing with ethnic diversity. The East African country of Uganda, for instance, is still reeling from the social and political shock of a bloody, state-sponsored effort in the 1960s and '70s to eradicate the rival power of the Kabaka, the traditional leaders of the country's Baganda people, and other tribal chiefs. Instead of unifying Ugandans, the catastrophic policies had the long-term effect of alienating the populace from the state and galvanizing rebel insurgencies.

In Ghana, the government of Chairman Jerry John Rawlings, who came to power in a military coup nine years ago but vows to return the government to freely elected civilian rule, regards the influence of the nation's village chiefs with such respect that he has endorsed an idea of giving one-third of the seats in a new Ghanaian legislature to "traditional leaders."

While some critics view chieftaincies as a wasteful and anachronistic impediment to national transformation, supporters argue that the system provides much needed cultural and social continuity.

"A nation without a culture has no soul. We are the custodians of our culture," says Nana Kwame Nkyi XII, paramount chief of the Assin Apimanim tribe of central Ghana, who serves as president of the central region's House of Chiefs.

"The people know their chief better than any government official," said T.K. Boakene, clerk of the central house. "That is why the government cannot do away with the system. The chief is everything in the community. He is judge, economist, planner; he is the link between the ancestors and the future."

Amakuade, paramount chief of the 70,000 Awutu people of Ghana's central coast, certainly sees himself that way. When asked to name a few of his predecessors, the chief promptly rattled off 15 names, some of them dating back to the arrival of Portuguese explorers in the 15th century. Upon invoking each hollowed name, the chief poured a drop of gin onto the floor of his office as an expression of respect.

A former stenographer who was chosen chief in 1956, Amakuade ensures the observance of customary laws, such as the provision of two fowls by a father to his neighbors exactly eight days after the birth of his child. But Amakuade says the modern tasks are more difficult. For two years, the chief has been trying to get the government to send a machine to dig out and empty the village's two overflowing and useless latrines, but without success.

Like most of the world's monarchies, Ghana's village aristocracies are laden with symbols of prestige and privilege. A chief just is not a chief without a scepter sculpted from the finest wood, a crown and pendants made of gold and other jewels and, most important of all, the painted wooden stool, which is handed down from previous generations of chiefs and symbolizes ultimate authority. Upon the stool, only a king may sit.

But unlike most other monarchies, a village chieftaincy does not necessarily mean material wealth. Each year during harvest festivals, the faithful sub-chiefs donate funds to their paramount leaders, but the donations usually do not amount to more than token living expenses. Indeed, many of Ghana's paramount chiefs, including Amakuade, seem to live humbly and labor in the fields as long and hard as any commoner. The power and respect they command from their followers seem to derive from their intelligence and wisdom and the model of behavior they set for the community.

Amakuade, for instance, lives in a fairly simple house that is not much different from or more comfortable than neighboring dwellings but is nevertheless called a palace because he lives in it. A gentle man, with sun-wrinkled skin and rough, calloused hands, Amakuade, who is known affectionately as Nai Odefi, or Old Chief, and says he is the father of "about 15" children, works six days a week in his corn field.

And while one's candidacy for the chieftaincy is usually determined by blood-line—most often matrilineally—a remarkably democratic procedure is generally followed in choosing a chief from among the contenders.

"There are many who believe that the traditional system of chieftaincy in Ghana was more just and more democratic than any modern form of government that has ever come to power in Africa," said sociology professor Assimeng.

A chief, he said, traditionally was chosen by a panel of elders. Those elders acted as advisers and served as a counterbalance to the chief's authority, a relationship much like that between the U.S. Congress and the president. "The chief was ultimately in charge, but he never acted alone. He had to consult the elders," Assimeng said.

"If a chief ever acted against the interest of the village or behaved unethically or irresponsibly," he could be dethroned, or in the case of Ghana's chiefs, "destooled," as Assimeng put it. Today, lunacy, theft and adultery represent a few of the leading grounds for a chief's certain dismissal by his people.

Assimeng calls the chieftaincy "a dynamic institution" but says it can only survive if it changes with the times. To that end, Assimeng regularly travels to various parts of the country to speak to seminars of village chiefs about their role in development. "I try to impress on them the inevitability of change and the need for them to take part in it," he said. "I also stress that if anything is to abolish the chieftaincy, it's the chiefs themselves and their behavior."

Assimeng pointed in particular to the old way of chiefly behavior, such as traveling with huge retinues and siring dozens of children. Assimeng says those customs should have no place in modern Ghana.

Recently, during a trip back home from Cape Coast, a port city 100 miles west of Awutu Breku, Amakuade sat in the back seat of a car, pondering the history of Ghana's chieftaincies and the nature of tribal identity here. "The people of Ghana can tell the exact village a man comes from just by his accent and the sound of his name," he said with pride. "That's what makes us what we are."

July 27, 1990

Thailand, After Two Decades of Growth, Is Poised to be the Next 'Little Tiger' of Asia

Keith B. Richburg

An American who first visited Thailand in the mid-1960s remembers when Silom Road was a klong, a smelly canal bordered on either side by a narrow lane of traffic—at that time mostly bicycles and pedicabs.

Today, Silom Road is one of Bangkok's main thoroughfares, lined on either side by gleaming new skyscrapers, department stores, airline offices and restaurants. The street is still clogged with traffic, but now it consists of buses, taxicabs, motorbikes, imported Japanese sports cars and motorcycles.

The sidewalks on either side are also packed, with vendors selling dried squid and fried pork on skewers, bootleg cassette tapes, fake Lacoste polo shirts, imitation Rolex watches and a variety of electronic gadgets.

The dramatic changes along Silom Road symbolize the economic boom that has transformed Thailand's crowded capital, Bangkok.

A city of klongs and rice paddies and bicycles has evolved over two decades into a bustling metropolis of 8 million people, with dozens of luxury hotels catering to a growing tourist sector and a corps of middle-class professionals in uniform white shirts and dark suits packing the city's restaurants, shopping centers and nightspots.

American policymakers once feared that Thailand would become Asia's "next domino" after communist victories in Indochina.

However, with its Bangkok-centered boom, some Thai officials are boasting that Thailand instead is poised to become the region's next "NIC," the latest East Asian country to achieve the status of "newly industrialized country." That would put it behind the other "Little Tigers": Hong Kong, Taiwan, South Korea and Singapore. "I think Thailand will emerge rather quickly as the third wave of Asian NICs within the coming decade," Phisit Pakkasem, a government economist, predicted recently.

However, other foreign economists and Thai business leaders are not so certain. While acknowledging Thailand's enormous economic strides, these skeptics believe the country's infrastructure is too antiquated, the number of graduating engineers and other professionals too low and the income differential too great to make Thailand a likely prospect to join NIC ranks soon.

They also point out that Thailand's boom is almost entirely centered in Bangkok, while two-thirds of the population live in the rural countryside.

Thailand's growth—its gross national product rose 7 percent in 1987 and will likely top 8 percent this year—seems even more impressive because it has occurred despite the regional turmoil that has affected almost all of Thailand's borders.

The communist victories in Vietnam, Cambodia and Laos disgorged a massive influx of Indochinese refugees fleeing to Thailand in the late 1970s. Vietnam's 1978 invasion of Cambodia brought a new wave, and Cambodian guerrillas still use base camps in eastern Thailand as their sanctuary. Until last year, Thai troops regularly engaged the Vietnamese occupation forces in Cambodia in border skirmishes over disputed hills.

Earlier this year, Thailand and Laos fought a brief border war, and the turmoil in Burma has sent a new group of refugees streaming over the border. Burmese rebels have long operated from camps along the border with Thailand, and students seeking training to fight the military government in Rangoon have recently flooded into these border camps.

"Thailand's long-term ability to balance the winds of change in the region is so astute that they always manage to work it out," observed Thomas A. Seale, executive director of the American Chamber of Commerce in Thailand.

Thailand's economic growth has remained steady despite the country's somewhat outdated reputation for military coups, and a strong Army role over political affairs. The economy has flourished because successive governments have adhered to a remarkably consistent policy of free-market nonintervention.

For example, the business community and some technocrats expressed anxiety last July when Chatichai Choonhavan unexpectedly became prime minister and stacked his Cabinet with political veterans who had little economic expertise. But those jitters were soothed when the government pledged to follow the same economic path as the last one, and the business community appears to have adopted a wait-and-see attitude.

In addition, foreign and domestic investors were largely willing to ignore coups and coup attempts in the 1970s and early 1980s because changes of government here have not affected the economy. Real power has always rested in the armed forces and in the widely revered monarchy, the main focal point for stability.

Thailand has prospered by following the classic export-led growth strategy that has become the textbook model of Asian economic development, but it has some advantages over Japan and the other NICS.

Thailand's economy is more diverse than the economies of the other countries, with a strong agricultural base, a growing manufacturing sector and a tourism industry that is now the country's largest foreign exchange earner. The diversity makes the economy less vulnerable to fluctuations of the global marketplace.

In 1986, Thailand, a leading rice exporter, for the first time exported more manufactured goods than agricultural products. Agriculture's share of the gross domestic product has dropped from 30 percent in 1975 to half that today.

Thailand has also diversified its manufacturing exports, including shoes, toys, jewelry, leather products, semiconductors, and, under a new contract with Chrysler Canada, automobiles, with the export of 15,000 to 20,000 Thai-made Lancer Champs. "This represents a dramatic export diversification," Phisit said.

Thailand has one other key difference from some of its neighbors: It has left alone its industrious ethnic Chinese population, which is the engine for Thailand's growth. Most of the major conglomerates in the country are still closely held Chinese family businesses, and many top bankers and businessmen in Bangkok are ethnic Chinese.

But Thailand's sudden economic boom has brought about its own set of new problems.

The growth was so unexpected and unplanned that the country's infrastructure is feeling the strain. Universities are ill-suited to meeting the economy's demand for engineers and technocrats. The system of Chinese family businesses seems incapable of competing internationally. Some analysts are worried that since it is almost exclusively centered in Bangkok, the boom is worsening the income difference between the capital and rural areas.

Some economists say the income gap alone will delay Thailand's entry into the club of NICs. The Bangkok metropolitan area, for example, now has an annual per capita income of $2,000—high enough for NIC status—but two-thirds of Thais live in the countryside and are largely unaffected by the expansion. Thailand's overall annual per capita income is only $900—less than half that of South Korea.

A more immediate problem is the country's sagging infrastructure.

"The country has been growing so fast it's like a great big ball of yeast," said a western embassy economist. "The port is overwhelmed. The roads are overloaded. Telephones are not quite what they should be. The spare power generating capacity is starting to shrink. The water supply is stressed. There is a desperate need for more infrastructure."

The infrastructure problem is evident to even the first-time visitor to Bangkok. Traffic is a nightmare. Traffic jams, sometimes several miles long, often turn a simple trip across town into a two- or three-hour odyssey. In most major world cities, streets account for about 11 percent of the total land area; in Bangkok, they account for only 4 percent.

The overburdening of Bangkok's port is having a ripple effect throughout the economy, slowing deliveries and causing handling costs to soar. The port is capable of adequately handling 600,000 tons of cargo a year, but now handles 700,000. By 1991, it could be overwhelmed with an estimated 1 million tons.

The telephone system is antiquated. Crossed circuits are common and long-distance lines are inadequate. In one central business district, the entire telephone system recently failed, leaving hotels, embassies and offices without phones for two days.

Foreign investors also are feeling a shortage of trained talent. One foreign economist estimated that Thailand needs 7,000 new engineers annually—but universities are producing only about 2,300. At the same time, social science graduates are taking jobs below their qualifications. "There is a problem between labor supply and demand," he said. "It poses a problem for foreign investors."

In the view of many economists and business observers, all of these problems make it unlikely that Thailand will soon achieve NIC status.

"It's a question of government and of infrastructure: can government respond to the problems?" said Bill Black, general manager of the Regent Hotel, which has seen its business jump from 50 percent occupancy in 1986 to 80 percent last year. "Thailand has developed very quickly, but if you're going to become the fifth dragon, you have to have the infrastructure to support that—the telephone system, the communications system, the transportation system."

October 9, 1988